The English Terraced House

Colour plate 1 (frontispiece). **London**, Uplands Road, N8, *c.* 1900.

THE ENGLISH TERRACED HOUSE

Stefan Muthesius

Yale University Press
New Haven and London
1982

For B. H.

Copyright © 1982 by Yale University.

Third printing, 1985.

Designed by Caroline Williamson.
Filmset in Monophoto Photina and printed in Great Britain by BAS Printers Limited, Over Wallop, Hampshire.
Colour plates printed by Cambus Litho, East Kilbride.

Library of Congress Cataloging in Publication Data

Muthesius, Stefan.
  The English terraced house.
  Bibliography: p.
  Includes index.
  1. Terrace houses—England. 2. Row houses—England.
I. Title.
NA7328.M88   728.3′12′0942   82-50442
ISBN 0-300-02871-7 (cloth)   AACR2
ISBN 0-300-03176-9 (paper)

Contents

Acknowledgements

My special thanks go first of all to Don Johnson for his plans and his marvellous co-operation, and to Stella Shackle and Michael Brandon-Jones of the Fine Arts Photographic Department at the University of East Anglia for their endless expertise and patience. I also owe special thanks to Harry Long who read the manuscript at an early stage, as well as to Andrew Saint, John Nicoll, Richard Hill and most of all Caroline Williamson, who read it later. I was specially assisted in my research by Peter Aspinall, Charles Clark (Portsmouth), Antony Dale (Brighton), Martin Daunton, Prof. H. J. Dyos†, A. F. Kelsall, Mr. and Mrs. Ross (Ilford), members of the Tusting Family (Builders' Direct Supply Co. Ltd, Norwich), Jane Wight, Robert Wyburn, and Alison Wardale for typing; the Norfolk and Norwich Record Office, the Library of the University of East Anglia, the Library of the RIBA, London, and the Map Room of the British Library, London.

Thanks are also due to local libraries and archives in Birmingham, Bradford, Brighton–Hove, Bristol, Cambridge, Colchester, Cardiff, Folkestone, Great Yarmouth, Ipswich, Leeds, Leicester, Liverpool, London (British Library, Dept. of the Environment Library, GLC Archives, Guildhall Library, Public Record Office, Vestry Museum Walthamstow (D. Mander)), Lowestoft, Manchester, Nottingham, Norwich, Newcastle-upon-Tyne, Plymouth, Portsmouth, Preston, Peterborough, Reading, Rochdale (Jack Milne, and in the Town Hall J. M. Russum), Sunderland, Sheffield, and Wakefield; the municipalities of Easington (County Durham), Hartlepool (F. A. Patterson), London—Walworth (D. Jaques); museums in Beamish (Stanley, County Durham), Bristol, Norwich (Bridewell Museum), Cromer; the firms of R. G. Croad, He. Jones & Jones & Son, D. A. E. Snow, Privett (Portsmouth).

Countless others helped and I can only mention a few: Lucie Amos, Nicholas Antram, Robert and Jill Bage, Nicholas Bullock, R. E. and H. Butterworth, Jno. Croad, F. Cornwall, Alan Carter, Heik and Heather Celik, Moira Coleman, E. Collingwood, J. Collins (Romford), Alan Crawford, Roy Church, Roger E. Dixon, Cliff B. Elliott, Trevor Fawcett, Ulrich and Carin Finke, Adrian Forty, G. Foyster, F. Forrest, George and Olive Garrigan, Andor Gomme, Terry Gourvish, Sally Gritten, Alistair and Heidi Grieve, Willy Guttsman, Ivan and Elizabeth Hall, A. Heinlein, Stephen Heywood, Tanis Hinchcliffe, G. Hines, Miles Horsey, J. House, A. Ireson, Neil Jackson, Wavell John, Judith M. Kinsey, Günther Kokkelink, Helen Long, Robin Lucas, Gordon Millar, R. Macdonald, Rodney Mace, J. C. Miles, Victor Morgan, Mr. Morrish (Plymouth), P. and J. Morris, Bianca Muthesius, The National Housing and Town Planning Council, John and Elizabeth Onians, Patrick Page, A. J. Parkinson, A. C. Piper, Alexander Potts, Helmut and Ulrike Proff, Jill Quantrill, Jonathan Ratter, R. C. Riley, Michael Sanderson, Michael A. Simpson, S. Skipper, Geoffrey Stell, Michael Stratton, Sir John Summerson, Anthony Sutcliffe, Mark Swenarton, Mary Trenchard, Paul Thompson, David Thomson, Robert Thorne, Clive Wainwright, Chris Wakeling, Barnaby Wheeler, Suzette Worden, R. Wood, David Young.

Introduction

In many ways, the rows and terraces in which millions of English people still live make a curious subject for a book. One row looks much the same as any other. Do we really need a book to tell us that old drainpipes are liable to leak; that almost all of these houses have two main rooms on each floor? Do we want to be reminded again that house prices were so much lower in days gone by? Do we need a book with illustrations of what we can see every day in almost every street?

But, of course, our environment is not just there, it has not come about automatically. It was created by ourselves, by our parents and grandparents. We are constantly concerned with it, consciously or unconsciously, and we keep changing what does not suit us any more—such as the backs of older houses. According to many foreign observers the English live more cheaply and in better kinds of houses than do people in other countries; we are still more lavishly housed than many continental nations who have lately surpassed us in their standard of living generally. Architects and planners from abroad still come to study the English set-up, as they have done for the past hundred years. We have those better dwellings because we seem capable of a more judicious, small-scale kind of planning than other countries; of more feeling for the landscape, more artistic sense even. And this does not just refer to architects, builders and developers, but to the clients as well, to all of us.

Thus most of what is said and illustrated in this book is common knowledge. On the other hand, the obvious often escapes notice, precisely because we take it for granted. Our attention needs to be drawn to the individual features, as well as to the story of the type of house as a whole. This book is conceived as a detailed account of the terraced house, beginning with its inception by the developer and ending with the shapes and meanings of its decoration.

Our study of a Victorian house, perhaps our own house, should begin by thoroughly reading the deeds. What happened before the house was built, who were the developers and builders, what was the financial situation? All deeds contain stipulations as to what the builder, and the inhabitants, were not allowed to do, especially in relation to lowly trades like pig-farming or bone-boiling. In addition, we want to learn about the influence of the building regulations on the shape of our house. We should then try and find out more about the people who lived in the house when it was first built. What were their incomes? How many servants did they have? What is the history of some of the main rooms of the house, the drawing-room of the middle classes, and the parlour for the upper working classes? After this, we must turn to services and to more technical aspects: bathrooms, toilets, the construction of walls and roofs. What were the costs, which innovations occurred when, when did these conveniences become generally available? We can then discuss the plans in detail. Having stressed their general similarity throughout, a closer examination will reveal many variations, some of which are well known. How did the back-to-back type develop in Yorkshire, how did the back lane become a typical feature in Lancashire? How were plans affected by changes in what was considered convenient or desirable, for instance direct access to the back garden from the main living-rooms?

At this point it must be stressed that if all these developments belong to history, the product itself does not. We do not just inhabit these houses because we cannot afford newer ones, but also because we still approve of them, at least in general terms. At the end of the historical development sketched out in this book, by about 1910, stands the house which still fulfils today's demands in almost all respects: the small-to-medium-sized, two-storey three-bedroomed family house, with upstairs bath-room and toilet, with full drainage, with water heated from the kitchen boiler, with possibly a gas cooker, with electric light, and possibly even a telephone, with a private garden at the back (e.g. plate 48). Only the central heating is missing; one has to remember that this was not installed generally before about 1960. This sort of house could be afforded by the great majority of the lower middle classes and even by many members of the working classes. Though conscious that the poor carried on living in bad old houses, one has to bear in mind the tremendous levelling, or convergence, that had happened with new houses from about the middle of the nineteenth century onwards, filling in or reducing the gap between a mansion or a large terrace and the minuscule and miserable cottage for the poor. In that sense, most houses built from the late Victorian period onwards *are* modern houses.

We did witness a period, roughly from the 1940s to the early 1970s, when some planners and architects condemned the suburban row house and advocated other types of dwellings, like high-rise flats. Now we have returned to modified forms of the terrace and have reacted violently against the new types. Surely one of the reasons for this rejection of the new types was that they had not been tried for long enough. It was, and is, the advantage of our old–new type that it evolved over centuries. In that sense, history can assume a direct and positive value for the present.

There are, of course, less practical aspects to the house. It also has more subtle emotional and artistic values attached to it. We want a 'comfortable house', a 'pleasant' house. A well-kept garden with varied features, a neat front—these are the images we constantly keep in mind. Yet many people are surprised when small houses and terraces are described as 'architecture'. Although the major Georgian and Regency terraces have for a long time been classified as architecture, most people still associate this term chiefly with buildings of the scale of the Forum Romanum, of Salisbury Cathedral or Blenheim Palace. In addition, most of us appreciate the charm of the accidental in the old vernacular rural cottages. A closer look at many towns in this country will however reveal at least some nineteenth-century terraces of great architectural beauty; while others seem to perpetuate the vernacular elements of older houses. At this point, the question arises how these terraces can merit special architectural attention, if they are so much the same everywhere? It is true that because of the growing standardization—which was, we have said, an economic and social necessity—houses did become more alike later in the nineteenth century. On the other hand, there was not yet anything like the standardization of components which we see in much twentieth-century building.

The fact is, we simply have not looked at our smaller nineteenth-century houses. Probably never before had builders used such a wide variety of materials. On the one hand, strong local traditions continued; on the other hand, builders increasingly provided a conscious mixture of materials. And there is another area of contention about the way the history of architecture and building has been written so far: it has been oriented far too much towards London. Of course, this book, like so many others, constantly refers to London as the hub of architectural and all other kinds of fashion. But as regards traditional materials and crafts, London had in many ways far less to give than most provincial towns. This is particularly true of brick: one only needs to go just outside the capital to be confronted with the loveliest patterns and colours, like the Luton 'purple' (colour plates 31, 32) and the Reading 'silver grey' (colour plates 29, 30). By contrast, London brick looks drab, or at best—if cleaned— pleasantly rough-and-ready. For the most superior white-creamy brick, as well as the finest 'gauged' arch work, we must go to Norfolk (plate 191); and for the most exuberant late Victorian moulded bricks perhaps to Liverpool (colour plate 14). It was only in the early twentieth century that brick-making became a national industry and regional production was largely phased out. The tradition of delicate carving of stone continued in Bristol (plates 184, 185, colour plate 21); in the North it is the heaviness and solidity of stonework which is impressive. In the Midlands, not surprisingly, we find more of a mixture of materials: brick, stone and wood (plate 195). The exuberant woodwork of so many Victorian houses in Hull (plate 209) and Sunderland (plate 211) is in a class of its own. There are contrasts between adjacent towns: Liverpool houses are generally different from those of Manchester in many respects; those in Norwich are different from those in Ipswich. Some even say that south London houses differ from north London houses. For anybody in search of regional variety, the medium and small houses of the later nineteenth century provide a good starting point—while at that time the better-class buildings were already to a very large extent dominated by national trends. This book was written by somebody conscious of his own town's provincialism—though provincials must admit that they are often no better than Londoners in looking outside their own town.

In many ways a regional approach is extremely important, even essential, in the study of the ordinary house. It ought to begin literally on one's doorstep. If there is any documentation, it is mostly of a purely local character. The reason that so many Norwich examples are included in this book, as illustrations of plans or facades, or as case studies in the argument, is simply that they were close at hand. This means that most illustrations of Norwich houses could be replaced by almost identical examples from many other towns. By the same token, illustrations from other towns are normally meant to indicate what is characteristic for that town or area. But far more research has to be undertaken in order to achieve a more coherent picture of regional characteristics.

From the realm of art we can come straight back to matter-of-fact concerns and finance. In many London house advertisements we now find that the preservation of original interior fittings such as fireplaces is remarked upon. Soon, similar elements of the exterior will become selling points as well. In fact, Victorian and Edwardian houses are becoming 'antiques', or 'period homes'. They do not have a scale of prices attached, but are simply divided into those which are preserved well and those which are not.

Having got this far, many people might still be inclined to say: very well, but all this is best left to the specialists, the professionals, the plumber, the builder, the estate agent. But here we finally do come to something that has changed since the Victorian period: we, as inhabitants are much more concerned with the houses ourselves, not only with improving their fabric, but also in a general sense, in trying to improve what is characterized by that vague but indispensable word, the environment. It is here that a glimpse of history can bring a recognition of individuality, a sense of identity. Our street, our house is not just one of millions of the same, but has its own history and its own architectural value.

1. The common English row house

The ordinary English terraced house is vastly superior to the German dwelling, economically, socially and healthwise.

Rudolf Eberstadt, 1908[1]

By 1911 only about 3 per cent of all dwellings in England and Wales were flats;[2] perhaps up to 10 per cent stood as detached or semi-detached houses. The vast majority of English houses were built in one sort of row or another, houses of all sizes and in all price ranges. An overwhelming proportion of these had been built in more or less tight and regular rows since the eighteenth century. In the south, neat rows of houses can be found in small towns and villages with a population of 500 or less (colour plate 5); in the north, the midlands and Wales, even the smallest settlement in the countryside can be made up of one or several regular rows. What is even more significant is that the same type of small or large terrace was built in, or very near, the centres of large towns right up until the end of the nineteenth century (cf. plates 61, 67, 88, 89). England thus lacks, at least until the early twentieth century, the pattern of housing which we find in almost every other country (one only needs to go as far as Scotland): widely spaced, detached houses in the outer suburbs and in the countryside, contrasting with dense blocks of flats in the inner urban and suburban areas.

The explanation of this phenomenon is extremely difficult. It seems impossible to indicate one, or several, precise causes for the existence of the English pattern; certainly one cannot pinpoint specific events in time, as in the case of the more purely architectural developments. It would be particularly helpful, in our case, if we could refer to more detailed research into the development of other, contrasting types of dwellings in other countries.[3] A proper investigation of our type would also have to go a long way back; here we can only try and mention a number of later elements of custom, of law and economic practice, as well as some social–architectural factors.

First of all, we must remember that the contrast between town and country was much less decisive in England than elsewhere in Europe. Most town walls had lost their importance by the sixteenth century, and there was no need to squeeze into a narrow area within these walls, as there was in so many continental cities. Neither were there strong contrasts as regards ownership: the leading 'estates' in the country were often the most important developers of 'estates' of houses in the towns. The use of the same word in both contexts is significant and seems peculiar to the English set-up. Likewise, the suburb developed early in England; yet it was only during the nineteenth century that it became a separate entity between town and country. Initially, the basic kind of house discussed in this book was not confined to any particular kind of surrounding.

The early beginnings of the process of 'suburbanization' in England correspond to

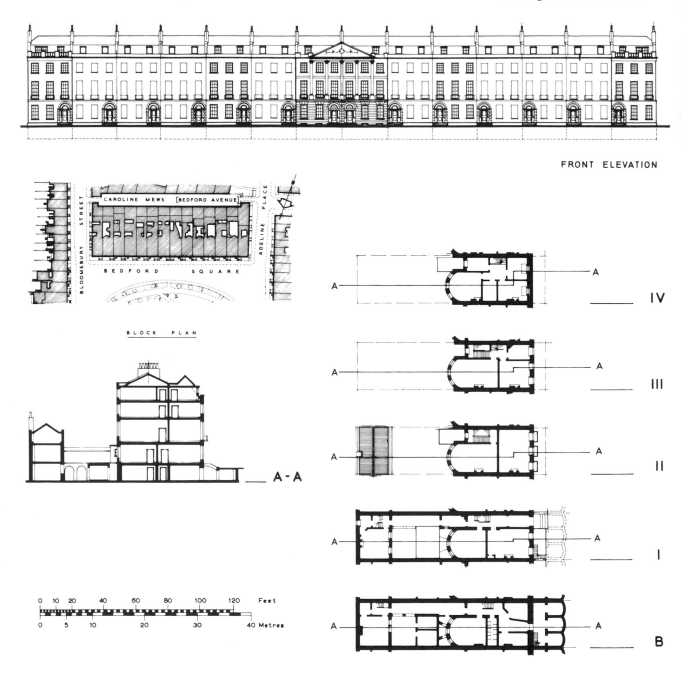

FRONT ELEVATION

BLOCK PLAN

A-A

IV

III

II

I

B

1. **London WC1.** Bedford Square. The most complete and best preserved of all Georgian squares in London, built 1775–80, probably to the designs of Thomas Leverton for the Duke of Bedford's estate (cf. plate 3). The block plan and the facade are of the south side of the square. The plan and section show a basement, for kitchen, servants' rooms and cellars, which reaches from underneath the footpath of the square through to the yard and ends with the stable buildings, which give out to a mews street. The ground floor usually contains the dining-room and a sitting-room; the first floor, whose ceiling is slightly higher than that of the other floors, accommodates the drawing-room in the front. The rest of the house was mostly taken up by bedrooms, and the attic usually reserved for the servants. Note the smaller staircase leading up to that floor. The facade, though impressively regular in its overall appearance, with all the elements of palatial Classical architecture, shows the doors of the two central houses placed side by side, which necessitated a central pilaster beneath the gable—much criticized at the time as illogical (cf. also plate 6).

the growing desire to live away from work, perhaps from as early as the sixteenth century. A house is a dwelling and nothing else. This was certainly a strong tendency with the better classes from the seventeenth century onwards. In these new residential suburban districts we also find a strong desire for class separation, made evident in the way that the squares and some streets were reserved for the 'best' circles (plates 3, 135). Indeed, the two elements went together: to be seen in conjunction with work or trade was precisely a sign of not belonging to the best circles. Increasingly, English merchants avoided living over their shops. Lastly, the house was more and more seen as the home of one family, which, from the later eighteenth and nineteenth century onwards, came to mean the nuclear family. There had been attempts to prohibit sub-letting by law in London in 1589 and 1602, and middle- and upper-class families seem to have avoided it more and more.

The pattern of ownership of English houses was always simple, in the sense that, until recently, owner-occupied flats in terraced houses hardly occurred; whereas in Scotland from a long way back individual ownership of flats had been common. The early development of the Scottish pattern was marked by the fact that the gentry owned flats in the lower parts of the block. In London, separate ownership, or lease, of the individual floors of a house would have led to chaos in the leasehold system. In fact, around 1800 we can observe a streamlining process in the timing of leases of houses: in each development they were all timed to 'fall in', or terminate, at the same time, in order to facilitate redevelopment.

On the continent dense blocks of flats for the lower classes were usually considered the inevitable result of the Industrial Revolution and the rapid growth of towns; though this does not explain why high blocks of flats can appear in secluded country situations, or why middle-class people did not seem to mind living in such blocks in towns. In England, on the other hand, even in most urban industrial regions, working-class families normally inhabited a separate small house. In late eighteenth-century Birmingham the workers of small firms did not crowd into the back or the upper storeys of the master's house, but small houses were built for each family in the yard behind—though, of course, at first these houses were very small indeed and much like the poorer peasant dwellings in the country.

However, subletting was very frequent in England. It must be stressed particularly to continental observers, with their admiration of the English custom, that there were very substantial regional exceptions to the one-family-one-house pattern. In 1911, 40 per cent of all London families had to share a house, mostly of an older type and not adapted in matters of sanitation. It seemed that land and building costs were simply too high to produce a suitable small house. In Plymouth the situation seemed similar. Although the dwellings looked like medium- and larger-sized terraced houses, and showed hardly any variation in their plans, they were immediately occupied by several families. Single lodgers were very frequent in the smaller houses of many regions. Also, in difficult times working-class families 'doubled up', i.e. two families lived in one small house.

Another consideration is that very high densities could be achieved with variations of the terraced house type itself. In Liverpool, a combination of back-to-backs, courts and cellar dwellings led to densities of up to 700 persons per acre (about 1730 persons per hectare) (plates 67–8). However, this pattern was phased out by the 1850s—and it still produced only half the normal density of the later, 1900, Berlin block of flats. In England, more than anywhere else, high density was associated with unhealthy and unsystematic multi-occupation. The large working-class blocks of flats which were built in the central parts of London and occasionally elsewhere were at first thought to bring some advantages, but were soon disliked

because of their usually grim appearance and because of the degree of control of the
inhabitants' lives which the owners thought necessary—because they themselves
distrusted the effect of the type on the tenants. The advanced type of apartment
block, which was developed in the later nineteenth century in the inner London
suburbs, could only be afforded by the upper-middle classes.

For most of the middle-middle classes and lower-middle classes there was virtually
no other type of dwelling that was desirable or available. In the new wave of
vehement discussions of the housing problem in the 1880s the solution for the lower
classes was generally seen to be the introduction of cheap commuting tickets by law,
and the building of ordinary terraces in the outer suburbs, at a density of 60–200
persons per acre (about 150–500 persons per hectare). As the *Builder* commented in
1883 on the type of house in Noel Park, one of the first distant London commuter
suburbs: not a 'specially new arrangement . . . but . . . the universally adopted type in
all towns and suburban terrace dwellings, as giving the greatest accommodation at
the cheapest rate' (plate 54).[4] In all but the most overcrowded inner urban districts
English housing densities remained low. The average number of persons per house
fluctuated during the nineteenth century. It had reached a peak of 5.75 persons per
house in 1821; but later on it fell steadily from 5.38 in 1881 to 5.20 in 1900, and to
5.04 in 1911—whereas even in Holland it was rising: from 5.50 in 1881 to 5.73 in
1901.[5] The average family size in England was about 4.5 for most of the nineteenth
century.

Factors of relative cost were equally important. Again and again, German
observers noted the low cost of English building land—probably a reflection of the
comparative lack of contrast between town and country—and its small share in the
total building costs, about 10–20 per cent normally; whereas for a big Berlin block of
flats it would amount to one-third to two-thirds, which made five or more storeys
inevitable. Only in the central London locations, and very occasionally elsewhere,
did the unusually high land prices among other considerations lead to the building of
high blocks of flats. However, construction costs were higher for these blocks: 7–8d
per foot cube, instead of 4–6d for small houses (£1.03–1.17 per m³, instead of
£0.58–0.88 per m³).[6] One of the chief inducements to build houses with no more
than two storeys was the nine-inch or one-brick-thick wall that could be used
throughout (plates 40–1). Continental observers, again, often remarked about the
lightness of English housebuilding generally. This lightness of construction was also
related to the carefully calculated life span of a house. In the case of many leasehold
developments, the life expectancy of a building was linked to the duration of a lease:
when the lease expired, redevelopment or restoration was envisaged. Even under the
freehold system the returns from investment in working-class houses were
calculated differently from those of the better houses, according to their shorter life
expectancy.

Standardization of plans and of the building process was one of the chief reasons
for the permanence of our type. From the late seventeenth century onwards
practically all houses in London were built speculatively, and the provincial towns
followed on from this at latest by the beginning of the nineteenth century.
Speculation means building without a client, in the hope that the house will sell for
the best price as soon as it is finished. Thus builders had to operate with the strictest
calculations and limit their options in order to reduce uncertainties. When W. H.
White tried to prove the superiority of the French type of flat for better-class
residences in inner town situations for reasons of convenience, he complained
bitterly about the conservatism of builders and estate managements in adhering to
the old type. England was far ahead of the continent in the organization of

speculative building. It was only in the second half of the nineteenth century that massive speculation took hold of towns in Germany and Holland, and again helped to entrench a particular type of dwelling—only here it was the multi-storey flat. Soon the housing reformers in those countries also complained about the obstinacy of the common builders and developers.

Not only for the builder and the developer, but also for the user, houses were simply a commodity like any other. Mobility seems already to have been high in the nineteenth century. There was much less sense of permanence attached to one's dwelling than on the continent, at least compared to the individual house in those countries. The continental term 'immobilier', or even the American 'real estate' are not used in England. Even with the vast increase in home-ownership in this century, English attitudes have hardly changed.

When builders and developers wanted to maximize profits, they had to be held in check by legally enforceable stipulations, issued either by the original landlords or by the government. Building regulations and building types are closely interrelated. But it is often difficult to disentangle cause and effect. Was a new building type introduced by a new regulation, or was the regulation phrased in such a way so as just to reform a pre-existing type, to bring about better construction and more salubrity? In chapter 12 on small houses we will deal with both processes. But once enacted, basic building laws were normally adhered to; there was no time for argument.

The most basic stipulation was the 'building line', that is, all houses must keep a common line at the front with their facades. Next in importance was the 'party wall' between the houses (plates 17, 41, 49, 60). In leasehold developments this was held to belong to the original ground landlord; it had to be carefully maintained and was not allowed to be broken through—especially, of course, as a precaution against fire. W. H. White, when advocating flats, somewhat jokingly recounts a case where His Grace the Duke of Bedford himself had to be asked for permission to break through a party wall;[7] to White this rigid regulation thus seemed a hindrance to progress. A party wall could never serve as any other kind of wall; conversely, no other kind of wall could serve as a party wall. Later on, from about the mid-nineteenth century onwards, the simple straight party wall was introduced for small urban houses in the north as well, where previously many mixed agglomerations, like the back-to-backs or complicated corner solutions, occurred, with angled party walls etc. This regularity was not introduced by specifying straight party walls as such, but by demanding regular space at the back of each house. This was a new kind of regulation, by far the most decisive one in the late history of houses in rows. Finally, it was characteristic that builders never quite knew how to design the side of the house when it was exposed at the end of the row; in most cases the unperforated party wall was simply left on its own—a major target of the critics of terraced house design in the twentieth century.

So far we have discussed elements which helped to establish and perpetuate our type. But it was also the plan itself, with its flexibility, which assured its continuity. In later chapters we shall discuss the variations of plans in greater detail. What needs stressing here is that the flexibility occurred within a strong basic similarity.

There was hardly any limit to the length of a row; Silkstone Row, at Lower Altofts, Yorkshire, of the 1860s, was over 800 feet long (244 m); along railway tracks in London one might find even longer terraces. The range of sizes varied enormously, but lords and peasants lived in the same type of house. In many other countries the situation was far more complicated. In Vienna, for instance, the town palace of the nobility and the middle- and lower-class flat remained completely different types, as

regards plan and facade treatment, until well into the nineteenth century, when they were combined in a complicated development.[8] In England, if one took off their yards and roofs, four small two-up-two-down houses (plate 94) could be fitted into the front drawing-room of the Albert Houses in South Kensington (plate 43). What is, however, more significant in this comparison, is that the largest house is only twice the width of the smallest house, and that its basic plan is arranged in exactly the same way: there are two rooms on each floor, one front and one back, and the entrance and staircase are placed on one side. Variations of this pattern, say, the placing of the entrance in the centre, are rare. Especially in London there was very little variation at all in the width of the houses. The depth, on the other hand, could be varied more; in fact, during the nineteenth century the tendency was to make houses deeper and narrower in general—though England hardly ever adopted the three-room-deep plan so common in Holland. Height was clearly the chief variable: there are quite comfortable versions of the row house on only one storey; on the other hand, four, five, even six storeys could be piled on top of a basement. One has to remember that normally only the servants had to climb all these stairs. All the same, by the later nineteenth century it was felt that height was getting out of hand and builders resorted to bulky back extensions as a more convenient solution. Again, the 1870s and 1880s can be seen as a crucial period: when in most countries the average number of storeys in a dwelling was rising, in England it was actually falling. Even after the first world war, the two-storey self-contained house remained the norm, less often in tight rows, and more frequently in narrowly spaced detached and semi-detached versions.

Reasons given so far have been chiefly of a material, practical kind. Given the basic desire of each family to live apart, on a separate piece of ground, the densely built rows of houses seemed the most economical solution. But there are other explanations which lie outside these spheres. Architectural elements will be considered in greater detail later on, but they are of interest here in that they are linked with certain social considerations, which seem as important as practical ones in the explanation of the occurrence and acceptance of our type of house. If we study more specifically the houses at the upper end of the social scale, we find that they were not adopted simply through economic necessity, but because of a positive liking for certain architectural consequences of the plan. A relatively high density of houses was not only the consequence of economic stringency, but also of a desire for certain architectural arrangements.

In order to understand the early developments of the modern terraced house in London, one has to remember that the squares of the seventeenth century were originally meant to be lined with the great palaces of the nobility. Bloomsbury Square was dominated at its northern end by Bedford House (plate 4). However, the building of these palaces was slow and irregular. The lack of demand stemmed from the fact that, unlike many of their continental brethren, the English nobility saw their main task to be in managing the land and embellishing their country seats, and they were content with a comparatively moderately-sized house in town. Thus the estates soon turned to the more rapid construction of large and medium-sized houses in rows. For thirty years the fourth Earl of Shaftesbury leased a terraced house in Grosvenor Square, which, though sizeable, was only one in a row of seven, and was infinitely outshone by his country seat in Wimborne St. Giles in Dorset.

It was the rapidly growing, or newly emerging, upper middle class (lawyers, successful doctors, civil servants, big merchants), as well as the minor gentry, which fuelled the booms in largish and medium-sized houses. They did not mind at all occupying a house similar to, and possibly not too far away from, those inhabited by some of the highest members of society. But very large houses were not built any more. By 1800, Bedford House seemed an anachronism in social and economic terms, and it had to make way for another street with tall, narrow terraced houses, called Bedford Place (plates 3–5). Even the Prince of Wales, in 1827, abandoned Carlton House, one of his London residences—albeit an unloved one; the chief Royal residence in London was transferred to Buckingham Palace, and in the place of Carlton House arose the magnificent Carlton House Terrace.

However, while London did not build large palaces any more, nevertheless a tight row of large houses could be made to look like a palace. In Grosvenor Square, during the eighteenth century, the facades surrounding this large space were treated on each side of the square as if they were a unified composition, with special corner and central accents. The fact that each grand palace or château facade was an agglomeration of houses inhabited by different families was not immediately apparent. In fact, these 'palaces' were larger than even the richest single one of their inhabitants could have afforded. In the later eighteenth and early nineteenth centuries this idea was eagerly adopted by the builders of slightly smaller rows of houses, such as Bedford Square (plate 1), and could even lend pretension to a row of decidedly medium-sized houses, such as Northdown Street, N.1., of around 1840 (plate 139).

Indeed, this type of terrace became so fashionable for a time around 1800 that a house within it seemed preferable to even a good-sized detached villa. One can thus find tightly grouped terraces of medium size not just in denser urban areas, but also in the leafy outer suburbs of provincial towns, placed in large semi-private parks, as for instance in the case of the terrace 49–69 Newmarket Road in Norwich of the 1820s, which was on a site big enough for all families to have been housed in their own sizeable villas with an ample private garden each (plates 6, 7).

Of course, when from the nineteenth century even working-class districts tried to acquire some of the elements or the look of the grand terrace, there was no money for any communal gardens, and the amount that could be spent on some extra decoration was usually pathetically small. But what could be done was to

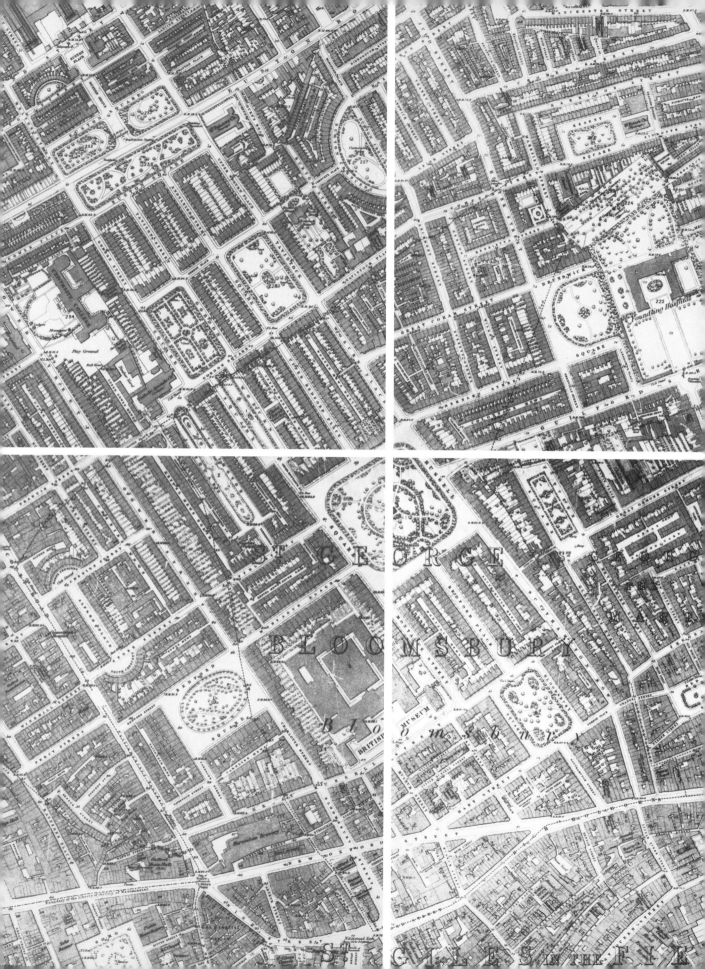

3. (facing page). **London.** Part
of the Bedford Estate on the
map of 1870; the model for all
later developments of terraces,
squares, and regularity in
general. Bloomsbury Square at
the south end dates from the
1660s onwards, Russell Square
from around 1800. Most of the
northern parts were built
during the 1820s.

4. **London.** Bloomsbury Square,
begun 1661, as depicted in the
middle of the eighteenth
century, with Bedford House at
its northern end.

5. The same northern side of
Bloomsbury Square; around
1800 Bedford House made way
for Bedford Place and its
terraces.

distinguish rigidly between the smarter front street and the poorer, everyday area at the back. Only in some early miners' settlements can one find situations where the front of one row faces the back of another (cf. plate 61). From about the mid-nineteenth century onwards this seems to have been avoided at all costs. Front and back doors now served different purposes. 'No such front street shall be constructed to be a back street on account of any such back door communicating herewith,' as it was specified somewhat clumsily in the 1867 Sunderland Byelaws; meaning that front street and back street should be distinguished as clearly as possible (plate 61). Regulations about the building line at the front became stricter all the time. Not even shoe scrapers were allowed to project (plate 28).

At its simplest level, the row house is derived from the better kind of narrow house with its front facing the better streets, traditional in London as in the rest of northern Europe. But the English row house of the eighteenth and nineteenth centuries does not just form a row of houses. It is in most cases something more than that; a row has an architectural unity which provides a heightened social image and which speaks of a special achievement on the part of those who planned and built it and those who bought or rented it.

The final definition of the terrace is clearly related to practical elements, as well as to social status and to architectural elements. It was, in fact, their effective combination which let the terraced house type continue for so long. Indeed, when the two elements parted, when it was no longer fashionable to live in a terrace, and the villa and the semi-detached house took over as the most desirable types of residence, the terrace was relegated to the lower classes, and after 1920 it was largely phased out even there. Regularity was no longer the result just of style, but also of economy.

Nevertheless, by the end of the nineteenth century the vast majority of Englishmen, including the middle and lower classes, lived in neatly ordered and at least moderately ornamented terraced houses. The terrace had become the common type of house. When in the late nineteenth century the popularity of the new large working-class blocks of flats was at a particularly low ebb—although hygienically they were often rather superior—the south London builder John Dudley commented on a particular type of medium-rise block of flats quite frequently met with in inner south-east London: 'All our houses face streets like ordinary terraced houses. I believe in that as it appears to people as much as ordinary houses as possible' (cf. plates 106–10).[9] Indeed, the vast majority of the 3 per cent of flats in England, mentioned at the beginning of this section, consisted of the purpose-built 'cottage-flats' and 'terraced flats' of London and Tyneside (plates 100–10), which were of two storeys only and which, on their facades, looked almost the same as the ordinary two-storeyed terraced house.

6. **Norwich.** Terrace in Newmarket Road, late 1820s. A considerable area of semi-private parkland separates the terrace from the public road.

7. The back of the same terrace; a typical example of 'Queen Anne Front and Mary Ann Back'. There is a semi-private roadway which gives acess to the back yards, as well as to the short, enclosed gardens of the houses (cf. plate 37).

2. The Georgian terrace and its Classical origins

While other countries have contributed more to the art of painting, sculpture and music, or monumental architecture, the English have cultivated everything connected with daily life . . . English domestic architecture always had a stamp of its own.

Steen Eiler Rasmussen, 1934[1]

Royal permission had to be obtained for new buildings in London during much of the seventeenth century. In 1630 the fourth Earl of Bedford was granted such a consent by Charles I for his estate in Covent Garden. The Piazza Covent Garden (plate 8), which no longer exists in its original form, was the first English example of a modern, that is to say, Italian Renaissance, urban layout: a regular, symmetrical square with regularized facades. Soon all the best new quarters of London, Bristol and Bath were beginning to be laid out in this fashion, each square or street as regular and as straight as possible.

There was a desire for grandeur on a large scale, to embellish the city in an ordered fashion. One of the conditions under which Charles I granted permission to develop Covent Garden was that the Earl would employ the King's own architect, Inigo Jones. Both he and the King were leaders of fashion. Jones was the first English architect to study and comprehend the new systems of the Italian Renaissance as well as of some new urban developments in Paris. The facades of Covent Garden, in fact, closely follow Palladio's models for grand *palazzo* facades (plate 8). This consists basically of a large Order of columns, or pilasters, with their appropriate cornices and further ornaments; because this order of pilasters comprises more than one storey it was called a Giant Order. To make this Order even more impressive, it was put on a high pedestal or podium, which, in contrast to the elaboration of the pilasters, showed a purposely rough treatment called rustication.

As it happened, the buildings around Covent Garden Piazza did not consist of rows of houses, but were divided into flats. But the new kind of facade was soon fitted on to the narrow front of the common London house (plate 1). The ground floor would be placed behind the rustication. The first floor now contained usually the main reception room, the drawing-room, in a more specifically urban fashion, but no doubt also influenced by the southern architectural model of the *piano nobile* as well as the French *bel étage* (plate 41). This unusually high storey, plus another, much lower storey above, were fitted behind the Giant Order, below the main cornice of the facade. Above, there was room for another low storey in the roof.

A major traditional northern feature was given up, the gable, and replaced by the cornice, or at least by a straight line, behind which the roof was usually no longer visible (plates 29, 41). England took this step in line with strict Classical doctrine, a step which the contemporary Dutch architects, who had many similar concerns, did not dare to follow.

The trick of the London *palazzo* facade was, however, that the Giant Order could be

8. Right: Andrea Palladio, Palazzo Thiene, Vicenza, elevation of courtyard, 1540s, from his own *Quattro Libri dell' Architettura* of 1570 which was frequently used as a pattern book. Together with other Italian Renaissance palaces as well as the Place Royale (now Place des Vosges) in Paris, it provided the model for the houses on Covent Garden Piazza, London, of the 1630s (left), shown here in a detail from an engraving in Campbell's *Vitruvius Britannicus*.

left out and yet that the facade still retained its character of a grand *palazzo*, because the proportions were faithfully adhered to: the medium-sized ground floor, the high first floor with its windows twice as high as wide, and the smaller third floor. In addition, there was always at least a token of rustication on the ground floor; always, at least in London, a firm line terminating the ground floor and suggesting a baseline for the main floor, as well as a firm cornice at the top. Thus really only the expensive columns or pilasters were left out (plate 5).

However, the fully expressed Order with columns or pilasters came back with a slightly different function: to give special emphasis to the centre and ends of a row of houses. Early on, the central accent in a terrace, as in Queen's Square, Bath, or Grosvenor Square, London, would be marked by a wider house to fit under the large portico with its gable. Later all the houses in a terrace are normally of the same width, as, for instance in Bedford Square, London (plate 1, cf. 6), where the central gable embraces two houses and is thus entirely decorative. This way of 'pulling together' a long range of buildings was mainly derived from French seventeenth-century palaces, and Elmes could claim that the grand terraces in Regent's Park were actually reminiscent of a 'Sovereign's Palace facade' (plate 112);[2] indeed we need not look far for a real palace with much the same disposition: Buckingham Palace, as it was built from the early nineteenth century onwards. The contrast between the elaborate centre and corner accents and the plain house facade in between became an essential element in the design of street elevations. Designers gave up the earlier practice of applying a Giant Order continuously between all windows, as in Covent Garden (plate 8), or to cite two late examples, the Royal

Crescent in Bath of 1767 (plate 125) and The Crescent in Buxton of 1779–81 by John Carr.

The basic definition, or architectural intention, of a terrace from the eighteenth century onwards is thus to bind together a row of houses as tightly as possible, to give an impression, an illusion, of unity. It was precisely because one was concerned with something less than a complete *palazzo* facade—because the Orders, the decoration, had been abstracted, or abbreviated—that one had to be all the more careful with correct and consistent overall proportions. Ultimately, even the centre and endpieces could be built without pilasters or columns, as in Bedford Place (plate 5)—where they must project very slightly—if only one kept rigidly to the proportions and the lines of the cornices (plate 2).

The unity of such a row of houses was often stressed further by a plaque, usually fixed on to the centre house, proclaiming the name of the terrace (cf. plate 2). Nash's lettering for Chester Terrace (plate 113) is unusually large, and as time went on plaques became increasingly a small feature on cheaper developments. The names were taken from a fairly narrow range of fashionable personalities, first and foremost the Royal family, and from localities of high standing, like Kensington, or Lansdown, an estate in Bath; sometimes military campaigns were celebrated, whence we have Trafalgar Terrace, and occasionally more abstract terms were used, as in the case of Onward Terrace, Wolverhampton, or Progress Terrace of 1884 in Preston.

It is odd that the term 'terrace' as such has never really been fully accepted. The more common and original use of the term refers to a piece of elevated ground, perhaps walled or fenced in; it is sometimes used for a street, in those cases where the street simply takes its name from the terrace along which it runs, for instance in Clifton. Further, according to the *Oxford English Dictionary*, a terrace can be a 'row of houses on a level above the general surface, or in the face of a rising ground. Improperly, a row of houses in a uniform style, on a site slightly, if at all, raised above the level of the roadway.' The Adelphi Terrace of 1769, on its platform above the Thames, seems to mark the beginning of this usage (plate 9). Earlier on, the word 'row' seems occasionally to have been used with something of a distinction attached to it, for instance in the case of the very regular Minor Cannon Row terrace of houses in Rochester of 1736 or the somewhat later Prospect Row in Chatham.

It appears that the English were placing themselves firmly within the European context: the Classical style, the imposing size and regularity of these houses proclaimed the glory of the King and the nobility, as did their inhabitants' polished manners and modern dress. But no other country took regularity in its ordinary houses to the same degree as the English; there is no equivalent to the grand English terraces anywhere—except perhaps for the occasional imitation, as in Kenau Park in Haarlem in the Netherlands in the 1830s. In the centres of most French towns we find more overall control, exercised by the King or the municipal authorities or both, as regards the layout of the streets and the overall contour of the buildings. Thus the town takes on a much more unified character in its plan, with long calculated vistas, axes, diagonal connections and so on. In England this very seldom happens, and although there is much ordered layout within each of the large London estates (plates 3, 4, 135), there is rarely any correspondence between the estates. But if one looks more closely at the individual facades of the Parisian streets, one seldom finds the individual house—or rather *immeuble*—to be an exact copy of its neighbour. There are far more ordinary houses in Paris with full-scale classical decoration, yet minor houses without this classical decor in Paris are far less rigidly controlled and proportioned than their London counterparts. Passing on to the Netherlands, one finds that the tradition of the individual family house was almost as strong as in

9. **London**. Adelphi Terrace, by
Robert and James Adam. The
architect's own description
from his publication of his
buildings: 'The above print
exhibits the Royal Terras, the
Houses and Openings of the
streets leading to the Strand;
Together with the Wharfs,
Arcade and entrance to the
Subterraneous Streets and
warehouse of the Adelphi,
which is a private undertaking
of Messrs Adam designed by
them, and begun to be carried
into execution in July 1768,
being so contrived as to keep
access to the houses level with
the Strand, and distinct from
the traffic of the Wharfs and
Warehouses'. This was the first
row to adopt the term 'terrace';
note the contrast with the
irregular, older houses on the
right.

English towns, yet it seemed to lead to completely different results visually: each
house is stressed in its individuality. Even in periods when strict Classical order was
dominant, as in Brussels in the early nineteenth century, there is mostly a slight
variation of the height and shape of the cornice for each house in the row. One also
notices on most continental facades that the actual facade, in a material sense, the
'face', is individually attached to each house, even if the projection is only slight. In
the post-Palladian English terrace, the emphasis is, on the contrary, on the smooth,
continuous surface and careful bonding, that is, laying, of the facing brick or stone
throughout the length of the row. Only some later working-class rows in the Low
Countries show some measure of repetition. What seems to have been lacking in
those countries was the strong control of one dominant fashion under the influence
of a small number of large estates. One might thus argue that the exceptional degree
of control in many English streets and terraces stems from the desire to have both
self-contained houses and palatial unity.

Another factor, already mentioned, was of decisive influence in English towns
from a comparatively early date: the separation of work and trade from the living
areas. Fewer and fewer members of the English mercantile class resided over their
shops. The size of the major London estates and those in the resorts made it possible
to allocate special areas for markets and workshops so that the main streets and
especially the squares were purely residential. Social and architectural aspirations
were closely interrelated: if the square or street was to be inhabited by the best
clientele, the architectural model had to be of the highest order. The facade of a

grand *palazzo* could not be imagined with a shop window. The continental system of mixing several classes in one large block was abhorred by the English. Increasingly, the 'best' quarters of London were those which had the most exclusively residential character. During the nineteenth century this principle was applied to medium-sized and even to lower-middle-class houses. In this respect England was completely at variance with continental Europe: there the most important and architecturally imposing streets were the main thoroughfares with the major shopping areas and often the best houses, closely adjacent to the centre of the town and the public buildings. In England we witness the development of the splendid secluded residential area and suburb; the centre or even the main thoroughfares and shopping streets in the suburbs receive hardly any overall architectural attention. Bristol's suburb Clifton is a telling example of this kind of contrast.

The 'terrace' can thus be called England's major contribution to Classical urban design. However, by 1800 one begins to doubt the label 'urban'. By then there was a strong tendency to live far outside the town, to surround oneself as much as possible with greenery. It is part of the pioneering English movement of the Picturesque, which led ultimately to the preference for the detached house, or at least the semi-detached, as the fashionable type of residence; and we shall come back to this development at the end of the book. Meanwhile, the terrace in some ways adapted itself to this new movement, beginning with the grand terraces by Nash around Regent's Park (plates 112, 136): they no longer form part of a rigid street block, but are separate units, just one long range of houses, all with their own back or front access. Even in the denser urban situations terraces do not form square blocks any more but appear as single rows, as in the later, northern, parts of Bloomsbury (plates 3, 4). Architecturally speaking, it is at this point that the 'terrace' comes fully into its own, and we witness a number of monumental structures, large by any standards, with which we shall begin our story of the facades. But first we have to turn in more detail to the practical aspects.

3. Demand and supply

Developments of the ordinary English house, owing to cheap land, plentiful capital for building, and an independent and resourceful building industry, adequately satisfy the demand for dwellings for the great majority of the population.

Rudolf Eberstadt[1]

From 1801 to 1911 the population of England and Wales grew from 9 million to 36 million, and the number of houses from 1.6 million to 7.6 million. We have, in the previous chapters, discussed the general issue of one-house-one-family, the ideal and the reality, and in chapter 6 on the house and home we will deal in detail with the sizes of houses and with their inhabitants. Here we are concerned with economics: firstly with the economics of renting itself.

Renting

Until the beginning of the twentieth century 90 per cent of all houses were rented from private landlords. The number of houses owned by one person varied considerably, from one or two to several hundred. Houses of all kinds were owned by builders and speculators themselves. Many smaller houses were owned by small shopkeepers, traders, and so on. Conditions of letting varied greatly: the middle classes generally paid their rent quarterly or half-yearly, the working classes had to pay it every week. The owners of small houses often faced considerable difficulties with the collection of rents and the upkeep of the houses, because of the poverty of the inhabitants and their high degree of mobility. This led, by about 1850, to the employment of special rent collectors, or house agents, who were also dubbed 'house jobbers', or in London, 'house knackers'.[2] These officials followed the mode of the 'agent', the general surveyor, manager, and supervisor in the big London estates, who also undertook the sale of houses or leases. By 1900 the term 'estate agent' had been established for this whole branch of activity.

As to the rents themselves, we can perhaps begin with some early colliery-owned miners' houses in the north-east: these cost 3d per week, or 13s per annum. A one-up-one-down house in Norwich claimed, around mid-century, a rent of 1s 2d per week, or about £3 a year (plate 61). 'Two-up-two-downs' cost 3–7s a week (£7–15) (plate 94). Five- and six-roomed houses 6–10s (£16–26); the medium-sized late-standard house at the end of the century in the home counties cost about £20–40 a year to rent (plate 48). Very large terraced houses could fetch a rental of £100 or more a year. As with house prices today, rents varied considerably from region to region. The *Cost of Living Report* calculated the differences for smaller houses on the basis of a house with the same number of rooms regardless of their size, and taking the average London rent to be 100, Plymouth rents averaged 81, Tyneside around

70, Liverpool 65, Manchester 62, Birmingham 59 and most industrial towns between 50 and 60, while some midlands and eastern towns came below 50. Macclesfield marked the bottom with 32, in other words less than one-third of London rents. But the *Report* does not mention that the stagnant industries and population in that town meant that houses were rather small and old (plate 201). Generally, and in contrast to the cost of other necessities like food, rents of new houses rose considerably during the course of the century; from 1790 to 1840 they doubled and then rose again by about three-quarters until 1910. The increase was due both to increased building costs, and to the increased size and quality of the houses. As a proportion of family income rents were calculated at 8–10 per cent for the middle classes, and more, sometimes much more, for the working classes and the poor (not taking into account any subletting). For the owner, rented property was considered a safe if unadventurous investment, usually of a strictly local character, at least until the early 1900s. The rent was calculated at about 10 per cent of the purchase price of the house and meant to yield about 4–7 per cent profit, or 10 per cent in the case of working-class houses with their shorter life-expectancy. There were, however, ups and downs similar to those in the 'cycles' of house-building itself. These expressed themselves in the number of empty houses, which could go up to 10 per cent or more of all houses, and rarely went down below 5 per cent. Occasionally rents had to be lowered temporarily, for instance in the 1830s and mid-1880s.

As regards home-ownership, we do not yet find the ideological overtones which it has acquired in the twentieth century. When William H. White, a late nineteenth-century architect, talks about the system that allows every family its own 'plot of land and . . . space above it' he seems to have not home-ownership in mind but the physical shape of the house.[3] In some cases owners of rented property were renting their own houses from somebody else.[4] However, in some provincial towns, like Norwich, home ownership was fairly frequent among the middle classes. In the 1840s and 1850s we witness what was called the 'freehold movement', but its main aims were to obtain franchise for the small man through possession of property, and it mainly concerned rural areas. In many working-class areas 'building societies' or 'building clubs' were operating, as in Leeds, Burnley, Swansea and the west midlands. In Birmingham one in six houses was owner-occupied by 1860. The role of these societies was strictly local and mostly temporary ('terminating'), and they frequently loaned to small investors and speculators as well. However, a few of the societies have continued as 'permanent building societies' to this day. In London it was only from about the end of the nineteenth century that the building societies took on their modern role—after much financing of big building speculations. A typical example of the early 1900s is a three-bedroomed house in Ilford, costing £300, out of which the Co-operative Building Society advanced £290, to be paid back monthly at £1 14s 4d over 25 years, which, taking into account some previous savings, was a little more than half of what the ordinary rent would have been.

There were many additional outgoings for the occupiers. Mid-nineteenth-century sanitary and municipal reforms added a number of new rates to the old poor rate, which kept going up: in London, for instance, from 1s 1½d to 1s 5d in the pound between 1900 and 1907 alone.[5] For smaller houses, i.e. those under £10 annual value, in most districts the rates were paid *en bloc* by the landlord ('compounds'). In addition to rates there was the Inhabited House Duty, deducted with income tax, with the threshold being raised to the £20 house in 1851, and amounting to 4s 9d for such a house in 1874. Lastly, there was the infamous Window Tax, which amounted in 1821 to 3s 3d for houses under £5 with not more than six windows, and £1 8s for houses with ten windows. But in 1823 it was abolished for houses with fewer than seven windows and in 1851 it was scrapped altogether. Insurance was usually compulsory, at least in the London leasehold estates.

The speculators

The story of speculative house-building from the seventeenth to the twentieth century has fascinated many urban as well as economic and architectural historians. It often concerned financial undertakings of the highest order and Britain was far ahead of the continent in these developments. In nineteenth-century London something like 99 per cent of all houses were built speculatively.[6] This meant not for a specific client, but in the hope of selling or letting when finished, and it included all types of houses, terraces and villas up to an annual rental of £1,000. Borderline cases existed earlier on, for instance in many very large Georgian and Regency terraces, where individual houses were left unfinished, as 'carcasses', until a suitable purchaser was found who completed the house according to his own wishes, as for instance in the case of the Duke of Devonshire's residence, 1 Lewes Crescent in Brighton.

Many speculative undertakings are characterized by vast size, made possible by the absence of restrictions on suburban development, and by the large size of so many land-holdings. One estate could comprise a quarter or more of the land surrounding a town. There was an ever greater tendency towards overall organization in matters of finance, in the allocation of social and architectural functions. Even some of the largest terraces discussed in this book form only a small component in a larger development. Developers of adjacent estates often co-operated.

It was, of course, the larger London estates who set the pattern. Almost all the land north and west of the old parts of London belonged to a small number of 'great estates': the Duke of Bedford in Bloomsbury and north of it; the Crown around Regent Street, the Duke of Portland in St. Marylebone; further west in Paddington and North Kensington the Bishop of London and the Ladbroke Estate. The Earls of Grosvenor (later the Dukes of Westminster), developed Grosvenor Estate in Mayfair in the eighteenth century, and in the following century Belgravia and Pimlico. In Chelsea there is the large Cadogan Estate. Most of these London landowners have profited from their developments to this day.

Except for Bath and Bristol, most provincial undertakings were at first of a far more modest nature. But by the nineteenth century they could be as rigidly planned as many of the London estates. An area of extreme repetition can be found in the later nineteenth-century streets around Orchard Street, Pendleton, Manchester: there are eight rows of 16 × 2 identical houses on a grid pattern. In Morecambe virtually all houses show the same characteristics; only their height varies. Other towns with a strong degree of unity in their plan are Ashton-under-Lyne, Mauricetown (Devonport), Birkenhead, Middlesbrough (plate 89) and especially nearby Grangetown, Barrow-in-Furness and Cardiff, not to mention the much rarer cases of small towns developed and controlled completely by the actual employer of the inhabitants, such as Saltaire, built by Sir Titus Salt near Bradford from 1850 onwards. It would, of course, be equally interesting to investigate examples where overall control appears to have been particularly lacking, as in many districts of Southampton (in contrast to organized Portsmouth), Ipswich, Peterborough, and Cliftonville near Margate (in contrast to Southend across the river).

Who were the actual speculators? Basically they were the estates themselves, the

'noble landlords with a greedy purse', as Summerson wrote. The initial impulse
could also come from somebody who bought or leased the land from one or several
established families. It was he who was usually called the developer, or speculator, in
the narrower sense of the word. In every development there had to be somebody who
had the roads laid out (plate 10), the sewers dug and the plots parcelled out for sale to
individual builders. In many cases this developer–speculator was simply the estate
surveyor; in other cases a person from outside took on this job, often a builder, but
members of many other professions, or no professions at all, were also found. A
subsidiary role was played by architects, surveyors, agents and auctioneers, if they
were not actually acting as developers. A very important person in many
developments was the solicitor, not only for the voluminous paperwork, or
parchment work, charging something like two pounds for a conveyance, but
especially for procuring finance for the builders. He was really the mortgage
broker—the word mortgage was chiefly used for builders' credit—and his investors
were all kinds of private individuals—spinsters, businessmen, or shopkeepers, like
George Penson, the City of London cheesemonger, whose personal estate by the time
of his death in 1879 was valued at £120,000, largely derived from his investments
in housing in North Kensington. The rate of interest for these investors was 5 per
cent, and it seems to have remained the same throughout the period, except that in
slack times it could drop to 4½ per cent. Later on, banks and insurance companies
grew rapidly in importance as investors.

Characteristic of speculative housing development was its uneven progress.
Booms and slumps followed each other rapidly: the 1790s and the years
immediately after Napoleon were extremely busy; they were followed by a severe
slump from the mid-1820s, with things picking up a bit in the 1830s, minor booms
in the 1840s and early 1850s, and a higher peak in the later 1860s which was
followed by a steep fall. Then came the tremendous boom in the middle to late 1870s,
which was followed by the quiet 1880s; then a new and absolute peak around
1900. For several years something like 160,000 houses were built annually (a figure
not surpassed until the mid-1930s) at a time when the population of England and
Wales stood at 32,500,000. It was again followed by a rapid fall towards 1914.
There were, of course, considerable local variations in this pattern, based mainly on
the London story. Urban and economic historians are still in disagreement as to the
reasons behind the 'building cycles';[7] they certainly were not simply based on the
demand situation in each town, but were also dependent on whether or not creditors
found other kinds of investment more attractive. The price of land varied
considerably, from a few pennies to a few shillings per square foot—though
generally the cost of the land did not exceed 10–20 per cent of the total building cost.
What are particularly difficult to assess are the profits made from the sale and resale
of the land. Clearly the kind of speculation which multiplied the price of land long
before building started, as in some German cities, was absent in England. Of course,
developers often bought land cheaply in anticipation of building, but its value rose in
line with demand, and the only way to help demand along was to build what was
called a 'strategic' road, or later a suburban railway line. In addition, land prices rose
generally, in line with generally improved building and the increased sizes of houses.
But in its most general sense the 'improved groundrent' was only achieved when the
houses had been built and sold, or let.

There were several ways of disposing of land for building purposes, ways of getting
the process of development going. In most parts of London the estates were normally
entailed, or held in trust, and the land had to remain in the family. Plots were
therefore let on long leases. The estate usually laid out the streets and later also the

sewers. Builders would then take out leases, usually on a small number of plots, to build a number of houses. The rent during the period of building would be very low—sometimes it was called peppercorn rent—so that the builder did not need a large capital outlay and could be more easily controlled by the estate. The builder would then sell the lease of the plot with the house, or let the house himself. After the expiry of the lease, usually after 99 years, 'three lives', the plot, with the house, reverted to the original ground landlord, so that the house had not cost him anything to build. He could then repair or redevelop the site and start the whole process again, or he could let the property himself at a very profitable rent—often called rack rent.

Some major provincial towns like Birmingham and Sheffield also used the system of the 99 years' lease. In a few other towns and regions, for example in Lancashire, the lease was 999 years, which amounted to virtual sale. But most provincial towns adhered to the simpler 'freehold' system, the outright sale of the land. As we have seen, the early development of speculative house-building was found in conjunction with the London leasehold system, and it has often been said that the tight control which the original ground landlords or the developers exercised over the individual builders—and the resulting order and conformity of the terraces—was peculiar to this system. However, the mechanisms of control could be just as efficient in the freehold system, by applying the 'restrictive covenants' which were contained in the conveyances. We shall come back to mechanisms of control in a further chapter. The equivalent of the peppercorn rent in freehold developments was the custom that the builder could defer payment for the plot until the houses were begun or finished. In some towns, as for instance in the grand developments of Regency Brighton, builders were given a choice of freehold or leasehold.

The cost of building houses in the later nineteenth century was reckoned to lie between 4d and 10d per foot cube (£0·58–1.39 per m³) according to the class of house—and we shall discuss its components below. London prices were usually about 20 per cent above those of the country. The value of a house was usually expressed in its annual rental: a '£10 house' or a '£50 house', which normally amounted to one-tenth of the total cost of a house, including land. Prices and rentals of existing houses very rarely rose during the nineteenth century.

In the end, the profits of the speculators and builders are extremely hard to assess. They were expected to be greater than those for the owners of rented property, with their 4–10 per cent, and above those for the providers of mortgage money, the silent investors, with their steady 5 per cent. In actual speculation there was, of course, no certainty. Vast fortunes could be made and lost. In many cases progress seemed sluggish: the well-known speculator Charles Henry Blake at times only managed $1\frac{1}{2}$ per cent excess of income over outgoings with his west London developments. Bankruptcies were very frequent, such as that of James Hall of North Kensington, who had liabilities amounting to £340,000 in the mid-1850s.

A more specific question is that of the profitability of working-class housing. We must exclude here the tradition of direct provision of houses by employers, like many miners' houses, or the especially well-known developments like Saltaire—which, in the long run at least, were by no means unprofitable. Most commentators in the nineteenth century agreed that small houses ought to be supplied by the same speculative, capitalist process as any other kind of house. There was no doubt that in areas of little middle-class demand, such as in the districts close to the Liverpool Docks, the building of working-class housing was highly profitable. In London, on the other hand, some large builders, like Thomas Cubitt, professed that they never built this kind of house. There were enough redundant old houses the poor would squeeze into which were eminently profitable to the owner. In many cases the poor would pay exactly the same rent per square foot as the rich. When strict building legislation came in around 1850, a hiatus is said to have occurred in Liverpool, when it did seem to be unprofitable for a time to build small houses. But by the 1870s everybody took the building restrictions for granted and later the great majority of houses exceeded the minimum stipulations of the regulations anyway. Working-class houses did not seem to form a special category of speculative housebuilding any more, as they did in the earlier period when skimping was often considered to be necessary to make a profit. For the lowest paid and the poor, about 15 per cent of the population, the old situation remained; they could not pay for an adequate dwelling.

It would be pointless even to try and give an account of all major speculative developments. Most speculators must be seen in a purely local context. There were some, however, who became well known nationally, even during their lifetime, and who deserve to be seen in the company of other great entrepreneurs of the period. According to Summerson, the first great speculator was Nicholas Barbon in the later seventeenth century. He seems to have achieved a certain degree of standardization and speed of development. Although on the whole a successful man of many activities, which included writing a book on the principles of capitalism, he died deeply in debt.

The greatest success in luring people to grand new houses, or 'second homes', were the resorts, above all Brighton (plate 115).[8] Residents were attracted by the sea-air—near magic effects were attributed to it. The other attraction was Royalty, though in the case of Queen Victoria this remained largely hypothetical, as she did not particularly like to be eyed by the public. Thomas Reed Kemp, a Lewes man of middle-class background, almost single-handedly developed new towns east and west of the old town from the mid-1820s onwards. Progress was extremely slow, and some parts took over thirty years to complete. The architectural results are striking, but in terms of finance there was no overall profit for the developer. In 1837 Kemp had to leave the country temporarily to escape his creditors. He was, however, finally rewarded by the naming of the eastern part of his development as Kemp Town. The chief developer in Cheltenham was a retired London merchant, Henry Thompson, who began the Montpellier and Lansdown Estates. His son, Pearson Thompson, took over in 1820. He did not fare particularly well and sold the unfinished terraces around 1830 to two architects, the brothers Jearrad. Thompson was later involved with some of the main North Kensington developments, the Ladbroke Estate. In Royal Leamington Spa many of the speculators and investors were midland-based. However, by the mid-century the great time of the fashionable big resorts was already over, and their functions for daytrippers and for commuters belong in a different story.

In London, the ups and downs of John Nash,[9] mostly on land owned by the Crown, have been well charted. The career of Thomas Cubitt, the most successful of all nineteenth-century builders and speculators, has been investigated;[10] son of a Norfolk carpenter, he died a millionaire. In conjunction with other entrepreneurs and builders such as Seth Smith, he and his successors built over five thousand houses in the estate of Lord Grosvenor, the Duke of Westminster, alone: practically the whole of Belgravia and Pimlico are due to his efforts and business acumen. Two of the most important speculator–builders of the 1850s and 1860s in Kensington, Charles Aldin and William Jackson, had begun their business under Cubitt. Another Kensington entrepreneur in housing was C. J. Freake, probably the first member of the trade to obtain a baronetcy—while Cubitt was certainly the first to reject a knighthood.

10. **Cromer.** An advertisement aimed at investors and builders from the early 1890s. This small resort had developed very rapidly in the previous years, owing to Royal patronage and a new railway to Norwich. The structure on the left, the Grand Hotel, dated 1891, still exists. Cromer Hall, a minor seat, is about half a mile away and has no visual relationship with the site; its inclusion was clearly aimed at those who did not know the locality. However, some of the roads, especially Cabbell Road, in the centre running towards the sea, were soon to be flanked by substantial terraces, probably used as boarding houses from the beginning.

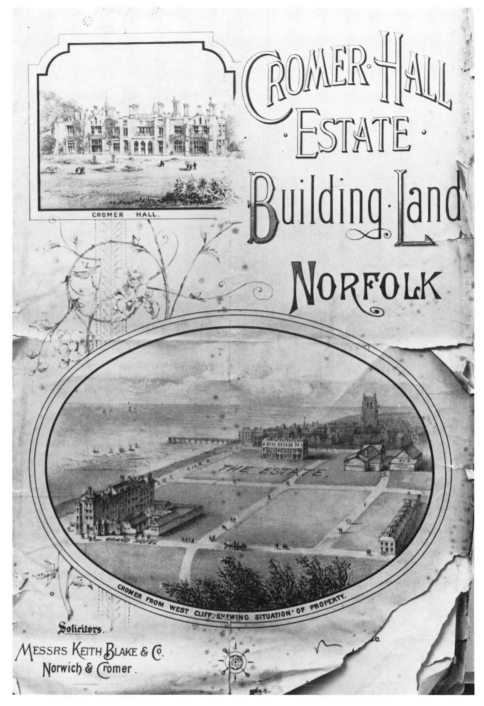

Others have dealt with the more humdrum stories of many provincial speculators.[11] These need not necessarily be dull, but it is only the most painstaking reading of deeds that reveals all the intricacies. In Norwich, for instance, in the early 1860s, the situation was 'right' for the area between Earlham and Dereham Roads. There was a demand for both small and middle-sized houses; the site was moderately attractive, at least at its southern edge; there were good roads connecting it with the centre. An owner of large tracts of land, W. B. Humfrey, sold almost 10 acres (4.05

Colour plate 2. **Brighton**, Brunswick Terrace, *c.* 1830. To decorate each house with pilasters was by that time somewhat unusual, and peculiar to Brighton.

hectares) in one piece to S. H. Meachen, as builder–speculator, in 1861, for £4850, that is for just over 2d per square foot (£0.09 per m²). Yet, for the time being, Meachen only paid him £350, presumably for the plots he went on to develop himself. He began to make the new roads, at least staked them out, and gradually sold most parcels to other builders. He charged his fellow builders just over 4d a square foot (plate 37, cf. 50, 191). But by no means did he pocket the difference; it all went straight to Humfrey; Meachen kept only 10s in every transaction. Within seven or eight years three new streets with about 230 small but orderly houses were built by about eighteen different builders (e.g. plates 37, 191). In many cases the development is straightforward: the builder buys the land, obtains a mortgage from a solicitor, builds five or ten houses, and within a year sells them individually or as a group, repays the mortgage and turns to his next development.

In other cases we can find the most tortuous story, as with a row of five small houses in Alexandra Road within the same development. It took nine months to build the first house, then the builder, J. Youngs, had to sell the whole undertaking to another builder for less than he had paid for it initially to Meachen, in order to repay a local solicitor, J. Winter. He in turn lent to the second builder, who, only three months later, found he could not go on either. He sold everything back to Youngs, again at a loss. Shortly afterwards, Youngs sold everything back to Meachen. All three of them were now paying back some of their debts to Winter, and after renewed borrowing from the latter, Meachen was now 'building' the rest of the houses and completed them about eighteen months after the first resale of the land. In the end, even the purchaser of the houses, Bernhard Zipfel, from whom the terrace subsequently received its name, borrowed from Winter. It is unlikely that anybody made any substantial profits in this particular development, except the original landowner, Humfrey.[12]

Later on, we encounter other kinds of developments, where one feels this sort of performance was less likely to occur. In the late 1890s the British Land Company advertised the sale of plots on the Rectory Manor Estate, Church Hill, Walthamstow. First came the usual praise of the 'elevated position', which was 'charming' and 'healthy', as well as 'central'. Then it was claimed that the area was 'fully ripe for building operations', and suitable for 'builders, tradesmen, small capitalists, plot buyers, speculators'. They could acquire it either for 'profitable resale, or for building on their own account, or for their own occupation'. The vendors would consider applications for advances for freehold buyers. The land could also be let on lease, again, with advances, if required; nine-tenths of the purchase price might remain on mortgage. It says further in the advertisement sheet that new roads and sewers had been carried out. There was no charge for a normal-type conveyance prepared by the vendor's solicitor. Thus this company did everything except the building, and even that could be tightly controlled. Designs for the houses were supplied, which, in any case, did not differ from the tens of thousands of houses built around London at the same time; and the plans fitted, in turn, into the parcels into which the company had divided the land (colour plate 11). Thus everything was now predetermined.[13] The days of the daring developer seemed over.

In the end, assessments as to how well the supply of houses met the demand vary a lot. Clearly, there were not enough houses for the poor and lowest paid. On the other hand, for all classes above there was often a glut. What was often lacking was a more precise tailoring of the supply to the demand of a particular moment. One has to admit that the English speculating builder set himself a particularly difficult task. If he built a block of flats, there was, at least notionally, a degree of flexibility within the block, in dividing it up. But to build a whole house without a client, with ten rooms

or more, or even a row of such houses, meant that thousands of pounds could be buried in bricks and mortar. The most difficult decision that every developer faced before every new undertaking was clearly the size of the houses. There seemed few general considerations or rules which could be relied upon. The natural inclination was towards larger houses, due to initial optimism, reasons of prestige, social and architectural, and the desire to predetermine the 'tone' of as large an area as possible. Bigger houses would be more expensive to build—absolutely and relatively—and thus profits would be higher. But in a situation where the nature of the demand could not be easily gauged the question as to whether, on a given piece of land, a smaller number of bigger houses, or a bigger number of smaller houses would be more profitable, could depend on a host of factors: the particular situation, the desire for gardens, customs of subletting, etc. In any case, for most developments the decisive factor lay elsewhere in the calculations, namely speed of sale. Thus we find so often, in the Regency and mid-Victorian years, the beginning of a street in grand eloquence, which soon peters out into mediocrity; and we shall never learn of all those grandiose projects which remained entirely on paper. David Cannadine recently argued that the actual influence, or will, of the great developers to shape their estates according to their conceptions of high-class districts has been overstated, and that natural factors were far more decisive. For instance, a pleasant hill site would always attract the best clientele, and a working-class town, or an area close to a factory, would always produce working-class houses. However, the question of size, within a smaller range and in areas of middling attractiveness, always remained a difficult one for speculative developments. The idea of advertising more widely specific estates and developments seems to have occurred only from the late nineteenth century onwards (plates 10, 108).

From about the middle of the nineteenth century the problem was eased a little, in that the best classes began to prefer to live in separate houses; individual detached houses could more easily be sold one by one than houses within a large terrace. The range of sizes for terraced houses became more limited. It is all the more remarkable that builders did not take to an easy, natural solution, namely to mix sizes within one development, which surely would have been conducive to more rapid sales. This was how large continental blocks of flats were planned, each containing a wide range of sizes of dwellings. But the English increasingly disliked the close proximity of different classes; even the middle classes did not want to be too close to the lower middle classes. Many large estates in the later nineteenth century do show a carefully graded range of sizes, though the different sizes were kept out of sight of each other as much as possible; preferably each street kept to one class only. By the end of the century, as we have already indicated in the case of the Walthamstow development—and we shall see it further in the discussion of the plan—the 'late standard' types of house meant a further convergence of sizes. Also, at the lower end of the scale, the 'working class' house, in the older sense of the word, which meant using specially reduced plan types and often a skimping on materials, no longer existed. Not only the plans, but the methods of construction were very much alike in all sizes of terraced houses, as was the provision of sanitary facilities. Houses were now carefully differentiated in rentals of, say, £8 houses, £8 10s houses, £10 houses, etc. (cf. plates 37, 90). The question remains as to how class differences were marked, and in the last chapter we shall discuss methods of differentiation through external ornament.

4. The economics of building: from craft to industry

An Arkwright is wanted for the building trade.

James Hole, 1866[1]

After discussing the mechanisms of speculative development we must examine some of the factors in the building process and the provision of materials. Later chapters will deal with the actual fabric, with the question of what is good and what is bad construction, as well as with the different techniques of decoration; at this point we are interested in building purely as a business.

In every respect, building was one of the most important trades. It recruited an increasing proportion of workers, numbering over one million in England and Wales by 1901. One can fairly assume that houses were the bulk of the output. What kinds of people were involved in the building process; how was it organized and controlled; what were the chief problems of production, transport, marketing and pricing?

In the early nineteenth century we witness a fundamental change in the methods of assessing and controlling building work. Traditionally this was done by measuring and valuing as the work went up, or when it was finished—a method which seems to have carried on much longer elsewhere, for instance in France.[2] It was the general increase in the size of operations, the greater demand for speed, the bitter rows between clients and builders as to the true costs, which led to a radical change in the methods of assessment. Builders and clients now worked out all the costs before operations began, and the builder went into a contract to do the job at a fixed price, within such-and-such a time and according not only to detailed plans, but also to minute 'specifications' and estimates. 'I would even build a dog kennel by contract,' ran a comment in 1834.[3] Building firms now competed with each other in a much more organized fashion, by sending in estimates, or 'tenders'.

On the face of it, the situation was different for builders of speculative houses, as there was, strictly speaking, no client. But in effect, 'building agreements', 'restrictive covenants' and the building legislation, as well as the stipulations often attached to the borrowing of capital, amounted to much the same as a contract. As regards borrowing, we know that Thomas Cubitt in the mid-nineteenth century, for instance, when he acted as a developer, divided his advances to his builders and waited each time until the builder had satisfactorily completed the specified part of the house. In other cases, however, a strong developer or builder could negotiate the contents of agreements with the ground landlord, and occasionally agreements would be altered when general economic conditions changed.

There were, basically, two kinds of contract: those with representatives of several trades for different parts of the building, and those with one builder, or contractor, for all aspects of building. In speculative house building it seems that it had already become customary for one firm to undertake all the essential parts of construction by about 1800. The old practice of putting up just the shell or 'carcass' of the house and letting each buyer organize the rest of the trades seemed to be on the way out. There was, however, a continuation of the method of contracting labour only, especially by speculative builders who themselves did not belong to one of the trades; it was called the 'taskmaster' system,[4] and was apparently a source of acrimony and much bad building.

'Merchant builder', 'contractor', and 'master builder' were the words used for those who contracted for all trades. The term 'builder' as such, a man of several trades, was only adopted during the eighteenth century, to distinguish him from those who practised only one trade, such as bricklayers and carpenters. The speculative builders became more and more a separate race, especially in London — and the term was used at least from the 1830s onwards. In addition there was the 'jobbing builder', usually a very small firm concentrating on repair work. Most building firms remained small, though by the end of the century there were already large firms in most towns: at that time 17 per cent of the firms built 40 per cent of the houses in London, and in Sheffield and Norwich the concentration seems to have been slightly higher.

Work on the building site was generally well paid. In all, money wages rose by about 50 per cent from 1790 to 1850 and then again by 80 per cent until about 1900. More importantly, wages as a proportion of total building costs for ordinary structures rose from under a quarter before 1850 to nearly half by 1914. On the other hand, building workers were particularly vulnerable to seasonal fluctuations. The new stricter methods of organization brought a greater degree of differentiation and control among the ranks of workers, with 'clerks of works', 'foremen' and the like; but the methods of contracting also gave greater freedom of movement between trades. The great building boom of the late 1890s brought greater unionization and a reduction of 'piece work'. The larger firms usually had a greater permanent workforce. Thomas Cubitt — who was rather an exception in being active in speculative housing as well as in major architectural works — became well known for his paternalistic concern for his workers, coupled with very strict organization of the building process.

Bricks were still laid upon bricks; basic building methods hardly changed. But there was considerable development in the production of many building materials, and in their preparation for the site. As the *Builder* reported in 1854, Cubitt's workshops produced almost everything by machinery.[5] In Bedfordshire from the 1830s, simple machines producing agricultural drainpipes like macaronies reduced their price by more than half.[6] The tremendous demand for sanitary pipes soon afterwards could hardly have been satisfied by handwork alone. Brick-making machines were slowly introduced from the 1830s onwards. In the 1870s one machine could produce 10,000 bricks a day, that is about six times the output of one brick-maker with the old hand process. By 1900 a machine could churn out 60,000 bricks a day.[7] The continuous Hoffmann kiln could, from 1859 onwards, burn larger numbers of bricks more quickly and cheaply, and greatly reduced the number of badly burnt bricks inevitably produced by the older kinds of kilns or clamps. The effects of the new production processes on the look of the bricks can, in most cases, easily be described, but their effect on prices is much harder to assess. Generally the price of ordinary bricks varied from £1 to £2 per 1,000. After 1904 prices fell dramatically, especially for the new 'Fletton' bricks, to about 13s per 1,000; this was due to more efficient manufacture, as well as to overproduction and a slump in building generally.

Treating stones with steam-saws and preparing them in the quarry itself greatly facilitated their use. (By 1900, it has been claimed, one in six of the British population could afford a proper gravestone.) While local stones were used less and less in ordinary walling—brick proved more practical and thus cheaper—dressed stone decoration became universal, even for small houses. The greatest increase in efficiency was found in the woodworking industry, amounting to about 60 per cent. Partly under American influence, the use of machinery in woodworking grew in the 1840s and particularly in the 1870s as a response to a strong rise in carpenters' wages. At about this time, Laxton reckons the cost of setting up a joiner's shop with four machines and one steam engine at around £1,000.[8] In addition, ready-made windows, doors and mouldings—the actual 'machine joinery'—began to be supplied by the countries who grew the wood, like Canada or Sweden. As in actual building, firms of producers of building materials generally remained small, but by the end of the century a number of companies were amalgamating, especially among the London and Fletton brick-makers and the Bath stone quarries.

Traditionally the great majority of building materials were produced near the building site, or in some cases, like bricks and lime, on site. Transport was extremely cumbersome and expensive and severely limited the distribution of materials. However, because of the shortage of wood in Britain, timber had been transported from overseas for some time, and in the better houses stone for sills and copings, as well as slates, usually had to be transported over great distances. Whenever possible, this was done by river or by sea, or later by canal. Elsam cites prices for Portland stone and slates as including wharfage in London, but no transport beyond. It was overland transport that proved the main problem. Many of Elsam's prices include transport for one mile only. Early on, in Bedfordshire transport for one mile added 2 per cent to the price of bricks, but five miles added 40 per cent. A horse could transport only about 600 bricks in good road conditions and as late as the beginning of the twentieth century boys pushed barrows with small quantities of bricks from one end of Norwich to the other. It was only after 1900 that steam lorries came into use, while motor lorries became common only after the first world war.

The real revolution had, of course, already come with rail transport. It only started in earnest when the railways themselves became more interested in bulk freight in the 1850s and 1860s. Most kinds of stone could now be supplied to London from all over the country, those from Yorkshire often by sea and rail combined (on 'low through rates'). This usually added 1s, that is one-third, to the end price per foot cube. All the modern producers had a siding, such as the Flettons in Bedfordshire and near Peterborough, though it took the latter until after 1900 to compete successfully with cheap London bricks and their methods of barge transport from Kent. By 1900 transport for many goods, if ordered in bulk, was advertised as 'free'.[9] What mattered most was that transport costs and the end price of materials could now much more easily be calculated for a far greater number of places and could be quoted instantly by the supplier.

Lastly, there was a new process of selling materials. Earlier on, the ground landlords, builders and architects themselves were often involved in the production and supply of materials. Itinerant gangs of brickmakers moved from site to site. For more specialized materials, like paint, Elsam and Webster advised the architect or builder to travel around and examine them at their place of manufacture. On the other hand, slates and timber were already supplied in standard sizes by larger firms with their own depots. There were also the more specialized showrooms for better-quality fittings, like marble chimney pieces, and some firms, like Coade with their decorative stone, also produced illustrated catalogues. Ironmongers were also important for building supplies. But after about 1870 a new species of trader developed very rapidly: the general builders' merchant. Kelly lists 100 in that year, in 1910 there were 1,300. A prominent London one is Young and Marten, founded in 1871; somewhat later Broadbent of Leicester had branches in London, Liverpool, Cardiff and Hull, and sold tiles, bricks, stone, sanitary ware—almost everything needed.[10] Many firms began to produce lavish catalogues (plate 208) which took over some of the functions of builders' price books, and even of the pattern books: Young and Marten's called theirs a 'Builders' Manual' (plate 208). To keep sufficient stocks in a market 'flooded with novelties'[11] and to help generally with the efficiency and flexibility of the building process were the functions of the builders' merchant. In addition he gave generous credits, a practice which seems to have begun among some suppliers after 1815[12] and which applied to a 'good proportion of materials' by the 1880s.[13] Thus the builders' merchants also took over some of the functions of the ground landlords and the other creditors. The visual results of this intense competition between some materials we shall discuss later on.

On the whole, the development of building costs is difficult to judge. Wages rose considerably; and the cost of materials fluctuated, with a peak in the 1870s. Up to the middle of the century another factor was taxation on most materials, especially on bricks: 5s for a thousand ordinary ones, and more for larger ones. This tax was lifted in 1850. But the effect of this abolition is difficult to assess, as the fluctuations in price due to other factors, such as transport costs and the changes in demand generally, could be much greater than the tax proportion. Over the nineteenth century as a whole, the cost of materials (cf. plates 53, 92) remained more or less the same, but because of the rise in wages, building costs as a whole rose considerably overall. In many ways, however, this does not say very much, because of compensating factors in the form of increased reliability and variety, and improved methods of construction.

The most important factor in the overall development of the building process was standardization. In plan and elevation it was caused by the new insistence on drawing detailed plans, even for the smallest house, where variety would simply have meant additional expense. As regards the parts and fittings of ordinary houses, standardization had, according to the *Tudor Walters Report* of 1918, gone quite a long way in carpentry and joinery, but less far in plumbing. In its most general sense, standardization can be observed in the look of the houses. Whereas with the better Georgian and Regency houses, architectural style demanded the utmost accuracy and repetition on the facade, the backs were usually left to the individual resources or preferences of the builders and clients. After the mid-century, the opposite applies: intentional variety at the front, but strict uniformity and repetition at the back. Even such poor performances in economic terms as Zipfel's Terrace in Norwich did not have to result in an irregular appearance. There were other ways of enforcing regularity to which we must now turn.

5. Control

When contemplating an ugly, ill-built town, where every little freeholder asserts his indefeasible right as a Briton to do what he likes with his own; to inflict his own selfishness, ignorance and obstinacy on his neighbours, and on posterity for generations to come; and where local self-government means merely mis-government — we are apt to wish for a little wholesome despotism to curb such vagaries.

James Hole, 1866[1]

The deeds

It is usually when we want to sell our house that we begin to look for the deeds. We know that they can give us more information about its history than any other source, written or printed. Alas, too many old documents have lately been destroyed or dispersed; one can even find them in antique shops nowadays. This is all the more disturbing as these documents are by no means of purely historical value; often some of the stipulations could still be binding for any present or future owner of the property. We are also aware that if we want to substantially alter our house, or add to it, we cannot just draw up plans and let the builder go ahead, but we have to ask the law, or rather the local authorities, for permission.

We have already dealt, in the previous chapter, with the rapidly growing organizational rigour in all matters of building; with financial stringency, with contracting, with standardization in quality and price. Minute specifications and estimates were drawn up, and these grew longer and longer, as the buildings themselves became more complicated through new demands for comfort by a greater number of people. Building had become an economic activity whose success depended on everything being minutely predetermined. However, in the case of the common house, there was no need for a detailed specification or estimate for each one, as it would merely be a repetition of the house next door and of so many others elsewhere. Detailed estimates were, of course, expensive in themselves. What was needed was a general framework of stipulations which could be applied to as many houses as possible.

Nothing could be more effective for this purpose than the law. To attach legally binding conditions to the sale of a property was a very old concept, and more recently there had been decrees from above, from the state. In concrete terms, there were the 'restrictive covenants' in freehold conveyances, or the restrictive clauses in leasehold building agreements; and there were the building regulations, or, as they were called earlier, the Building Acts and Building Byelaws. As they concern almost every aspect of the plan, the construction and the architecture of the house, we shall refer to them again and again; here we shall give a summary of their contents and discuss the way they developed and how they were enforced.

First of all the deeds demanded that the house must be a 'dwelling house' and that nothing else could be permitted on its grounds. Often even subletting was forbidden. The house or its grounds were not to be used for any trades, especially 'low' ones, like bone-boiling, brick-making, lime-burning, or pig-rearing. Some Bedford Estate repair leases in London specify all conceivable trades in the most minute fashion, up to sixty or more—'. . . coffee house keeper, coffee shop keeper . . .'[2]—so as not to leave any loopholes. Only as regards schools, doctors' surgeries and, in resorts, boarding houses, was there less stringency. In addition, the street, or at least the front garden, was minutely controlled: all gates had to open inwards, fences were not allowed to exceed a certain height. The most decisive stipulation usually comes after that: the size of the house, expressed in the figure for the annual rental, or sometimes in 'class' or 'rate'. In larger estates there could be a carefully planned range of rentals. As regards the fabric itself, the most frequent stipulation was that of the 'building line', that is, all houses had to keep to one line at the front. Often the precise height of the roof line ('wall plate') was also given, and sometimes even the height of each storey, which amounted almost to giving an elevational drawing for the facade. If the house were to burn down, the facade had to be rebuilt exactly as it had been. There was a wide range of stipulations about workmanship, from general exhortations like 'workmanlike' to categories such as 'best' or 'good' work,[3] down to specifying the kind of bricks, timbers and even nails.[4] For many Regency terraces, deeds prescribed the colours in which the front had to be painted, as well as how often it had to be repainted, usually every three years (cf. plate 111). There were, of course, always the subtle legalisms as to what was left out of the covenants or restrictive clauses.

Of course, all this applied at first only to the better kinds of house. In towns, the absence of covenants almost invariably meant the prospect of a slum. In a poor area too many expensive stipulations would have prevented builders from taking up the plots in the first place. But in this as in so many other respects, it was an age in which standards percolated downwards, and from about the mid-century onwards we can find detailed prescriptions almost everywhere. The Duke of Bedford's estate Figs Mead, around Oakley Square, London NW1., was developed with medium-sized houses for the higher clerks, better tradesmen and such like in the 1830s and 1840s. Here the stipulations are unusually long, and the motive is clear: because the houses were not of the top rate, one had to be even more careful not to let them slide down to the level of, say, neighbouring Somers Town. In Norwich, in the late 1870s, £8–9 non-hall-entranced houses have covenants running into several hundreds of words, and later small houses in Preston have hardly fewer. Some towns, though, such as Portsmouth, tended to have shortish covenants throughout—and yet housing is particularly regular here.

Covenants and restrictive clauses not only controlled the building of the house, but also what happened to it afterwards. There were cases in leasehold areas where the estate itself did not bother to enforce standards, with a slum as the inevitable result. On the whole, not many cases of dispute as regards the actual enforcements of covenants are known. The cost of lawsuits probably deterred many landlords from prosecuting. The question of the enforcement of anachronistic covenants today is a difficult one; occasionally they seem to cause embarrassment, as in the case of the semi-private lawn, protected by covenant, in Norfolk Square in Great Yarmouth; 'Victorian Covenant sparks sharp criticism', ran a heading in the local paper in 1980.[5] Many of the Georgian London squares are also still closed to the general public.

As regards the tenants in rented property, we have already pointed to the generally more efficient administration and control after the middle of the nineteenth century. There was also the growing notion of tenant's rights. As Marr wrote, the occupier could expect good repair as a rent payer, and as a rate payer decent surroundings.[6] Occasionally the tenants were more strict than the owners, as in the case of the West Brighton Estate, where the inhabitants successfully prevented the Estate from erecting a pier which would have lowered the tone of the neighbourhood.

The landlord was not always a source of complaints. In the case of a row of ordinary late Victorian lower-middle-class houses in Gillingham, Kent, all the doors and windows, front and back, are today still painted in the same colour. Even the curtains are much the same colour, although there is nothing about this in the rent agreement. This agreement dates from about 1900, and also stipulates no noise at night and makes a number of other restrictions. The landlord lives not far away and regularly walks by 'to keep an eye' on his houses. It is felt that 'he cares'.

At this point the issues of control and enforcement become blurred. Why was there so little apparent difficulty in enforcing a great number of stringent conditions? The answer is that there was little antagonism between the 'controllers' and the 'controlled' in the first place. Both the owners and the residents considered it in their own interest to keep up 'respectability'. In a previous chapter we discussed the issue of the owner–occupier, and the fact that there did not seem to be much of the twentieth-century style of ideological desirability of home-ownership. Clearly, it seemed less important when both parties subscribed to the same ideals of respectability.

Building regulations

Although the social and political framework of Parliamentary Building Acts and local byelaws differs from that of private stipulations, their overall purpose is similar. In fact, their early history in England strongly overlaps. The earliest large-scale legislation in London was to serve, as in other European cities, towards the glorification of the king. Yet it was put into practice first in the new estate of the Duke of Bedford in Covent Garden. When in 1844 the new Metropolitan Building Act greatly extended the area of the London building legislation, the metropolitan surveyors simply took over some of the tasks of the estate surveyors. In many London building agreements the stipulations are abbreviated by stating: '... in accordance with the Building Acts'. The laws could thus act as building specifications.

The history of the London Acts goes back to the Middle Ages. By the late seventeenth century there were already very comprehensive attempts to ensure, above all, fire-proofing, stability, and even health in building. The 1774 London Building Act was valid for much of the nineteenth century, and in some respects is still valid today, for instance in the construction of fireplaces. Buildings were divided into seven classes (plates 40, 41): houses costing more than £850 came into Class I, those above £300 into Class II, those above £150 came into Class III and those below £150 into Class IV. There were numerous other elements of classification, but as in the case of the rentals, they were not always strictly adhered to. What really mattered was the wall-thickness specified for the different sizes of houses from two or more bricks thick down to one brick thick for Class IV. Classes V, VI and VII do not concern us here, as they largely related to free-standing buildings and very few details were given as to their workmanship. There were no restrictions at all in the Act as to the height of buildings and the width of streets. (Summerson's contention, that in effect the Act contained minimum stipulations for working-class housing, seems difficult to support (cf. plate 66).[7]

There were fines for non-compliance with the Acts, and all buildings were examined by official surveyors during building or after completion. Later these agents were called district surveyors; they received a fee for each building they examined, which ranged from £3 10s for a first-class structure down to 2s 2d for those of Class IV and only a few pence for Classes V to VII. Almost all these guardians had their own practices as architects or surveyors—and there is no shortage of stories of negligence and corruption. As a *Punch* cartoon indicated in 1890, the problem of £10 a builder was found to have underspent on foundations might well be settled over a bottle of Heidsieck and £5 into the District Surveyor's pocket, '. . . as to the underpinning well nobody will be a bit the wiser and the building wont be half penny the worse I'll bet my boots. Come, it's a bargain.'[8] Basically the system of control remained intact into the twentieth century.

It is hard to give a date for the beginning of provincial Building Acts. The numerous 'Improvement' Acts from the later eighteenth century onwards usually dealt with streets and public order. Sometimes covenants contained elements of the London Acts. The Brunswick Square Act of 1830 for that part of Brighton helped, among other things, with the enforcement of covenants for the individual houses. By that time many large towns were obtaining comprehensive Acts, dealing not only with streets, but also with 'areas', that is the space between the footpath and the basement, and with 'building lines'.

We gradually find the beginning of a completely new attitude to building legislation: that it should benefit everyone, including the poorer parts of the population. The purpose of covenants and agreements was to control the builder, but it was up to the ground landlord or the developer whether they wanted to do so. Now the building regulations would control the speculators and landlords as well. From the 1830s onwards there had been a tremendous concern for the health of the poor, buttressed by scientific reports. Its main motivation, apart from shame and philanthropy, was the simple realization that contagious diseases did not respect class barriers. The ensuing demand for healthy houses for all—only one aspect of a larger health movement—can thus be seen in the same light as the earlier demands for the fire-proofing of all houses. There was, of course, a good deal of 'laissez-faire' objection to all this; as late as the 1890s an R.I.B.A. memorandum objects to some new demands for more light and air at the back of houses, as rights in these matters partake of 'the nature of private property'.[9] On the whole, though, English building legislation of that period was held, at least by foreigners like Rudolf Eberstadt and Hermann Muthesius, to be brief, flexible, lenient, but strict and detailed where it had to be, i.e. in all sanitary matters.

In the 1840s many large towns vied with each other to be ahead in health legislation: Liverpool in 1842 and 1846, Manchester in 1844, Nottingham in 1845—though there was little in Birmingham before 1876. The most comprehensive piece of legislation was the Metropolitan Building Act of 1844. Though in many ways a continuation of the earlier London Acts, it concerned itself also with drainage, with cellar dwellings, and with the height of buildings in relation to street width; and it stipulated a free space at the back of each building, 100 square feet (9.92 m²). Plans for new streets and general drainage had to be handed in to the local authorities before the beginning of any work—an important amendment to the tradition of inspection of buildings after they had been started. On the whole, legislation developed and changed far more rapidly, and as early as 1855 the Act was brought out in a revised form.

Purely local Acts, however, were on the way out. Legislation was to be first and foremost a national affair. Earlier on, there had been the occasional national Act concerned with buildings, such as the chimney and chimneysweeper Acts (plate 17), and also the taxation Acts. After long debates the Town Improvement Clauses Act was brought out in 1847, which consolidated earlier local Acts, and in 1848 the Health of Towns Act emerged (also called the Public Health Act 1848). It resembled the London Act of 1844 in its concern for drainage, toilets and the like, but it went further in stipulating the handing in of plans not only for streets and drainage but for all buildings before operations began (plate 50, colour plate 11). Above all, it changed the whole pattern of law-making in all matters of building and health. Local Boards of Health were created in all towns, and although the laws were still drawn up by these local bodies for their individual towns, they no longer had to be sanctioned by Parliament—always an expensive process—but by the newly created National Board of Health, the nucleus of the Department of the Environment. By and large, the local legislation—the 'byelaws'—followed the National model legislation. It must be remembered that at about this time the municipalities themselves were reformed, as regards their government and their administration.

Much of the further housing legislation, though important in social and political terms, does not concern us here, as it dealt with slum clearance. It was the Local Government Act of 1858 which went into much greater detail about new houses. All new carriage streets had to be 36 feet (10.97 m) wide; at the rear of each house there had to be 150 square feet (13.94 m²) of clear space, and the distance to the next building had to be a minimum of 10 feet (3.05 m), or 15 feet (4.57 m) in the case of a two-storey building—perhaps the most crucial regulation of all as regards the plan of the house (plate 60).

Almost all major towns issued byelaws according to the 1848 and 1858 Acts within the next ten years or so. But science and legislation proceeded more and more rapidly and new Model Byelaws were issued in 1877, based on the Public Health Act 1875, which amounted to 17,000 words, largely elaborate details about drainage. It was now argued that while greater municipal power was inevitable, stipulations should be clearer, explicit and open to anybody, and not resort to the phrase, so frequent in earlier legislation, '. . . as the authorities shall determine . . .'. It was also regretted that legislation still varied to some extent from town to town[10]—though, as we shall see in the chapter on small houses, this variety was a reflection of different local and regional housing patterns. By the mid-1880s virtually all municipalities had issued new byelaws. Laxity in legislation and enforcement—as reported in the 1880s by Barry and Smith for some West Yorkshire towns—was probably rare. Meanwhile London still remained outside the national legislation, but gradually caught up, for instance, with the 1894 Building Act. There is ample evidence for the strict enforcement of byelaws, at least at the planning stage, shown by the considerable proportion of rejected plans. In some ways, the laws were as strict as in the 1980s, if not more so. In order to add a bay window to a house in Connaught Road, Norwich, in 1891, a design had to be handed in, with consenting letters from the neighbours, as well as a statement that there was nothing in the covenant against the proposal; this was a late example of the sensitivity about the building line, the covenant dating from around 1880. In this situation the municipality acted as a kind of co-ordinator of private and public stipulations. However, by the end of the century it was widely felt that some of the byelaws were in effect over-restrictive, especially as regards fire precautions, and the 1901 Model Byelaws for Rural Areas were considerably more lenient. Soon the new science of 'town planning' was to extend the building byelaws into new directions.

We have previously stressed the importance of speculation, the freedom of the developer and speculator to make as much profit as possible out of the building of houses, without much knowledge as to who was eventually going to live in them—and hence the necessity for control. But in this chapter we have also maintained that, in the end, the developer and inhabitants do share an interest in the state of the property—even if that idea of 'respectability' only consisted of maintaining a certain level within the class hierarchy. In most groups of houses, streets, or estates, there is still at least a small residue of the Classical Utopia, as it was created, or dreamt of, by the writers and architects of the Renaissance. The chief expression of this ideal lay, of course, in the unified architectural treatment which seemed so desirable until the end of the nineteenth century.

The question of the need for control was posed especially in regard to the smallest types of houses for the working classes. In previous chapters we have emphasized that working-class housing had to be profitable like any other housing, but that as regards standards there were important changes after mid-century. Most writers on the subject of working-class housing in the nineteenth century apply a basic differentiation between 'reform' and philanthropic housing on the one hand, and ordinary speculative housing on the other. The standards of the first group are seen as vastly superior. It must be borne in mind that the model estates formed an infinitesimally small proportion of all working-class housing. As regards their standards, a study of later nineteenth-century speculative housing, in which the great mass of the population lived, reveals a rapid convergence with those of the reform colonies. One such colony is Saltaire (plate 94), a model estate built entirely by one employer, Sir Titus Salt, from the 1850s onwards: its new planning elements and sanitary improvements were rapidly absorbed into speculative housing, if not in Yorkshire then at least in Lancashire and most of the rest of the north. It might even be possible to find speculative estates of comparable houses before 1850, for instance in Preston. In fact, the smallest houses in Saltaire amounted to hardly more than what was soon to be specified by most housing byelaws. There were, of course, certain elements in model colonies, like restrictions on alcohol, which one would not expect in ordinary speculative estates.

The terms 'byelaw' street (e.g. plate 180), or 'byelaw house' with their connotations of space, order, and also of commonness, underline the point that these laws were rigidly enforced. The way they caused extra expenses to the developer in land, street and drainage costs could be seen as part of the rapidly growing power of the municipality, or, to use a catchphrase of the late nineteenth century, 'municipal socialism'. The mistake made by so many housing reformers of this century was to fail to distinguish between the bad conditions of the crowded dwellings of the earlier nineteenth century, and the better dwellings of the later years. In the case of the later houses, it was chiefly an aesthetic dislike on the part of the housing reformers of their overwhelming repetitiveness; all houses were thus lumped together and declared unsuitable.

An illustration of the changing procedures of town planning and housing from the early to the late nineteenth century is provided by the development of Middlesbrough (plates 33, 89). This huge 'company town' was created out of nothing in the 1820s. The oldest part, built before 1850, consisted of a very regular grid with a central market place. But behind the regular street fronts soon came the irregular growth of courts and back-to-backs. After 1850, for the vast new extensions to the south, the reverse can be observed: there was hardly any plan for the overall street pattern any more, but only one type of house was built, and one type of street and back lane—according to the byelaws—and the same pattern sprawled further and further out until the early 1900s. The fact that the developers were still relatively firmly controlled by the large iron and steel firms did not cause the town and the housing to look any different from the speculative estates of other towns in the same period.

As was stressed before, the byelaws meant for the lower-class house what the covenants had meant for better-class houses. But even in lower-class houses standards could not have been enforced if the inhabitants had been unable to pay for them. By the end of the century the vast majority of new houses exceeded the minimum stipulations of the byelaws. There were enough substandard older houses for the poor to squeeze into; for new substandard houses there simply would not have been any customers.

6. The house and the home

As with the commander of an army, or the leader of an enterprise, so it is with the mistress of a house.

Mrs. Beeton, 1861[1]

The chief question in trying to understand the history of a house, its type and its plan, is to find out who lived in it and how it was lived in. We have so far been told about how houses *should* be kept; we must now try and reconstruct what actually happened. This is not an easy task in many ways, because historians have generally not concerned themselves much with the history of ordinary life. On the other hand, the analysis may often sound trivial and unnecessary, for the simple reason that life in the nineteenth century was in many ways the same as it is today. On balance, there seems more that separates the ordinary house of the nineteenth century from the ordinary houses of the previous centuries than from those of today. Nevertheless, there are some essential differences between the nineteenth-century and the twentieth-century and Domestic Revival view of the home, which can only marginally be indicated here. To begin with we must briefly investigate the relationship between the house, as a dwelling, and other aspects of life and work.

Suburbanization

The division between the town, or town centre, and the suburb is something we take for granted today. The first means work, the second refers to where we live when we are not working. Exceptions to this pattern are now rare in the Anglo-American urban set-up. But in pre-industrial Britain a combination of work and dwelling place had been the rule. In the better quarters of London a certain degree of suburbanization had already taken place during the eighteenth century. By the 1820s in the remoter provincial towns the middle classes would choose more suburban situations for their new houses, whether terrace or detached, though the distance from their place of work would depend on the size of the town. By the middle of the century the lower-middle class had begun to follow suit. The neat rows of small houses banished all trades and crafts; shops and workshops were normally placed on corner sites, or as ribbon development along older roads.

The development of lower-class houses in this respect is much more complicated. Even after the large-scale introduction of factories some work was still carried out inside the home. In the early manufacturing districts such as Birmingham, or the early textile towns such as Nottingham, and also in some parts of Lancashire, houses were built with special rooms for work, usually placed at the top. Unusually large windows sometimes still betray the original function of these houses. Very curious combinations of home and factory were the so-called cottage factories, built until the

1850s in Coventry; long rows of individual houses with extensive workshops at the top—called 'top shops'—where the looms were driven by a central shaft which was powered by machines situated at the end of the row.[2] Later in the nineteenth century the separation of work and dwelling place became common even for the working classes. What did continue at home was women's work, such as hat-making in Luton, or stay-making in Portsmouth, for which no special rooms were needed, and which were not affected by the generally very strict Factory and Workshop Act of 1901. Similarly, the 'rural connection'—the keeping of livestock such as pigs in the backyard—was largely phased out; the neighbours did not like it, the deeds did not allow it, and self-reliance in food was no longer needed. A much firmer distinction was drawn between town and rural life; only superficially does 'suburbanization' mean a move from the town to the country.

The final development of the suburb, as a guarantee of effective separation from the noisy and dirty surroundings of work, came with more efficient urban transport. The move to more distant and secluded country surroundings had long been under way for the best classes in London, and in Manchester and Liverpool it began in the 1820s and 1830s. Private carriages and improved roads, omnibuses and steamboats, and from 1861 horse-drawn trams, as well as some railways, helped with the commuting. Even before the construction of the railway, some travelled daily by coach from Brighton to London. But it was not until the 1880s that many of the working classes were convinced of the advantages of suburban living (plate 58). There had to be an improvement of, and more stability in, wages and shorter working hours. The men had to get accustomed to not having their midday dinner at home. From the 1860s some London stations offered reduced commuting fares aimed at the lower-middle classes, and in the 1880s central legislation began to introduce 'Workmen's Fares' (Cheap Trains Act, 1883), which lasted until the 1960s. They amounted to about a quarter of the normal fare, but strenuous efforts were made to keep the classes apart by making the workers travel at five and six in the morning. The real breakthrough in suburban transport came with the electrification and—in most cases—municipalization of trams around 1900, with reduced return fares. Even in many medium-sized towns of around 50,000 inhabitants, long daily journeys became common for workmen (plate 108).

Home, Sweet Home and domestic economy

It is difficult to imagine today what life was like in the urban houses of pre-industrial Britain. There was a far greater mixture of people and activities: the extended family, friends, servants, apprentices; the private sphere, work, recreation, the care of the sick; all co-existed and overlapped. The master bedroom could, for instance, serve as the most important room of the house generally, or be immediately adjacent to it. Modern society, from the eighteenth and nineteenth centuries onwards, began to dislike this mixture, and the private sphere of the family—increasingly the nuclear family—and the individual became much more carefully demarcated. Work was performed elsewhere, the roles of the different kinds of servants became more closely defined and at the same time they were segregated as much as possible from the family. There were now far more opportunities for entertainment outside the house; pubs and later restaurants assumed their modern role during the nineteenth century. In short, there was a relentless process of differentiation and segregation. One might say that the home became more specialized.

'Selfcontainedness', the clumsy but precise term used by Stevenson,[3] meant a concentration on the running of a house as the dwelling for one family. This 'running' was considered an immensely serious matter. The purpose of the sentence we quoted from the beginning of Mrs. Beeton's book was, of course, primarily to buttress the self-confidence of those it was addressed to, but it also served to underline the scientific and managerial nature of conducting the business of a house. 'No one can live without the complete knowledge of the principles and practice of [domestic] economy,' is claimed in another, similar book by Walsh. These are only two of a large number of similar publications about matters concerning the family house and home, appearing throughout the nineteenth century. Many of them indicated in their titles the range of incomes to which they addressed themselves, say £100, or as in Walsh's case, a range of £100 to £1,000. Clearly, one reason for the proliferation of this kind of book was the increased desire for status. Those income groups which previously did not aspire to any trappings of wealth now wanted to be told with precision how to behave and how to plan their budget. Secondly, houses did become more complicated. There was more space, there were more different kinds of rooms; 'the great amount of space *now* required', as Stevenson put it in 1880.[4] When the Sanitary Movement developed after the mid-century, health and cleanliness acquired a new meaning. We can therefore understand that there was a need for instruction in all those things which we now take for granted (plates 11, 27).

On the other hand, organization was taken to enormous lengths. At least the larger households seemed to follow a strict and sometimes complicated timetable. In her chapter on the mistress of the house, Mrs. Beeton gives the

ORDER OF THE HOUSEHOLD

Morning Prayers, 8.45 A.M.
"Forsake not the assembling of yourselves together."

MEALS

Breakfast (Kitchen & Nursery) . . . .   8 a.m.
,,   (Dining-Room) . . . . . . 8.30 ,,
Kitchen Dinner . . . . .12.30 p.m.
Luncheon . . . . 1.30 ,,
Kitchen and Nursery Tea 5   ,,
Dinner . . . . 6.30 ,,
Kitchen Supper 9   ,,

POST ARRIVES   8 A.M.
"Kind words in which we feel the pressure of a hand."
POST DEPARTS.   8.30 A.M. & 6 P.M.
"A timely written letter is a rivet in the chain of affection."

Pleasures and Duties in due order linked.

Evening Prayers, 10 P.M.

It was, of course, the servants who ran the complicated 'machines' of the larger houses. The number of servants in Victorian Britain has always been called phenomenal. About one in five families had at least one servant. In the 1890s an absolute peak was reached with about 16 per cent of the working population in England and Wales in service, whereas in 1851 it had 'only' amounted to 13 per cent. In London female servants numbered 1 in 15 of the whole population, in

11. Illustrations from the 1880
edition of Mrs. Beeton's
Household Management.

The Mistress

Domestic Servants

An English Breakfast-Table

Luncheon at Home

A Family Supper

Going down to Dinner

Brighton 1 in 11, and even in industrial Jarrow the proportion was 1 in 43. Their wages were generally low, but later in the century their circumstances, such as the quality of their accommodation, improved, and their wages rose considerably. The borderline between servant-keeping families and those who had none rose from an annual family income of about £200 to about £300, at least in London. There was, however, a wide margin, with the employment of occasional help, the 'young girl for rough work', or the 'pauper slavey' for about 2s a week.

The household became a focus for quasi-scientific economics; the house and the family as a whole became an object of moral considerations. It was seen as a necessary haven, a refuge from the growing pressures of professional work. The distance between the inner town and the suburb as the living quarter was a welcome one, because it was felt that towns were ugly, uncomfortable and liable to harbour immorality. Old Protestant values were newly emphasized by the Evangelical Movement from the late eighteenth century onwards. Social commentators, above all Charles Dickens, associated the virtues of sobriety, cleanliness and thrift with the notion of 'home, sweet home'. The saying was popularized in an opera by John Howard Payne in 1823.[5] The patriarchal image of the family was strengthened: it was the working father who was meant to use the home as a refuge, forsaking the entertainment of the pub or the club; the mother's task was to help make it such a refuge. In larger houses the mistress ruled over the servants, and the upper servants ruled over the lower servants.

There had always been symbols of togetherness in the 'home'; the 'hearth', the fireplace, was the most important one. There were others, like 'puss: they keeps the varmint away and gives a look of home', as Henry Mayhew reported from the inside of a poor home.[6] However, it needs to be stressed that the plans of terraced houses (and other kinds of houses) of the Georgian and nineteenth-century tradition did not necessarily emphasize family togetherness. In fact, separation and differentiation were the guiding principles in the development of the domestic plan. There was now more than one fire in the house, for example. Throughout the century the working-class home tended to develop beyond the general one-room plan, which was considered to be old-fashioned and unsuitable. It was only in the plans of the architects of the Domestic Revival in the later nineteenth century, for middle-class detached houses, that we find a new concentration on a central, large room, usually the 'hall'; and it was not until after 1900 that housing reformers like Raymond Unwin tried to reintroduce the idea of the main kitchen–living-room into general working-class housing. We shall come back to the latter trend in the ideology of the 'home' and its message for the plan and the design of the house. It was clearly derived, in part, from earlier moral and practical concerns, the notions of salubrity, convenience, and privacy, but there were also new kinds of emotional and artistic values. In any case, in this context our concern is less with what the writers on morals and art held, but with the more practical elements of the house: its size, the precise plan, how it was provided with modern conveniences, how physical comfort was improved and privacy achieved. First of all these factors depended on class and economic circumstances.

Though the upper classes continued to be admired and aspired to, they could not usually serve as models for close-knit families. Likewise, their very large houses, of which they often had several, usually stressed separate occupations and outward socialization more than family togetherness. Indeed, some large, later country houses built special 'family wings'. A strong interdependence of family members was most likely to be found in the medium-sized house of the middle-class family, in those income groups where there was little entertainment outside the home, where the children did not go to work and did not go to boarding school either, and where the mother had one or two servants, who took away the drudgery but did not leave her unoccupied with household matters altogether, as in the upper-class houses.

The values of home life in working-class houses, are, again, more difficult to assess. Here, an important factor was women's work. A considerable proportion of married women went out to work throughout the period, though there were strong regional variations: many worked outside the home in the cotton areas, few in the heavy industry areas. The mother's absence was generally felt to be detrimental for the well-being of the family, though Anderson has questioned this view. What is certain is that it did bring in more money and thus better houses could be afforded. Women could also take in occasional work, such as sewing and washing. Children were important as helpers in the household, and compulsory schooling after 1870 probably led to more of this help, as it reduced the numbers going to work. As the social critics maintained, very little wealth was needed to create a 'home':

> Mid pleasures and palaces though we may roam,
> Be it never so humble there's no place like home.

—or so it was sung in Payne's opera. The few books on domestic economy for the lower classes sounded mostly like sermons: 'They never have anything fit to eat, but everything is always beautifully clean and served as for a banquet.' Cleanliness had become the most important issue, when H. L. Hamilton held up this ideal of family life in the 1880s.[7] There were courses in household management in some Board Schools from 1873 onwards, and there was the important channel of middle-class influence through the former maidservant setting up her own home.

Working-class women, it was stressed, simply did not know what it meant to 'run' a house. As far as relaxation, comfort and social life were concerned, these depended on how much the husband relied on the pub for the small amount of free time allowed by his long working hours. For the women who stayed at home, socializing often still meant close contacts outside the family, the communal washing days, the popping in and out through each others' back doors—elements to which we must come back when we discuss the precise size and shape of the houses.

There was one more aspect of the home. If you work so hard to keep it up, you want to show at least part of it to people from outside. Middle-class entertainment at home was on the increase, at least for a time, especially as the reputation of so many outside places of entertainment such as pubs was going down. According to D'Aeth in 1910, small shopkeepers and clerks generally entertained at home, whereas the working classes usually did not, except on feast days. As we shall see, the rooms for entertainment and their relationship with other rooms are crucial elements in the plan and the architecture of the house. It is here that we find also the strongest degree of class division and hierarchy, as well as the most persistent imitation of the upper classes by the lower classes.

Household and house sizes

Our very rough division of society into upper, middle and lower classes has served us so far, but in a more detailed description of house sizes these categories are far too broad and imprecise; and the same must be said about the four 'classes' into which London houses were normally divided. Our survey must begin at the top.[8] The very largest terrace houses in Belgravia, or later in South Kensington, were inhabited by knights, peers, judges, merchants, or simply 'gentlemen' with incomes of about

£3,000–5,000 or more. For long periods in the year many of these houses were only inhabited by their servants, as their masters spent much of their time in their other house in the country or in a resort. Some of these houses cost more than £5,000 to buy and annual rentals could exceed £500, as in the case of the 'Albert Houses' of about 1860. Servants, up to twelve—three of them male, though later the proportion of male servants generally diminished—far outnumbered the family. There were about twenty rooms, plus smaller rooms for the servants, not counting the rooms in the mews block behind. In short, we have the equivalent of a medium-sized country house (plate 43).

After the few very wealthy came the rich, with incomes of at least £1,000, making up something like 200,000 families by 1900: lawyers, merchants, upper civil servants and others. They inhabited the large terraces of Brighton, those in some parts of Bristol and many of the western suburbs of London. The houses cost about £1,000–3,000 to build and at least £100 to rent. There were about fifteen rooms, including the rather sparse bedrooms for the servants. There might or might not be a separate servants' staircase. A butler, paid £30–45, resided in his own room near the 'butler's pantry' in the front part of the basement; there was the cook (£10–25), two maids (£15–25), and a governess if there were children. In many cases there would be a coachman and horses, though later in the nineteenth century this could no longer be taken for granted, and fewer and fewer houses had their own stables (plates 41, 42).

The next important income group was formed by the 'professional man': lawyers, the successful doctor, the top range of clerks, in the earning bracket of £500–700. The house would be worth about £1,000 and the rent £100 or less. There were about ten rooms, kept by three female servants including a cook or a governess. In its accommodation there were crucial differences between the two top categories and this medium one. There were no servants' stairs, no mews, there was no butler's department, nor a servants' hall. The servants' living room was the kitchen, and their sleeping accommodation was likely to be poor in the older houses, perhaps with several sleeping in one bed.

Next in line were the lower-paid professionals, like the higher clerks, earning around £350, renting a £500 house at £40 to £60. There were seven or eight rooms, and one or two servants, whose accommodation could be extremely makeshift, such as a bed in the bathroom.

We then reach a borderline area, the lower clerks and the shopkeepers, earning around £200, with one servant, mostly a young maid, who was paid £20, to which the cost of her keep had to be added, as with all servants. After 1900, especially in London, there was an increasing shortage of this kind of servant. The house was of six or seven rooms, costing £200–300 to build, or £25–45 to rent.

With the lowest-paid clerks, at annual incomes of around £100–150, we reach the bottom of the lower-middle classes. These would have no servant, except the kind of occasional help mentioned above. The house, with five or six rooms, which included the kitchen but excluded the scullery, would cost £120–200, or £12–30 per annum. There was no firm dividing line, in many respects, between the lower middle class and the highest earners of the working class, the 'artisans', whose earnings could exceed those of the lower clerks. Particularly important was the considerable rise of these classes in absolute numbers: the proportion of clerks alone was 2.5 per cent of the working population in 1857, but 7.1 per cent in 1911. We shall have to come back to the phenomenal rise in the number of small-to-medium sized, standardized suburban houses in the later nineteenth century (e.g. plates 48, 58, 162, colour plate 1).

About three-quarters to four-fifths of the population belonged to the working classes. Their real earnings rose by about 30 per cent between 1850 and 1875, and later there was a continuous but slower rise. There were many who earned 40s a week, that is, over £115 per annum. Their houses in the late nineteenth century could be exactly the same as those for the lower middle classes, but in the north houses with three or four rooms were more usual, and in London families would usually occupy only one floor of a medium-sized terraced house. Apart from increased earnings, there was also increased job stability, as well as a greater readiness generally to spend more on the home. As it was remarked in the Housing Report of 1884–5: one ought to '... spend ... 3s not on drink, but on rent ...'.[9] However much this was true, the increase of the rent-proportion in all outgoings seems to have been particularly strong with this group, and the 1880s were probably the period when attitudes changed most rapidly.

Below, there was the great mass of the semi-skilled, like miners and textile workers (e.g. plates 61, 94), earning 20–35s a week (£52–78 a year), who would live in houses of 3–4 rooms costing about £100 to build or 2–3s to rent (£5–12). There were the smaller, older types of houses, in many areas of the back-to-back type, or the later regular through houses, with or without a scullery. The next class below, that of the unskilled labourers, had wages of 14–20s (or £33–52). They generally lived in the same sort of houses, though the proportion of older and smaller houses, many with only two rooms, would be larger. Here we are approaching the category of the poor; but this group, though of a sizeable 15 per cent or more of the total population, does not concern us here, as its members usually occupied older houses or the cheapest kinds of early nineteenth-century houses.

The main rooms of the house

The overriding principle in the planning of a nineteenth-century house whether country mansion or cottage was the same: the differentiation of functions, the allocation of a separate room for each and every purpose. Lack of evidence makes it difficult to chart the more detailed progress of these elements in the better houses. It seems clear, though, that in the eighteenth century divisions were still far less decisive. There was less precision in the names given to the rooms, as in the case of the 'parlours', 'drawing-rooms' and 'ante-rooms'—a term later to disappear. There was less determination as to their position within the house and relationship to each other, as there was less privacy as regards separate access to the rooms. There was also less of a strict division between family rooms and the more public reception rooms. No. 26 Grosvenor Square, as remodelled by Robert Adam in the 1770s, still shows all these more old-fashioned elements of the plan.

The proportion of 'reception rooms' to the rest in the later nineteenth century—the term was already used in advertisements in the 1870s—was about one in two, or one in three in larger houses, and one to one in smaller houses. In a house of sixteen to twenty rooms there could be five to six living-rooms: the drawing-room, the dining-room, the breakfast-room, a study, and a boudoir or a library. In ten-roomed houses there would be a drawing-room, a dining-room, a breakfast-room and a study. In an eight-roomed house the study could become another bedroom. In a seven-roomed house there were only three main living-rooms. At the lower end of this range the figures are rather imprecise, because the kitchen was sometimes included in the counting.

The most prestigious room was clearly the drawing-room (plates 13, 41). The

12. (facing page, above left).
The hall of a fully hall-
entranced, small-medium-sized
house. The ceiling light above
the stairs is somewhat unusual.
(Norwich, *c.* 1870, see
pp. 86–8.

13. (facing page, above right).
Brighton. A typical first-floor
drawing-room, seen towards
the bow window, *c.* 1840
(Brunswick Square; the house
is similar to that shown in
plates 42, 117.)

term was derived from the 'withdrawing room' of the seventeenth century, usually situated near the bedrooms, where the ladies withdrew after dinner. This pattern continued to some extent into the nineteenth century, when after dinner the men stayed on in the dining-room—or went to the study or the library, the male preserve—but were allowed to join the ladies in the drawing-room later on, after having sobered up a little. In addition to large formal dinners there were many other occasions of a greater or lesser formality, like 'morning calls' (always in the afternoon) or 'at homes'. Etiquette was strong throughout; specific activities were allocated to specific servants, like receiving guests at the door (plates 11, 13); special attention was paid to the differing social ranks of the guests. The dining-room was usually on the ground floor (plate 40), and the drawing-room on the first floor. In very grand houses the latter took up the whole of the first floor, from front to back (plates 42, 43); in smaller houses there were often folding doors between the front and the back room, even when there were only two reception rooms on the ground floor. By mid-Victorian times the country house had abandoned the Renaissance custom of placing the main rooms on the first floor, but the bigger town houses adhered to it for longer. There were important advantages in this arrangement as it kept the drawing-room away from the dining-room and the kitchen smells and allowed for a longer 'processional' way from the latter to the former (plate 11).

The seven- and six-roomed houses marked an important borderline. It was very desirable, almost imperative, to have a dining-room, so as not to have to eat in the kitchen. It was also essential to have a room for 'best', always 'in a condition fit to receive strangers'. Thus, unless the dining-room was large enough to allow for various activities, like sewing or sitting by the fire, 'the many untidy kinds of work that have to be done in all households', it was highly desirable to have a third room, at least a small one.[10] In older London houses this was usually the front room in the basement—called the breakfast-room—and in later houses it could be found at the beginning of the back extension, before reaching the kitchen (plate 11, cf. 48, 55). the respective use of dining-rooms and kitchens depended, in turn, to some extent on whether the kitchen had been divided into kitchen proper, for cooking, and a scullery, for all the more dirty work, like washing up and cleaning food. It is hard to say when sculleries began to be introduced; it is probably fair to expect them in all medium-sized houses of about seven or more rooms by the mid-nineteenth century.

In every respect the situation is simplified in the five- to six-roomed house without a basement: there are just two reception rooms, one front, one back. The word 'drawing-room' was rarely used here: 'sitting-room', 'best room', 'parlour' or 'living-room' are the usual names for the front room. It was clear that the back room was for ordinary living and the front room for 'best'.

The story of the drawing-room was mirrored lower down in the reception room of the small house. All the words just mentioned were used for the best room in those houses as well, but the term parlour was by far the most important one (e.g. plates 14, 48, 61, 94). It was derived from 'parler' and referred to those rooms in monastic set-ups where strangers could be received; it was adopted in the seventeenth and eighteenth centuries for the best room in good farmhouses, or tradesmens' houses— where it could be the master bedroom. In the early nineteenth century, Humphry Repton already considered the word old-fashioned and it was hardly used in larger houses any more. But with small houses the term continued into the twentieth century—the unheated, unused working-class parlour of small houses, with only two rooms and a scullery on the ground floor (plate 14); the TV is in the back room which is also of course the dining-room. One has to remember here the primary Victorian principle of differentiation of room use, and the separation of common and

14. (facing page, below). The
front parlour of a late
nineteenth-century non-hall-
entranced house. The door
leads straight out to the front
garden or the road. There is a
small wooden bay. (Norwich;
see plate 183 for the outside,
plate 50 for a plan; the
fireplace is not the original
one.)

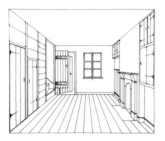

15. The back room, or kitchen–living-room, in a small two-up-two-down house. On the left the beginning of the narrow, steep stairs. The other door leads into the small scullery. (Norwich, c. 1860–70.)

everyday activities from the more formal and rarefied ones, like receiving strangers, was a very basic one. It must also be noted that the parlour was, and is, used for a number of disparate purposes: piano playing; the courting couple; there may be a desk for writing letters; when the family is large, children can play there, at least occasionally; perhaps there is a small bed in the room. By which time the parlour is not a parlour any more, but a general-purpose room.

In any case, having a parlour or not marks an important social distinction. In Belfast there were 'parlour houses' and 'kitchen houses', that is, houses with only a kitchen–living-room and a scullery.[11] James Hole tried to differentiate between the two types by calling the smaller one not a house but a cottage. By the later nineteenth century few houses were built without a parlour. The very carefully differentiated range of sizes for small houses in Noel Park, North London (plate 54), shows a parlour even in the smallest non-hall-entranced, four-roomed house[12]—a type which was the norm in many provincial towns (plate 50). About the four-roomed houses without scullery in Manchester we are told—at the end of the century—of 'washing, cooking, children playing, all in the same room'.[13] Hole reports some three-roomed back-to-back houses in Leeds in the 1860s, where the cellar was used as the all-purpose room and the ground floor room was kept as the parlour, 'commendable feeling . . . but really impractical', he thinks, which was perhaps the first criticism of the rigid insistence on the parlour.[14] Lastly, even in three-roomed ground-floor flats, the *Cost of Living Report* tells us there is the kitchen, a small bedroom and the front room as 'best or sitting room'.[15]

All this depended, in turn, on how exactly the main living-room was used (plates 15, 26, 50, 54). Originally, in older and poorer dwellings, everything was done in one room. There was usually only one fire in the house. The two-room-deep house was a major step up from the old one-room-deep one. Then there was the extension at the other end of the house, which contained a new kind of room—new, at least as far as small houses were concerned—the scullery, also often called 'wash-house'. In the south, few houses were built without sculleries from about 1870 onwards, and the same can be said about the north after about 1900. From the 1890s the very popular gas-cookers were installed in the scullery, especially in small houses (plate 19). Thus the kitchen–living-room became more and more restricted to a living–dining-room; and the front room was all the more likely to be kept 'for best' (cf. plates 14, 54).

About the other half of the house, the bedrooms, little needs to be said. Before our period, bedrooms were often used as living-rooms too. The nineteenth-century desire for privacy phased this out completely, and also increased the number of bedrooms. There were probably also more dressing-rooms; in four-roomed houses at least the front bedroom—the 'master bedroom'—had a small dressing-room on its side, which could, of course, easily be turned into a bedroom itself (plate 42). Around the mid-century, many dressing-rooms were adapted as bathrooms. The great majority of small houses had two bedrooms. But the sanitary reformers of the nineteenth century thought that three bedrooms were the minimum for a family, in order to keep the children of different sexes apart (plates 50, 99). By 1900 a third bedroom in the back extension was the norm for even the smallest new house in many parts of the country. In Spinks Street, Oldham, we find houses with one- and two-storey back extensions alternating. The problem of separate access to the small third bedroom in the back extension must be left to the discussion of the plans themselves.

7. Comfort

The five priorities of a British heating appliance: 1. safety 2. economy 3. ventilation 4. looks 5. heat.

Anonymous continental observer, twentieth century

Light and air

The next chapters will continue to deal with the history of the obvious. 'Aspect' and 'prospect' were two traditional principles in the planning of a house. 'Prospect' will concern us when we discuss the street, the garden, the layout of a terrace generally. 'Aspect' denotes the orientation of the house according to the functions of the different rooms, ensuring for example the presence of the morning sun in the breakfast room. For most of our smaller houses, of course, these considerations could hardly ever be taken into account; but a new concern for light and health generally affected all types of dwellings.

Our modern craving for light and fresh air simply did not exist before the nineteenth century. It was largely based on the new belief that they were essential for health. It was the time of the 'invention' of the seaside resort, with its monumental architectural consequences. Then there were legal developments, which reflected the general climate of opinion. We have already mentioned the 'taxes on light and air', as they were called at the time they were abolished: the Window Tax and the Duty on Glass. The precise effect of their abolition in 1851 and 1857 respectively still needs to be investigated. From 1823 the Window Tax was only levied on houses with more than six windows; thus it did not concern the smaller, poorer houses. The sort of house which had been affected most severely by the tax was probably the larger, older house, multi-occupied by the poor. From the 1850s onwards, the laws went in the opposite direction by stipulating minimum sizes of windows for small rooms.

Far more important than legal stipulations were improved technology and its availability. The sash window, introduced from Holland in the seventeenth century, came in two versions: the kind with the mechanism hidden behind a recess in the wall, common in London, chiefly because of fire regulations, from the eighteenth century onwards; and the more primitive version that exposed the frame, leaving it almost flush with the outside wall (plate 69). This method continued in small provincial houses until after the mid-century, and at the backs of small houses for some further decades, as did the even more old-fashioned small casement windows (plate 52). 'The abundant introduction of light, by means of large panes of glass, adds a cheerfulness formerly unknown,'[1] wrote Webster in 1844. By then the fashion for greenhouses, verandahs and balconies was in full swing. The price of glass had already come down considerably, and between 1840 and 1910 it fell again by

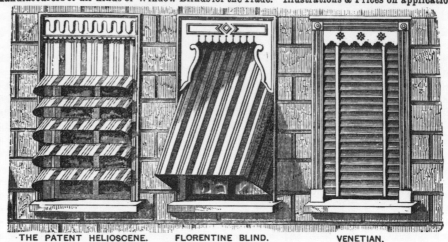

R. LOWTHER & CO. Limited, 38 & 40, South Lambeth Road,
VAUXHALL S.W.
Manufacturers of all kinds of Window Blinds for the Trade. Illustrations & Prices on application.

THE PATENT HELIOSCENE.   FLORENTINE BLIND.   VENETIAN.

two-thirds. Large panes were no problem any more. The twelve-pane Georgian and Regency sash-window was replaced around the mid-century sometimes by six upright panes, but then universally by four panes. There were many processes of making cheaper kinds of glass, with a very confusing terminology. The most widely used type was 'sheet glass' (also called British Sheet, German Plate and Cylinder Glass), introduced in 1838 and later of Crystal Palace fame. Later 'Patent Rolled Rough Plate' was also widely used.[2] However, just at the point when larger panes could be afforded by all, the Gothic and Domestic Revivalists began to dislike them, as they wanted more 'cosiness' inside the house, and therefore re-introduced small frames and in some cases the old-fashioned casement frame. Late Victorian and Edwardian windows are usually a compromise between a cheerful outlook (the large pane of the lower half) and cosy enclosure (the small panes of the upper half). Leaded lights were on the increase again in better houses, though the trellis-work lead strips stuck on to the glass of so many small houses in the north were only developed around 1930.

At times, however, light had to be kept out. A variety of curtains protected the furniture from fading. The custom of protecting the paint on the front door from that fate by hanging a curtain in front of it during the summer can still be found today. The most effective means to keep light, and onlookers' eyes, out were the blinds. The simple old Venetian blind was supplemented by more complicated outside protective constructions (plate 16). Inside shutters were also used for those purposes, as well as for security reasons. When not in use they folded back into neat compartments in the splay of the windows near the edge of the wall, or slid down like sashes below the window. By the end of the century these shutters seem to have gone out of fashion. Wood and metal 'self-coiling' shutters, the continental 'jalousie', were available perhaps from the 1860s, though, like the traditional kind of simple external shutters,[3] they were rarely used in terraced houses.

'We now hear such an outcry for ventilation,' wrote Walsh in 1856.[4] A smelly house, a 'rancid whiff', was not helpful in matters of social status, and in the chapter on sanitation we shall be further concerned with various kinds of smells. Foreigners were forever complaining about the draughtiness of English rooms. Hermann

Muthesius wrote that it was not considered polite for English domestic servants to close the door after they left a room.[5] There were several means of providing ventilation. 'All heating arrangements must be subservient to the scheme of ventilation,' wrote Bannister Fletcher, who maintained that in 'healthy places of worship there should be no sleepers among the congregation'.[6] Special openings connected with flues and placed below the ceiling were introduced. For very small rooms, so-called 'registers', small openings to the outside, were made compulsory by the 1875 Act. All ordinary domestic windows had to be fully openable in their upper half from 1858; windows other than double-hung sashes were rare in the late nineteenth century, except in kitchens and sculleries. Characteristic of sash-windows from the later Victorian period onwards are the 'horns', small projections from the upper and lower ends of the sash frames respectively; their function is partly to strengthen the construction of the frame, partly to ensure a gap at the bottom or the top of the window when the frames are fully pushed up or down respectively. Lastly we must mention here the early attempts to make the outside air itself more breathable, beginning with legislation in London in 1851.

Energy

Although aware of the voraciousness of English fires, Webster talks about the 'abundance' of coal in the 1840s,[7] and Stevenson writes thirty years later, a little more cautiously, of 'as long as the coal lasts . . .'.[8] The total output of coal rose from about 10 million tons in 1790 to 240 million in 1900. Prices fluctuated and varied greatly from area to area; 15s to £1 5s a ton in London, 10s in a coal area. Miners received around 12 tons per annum free, and each house could store about two tons at a time. There were several other fuels. Paraffin became popular from the 1860s and cost 6–10s a gallon in 1900.

The success story, of course, was gas. From its beginnings in 1807, when the National Light and Heat Company was established, largely for street lighting, we reach a state of constant underground supply and reliable meters by 1820; houses began to be lit up in great numbers after the 1830s. The price of gas fell from 15s per cubic foot (£26.57 per m³) earlier to 3s by 1870 (£5.31 m³). By 1885 there were about two million gas consumers in England and Wales. At the end of that decade penny slot-meters were first introduced, installed by private and municipal companies at varying charges. By 1920 there were about 7 million consumers, half of them on slot-meters. The average working-class family spent about £1–2 per annum on gas.

Electricity for private use was first produced in Brighton and in Holborn in 1882 and then in 1887 for parts of Kensington, but its progress was slow before 1900. By 1910 most new medium to large houses had it installed. The price in 1913 was about one-ninth of that of 1891, though gas, on the whole, was still cheaper. There were still only one million consumers in the whole of the United Kingdom by 1920. Much of the early electricity was in fact used for the new trams. All these figures demonstrate that the majority of houses were still without electricity or gas before 1914, even, for example, some of the houses in the relatively very modern late nineteenth-century district of Noel Park in North London.

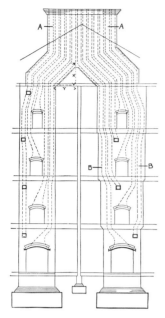

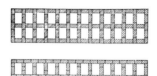

SECTION THRO: AA

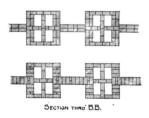

SECTION THRO: B.B.

17. Section through the chimneys of a London-type terraced house, with all the fireplaces built into the party wall. The horizontal sections are drawn through the flues of two adjacent houses.

Artificial light

Candles seem to have remained the universal source of artificial light until the mid-century. Among the cheapest were the smelly tallow lights—though in 1822 even these were still considered too expensive for labourers by Cobbett. Even later in the century we still hear that 'one lamp serves for the house'.[9] It was usually fixed in the living-room, and was then most likely an oil or paraffin lamp, for which there had been new designs from Argand in the eighteenth century to Hink's Duplex burners in the 1860s. According to Walsh, they cost about the same to run as gas and twice as much as tallow candles (plate 18). But gas gave five to ten times the amount of light and it could be fixed in every room. Its disadvantages were smell and dirt—though the system could be installed with built-in ventilation. From 1887 the much more efficient incandescent burner, invented by the Austrian Baron Auer von Welsbach, replaced all previous ones. Stiff competition with electricity as regards lighting began a little later.

Heating

Estimates as to how much heat went up the chimney in British fireplaces varied considerably; 80 per cent seemed a fair figure. But the 'cheerful blaze so dear to the heart of every Englishman', to cite only one of the many writers,[10] could not be abandoned. The fireplace was the most important fitting in the architecture of the interior. Even the actual heating methods were susceptible to the changing decorative fashions, as Stevenson claims about the more than usually inefficient Gothic and Queen Anne Revival fireplaces. It was its very simplicity that recommended the fireplace, especially when one could rely on the servants to light the fires before their masters got up. And when the ventilation craze came the old methods had even more to recommend them.

However, there were improvements. The new science of fireplaces around 1800 can be seen as the beginning of the science of the house, which after 1850 mainly continued in the sanitary field. The early and most important changes were devised by the American-born Benjamin Thompson, who later acquired the Bavarian title Graf Rumford, and consisted of the reduction of the width of the back of the fireplace to one-third of that of the front opening. By the mid-century there was the Register Grate: the iron basket holding the fire was linked with the iron opening and often with the surround of the fireplace as well. In 1884 Dr. Pridkin Teale helped to perfect the arrangements for the space at the bottom of the firebasket with a better regulation of the airflow, which was widely adopted by the early 1900s.[11] Other types of heating, even if used only in addition to fireplaces, were rare in the houses under discussion. In smaller houses there would still be rooms without a fireplace. In older two- and three-roomed houses there was usually only one; there would be two or three fireplaces in the later three- and four-roomed houses (plate 94) and four in most five-roomed houses (plate 50).

While simple as a method of heating, the fireplace and flue usually formed a complicated part of the construction of the house as a whole. This was largely due to the fact that each fire had to have a separate flue right to the top (e.g. plates 17, 86). Regulations in other countries seem to have been more lenient in this respect. There were two major variations of the position of the fireplace in the main part of the terraced house. The older one, still to be found in medium-sized houses in the provinces, placed the front and back room fireplaces back-to-back in the centre of the house, so that each house had one double (main) chimney (plate 6). The one traditionally used in London was to place all fireplaces in the party walls (plates 17, 41). They would often be combined into one construction, which also helped to insulate one house from the next. All the constructional and spatial details were minutely prescribed by the London Acts, notably the one of 1774, which was by and large adopted nationally in 1840: the construction of the chimney-breast, the floor in front of the fire, the flues—12 inches in diameter (305 mm)—the minimum angles for turning the flues, the minimum and maximum heights of the chimney (at least 3 feet (914 mm) above the roof, but less than six times the width of the chimney). Successive national laws of 1840 and 1875 also phased out the notorious employment of child labour in chimney sweeping.

Cooking and other services

More innovations can be found in the kitchen. Yet the fundamental reform proposed by Webster and Soyer (of Reform Club and 'Relish' sauce fame), the attempt to introduce the free-standing stove, common in many parts of the continent, had little success. The reason, as has been pointed out, was the English adherence to the fireplace and open-fire roasting (plate 18).[12] From the late eighteenth century onwards the standard British custom was to combine room heating with oven and water heating in one 'range'. By 1820–30 there was the closed range, and after 1870 the open and closed 'Yorkshire Range' with the oven well above the fire was introduced. Gas cooking, first demonstrated in the 1840s, was only slowly catching on as an alternative to range cooking. There were still enough servants to operate and clean the cumbersome apparatus (plates 24, 26). How the lower classes cooked is more difficult to assess. In the eighteenth century meals were often cooked outside the home because coal was dear. Even after 1900 the Sunday roast was often given to the baker for cooking. The open fire in the kitchen–living-room was slowly made more flexible, with small aids like hooks and shelves. The real breakthrough for the lower classes came with the gas slot-meters after 1890. At the beginning not only

18. Kitchen, probably in the basement of a town house, of 1855. Note the old-fashioned open fire and, on the other hand, the modern gas lighting.

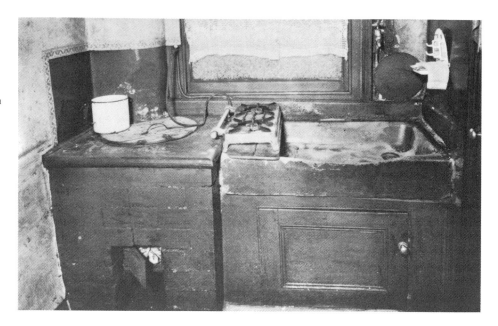

the meters but also the stoves could belong to the Company (plate 19). Baking went on being done outside the house for longer; sometimes larger estates had communal bake-ovens. Sometimes there were also special bake-ovens in the scullery, placed into the chimney breast, and pre-heated by a wood or coal fire.

The terms pantry and larder are today often used interchangeably. The latter, however, was only the place for food, and it diminished in size all the time, as more and more food was bought at shorter intervals. The pantry was for storing household goods, especially the silver, and in large houses this was the butler's province, hence the 'Butler's pantry' (plate, 43). Generally more and more built-in cupboards were introduced, usually in the recesses of the wall near the fireplace. One more service available in all houses with servants was bell hanging. First introduced probably in the late eighteenth century, from the 1870s battery-powered electromagnetic mechanisms rapidly replaced the complicated wire pull systems. Bells had implications for the plan and use of the house, in that servants could be kept on call, but would also remain distant when not needed.

8. Sanitation

The bathroom is a perfect boon to those who like washing.

Builder, 1904[1]

Cleanliness was one of the most important new concerns of the nineteenth century. Today, we take it for granted that all our toilets are flushed with clean water into the public sewer. We forget that in the nineteenth century all these installations had to be invented, propagated, financed and universally installed. Britain and the USA were the leaders in the field. Old English WCs can still occasionally be met with in remote places on the continent; and British engineers like William Lindley devised the first major sewage systems in Germany from the 1840s onwards.

We have already referred to the way housing estates were kept relatively salubrious by excluding trades, and we shall mention street cleaning in due course; here our subject is the use of water. It grew from a trickle in the eighteenth century, when a few people, like James Boswell, were famous for insisting on a daily bath, to a stream in the Regency period, when Beau Brummel of Brighton began to associate cleanliness with elegance, to a torrent after 1870. It was the concern for the health of the poor and the warnings of the numerous epidemics of contagious diseases, which led to the scientific and statistical investigations in the 1830s and 1840s. But when the Prince of Wales nearly died of typhoid in 1871, and the source of the infection was said to have been bad plumbing—and that in a country house—the middle classes were finally alerted. In the event, the Prince is reputed to have commented: 'If I weren't a Prince I would be a plumber.'[2] The activity of cleaning gained a wider purpose: from merely polishing and brightening the front to a new comprehensiveness (plate 27). It was only at this time that it was fully recognized how disease spread. Cleanliness in a wider sense became associated with 'respectability', one of the new kinds of respectability, like sobriety, in which all classes were expected to participate. The image of lightness, cleanliness, naturalness and practicality was even linked with the 'High Art' tendencies in the 1870s and 1880s, at least with the interior design styles of the Aesthetic Movement; as they were with the 'Rational Dress' movement for a more natural and healthy style in women's clothes.

The services of the town

Early water supply took many forms: the poor begged and stole, people carried buckets from wells and pumps (plate 37), and there were cisterns to collect rain water (plate 20). After 1850 many public fountains were installed, for cleanliness as well as for sobriety. For the best London houses, a piped supply had been laid as early

DOCTOR TERRACE

20. **Bedlington, Northumberland.** Doctor Terrace, *c.* 1860s. Miners' houses in a relatively rural area, where this kind of water collection was frequent. We are looking at the back of the houses, which was—and is—also the main entrance, as the front door is hardly ever used (see also plate 65). The toilets and coal sheds are across the lane.

as the seventeenth century. After 1800 there were rapid improvements: steam engines for pumping (1810), cast-iron mains (1827), filtration (1829) and reservoirs. By mid-century most London houses had an intermittent supply, though the costs were high, up to 3s per week. From about 1850 onwards there came large-scale municipalization; Manchester was early in 1847 and London was late in 1902. Liverpool had a complete constant supply by 1878,[3] London 50 per cent in 1880 and 95 per cent in 1900. By 1876 Swansea had a constant supply, 'except in mid-summer'.[4] There were fixed charges according to the size of the house, with WC and bath costing extra. The average consumption ranged between about 15 gallons in the country to about 40 in London per head per day (68–182 litres). How far did smaller houses have their own supply? Ashworth laid water to each of his workers' houses by 1835, Saltaire and Akroydon followed suit in the 1850s and 1860s. The *Cost of Living Report* of 1908 gives a good survey: southern towns were usually more advanced, but Tyneside also had water 'usually laid on'. Sheffield still had mostly standpipes and in Kidderminster only the newer working class houses had it laid on individually, the older ones still existing on one tap per row.

Underground sewers were constructed in the best parts of London in the eighteenth century. Usually they were provided by semi-public 'Commissioners', among whom prominent landowners and developers played an important part, as in the pioneering work of Cubitt in Belgravia and especially Pimlico, with its difficult flat terrain. In 1855, when still only one in ten houses in London was linked to a proper sewer, the newly-formed Metropolitan Board of Works embarked on its monumental task of a comprehensive sewer system, which was completed in the 1870s. By 1875 councils were charged with a duty to provide sewers, though in most new housing estates the sewers were actually constructed by the developers, but to the strict specifications of the byelaws (plates 21, 50, colour plates 3, 4).

21. Cross section of a road, 1899, with sewers etc. (Compare also colour plates 3, 4; plate 50.)

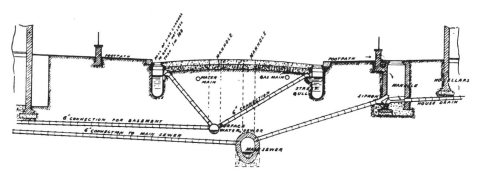

Methods of treating sewage—other than using it as manure—began in earnest after 1876. The progress of some provincial towns will be charted below.

Refuse was usually removed by the municipality, in many cases daily. They had a duty to do so after 1875. After mid-century the customary large open ashpits were limited in size, and had to be more solidly constructed. Ashes were separated from other refuse. Bins became frequent by the end of the century; in 1906 the better houses in Walsall, for instance, had them, whereas the poorer ones still used pits. The late nineteenth-century tippable bins in some northern towns, like Liverpool or Darlington, were interesting solutions (plate 22); ashes were also used for toilets. Refuse was generally re-used profitably, for roadworks, or in London for brickmaking. From about 1875 onwards we also find the installation of destructors; by 1906 Barrow-in-Furness produced electricity with it.

The toilet and plumbing

22. A tip-up bin (Darlington, *c.* 1900) of a kind still frequently to be found in the North, though no longer used. We are in the back street, looking at the rear wall of the yard. The bin was filled inside the yard, and the refuse collector opened it from the outside with his own key and tipped the contents into his cart. The other small opening leads to the coalshed.

The development of the WC has fascinated many historians. Our main concern here is the general progress of availability and the 'class hierarchy' of methods. Euphemism flourishes with the numerous terms: the 'accommodation', the 'necessary', from which probably the Geordie version of 'netty' is derived, and many others. The universal pre-WC type of toilet was the 'privy', which usually meant privy-midden and was occasionally called 'earth closet', which was misleading, as the proper earth closet was a new invention, to be mentioned again below. The 'midden' was, in fact a cesspit, placed more or less underneath the toilet. It was emptied, or drained, by 'night soil men', or 'scavengers', at first more for profit than for health reasons. Later in the century 10s worth of manure per person per annum was not considered enough to cover the cost of removal. By that time the middens had to be emptied more frequently, and they had to be smaller in size and more solidly constructed.

The most common WC in the nineteenth century was the pan closet (plate 23). It consisted of a funnel with a small pan at the bottom, which was tipped down after use and its contents swirled, with the help of water, usually poured in from a jug, into a larger container, whence it passed into the drain. The pan was later condemned because it was liable to accumulate dirt. The valve closet—first developed by Cummings and by Bramah in the 1770s and later improved by Doulton and Hellyer—was much more complicated than the pan. Its top bowl was permanently filled with water which, after use, would be let down into a lower bowl, through the valve. The top bowl would then be refilled with an automatically controlled quantity of water. The lower bowl was also separately ventilated or flushed. The disadvantages of the valve closet were its cost, the fact that it used a lot

Long Hopper Closet

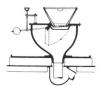

Pan Closet

Valve Closet

Short Hopper Closet

Pedestal Washdown Closet

Pedestal Washout Closet

23. The main types of WCs in the late nineteenth century. The Pan Closet also shows the dreaded 'D' trap. The Wash-out and the Wash-down are shown as 'pedestal' closets, of one piece of ceramic.

of water, and that the complicated mechanism had to be enclosed with a wooden box. Nevertheless many architects swore by it, and it was still sold in the 1920s. Then there was the 'Hopper' a 'long' and a 'short' version; what it amounted to was really only a funnel which ended in a drainpipe. The 'Short Hopper' however seems to have been the first toilet with an S trap, the simplest and most efficient water seal, and was thus the forerunner of the 'Wash Down'. This was brought into the market by E. Humpherson in the 1880s (according to Palmer) or by D. T. Bostel of Brighton in 1889 (according to Wright). It was usually made of one piece of glazed earthenware, including the 'pedestal', the base, a great advantage over the older types made of iron or lead. There were many other kinds of WCs in production around 1900, including the American 'Heber' Closet, the 'Syphonic' with extra ventilation, or the 'Wash-Out', which became the common type on the Continent. Not only that, each model had its special name, and often its own exuberant decoration, such as the 'Blue Magnolia', the 'Dolphin', the 'Epic Syphonic Closet' and the 'Closet of the Century' of 1900. All these names and types slowly disappeared, and only the white 'Wash-Down' remained. Characteristic of all British WCs is the 'waste water preventer', or cistern, insisted upon by the water companies because of the fixed charge system. One would like to have heard Claughton's 'Niagara'[5]— though silent ones were also advertized, especially with valve closets.

In 1822 Elsam wrote about WCs that there is 'no good house without one or more', and that the large houses even had one for the servants. The 'patent valve' cost £6 6s, the 'common pan' £3 10s, including fixing. Simon in 1874 gives £5 for the valve and £1 18s for the 'cottage pan'. In the 1870s *The Times* advertized houses with '5 beds, 2 dress., 3 WCs'. In the provinces these matters are harder to assess. Liverpool seemed advanced with WCs in all the better houses by 1850.

However, after the mid-century, the principal issue was no longer the WC as such, but how it was drained—in short, plumbing. In the foreword of his book on all matters of building Nicholson maintains that 'plumbing . . . does not admit of any very scientific treatment'. Webster in 1844 and Walsh in 1856 are still rather brief about the subject in their equally voluminous works. Even Simon in 1874 does not go to very much trouble about it. Plumbing at that time meant chiefly the making and putting together of lead pipes. But by 1866 Hole already talks of 'sewer gas', and says that the 'rich have no easy task to keep their water closets in order';[6] he doubts, like others in those decades, the validity of the entirely waterborne drainage and WC system. Soon the climate was to change dramatically. For the next thirty years books on house construction were almost entirely, and those on domestic economy very largely, concerned with sanitary matters. There was the scientific Dr. Pridkin Teale, or the arty Stephen Hellyer. Others tried a more popular line, like G. G. Hoskins with his book *An Hour with a Sewer Rat* of 1879. Catherine Buckton, a teacher from Leeds, tells us in *Our Dwellings Healthy and Unhealthy* of 1885 exactly how to use the toilet and even illustrates a toilet brush. Some better houses had their drainage plans displayed on a plaque engraved in brass.

The first problem was the position of the WC (plates 40, 41, colour plate 3). Many of them had been placed inside, hidden away and completely enclosed. The 1875 Act specified that there should be at least one outside wall with a window. Separate cisterns, that is a separate water supply for the WC, and a separate drainage system, the soil pipe, were gradually introduced. This soil pipe was fixed outside the house and its connection with the sewer had to be as simple and straight as possible (plate 21, colour plate 4). Manholes and inspection covers had to be constructed. The pipes had to be of glazed earthenware, first introduced by Doulton in 1846, or cast iron. These factory-made pipes could easily be assembled on site, replacing the old

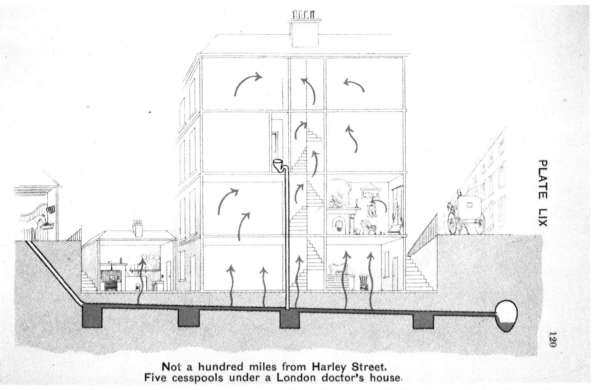

PLATE LIX

120

Not a hundred miles from Harley Street.
Five cesspools under a London doctor's house.

Colour plate 3. Unhealthy London houses. From Dr. Thomas Pridkin Teale, *Dangers to Health, A Pictorial Guide to Domestic Sanitary Effects*, 1879.
Colour plate 4. Section through a small, late nineteenth-century house in Liverpool, showing how it should be drained (see also plates 92–4). From W. Goldstraw, *A Manual of Building Regulations in Force in the City of Liverpool*, 1902.

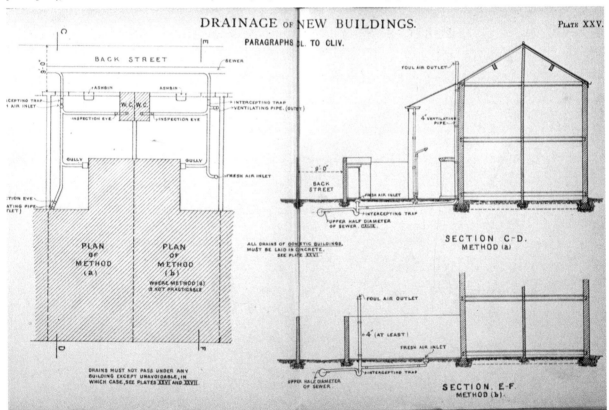

DRAINAGE OF NEW BUILDINGS.

PLATE XXV.

PARAGRAPHS CL. TO CLIV.

leadworking methods. What mattered most was the proper joining of the pipes, with the cement specified by the byelaws, except where the pipes had to be kept open for ventilation. This was again in contrast to the earlier methods, where everything was kept tightly closed. Likewise, the S trap, the simplest water seal, replaced the more complicated older D trap (plate 23).

Class differences as regards toilets were considerable. London building regulations of the early 1890s made a curious distinction between 'working-class' housing versus the rest, in that in the former the toilets could be placed in the yard, which caused an alteration in the complicated minimum stipulations for height and space in that yard (cf. plate 107). What these regulations really indicated was that the better classes expected their toilets inside. The class borderline between indoor and outdoor toilets moved downwards all the time, but even after 1900 some new three-bedroomed small houses in London only had one outside WC. In the case of those houses which had an upstairs WC as well as a downstairs outside one, we can assume that the latter was for the servants (e.g. plate 48). In the provinces, outside toilets appear to have been more frequent in better houses, especially in the north, for instance in Sheffield. But the most important class difference in most northern towns was not so much that between the outside and the inside toilet, but that of the WC versus the rest. Rochdale had only 750 WCs in 1906, in a total of over 10,000 houses. In addition we have noticed the wide price range, which meant differentiations such as a choice of mahogany or plain deal for the seat.

In any case, the older, small, working-class house was hardly big enough to have a toilet installed inside, and the fabric would often not have been strong enough to stand heavy plumbing. For those reasons, as well as for more purely sanitary ones, toilets were invariably placed in the yard, either attached to the house, or at some distance in a separate block, as was mostly the case in the north (plates 67, 74, 75). In Sheffield the 1864 byelaws specified a distance of at least 5 feet, and in the 1880s 15 feet (1.52–4.57 m); but most toilets are, in fact, much further away from the house.

By no means each house had a toilet of its own. In a report on some miners' colonies in the north-east we find remarks like 'unprovided with privies',[7] which meant that there were none in the proximity of the houses. In the older back-to-back districts there was sometimes only one toilet for every twenty houses, and as Hole describes, people had to queue on a Sunday morning. In 1848 the Health of Towns Act stated that 'No new house should be built without proper water closet etc, privy and ashpit,' which was sometimes interpreted as meaning that each house had to have its own toilet, as in Sunderland in 1867. The wording of the 1858 and 1875 Acts was much the same as in 1848. But by the 1880s, separate yards and individual conveniences were the rule for each small house, and areas of lax legislation, or enforcement, like Leeds (which still stipulated only one toilet for two houses until 1902), were rare. Even on Tyneside each flat had its own toilet, which led to some curious planning of the outbuildings (plates 100–5).

Lastly, we must come back to sewers. Many towns adopted the cheaper 'conservancy system', with the drainage limited to rain and slopwater (plate 50). The old cesspit method, however, was largely replaced by the 'pail system'—in Manchester, for instance, officially in 1871. These 'pails' were containers provided and emptied by the corporation. There were many local varieties, such as the 'Rochdale Tub' which used wooden oil casks sawn in half. Another method was the 'cinder sifter', which separated coarse from fine ashes and used the latter to fill the toilet. The actual earth closet—basically a box filled with earth—was first patented by the Rev. Henry Moule; in ordinary houses its use seems to have been limited

24. The bathroom with hot water from the kitchen range, 1875. The (abbreviated) description runs: 'B back boiler, G hot cistern, cased in and felted, F cold water cistern; H 5 feet 3 inches taper oval-end copper (or galvanised tinned iron) bath with full-way diaphragm bath valves with handsome levers and plates, mounted in deal panelled framing, with mahogany top. M trapped waste pipe. N Copper or galvanised tin iron shower bath, suspended from ceiling. PP hot and cold for hand wash basin.' The total cost, including fixing, was £41 15s. The system was called the tank system, in use from at least the 1850s. By 1900 it was considered a cheap system, the 'cylinder' system being the more advanced one.

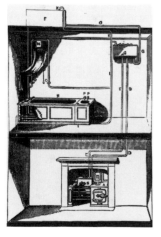

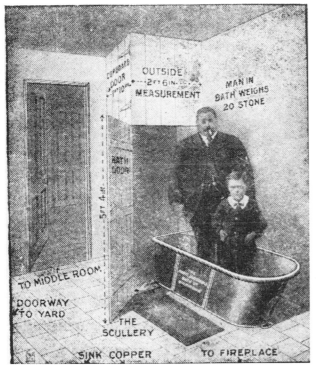

25. A folding bath in a scullery in a small, four-to-five-roomed house. Advertized by the Patent Adjustable Bath Company of Birmingham. It was of lead-coated steel; the water was heated in the copper or on the stove. The cost was around £3–4. 'Over 2000 were in use by late 1907.'

26. The most primitive kind of bath: a tub, to be set up in the kitchen–living-room. (Compare also plate 107.) Modern re-staging at Beamish Museum, Stanley, County Durham (See also plate 61b.)

(plate 61). One more type of closet needs mentioning: the 'rainwater', or 'waste water' closet, also called 'slop water', with a cistern, emptying automatically when full—quite frequently when it rained, so I am assured. Not surprisingly it seems to have been mainly used in the wet north-west, for instance in Burnley.

As regards WCs for small houses, Liverpool was ahead, with complete provision by the early 1890s; Preston and Barrow were also very advanced. Manchester by 1902 had 42,000 WCs, 14,000 pails and still 3,000 middens. In Yorkshire around that date, 50 per cent of houses with WCs in a town was a high figure. Later Tyneside houses had mostly WCs.

The diversity in the provision of conveniences for the lower classes was no doubt partly due to differing financial considerations, and perhaps also to differing geographical conditions; but one feels that it may also have been the early, experimental stage of sanitary science and engineering which accounted for the variety of provision—just as in the case of the more expensive range of toilets.

Washing

In better houses pipes began to be installed upstairs, and bathrooms and sinks—or 'lavatories', as they were usually called—were placed near the bedrooms. Pressurized water supply had progressed rapidly by 1840. Earlier there was usually only a tap in the kitchen or in the new kind of room for all dirty housework, the scullery (plate 19). In all smaller houses this arrangement remained throughout the century. Occasionally the sink could be placed in the yard of the smaller house, as in Tyneside. Indeed, it appears that—wherever the tap or sink were to be found—having a wash outside, in the yard, was customary well into this century. There were many different ways of washing clothes.[8] The better classes gave laundry out, or had special servants and special rooms for it. In some cases even smaller houses had special wash-houses, or shared them, as in the west midlands. Sometimes there

Cleanliness outside the house.

27. Servant scrubbing doorstep, *c.* 1872. The photographer was Arthur Munby, a wealthy lawyer and later a champion of the servants' cause, who was to marry the woman, Hannah Culwick. 'Steps and entrances of houses are washed and whitened every day in towns . . .' (Webster, p. 345).

28. Late nineteenth-century shoe-cleaners; the same model can be found all over the country (this example from Strood, Medway).

were also communal drying grounds behind the houses, as for instance in Leadgate, County Durham, or in Manchester. Mostly, however, the washing was done in the scullery (although it was sometimes said that washing indoors was injurious to health); and often the scullery itself was called the 'wash-house'. Hot water was produced in the 'copper' (though this was usually made of galvanized iron) (plates 19, 50). After 1900 there was a considerable increase in commercial laundries.

Bathrooms were slowly introduced, it seems, in the best London houses from the 1820s and 1830s onwards. Webster remarks in 1844 that they should be regarded as more than a mere luxury.[9] By 1879 the *Builder* states that some of the big mid-Victorian houses in Tyburnia in London still had no bathrooms. 'Hot and cold' chambermaids served the portable baths. But by the 1880s most new houses in inner London of a rental of £100 or more, and in the suburbs of £50 or more, had bathrooms installed.[10] After 1900 probably all but the smallest London houses were built with upstairs bathrooms, as were the six- to seven-roomed houses in the provinces and many of the small houses in the north-east (plates 24, 48). Plumbing was simplified and co-ordinated by placing the bath and the upstairs toilet above the kitchen and scullery in the back extension. Heating the water was done in a variety of ways, either underneath the bath itself, or by geysers (from 1868), but increasingly, from the 1850s, in combination with the kitchen range. In small houses a movable bath tub was used (plates 26, 107), or there were baths which could be folded. Other people went to the public baths for their 'weekly tub'. As there were as yet no pit-head baths for miners, they had to have their 'daily tub' at home. The problem of decency was solved by wearing a small pair of pants (plate 26), and by bending down into the tub as far as possible. Whereupon the question arose: 'When do you wash the possible?'

9. Improving the fabric

. . . To secure the complete isolation of each distinct house for the due prevention of the spread of disease.

Barry and Smith, 1888[1]

The health of a house's inhabitants can be improved not only by means of modern fittings but also through the quality of the fabric itself. In previous chapters we have dealt with ways of ensuring standards in building; and we have also mentioned new methods of production which brought a greater degree of reliability to the quality of materials. There are two ways of developing construction in order to achieve a sound structure: with methods already known, or with innovations in materials and techniques. Unfortunately the most important question—what was the actual extent of bad building in the nineteenth century?—is also the most difficult to answer.

Naturally the assessment of the quality of ordinary construction varied enormously. 'Never have cases become known, where, because of building lightly, property or lives have come to grief.'[2] This clearly impossible claim was made by Hermann Muthesius, chiefly to impress the value of light construction, in general terms, on his German readers. Booth, on the other hand, claimed that even in new London suburbs of the late nineteenth century there was much bad workmanship. The *Tudor Walters Report*, the most detailed investigation of all matters of house building, undertaken during the first world war, is divided in its opinion. On the one hand it says that speculative builders used 'neither skill in design nor science in erection'. But further on it maintains that improvements had been made and that certain standard types were 'cheap under general conditions'.[3] While cheap houses are, naturally, liable to bad or indifferent construction, what was probably new in the later Georgian and Regency period was that even good houses had defects which were covered by the paper-hanger and the stucco-worker. Nash decried the construction of some houses on the Portland Estate, but soon the same criticism was made about his own houses, and was repeated countless times again about all kinds of houses. Yet at the end of the century there are frequent comments about improved construction even in small houses. The extremely critical Barry and Smith, in their report which condemned the back-to-back types, found nothing to criticise about the bricks, the mortar and the timbers of those houses. Byelaws did not eradicate bad construction, but they seemed to reduce the scope for it.

Only a brief survey of the common methods of construction can be attempted here (plates 53, 92). We can begin with what holds the stones together: mortar. Poor quality mortar was made of badly burnt lime mixed with sand and 'road stuff', that is, dirt, and when dry it fell into dust again, or dirty sand. Good lime, however, always has some hydraulic qualities—that is, it stays firm even in wet conditions—

and it continued to be utilized into the twentieth century. But increasingly the much more durable and hydraulic cements were used, though at first more for decoration than for structural purposes. Portland cement, the most successful nationally and internationally, was patented in 1824. After the mid-century scientific tests were introduced, and also the use of mechanical pugmills to grind the clay became more common. By the late nineteenth century cement had become universal in all foundations and for joining pipes. Webster already mentions concrete, as pebble mortar, in its use for foundations;[4] later the byelaws demanded it underneath all buildings. A light variety of it was 'coke breeze', one-quarter of it cement, the rest a by-product of the rapidly rising gas industry; it was used for partition walls and also for lintels in lieu of stone.[5] Hollow building blocks, or breeze blocks, came to England rather later. The numerous early experiments in building whole houses of concrete had little effect on the general run of houses. Cement was also increasingly used to cover the outside of buildings, especially on rough stonework. Inside plastering was applied to all buildings by perhaps the mid-century, but which time rough walls simply were not accepted any more.

The regulations about foundations were at first concerned with strength in the sense of providing enough bulk, such as the carefully graded footings, the bases of the wall, in the 1774 London Act (plates 21, 41, 53). Later there was more concern for damp-proofing. Apart from using cement, damp-proof courses began to be introduced perhaps around 1850;[6] they were made of lead, stoneware, slate or asphalt. From 1890 all new houses in Manchester used them, and by 1900 new buildings included them almost invariably. Perforated 'air' bricks can be seen in most houses of that period, ventilating the space underneath the floorboards, which themselves were no longer permitted to lie on the ground, even in small houses, from the 1860s–1870s onwards.

Generally speaking, brick replaced timber in non-stone districts during the seventeenth and eighteenth centuries; in the nineteenth century brick largely replaced stone in the stone areas. Yet outside London, especially in the south-east, wood continued to be used to a considerable extent. Many nineteenth-century wooden cottages have been preserved to this day in Kent and Essex. To what extent houses in the poorer districts of towns were still built of wood as late, say, as the middle of the century, is hard to establish. Often the backs of houses are of wood, as in the relatively stately-looking Ordnance Terrace in Chatham of about 1820. Even in small and medium-sized houses in the metropolis we find slatted wooden mansard roofs at the back, while the facade is built completely in brick.[7] It was a method widely practised in Holland till the beginning of this century. Inside, wooden partitions, i.e. a framework filled with laths and plaster or with bricks ('brick nogging'), continued in small houses (plate 53), often even for load-bearing walls. Stone walls, according to Nicholson, in the early nineteenth century cost half as much in the stone districts as a good brick wall in London; but he also lists the advantages of brick: it is lighter, easier to use and less absorbent, and a brick wall can be one-third less in thickness than an ordinary rubble stone wall. Bricks soon became common in all towns, at least for the back layers of walls and for dividing and partition walls. In small houses, and for instance for the conveniences, where space was at a premium, it was far easier to achieve a degree of precision with brick than it was with clumsy, cheaper kinds of stone. But, of course, bricks had to be 'good bricks', or 'well burnt bricks', as the covenants and byelaws never failed to stipulate. Later on the new methods of brick making and burning reduced the number of inferior bricks on the market.

The thickness of brick walls could also be regulated more easily, as it had been in London from the seventeenth century onwards (e.g. plate 41). They had to be at least one brick, or 9 inches (228 mm), thick. In Class IV houses only the walls around the dustbins could be a half-brick thick. It was this $4\frac{1}{2}$ inch walling, for part or most of the walls, that was the bane of much small house construction, and not only there; a three-storey house in Clark Street, Scarborough, of *c.* 1850 has half-brick walls on its sides. Soon the byelaws phased out the most flimsy kinds of construction. They also introduced party walls reaching above the roof (or just below it), which had been common in London for a long time (e.g. plate 52).

There were many ways of bonding brickwork. English bond was considered best for stability, and was used by many advanced Victorian architects. But the Georgian tradition was Flemish bond, largely for aesthetic reasons. Because of the great disparity in the quality of bricks and the special emphasis on the features of the facade, like gauged arches, there was sometimes a severe lack of bonding in late Georgian and Regency facades, between the front and back parts of a wall. Wooden ties were used to overcome this. The good bonding of angles was another test for the quality of bricklaying. Cavity walls were dealt with in housing and building hand-books, such as Stevenson and Mitchell, and seemed fairly frequent by 1900.[8] Increasing care was spent on steps, floors and sills later in the century: there was more use of stone, slate and later new kinds of hard tiles. For sills in cheaper houses, cement over brick remained common, and often we still find wooden sills.

What was changing in the traditional craft of carpentry? Webster writes in 1844: 'The science of carpentry is now better understood and strength is made to depend on judicious framing combined with lightness using as little as possible of the so perishable and expensive material as wood.'[9] Hermann Muthesius marvels at the lightness of English timberwork, but finds the weight is generally well distributed. Three factors were vital in this development: the specifications of minimum thicknesses ('scantlings') (plate 53); mechanical saws from the 1840s and on a large scale from the 1870s—in other words, a much greater degree of standardization; and lastly, much harder to assess, the insistence on well-seasoned wood, though thinner timbers clearly need less time for drying. It is much less usual to find timbers of greatly varying sizes in the floors of late nineteenth-century houses; earlier on this seemed to be common.

However, as far as the actual constructions are concerned, there seems to have been little change. Floor joists were a minimum of 2 inches thick and 6 inches high (50–150 mm) and were spaced 12–16 inches apart (300–380 mm) (plate 53). The distances of the timbers from fireplaces were minutely regulated. The basic 'single floor' with one set of joists would only cover a distance of 8 feet (2.44 m). This meant that almost all floors needed some reinforcement, like diagonal battens placed cross-wise ('herringbone strutting') (plate 53). For gaps of over 15 feet (4.4 m) 'double (joisted) floors' were needed, that is, with a second set of joists at right angles; over 25 feet (7·62 m), only in the very largest terraces, 'treble floors'. By the nineteenth century iron ties and beams were increasingly used, though much less, it appears, than in contemporary France and Belgium. They were used especially in places where partition walls were placed over voids on the storey below. In the category of floor construction belong attempts at soundproofing: plaster, felt and sawdust were put between the joists, and the joists never reached through party walls, but always rested on 'wall plates', embedded into a recess in the wall.

Great economies in roof construction came with the new kind of covering with Welsh slates in London around 1800; in any case, a strict Classical style also demanded flattish roofs. An even lower pitch could be achieved with lead or zinc covering. From Nicholson to Middleton, throughout our period, single rafter construction, that is, one set of main beams, was considered sufficient for spans up to

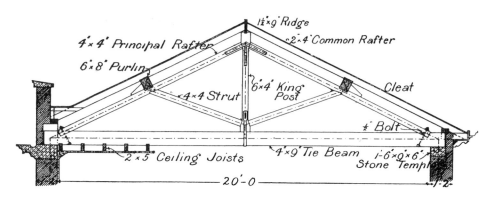

20 feet (6.01 m). In practice this was extended to 25–30 feet (7.62–9.14 m), the depth of a normal two-room-deep house (plates 56, 92). The partition walls could help with the support; there was also a collar (a horizontal cross-beam at mid-height), and there were diagonal struts, or purlins (beams running along horizontally behind the rafters). For wider spans double rafters had to be used, that is, the main beams had to be doubled, possibly with king or queen posts, vertical supports inside the roof.

One of the most critical parts of the fabric was the meeting point between the walls and the roof. A simple solution was the one almost universally adopted from the Georgian period onwards in London and Bristol (plate 177), but rarely for small houses elsewhere: a wall was carried up in front of, and above, the eaves. It was called a parapet or blocking course. The roof was mostly placed at right angles to this wall at the front, that is, its ridge ran with the depth of the house, which, by lowering the roof, simplified the timbers even more and thus reduced costs (plates 40, 41). Furthermore, the ridge of such a roof, its highest point, leant against the party wall. This high party wall, of course, had to be there by law, for fire protection, and thus it was only expedient to use it for supporting the roofs as well, and thereby save on timber. The great disadvantage with this method was, however, that the low point of the roof ran above the centre of the house and invariably caused problems of drainage, that is wet ceilings in the middle of the room below. This is the dreaded 'valley-gutter' in what is called the M-type roof. Occasionally one can also see an ordinary ridge—that is a ridge parallel with the front—which has its eaves at the front hidden by a low parapet wall.[10] The ordinary, traditional kind of ridgeline and eavesline, where the eaves project beyond the front wall, remained the rule in most provincial Georgian and Regency houses. By the mid-nineteenth century there was a revival of this method in villas and semi-detached houses, which soon reached ordinary houses as well. However, normally this does not expose the bottom ends of the rafters—fire regulations did not allow it—and the overhang is encased in slate or stucco, or sometimes wood; the whole was called the soffitboard. In addition there are 'trusses' at about one-foot intervals (300 mm). In reality these were decorative consols, or brackets, also called sprockets, which were embedded in the top layer of the wall and which had nothing to do with the real trusses behind. In the provinces we find yet another method in the later part of the century: the ends of the rafters are placed above a number of projecting courses of stone or brick at the upper end of the wall (plate 183).

Closely linked with these constructional details is the gutter. It was a source of constant annoyance in older streets that there was no gutter at all. In the earlier London and Bristol type of roof it could be placed behind the parapet wall. In the case of the eaves-drop traditional roof—with the roof projecting over the wall—it was fastened at the edge of the roof. Earlier gutters were made of lead or wood, but from the mid-nineteenth century onwards increasingly of zinc or iron. In later Newcastle houses the top edge of the front is always of stone and the gutter is embedded into it or placed above it (plate 103). Clearly with these features we are entering the realm of style and aesthetics: the older Bristol and London methods stemmed chiefly from the Classical desire for a firm roof line, combined with fire-precautions; the later method—which was really the traditional one—was part of the new cottage-fashion which wanted to make more of the roof generally—elements which will be discussed in the context of the facade as a whole later on.

Stairs changed considerably, mostly in the direction of simplification. Only in very small houses did the older methods continue, like the tortuous, steep stairs with several turns. Later the middle-stairs type of small house had only one straight flight, and in others there was one turn. Webster implied that turned stairs are of a lower status than those with a landing; this is curious in a way because it was, of course, far more laborious and difficult to construct stairs with turns. In the largest Regency and Victorian houses the steps were now of stone, several storeys up. Here the traditional craft of the carpenter was less and less in demand. This was even more true of handrails, a traditionally highly skilled branch of the craft: cast iron replaced much of the work. Fire-proofing, such a strong motive behind building legislation in the two previous centuries, was no doubt a factor in this development. However, regarding the choice of iron and wood, Stevenson maintains that wooden beams are generally safer in fires than iron beams—which shows that even in a subject as scientific as this there is room for opinions.

10. Outside the house

Les rues plus belles sont les plus droites et les plus larges.

D'Aviler, *Cours d'architecture* 1695

The estate

As this is a book on housing and not on towns, the subject of town planning is outside our concerns. However, it is impossible to understand a house and how it works without knowing about certain elements of the town as a whole. We have already touched on several of them: suburbanization, the increasing division of functions, especially the separation of living quarters from work, and technical innovations, such as water supply and sewage.

Although our view is biased by the fact that so many of the earlier, less regular streets and houses have been destroyed, we must stress again here the tendency towards greater organization, financial, social (plates 10, 58, colour plate 1) and architectural. The term 'estate' is used here in a vague sense. If there was no single, large estate, smaller landowners often collaborated in the layout of streets and the allocation of functions. In any given area, the first speculation often predetermined the shape of further developments. The power of the estate can chiefly be felt — apart from the degree of regularity in the street pattern — by the way shops and trade were separated from the houses. There were, of course, the pre-existing major roads with their 'ribbon developments' along them. Additional shops and pubs were usually placed only on corner sites — which also fetched higher rents than ordinary houses (plate 37). By the late nineteenth century, especially in the vast suburban areas of the south-east, shops were almost entirely restricted to the main thoroughfares. Green Lanes, Harringay in north London (plate 30), or London Road, North End, Portsmouth are typical examples of the massive turn-of-the-century shopping street. In the surrounding streets, shops cannot be found for miles. One must not forget, however, that much more street selling was going on in those days. Pubs, which used to be much the same size as houses, are now far more lavish, inside and out, but there are far fewer of them.

In a narrower sense the 'estate' sometimes meant a semi-private area, comprising one or several terraces, and the clearest expression of this was the existence of gates at the point of entry, sometimes with gate lodges attached (plate 31). At night, these gates were often closed, providing a kind of semi-private seclusion for the inhabitants. The gates for the Bedford Estate in London were notorious for hindering traffic between Holborn and Euston, and were only taken down in the late nineteenth century. More symbolic were the gates linked architecturally with actual terraces, like those flanking Chester Terrace in Regent's Park, or those in the Camperdown area in Great Yarmouth of the 1840s. It was not until the twentieth

30. **London.** Grand Parade, Green Lanes, Harringay; a typical late Victorian suburban shopping street; the long side streets are usually devoid of shops.

31. **Tynemouth.** Percy Gardens, *c.* 1860, in a favourite position, facing the sea. The lawn in front of the houses and the access road are marked 'private', and there is even a gate lodge, just as for a large estate in the country (compare also plate 113).

32. **Cheltenham.** The Promenade, built from the 1820s onwards (now Municipal Offices) in a view of *c.* 1840. The name of the street and terrace is an accurate description of its use.

century that the greater powers of public town planning created the English suburban 'estate' in its final, comprehensive sense.

The street

Few common types of dwellings are so intimately connected with their surroundings as is the self-contained house built on its own piece of ground. Houses always look out both front and back; houses without a front entrance are extremely rare.[1] Here we must briefly look at the normal type of street; the more unusual types like courts will be discussed below. Whereas the better eighteenth- and early nineteenth-century terraces always had very carefully made-up streets in front of them—often causing considerable moving of earth—most houses were reached by all sorts of bad streets or non-streets. There were never-ending stories about their misuse, their filth and their holes filled with ash and rubbish. For smaller houses a carriageway was often omitted altogether, especially in hilly areas: small handcarts and ponycarts only needed footways.[2] But even medium-sized houses of the 1830s where space was not lacking, as in Brandling Place, Newcastle, sometimes had no proper front streets. Total neglect of the front entrance can still be observed in the case of the Doctor's Row colliery houses in Bedlington of *c.* 1870 (plates 20, 65).

The widening, regularizing and cleaning of streets soon became one of the main objects of the sanitary reformers. In 1843 Maslen remarks about streets that private economy and 'private convenience should give way to public convenience and public security'.[3] Interminable local 'Improvement Acts' concerned themselves with the cleaning, paving, lighting and policing of streets, and especially with that important demarcation line between the private and public sphere, the 'building line'. Nothing was allowed to project, not even a shoescraper. By the end of the century Marr could state that every occupier, as a rate-payer, was entitled to a good street.[4] In addition to front and back streets, some towns, like Liverpool, stipulated 'cross streets', interrupting the terraces at specified intervals. Hole hoped for a minimum street width of 60 feet (18.29 m), though the common prescription from the mid-nineteenth century onwards remained 36 feet (10.97 m). Birmingham demanded 50 feet (15.24 m) from 1876 onwards and Halifax had four classes of streets: 54, 40, 30 and 24 feet (16.46, 12.19, 9.14, 7.32 m); the last one could not be a carriageway. The long straight 'byelaw street' became a common picture.

Great efforts were made to organize street cleaning. In some houses in Bristol in the 1880s wood-chopping had to be done inside the house to keep the street tidy.[5] According to Model Byelaws of 1877, footpaths had to be cleaned every day, except on Sundays. Public street cleaning became common, at least in better streets. In addition, much care was given to polishing door knockers and whitening sills.

The making of the roads, that is those in new housing estates, was a matter for the ground landlord or the developer. But the very strict byelaws, especially as to drainage, left little choice. Preferably the roads were made before the building of houses began (plate 10). In Barrow the maps show that roads, as well as schools and chapels, were built well in advance. But from many other estates it is known that the new inhabitants had to wade through the mud because the builders did not have the ready money to build the roads before they had sold most of the houses.

Roadmaking was an important new science (plate 21), as important as the others discussed so far in connection with the house. First of all there was the surveying, then the levelling, excavating and embanking, though Maitland recommends the use of a theodolite only for more difficult terrains.[6] When the ground was slightly

33. **Middlesbrough.** A reflection of the old use of the street as a place of social intercouse can still be found in many working-class streets in the north.

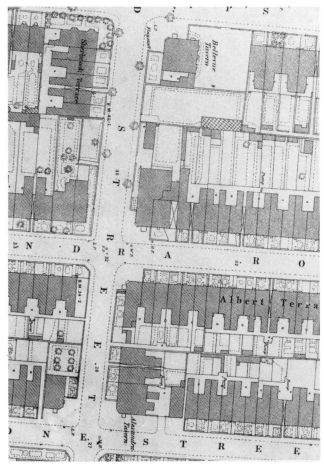

34. (far left). Another of the many functions of the street: the 'knocker up', a walking alarm clock (Rochdale).

35. (left). **London**. A mews street in Pimlico, c. 1850. The stables, with small rooms above, were often reached by ladders. As this street block is of rather irregular shape, the entrance to the mews is not in line with the terrace.

36. (far left). **London**. Eaton Place and Eaton Square, mews entrances, c. 1840 (compare also plates 135, 136). The houses on the right are new; most mews houses are now sought-after small residences.

37. (left). **Norwich**. Houses c. 1865–1880, from the detailed *Ordnance Survey Town Plans* of the 1880s. Note especially the varieties of rear access: the small houses have passages along the back, cutting through the access from the yard to the garden, accessible from the street by tunnels at irregular intervals (cf. plates 50, 183; colour plate 6). Somewhat larger houses have tunnels between every other house, and thus no need for a back passage. The medium-sized houses have passages leading to the bottom of the gardens. The chief reason for the rear access was the lack of a sewer for the toilet, though there was a sewer for rain and other waste water.

(B.M. bench mark; F.P. fire point; G.P. gas point; L.P. lamp post; W.P. water point. West is at the top.)

contoured, it made a great deal of difference to the orderly look of the terraces if that contour was levelled. Many street works were great achievements in themselves, as for instance those at the seafront in Brighton (plate 119). The early nineteenth century had brought great advances in road surfacing. There was Macadam's 'metalling', that is, broken stones or gravel consolidated by roadrollers. Then there was Telford's foundation set of tightly packed rough stones, which by the late nineteenth century was increasingly replaced by a concrete bed. Earlier, sandstone slabs or boulders formed the surface of better streets, but this was replaced by granite from the middle of the century onwards, though slabs can still be met with in sandstone areas like Bradford. To reduce the noise on granite paving, peat was sometimes strewn over it, for instance when somebody was ill in a nearby house. Wood was rarely used in residential streets; asphalt and tarmacadam became common in England only after 1900. Footpaths were usually covered with gravel or sandstone slabs; granite or blue Staffordshire bricks began to replace sandstone for kerbs. There were strict regulations about keeping the rainwater off the roads. In all, developers and builders had to spend £4–6 on sewers and roadworks per small house. Streetlighting was supplied by private or municipal companies; gas light had begun in 1807 in London and was widespread by the mid-century (plates 18, 69).

Finally, streets were places for communication, for promenading, or just for looking at what was happening. '. . . As if our families had nothing to do but to sit at the front windows to see the passing vehicles', wrote Papworth in 1857 (plate 32).[7] In working-class streets similar habits continued. As a German observer of English working-class habits said in the 1890s: 'one finds old people . . . outside, standing or sitting on the same spot for a couple of hours, till one thinks they must be waiting for somebody' (plate 33).[8] Tell-tale reflectors (called 'spies' on the continent), mirrors fixed near the window on the outside so that the street can be observed from inside, were known,[9] but probably not used very much. However, in better houses there seems to have been a very rapid change of these habits after the mid-century. 'Englishmen [in contrast to Parisians] do not desire to get out, or even look out of the windows; balconies are useless,' remarked William H. White in 1877.[10] The street and street life became devalued. Earlier on the best houses or terraces were usually placed along the best streets, or main thoroughfares, and the small houses tucked away behind. Later the opposite became the rule: the 'best' district of the town is found in a secluded, quiet position, often near a park; the main suburban thoroughfares are lined with small houses, no bigger than the ordinary houses behind: Ashton Road in Oldham is a good example of this development. Regular streets were no longer fashionable, and Stevenson even claimed that in straight streets the air was liable to become stagnant.[11]

Rear access and mews

The best Georgian and Regency houses had to have their own stables and accommodation for coachmen. This was placed at the end of the rear yard of the house and gave out to a small back street, which was usually shared with the row of houses and stables on the other side, forming the inside of a street block (e.g. plates 1, 3, 7, 35, 41). Later, as in Belgravia, these 'mews', as the back streets were called, were entered by splendid gates (plate 36). Outside London this sort of arrangement was rare, and only Brighton has a fair number of mews. But there they were often grouped at some distance from the houses, as in the case of Sussex Square. Later in the century those in Third Avenue, Hove, called King's Mews, formed a completely

38. Front gardens for small to medium-sized houses, late nineteenth century (Norwich). (cf. plate 169).

separate block, firmly enclosed. By that time, the inhabitants of London suburbs were less and less in need of private carriages, as omnibuses and cabs took some of the commuting traffic. It was also felt that mews were likely to harbour uncontrollable congregations of the lower classes. In denser parts of west London, as in the Portman Estate, most of the rear space behind the terraces was filled up with untidy additions. The feeling that the rear space of every house should be kept as much as possible free from additions grew rapidly, and with the 1844 Act came a compulsory 100-square-foot free space for every new house (9.29 m²). Occasionally the term 'mews' was misused, as in the case of the Royal Parade in Cheltenham, where it formed just a rear lane.

For houses of middling and smaller size the rear access was often a problem. It was largely to reinforce status differentiation that the entrance of a mews had to be placed away from the main entrance of the house and the major street. But for more ordinary houses in towns the old custom of each house having its own archway to the back, adjacent to the front door, had long died out. Thus those terraced houses which could not afford a mews generally had no separate rear access. In London the problem was largely overcome, as there was a separate front entrance to the basement (see below). In smaller houses there were sometimes coal-holes in the footpath for the front cellar. But later medium-sized and smaller London and south-east houses have normally no separate rear access (plates 58, 59)—though they at least have a corridor inside the house to carry the coal through and the bins out. In some other southern towns, like Plymouth, there are always ample rear access lanes. It was in the small corridor-less houses in the north that the rear lane became a very important issue, to which we shall return.

The garden

We know far too little about the gardens of ordinary English houses, and that in the country which contributed more than any other to garden design, and where, because of the lower housing density generally, more people have gardens of their own than in most other countries. We are not concerned here about the design of the ordinary garden as such—it contained then, as it does today, a mixture of formal and picturesque motifs; our question is a more basic one: was there a garden at all and how did it relate to the house?

To begin with, it must be stressed that in the centres of large English towns gardens were as rare as in those of most other countries. It was the later process of suburbanization which enabled the great majority of houses to have one. Furthermore, there are strong regional differences. In the north, gardens are less frequent, and most nineteenth-century small suburban houses have none. There are even late nineteenth-century larger-than-standard-sized houses in outer suburban situations in Manchester with only a small back yard and hardly even a front garden. Even when there was ample space around the houses, as in many miners' colonies of the north-east, it appears that there were few gardens. Nor were there proper streets; in fact there were hardly any delineations of the grounds at all (plate 61). It costs time and money to arrange proper surroundings for the house, and there was likely to be a shortage of both. In East Anglia, on the other hand, it seems that even the poorest houses on the outskirts of towns were always surrounded by ample gardens (plates 37, 50, colour plates 5, 6). Scattered examples of rows of small houses survive in Great Yarmouth, Colchester and Norwich, where only primitive paths or small carriageways lead to the houses amid the usually well-kept gardens.

39. **London.** Paddington, c. 1855. One of the new type of terraces where the back of the house does not give out to a bleak yard, but to a large private, communal garden—the sort of garden which in Georgian and most Regency squares is placed in the square (compare plates 1, 6, 7). The numerous levels and balustrades do not only lead down to the garden but also hide the access to the basement.

How much did small householders use their gardens in general, in a period when more and more food was brought in from outside? Artisans in East London were famous for their flower cultivation, but when Cadbury advocated home-grown produce for his workers in the late nineteenth century this was greeted as an innovation. There was, of course, also the allotment; Nottingham was famous for them already by the early nineteenth century, and later on towns had to provide land on demand. Finally there were the public parks, from the mid-century onwards, to cater for recreational activities.

From the vague, anonymous history of the garden we must proceed to the much more specific movements to introduce ornamental gardens into towns. In England this began with some of the large London squares in the seventeenth century. At first these were laid out in the precise and regular manner of the Renaissance garden, but later in the eighteenth century those squares were turned into miniature landscaped gardens. All the best late Georgian and Regency terraces gave out onto such a square or garden. They were, and still are in the case of many London squares, not accessible to the general public, but only to the residents of the surrounding houses who possess their own key. In London they are often called paddocks, in Brighton, enclosures (plates 1, 3).In some cases we find a compromise between a front garden and a square: the terrace is set back from the street and a stretch of greenery is placed between the street and the private driveway in front of the houses. There are good examples of this arrangement in Leamington Spa, like Lansdowne Crescent of around 1835 (plate 121, colour plate 12). Sometimes the best Victorian terraces of a town are situated in a proper park of their own, with a private access road, such as Blenheim Mount, Bradford, or Gambier Terrrace, Liverpool[12] of the 1830s to the 1860s (cf. plates 6, 7). In the case of Bede's Terrace of the same period in Sunderland, there are ample front gardens for each house, accessible from a private road. Occasionally we find that the street between the front gardens is replaced by a garden path and that carriage access is only at the rear of the house, even in medium-sized houses.[13] In Hull, all the later 'terraces', the smallest type of house, have ample front gardens, and no carriage access, front or back (e.g. plate 70).

Later in the century all medium-sized houses and more and more smaller houses were built with a front garden (plate 38), even those with basements. 'If kept in good order it improves appearance and adds privacy,' wrote Maitland,[14] and Banister Fletcher mentions them as status symbols (plate 110).[15] They became compulsory signs of suburbanity. Often they were enclosed by heavy iron-work, most of which was removed in the second world war. By the end of the century one can probably say that the majority of new houses had a front garden, or at least a 'forecourt' (plates 63, 103, 105, 169), that is a paved stretch of ground of the depth of the bay window. Even most back-to-back houses were built, by then, with a front garden, which was, of course, the back garden at the same time.

In contrast to the largely ornamental front garden, the rear garden was not valued much in larger houses in towns, at least by the middle of the nineteenth century. Gardens are 'usually uncared for' wrote White in 1877.[16] Large houses in Regency resorts seldom had back gardens. For these houses the back meant 'service' and the members of the family probably very rarely went into it. As late as the 1890s some of the large houses in Cathedral Road, Cardiff had splendid open front gardens (as well as a magnificent public park nearby) but only large yards at the back. There was, however, already a movement under way to give good houses their own back gardens. It probably began with Connaught Place, London W2, in 1807,[17] and on a larger scale we find it with some of the terraces in Regent's Park and in St. Leonards in the 1820s: the main entrance to the houses is at the back of the terrace, the front

giving on to ample greenery. In the case of Regent's Park this was devised to provide continuity with the park, the main asset of the development; in the case of St. Leonards it meant an unobstructed view of the sea. The notion is clearly derived from a new development in country-house planning, when direct access into the landscaped garden seemed desirable; there was also the idea, voiced by the Gothic Revivalists, like Humphry Repton and John Britton, that the main living-rooms should be placed on the ground floor, which was held to be the English custom, in contrast to the southern, and more urban, method of placing the main rooms on the first floor, the *piano nobile*, well above the sphere of 'common' activities on the ground.

The first attempts on a large scale to solve the problem for the terraced house came in the Ladbroke Estate in North Kensington and in parts of Paddington in the 1840s. The backs of the houses of Kensington Park Gardens give on to Ladbroke Square (plate 135, cf. plates 7, 39), the largest in London. This forms a communal garden, but it is no longer separated from the houses by a road, but accessible directly from the living-rooms at the back of the house—though the drawing-rooms remain on the first floor. Later in the century there are very large examples of similar arrangements in Earls Court, like Harrington Gardens or Barkston Gardens.

The crucial question, of course, was what to do with the service parts, the back extension? The answer in the early examples was to squeeze even more into the basement, which in fact in most cases spills out to the rear, and is carefully bridged over by terraces (plate 39). Decoratively speaking these houses must also have been more expensive, because they require an ornate facade front and back. In 1858 the *Building News* remarks about some newer London districts that it would be much better to arrange the land devoted to squares in such a way that each house could have a private garden at the back.[18] Indeed, hardly any squares or 'paddocks' were built after that time. One of the chief reasons must have been the intention to take children away from the street and supervise them playing in the garden. In the next chapter we will see how the late nineteenth-century medium-sized standard terraced house gradually turned itself towards the back garden; how the desire for a private garden with direct access helped to change the plan of the house (e.g. plates 48, 57).

Lastly, conservatories can be mentioned here: they occur at the back of many terraced houses, for instance those large houses in Queen's Gate which had no gardens at all, in the 1850s and 1860s (plate 43).[19] Small lean-to conservatories can be found in many medium-sized houses, especially in the south-west.

11. The plan: the regular type

Our plans must be compact and convenient, the rooms well proportioned and amply lighted. The various departments of the household must be distinct, with ready communications by doorways placed wisely to increase privacy . . .

F. Hooper, 1887[1]

The architect or builder has to bring together two basic elements: the clients' requirements, and the restrictions of the site and the type of dwelling which can be afforded. We have so far tried to sketch out what the clients wanted, what was required of a house, large or small, during the nineteenth century. We must now look at what the builders supplied, the way all those rooms were combined within the restrictions of the type. This chapter will deal with the whole range of houses though some special types of the smallest houses will not be discussed until the next chapter.

The basic plan of the regular terraced house is so simple that it can be summed up in a few words: two floors, with two rooms each. For variation and enlargements there are further floors on top, there is the basement and the back extension, or both. This regular plan had been accepted throughout the country before the beginning of the nineteenth century. Sometimes local variations are mentioned, but no systematic account of them can be attempted here. Only some special characteristics of London houses, and to a lesser extent, those of the terraces in Bristol, will stand out more clearly.

Far more important are changes over time. We have tried to characterize some of the changes in criteria for a suitable house: more light, more accommodation generally, the increasing demand for sanitary provision. We must now follow the way the plans adapted themselves to these changing demands. It is characteristic of the study of the terraced house, or indeed any other common type of house, that it continually fluctuates between stressing on the one hand the sameness of the plan, and its simplicity, and on the other hand its flexibility and adaptability (plates 40–2).

The double-fronted house

There is one major exception to the common plan, in which the entrance is placed not at the side but in the centre of the facade, with a major room on each side. Thus there are two major windows at the front on each floor—whereas the great majority of terraced houses has only one—hence the curious name. The origin of this arrangement is the detached Classical or sub-Classical house. In the smaller versions of the double-fronted house, whether detached or in a row, the stairway leads up immediately behind the front-door lobby; in the larger versions there is usually an ample corridor leading to the back of the house, and the stairs lead up at right angles

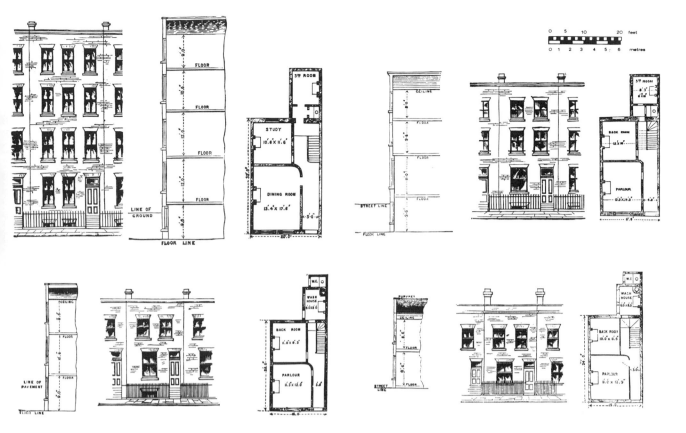

40. The four Classes of London houses, from Simon, 1875; in late and simplified versions. The plans are those of the ground floors. Class I still has a first-floor drawing-room, Classes II–IV all have reception rooms on the ground floor. Class IV has no basement. Note that the first floor in Class I is now of the same height as the ground floor. Note also the differentiation of indoor and outdoor toilets; this particular positioning of the indoor toilets was soon to be outlawed.

Colour plate 7. **London**, Harrington Gardens, SW7, late 1880s. So as to facilitate access to the private gardens at the back, the front of the terrace, towards the street, contains as much as possible of the service part of the house. Thus the customary front/back contrast is here confused.

to this corridor. Sometimes the double-fronted house was used in situations where there was not enough depth for a regular two-room-deep house, and this very often applied to corner plots, where one shallow house of this type is attached to the side of a regular terraced house (plate 37). In London, a whole area of medium-sized double-fronted houses dating from the 1880s can be found around Hampton Road, Woodgrange Park, E7 (cf. plate 161); a city where this plan is as common as the regular plan is Plymouth (plate 47).

Very large terraces

Amongst the most remarkable examples of our type are mansions with more than twenty rooms, but which are only 28 feet (8.50 m) wide. Within some of the grandest Regency terraces, such as Nash's Carlton House Terrace or Basevi's Belgrave Square, we find the occasional house which is more than 30 feet (9.14 m) wide and with more individuality in their plans. Those tightly packed palaces, however, with their multiplicity of large and small rooms, piled up in five or even six storeys on top of a basement, only appear in the 1850s and 60s in London, in Lancaster Gate[2] and in South Kensington around Princes Gate and Queens Gate (plate 43). Even these houses adhere to the regular plan: the entrance and stairway is at the side and there are basically two rooms on each floor. Only a few, like 31–57 Exhibition Road, South Kensington, show a version of an older type with a larger, top-lit staircase. At the back of some houses we find the curious feature of an enormously high chimney for the back extension, carried over to the main part of the house like a flying buttress; it prevents the kitchen smoke from blowing into the bedrooms (cf. plate 44).[3]

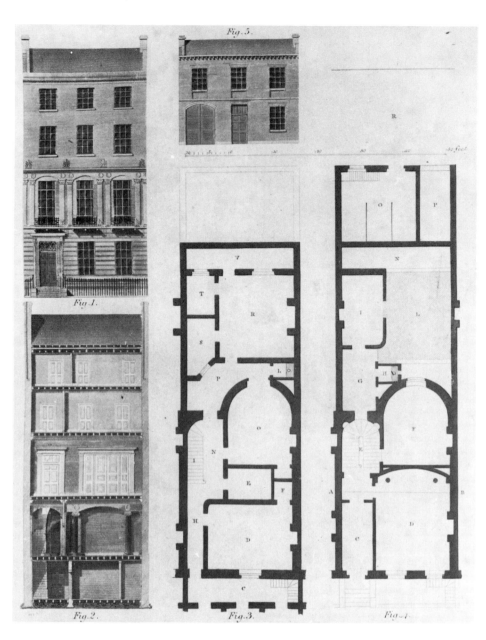

Fig. 5.

Fig. 1.

Fig. 2.

Fig. 3.

Fig. 4.

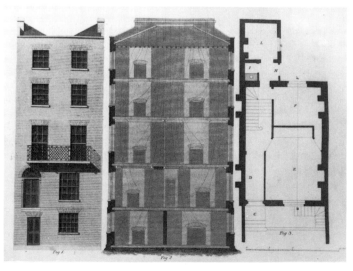

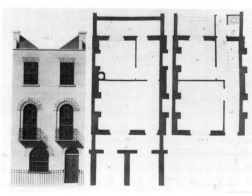

41. The four Classes of London houses, from Elsam/Nicholson 1823–5. The plans and sections are not very consistent and nowhere can a description be found. For Class I (facing page, above) there is an elevation of the front facade, the mews and a section through the house widthwise as well as a plan of the basement (centre) and the ground floor. For Class II (right, above) there is the facade, the same kind of section, a section through the front wall and a plan of the ground floor. For Class III (facing page, below left) there is the facade, a section through the house depthwise and a plan of the ground floor, and for Class IV (facing page, below right), the facade and plans of the basement and ground floor. There are also the rules for the wall-thicknesses for the four classes (right, below), according to the 1774 Building Act.

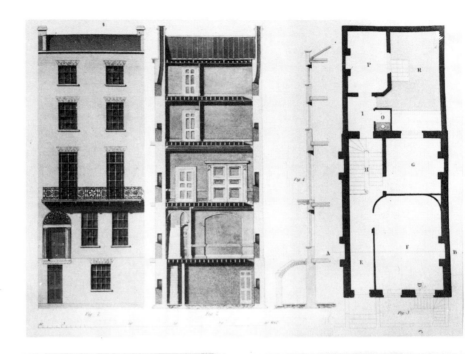

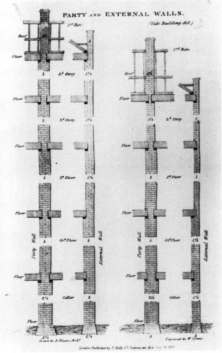

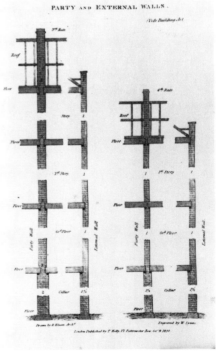

43. (below). **London.** South Kensington, 'Albert Houses', 44–52 Queen's Gate, 1859–60, by Charles Aldin (builder) for J. Whatman (client–speculator) and C. J. Richardson (architect). A mansion, 8 m in width. Note the additional servants' staircase from ground to second floor, and the way the planner managed to place the boudoir (for the ladies) and the study (for the gentlemen) well away from the other reception rooms. The 'mezzanine' is drawn at the level of the landing between first and second floor. (The facade is not to the same scale.)

V

IV

III

II

I

B

B = bedroom; D = dining-room; Dr = drawing-room; Dre = dressing-room; l'dr = larder; P = Parlour; K = kitchen; P'ty = pantry; Sc = scullery.

BASEMENT

GROUND FLOOR

MEZZANINE

FIRST FLOOR

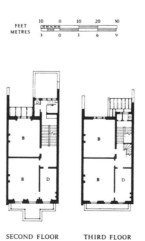

SECOND FLOOR

THIRD FLOOR

FOURTH FLOOR

ATTIC

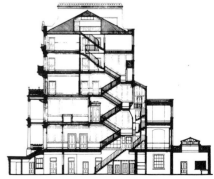

42. (left). **Brighton.** Brunswick Square *c.* 1830. The plans of the basement and ground floors do not correspond, presumably showing different versions that could be adopted by the builder. (See also plate 117, right; for a view of the back of very similar houses see plate 44; for an interior plate 13.)

44. (right). **Brighton.** Brunswick Square, *c.* 1830–40. The backs of very large houses. In the mews motor works have conveniently taken over from stables. While the facade was controlled, change was permitted at the back. For the front cf. plate 117; and see plate 42 for the plan of a similar house.

45. **Eastbourne.** Royal Parade, *c.* 1880. Extensions were now more regular and usually higher.

46. **Leicester.** Hinkley Road, 1864. Single back extensions of a medium-sized house.

47. (facing page). **Variations of plan**
A: a double fronted terraced house (Plymouth, Seaton Avenue, *c.* 1880–90)
B: large-medium London type with basement and shallow back extension for the whole width of the house (Morton Road, N1, *c.* 1865, Br = Breakfast Room).
C: Ground floor plan of a pair of semi-detached houses (Bristol 1850s).
Note the way the entrance is placed on one side, thus there is no need for a corridor along the front room (see also plates 147, 159.
D: Variations in the placement of the staircase, typical for Bristol terraces in the nineteenth century.

Slightly smaller houses of 'only' sixteen rooms or so can be found in many parts of South Kensington and Paddington. The largest houses in Brighton belong in this category (plates 42, 44), but there are very few elsewhere: some terraces at the seafront in Eastbourne, Warrior Square Terrace at St. Leonards and Elliot Terrace in Plymouth of around 1860. Both the latter form—not unlike the front range of Lancaster Gate—a complete street block in themselves with very high and ornate back extensions.

Later in the century there was the occasional large terraced house in the West End designed by Domestic Revival architects such as Norman Shaw or T. Wimperis,[4] with even more rooms, but their plans are too complicated and individual to be described here. Generally, however, regular rows of very large houses were hardly built after the 1890s. There is a great number of them in Earl's Court and their special garden-access arrangements have already been mentioned. Nos. 47–75 Harrington Gardens, of the 1880s, show an ingenious way of avoiding the back extension at the garden side by adding shallow extensions at the front and bridging the gaps between them with large screens, premonitory of similar devices in large blocks of flats (colour plate 7).

The regular type: the main part of the house

The vast majority of terraced houses range from a maximum of twelve rooms down to four or five rooms, not counting the smaller service rooms from the scullery downwards (plate 40). In London this range was divided, according to size, into four 'classes', though the borderlines between the sizes became more and more blurred as time went on. Height was the main variable in the terraced house. Victorian families generally wanted more bedrooms, thus their houses are normally one or two storeys higher than their Georgian equivalents. There were sometimes more floors at the back of the house than at the front, as in some of the late standard types. Occasionally the opposite occurred: three floors in the front part of the house and two in the back part, as in some late nineteenth-century terraces in Nottingham. As regards the width of houses, this was varied least of all; London houses in particular showed hardly any variation of it at all. Depth was more of a variable, though this could not exceed about four times the width of the house, as this would have cut off too much light.

There are only two kinds of access arrangement inside the house: those with a 'hall' (plate 12), as the usually long and narrow corridor is called, and those without (plate 50). It is difficult to trace the beginnings of this universal desire for corridor access; in the eighteenth century, we still find grand terraced houses, like 26 Grosvenor Square, remodelled by Adam in the 1770s, where most rooms had no separate corridor access. The second method, with direct access to the front room from the street, continued throughout our period for small houses, except in the south. Occasionally one finds very small houses, especially in the south, with a hall, as in Woodbury Lane, Bristol of *c.* 1850, where the front of the house measures $9\frac{1}{2}$ feet in total (2.90 m), which does not leave much room to do anything in the 'parlour'. The next step up from the non-hall-entranced house is the one where there is a corridor along the front room only; in order to get to the back door, or the back extension, one has to go through the main room at the back—an arrangement one might call 'half-hall-entranced' (plates 53, 54).

An interesting variation and development is the change in the position of the front door in relation to the front door of the next house. In the earlier version a door is

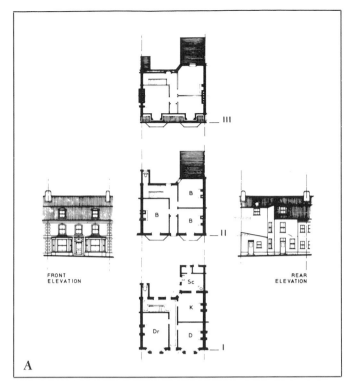

FRONT
ELEVATION

REAR
ELEVATION

A

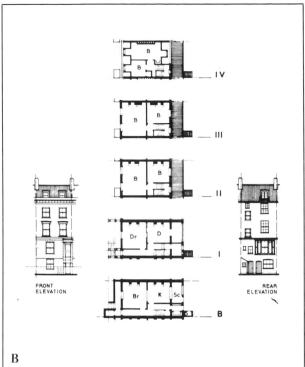

FRONT
ELEVATION

REAR
ELEVATION

B

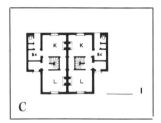

C

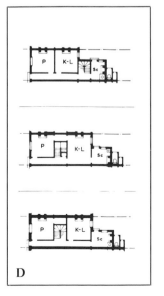

D

followed by a window, then by the door of the next house and so on. In the later mode, from about the mid-century onwards, a door was next to a door, followed by a window plus another window, followed by two more doors. In other words, the doors of two houses were now adjacent to each other. The reason for this change seems to lie with the back extension: with the earlier arrangement the back extension is either lacking or is a single one for each house. With the later method the back extensions are coupled; the extensions of two houses are under one roof. The communication core of the house has to be arranged along one line; access to the back extension has to be in line with the front corridor. Sometimes the resulting lack of privacy at the front doors of terraced houses is limited by wooden partitions projecting between the front doors (cf. plates 44, 50, 100–6, 117).[5]

The only major variations of the plan are to do with the position and construction of the staircase. An early mode was to place the turned stairs in the centre of the house between the front and the back room, accessible from a passage between the rooms. This seems to have been the rule in London until about 1700 and continued into the eighteenth century. In Bristol, however, it carried on until the later nineteenth century, with turned stairs usually in the smaller houses and those staircases with landings in the larger ones (plate 47). For very small houses with four rooms the traditional place of the stairs was in the back room, accessible only from that room (plate 15). In the smallest regular houses in the north it continued until after 1900 (plate 94). But elsewhere for small houses the one-flight middle stair became common, leading up in the centre of the house between the front and back rooms, as in the old type, though its construction was very simple (plates 50, 61). In Norwich, for instance, the changeover from the older back-room stairs to the straight middle stairs type occurred between around 1860 and 1880. Occasionally there is an intermediate solution: the stairs lead up in the centre, but are accessible from the back room.[6] In London the normal solution for the smallest house is to place the staircase at the side of the back room, with usually one turn at the top; these are called 'dog-legged' stairs (plate 48, cf. 12). For houses with basements the stairs are mostly double-flight with ample landings in between (plate 48). These landings always make themselves known on the outside, at the back of the houses, with their large windows which break through the level of the rest of the windows (plate 47). Finally there was the possibility of placing the staircase outside the main part of the house, at the beginning of the back extension. The access to them can be found either in the back extension (plate 47),[7] or, as in some small houses in Ipswich, inside the back room in the main part of the house.

Basement, area, back extension

The distinction between cellar and basement was by no means clear in earlier houses. Many urban houses had rooms below the level of the street or footpath, for storage in conjunction with trade, for coal and other purposes, with only a primitive window or access from the front (plate 158), or none at all. It was in these sorts of houses that the most dreaded examples of cellar dwelling occurred, which were slowly outlawed in the nineteenth century. Later the cellar came to mean an unlit and low room underneath part of the house, for storage only. It continued in many London houses—those without a basement, of course—until after 1900 (plate 48). In the provinces the position varied; in Nottingham, Northampton, Leeds and many other towns (plate 78), houses, even small ones, usually had cellars or basements; the distinction continued to be blurred and there was great flexibility in their use. Other towns, like Birmingham, had far fewer cellars.

The full basement was part of the space-conscious, urban Georgian terrace. Its layout was, for structural reasons, broadly that of the rooms above (e.g. plates 1, 41, 47, colour plate 3). The back contained the kitchen, the front the servants' hall, or in smaller houses the breakfast room. The basement always had a door at the back, to the yard. It was the fact that the London basement almost always had a door at the front that caused a great deal of complication and variation. As the level of the ground floor was usually that of street or footpath, the front part of the basement was normally situated completely below ground. To make a separate front access possible for the basement, and also to give it a proper window, a space was created in front of it, about 1·50 m to 3 m wide, which was called the area. Thus the front of the house was separated from the footpath by a gap which had to be bridged to reach the main, front entrance on the ground floor. The door to the basement was usually fitted underneath that bridge, and a small, steep flight of stairs in the area led up to the footpath. Cast-iron railings surrounded the area and the bridge to the main entrance as well. In London and its inner suburbs the basement remained the rule, even in small houses with only four main rooms above, until about the 1870s (plate 48, cf. colour plate 13). One of the main reasons for having the separate basement access at the front was the lack of a separate rear access. In the provinces such a rear access was much more frequent, and the basement was much rarer.

In most larger houses there were further extensions to the 'area'. As the street and the footpath do not normally represent the original ground level, but are filled up during building operations—the original level of the ground can usually be found at the back—there are a number of caverns underneath the footpath, accessible from the area. One is usually for coal, which is poured through a hole in the footpath, covered by a cast-iron plaque. Ornamental coal-hole covers are a well known feature of Georgian London, for all those who keep their eyes to the ground. A variation of this footpath–area arrangement can be found on sloping sites, where stables and workshops, normally found in a mews, are placed under a high walkway in front:

Royal York Crescent in Clifton, built from about 1790 onwards, is the most outstanding example (cf. plate 9). Nash's Carlton House Terrace has a storage space in the front, which carries a large terrace or balcony (plate 111); the entrance to the houses is at the back. There are some curious earlier solutions on a smaller scale, where the cellars or caves are built up from the ground, with complicated steps leading to the main front door above.[8] Another method is to cover the whole area with a roof, supported by a slender colonnade, which also provides for a balcony on the first floor, as in Eaton Square (cf. plate 43).[9] There is even a case where the roof or balcony covers the footpath in front of the houses as well.[10] In other terraces the balcony is smaller and covers the area only in part, as with Lansdowne Crescent in Leamington (colour plate 12). All these can be called typical Regency solutions which disappeared when the popularity of the basement itself waned after 1850. Later verandahs and porches were usually mere appendages to the facade and will be discussed below. From about 1840–50 onwards the basement was often raised, so as to be half above ground, especially in more suburban situations and in semi-detached houses and villas, but there are examples in terraces as well.[11] It was sometimes called a 'half-basement'. This gave more light inside, the bay window could be incorporated more easily, and there was the opportunity for a stately flight of stairs leading up to the main entrance.

The back extension is the most varied and complicated part of the terraced house. The later Georgian and Regency houses in London had their back yards usually filled up with a variety of extensions at various times, until there was hardly any uncovered ground left. The medium-sized Georgian house usually had a small extension at basement level, and perhaps one on the ground floor for what was called simply the 'back room'; the smaller houses usually had none, except for the small, lean-to toilet (plate 48).[12] A frequent later variation is the projection of the whole of the back, forming a scullery in the basement and a verandah on the ground floor, thereby depriving the kitchen and the main back room on the ground floor of their direct light (plate 47). In the provinces, where land was less at a premium, many terraces have long and bulky excrescences of varying heights,[13] often with later additions. In small and medium-sized houses there is often a one-storey extension.[14] Sometimes this is divided into two parts, even in small houses, with the kitchen–scullery in the larger part, and the toilet and shed in the smaller, further part. In all these cases each house has its own extension, built separately on to the house (see plates 36, 37, 45, 46). In Bristol this tradition continued long after the middle of the century, and in parts of Wales, such as Swansea, until about 1900. The roof of these extensions is either 'monopitched', of a single pitch, at right angles to the main roof, or pitched in the normal way, with either a gable or a hipped roof at the end, that is, a roof with its gable cut off by a small roof.

There are three major elements in the development of the back extension after 1850. They are coupled (plates 45, 49, 55): the extensions of two adjacent houses come under one roof (plate 51). The way this caused the front doors to be placed adjacent to each other has already been mentioned. It also meant that the back yards for each house were no longer separate, but adjacent: two houses shared a yard, though it was usually divided by a wooden fence (plates 49, 52). It was another retrograde step as regards privacy; on the other hand, space was gained and there was more air. Secondly, most back extensions were now two-storeyed, and there are even higher ones (plate 48). Increasingly, they replaced the basements. In country houses this had happened by the late eighteenth century. Kitchens and sculleries were now placed into the extension. The third element, due to the new stringency in building economy and organization, was that all extensions in a row were now

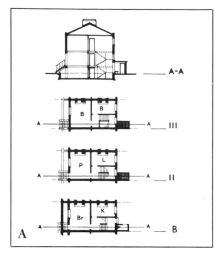

A

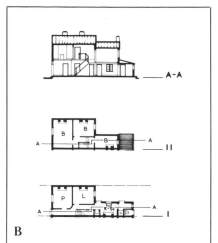

B

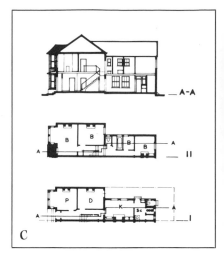

C

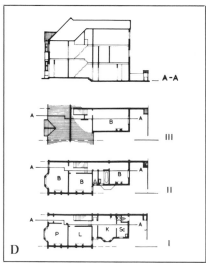

D

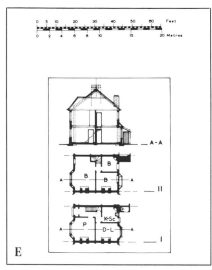

E

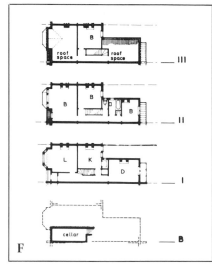

F

48. The development of the small to medium-sized house in London and the south-east
A: two storeys with basement and no back extension (Islington Park Street, N1, c. 1820).
B: frequent in poorer areas (Cordova Road, E3 c. 1870).
C: the late standard plan, the most common in the south-east (Southend, c. 1900).
D: a split-level solution (London, 1890s, see also plate 55).
E: the twentieth-century standard type: no basement, no back extension (Elmstead Road, Ilford, 1908, see plates 57, 58).
F: the dining-room in the back extension has access to the back garden (Cecil Road, N10, c. 1904).

exactly the same. Lancaster Terrace in Leicester of 1857 is an early example, with coupled two-storeyed back extensions. In Hull the fairly large terrace in Beverley Road (84 upwards) of about 1860 shows very large coupled back extensions, and squeezed into the yards between these extensions are smaller, coupled extensions, which presumably contained the sculleries. Thus each house has a share in two back extensions. Sometimes the extensions can stretch to a length of 70 feet (21.33 m).[15] A further variation can be found in Plymouth, where almost all the generally largish, coupled extensions have hipped gables not only at the end, but also at their junction with the main part of the house, and thus leave space for the upper windows of that part.[16] Lastly, we must mention the late nineteenth-century Railway Cottages in Parkeston Quay, Harwich, where one of the corners of the back extension is formed by a free-standing post around which the tenant can fit out part of the extension himself according to his own purposes. This, however, was probably rare and only possible in semi-benevolent Company housing, where employees would be trusted to make the best use of it. A more detailed variation is the treatment of the roof of the extension: smaller houses in provincial towns show a lean-to roof; in Norwich this mode was replaced by the more metropolitan and urban gabled roof between 1870 and 1890 (plates 51, 52). There is also a significant difference inside with these two kinds of roofs. In the former the back room is usually smaller, and always lower; the lean-to, indeed, strikes one as rather a rural feature, where often

49. **London.** Antill Road, E3, *c.* 1860–70. Two-part, coupled back extensions. Note the roofs, placed at right angles to the facade, hiding behind a high parapet wall.

the extension is far more closely linked with the house, and the roof is more prominent altogether (cf. plate 94). However, in the urban north-west and north-east both types of roof continue side by side until after 1900. Finally, the extensions can no longer be called such when they are separated from the house, as in the case of the kitchens and wash-houses of so many smaller houses in the west midlands (plate 61).

By 1850–60 the larger new houses in London had basements and back extensions. Houses in Walterton Road, W9, for instance, have three storeys plus basement, and short, three-storeyed back extensions. The height of the rooms in those extensions is only two-thirds of those in the main part of the house, and the result is a split-level construction throughout. But then, as indicated above, most London stairs have landings anyway. For smaller houses, however, the basement is increasingly given up. There were, of course, always very small houses in the poorest parts of London which never had a basement, though they could sport a small, single back extension, with a small, monopitched roof.[17] It appears that after 1850 this type served as a general model for the slightly larger, non-basemented house. It is significant that Class IV of the London house in Nicholson has a basement (plate 41), but that later on Class IV in Simon shows none (plate 40). The extensions vary greatly in size: one block with a gabled roof of two storeys, then a further small, lean-to extension for the toilet and shed. There are also double extensions, that is extensions in two parts, with a wider, higher part and a further lower one, each with its own roof and gable (plate 49). Some of these extensions take up considerably more than half the width of the house, and there is little room left for the windows in the back of the main parts of the house; the yard between the houses is of course rather dark and narrow, too. To achieve so much room inside the extension would

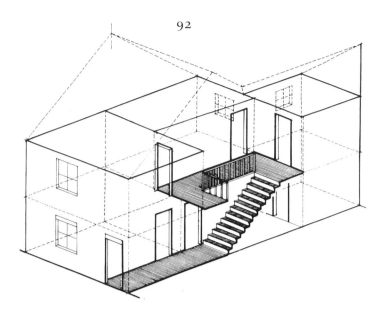

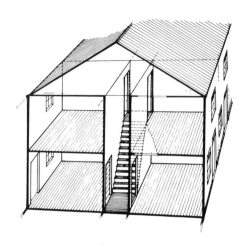

50. Late nineteenth-century standard types, small versions. The two sketches at the top contrast (left) the half-hall-entranced type (see plate 53) with (right) the middle-stairs type without hall entrance. The drawings on the right show the latter type in greater detail (Norwich, 1900). Note the way there is less privacy on the ground floor—but compare a more primitive type with stairs in the back room in plate 94. Note also the lack of separate access to the back bedroom (see p. 100). This plan is also an example of those handed in to the Local Building Control department, who, in this instance, faulted the drainage.

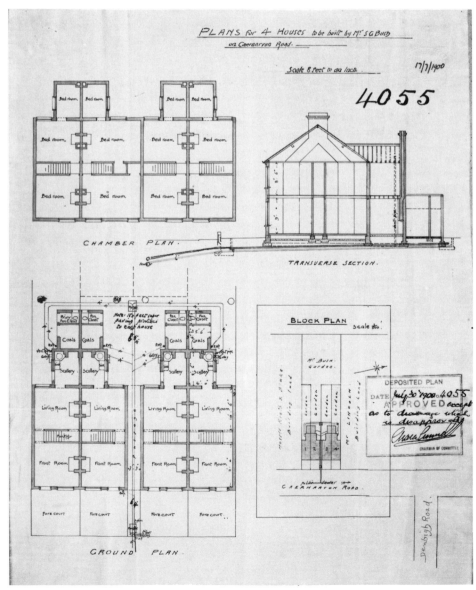

51. The older lean-to type of back extension. In this case the windows of the third bedroom were not allowed to be placed into the end wall because of the proximity to the toilet below (Norwich, 1880).

52. The newer type of back extension with a gable; the third bedroom is still very small. Note also the old-fashioned casement windows (Norwich, 1880s).

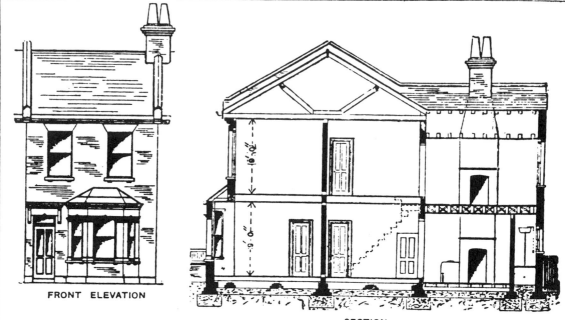

FRONT ELEVATION

SECTION.

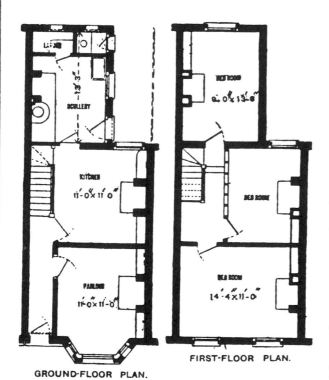

GROUND-FLOOR PLAN.

FIRST-FLOOR PLAN.

£150 HOUSE AT PLAISTOW, LONDON, E.

THE entire site is covered with a 6-in. layer of concrete, composed of one part best Portland cement to eight parts clean pit ballast. The brickwork of the external walls is of sound, hard, well-burnt grey stocks, the best and most even in colour being selected for facings; and there are red-brick dressings to the front elevation, the arches being turned in red bricks to the front elevation and in malm cutters to the back elevation. The sills to doorways and windows are of stone. The roofs are covered with Portmadoc duchess slating, laid to a 2½-in. lap, and secured with zinc nails; the ridge being of red tiles. The timber consists of second-quality Baltic fir and second-quality Swedish yellow floor joists, 7 in. by 2 in.; sleepers, 4 in. by 2 in.; ridge, 6 in. by 1¼ in.; common rafters, 4 in. by 2 in.; purlins, 7 in. by 2½ in.; ceiling joists, 4 in. by 2 in.; wall-plates, 4½ in. by 3 in. The windows throughout are 1¼ in., double hung in deal-cased frames. All the internal walls are rendered, floated, and set. All the windows are glazed with 21-oz. sheet glass. In the schedule appended to the specification in "Building World," No. 74. p. 364, the rate per hour for bricklayers and carpenters was stated to be 9½d.; that for labourers, 6½d. Bricks were 36s. per 1,000, delivered, and carcasing timber was £9 10s. per standard.

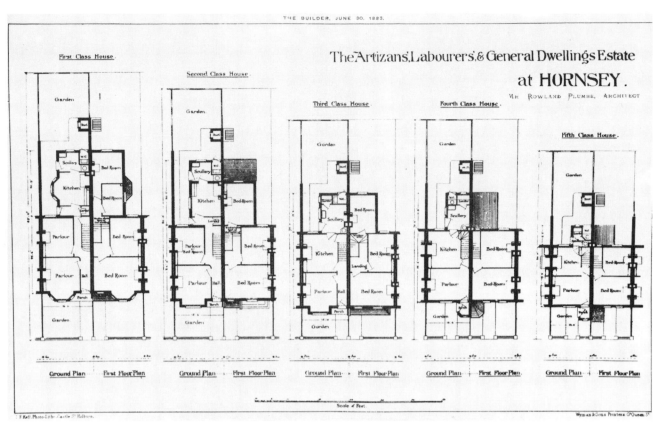

First Class House.

Second Class House.

The Artizans, Labourers, & General Dwellings Estate at HORNSEY.

Mr Rowland Plumbe, Architect

Third Class House.

Fourth Class House.

Fifth Class House.

Ground Plan   First Floor Plan   Ground Plan   First Floor Plan   Ground Plan   First Floor Plan   Ground Plan   First Floor Plan   Ground Plan   First Floor Plan

Scale of Feet

54. London. Plans for houses in Noel Park, North London (1883), built by a company with some philanthropic aims. A few features, like the porches, cannot normally be found in speculative London suburban houses of that period, and the smallest type in this series, the non-hall-entranced version, is rare in London.

53 (facing page). The most frequent plan in the poorer parts of the towns in the south-east, the half-hall-entranced type, *c.* 1900: one has to go through the kitchen–living-room in order to get to the back of the house. Another important distinction from the medium-sized house is the one-storey bay window (London). (See also plate 50.)

55. London. Tregarvon Road, SW11, *c.* 1890. A split-level back, closely corresponding to the plan in plate 48D.

56 (above left). **London.** Muswell Hill, Cecil Road, N10, *c.* 1904. The back extension, containing the service rooms, is turned to the side of the house, with a separate entrance from the front.

57 (above right). **London.** Elmstead Road, Ilford, 1908, the back of the house next door to the one shown in plate 48e. The outdoor toilet is on the left, then follows the door to the kitchen-cum-scullery and then a bay window for the dining-room.

58 (right). **Ilford**, a typical outer London suburban area, *c.* 1890–1910: the shops are centred around the station, surrounded by endless roads of houses of much the same size: the older ones with back extensions (see plates 48, 59), the later ones without (see plate 57).

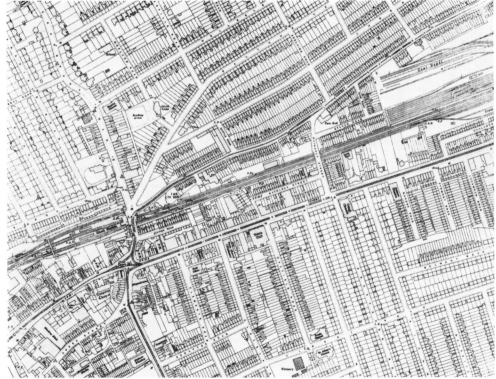

59. **London**, typical backs of late nineteenth-century small to medium-sized houses. The back extensions have further extensions, temporary ones, in the form of sheds, greenhouses etc.

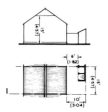

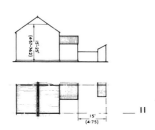

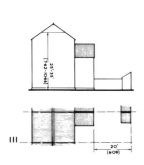

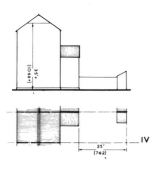

60. Minimum space at the back of the house, according to the Model Byelaws of 1877; similar but vaguer stipulations were already contained in the Local Government Act of 1858.

have been impossible with the older type of a single extension for each house, as the width of each yard would have been reduced to a mere passage and the light in the adjacent rooms to a flicker. One way of overcoming the problem of light is the bay window, which is now frequently found marking the main room in the extension, usually the breakfast room. Finally, no attempt can be made here to trace the immense variety of positions for fireplaces and chimneys in the back extension.

Late nineteenth-century standard types

For reasons of economy and more stringent legal control, standardization progressed rapidly during the nineteenth century. It is also because far more houses have been preserved that we have a much clearer picture of the kinds of houses built around the turn of the century. In 1901, 60.1 per cent of the population in England and Wales lived in dwellings of five rooms or more. A further 21.9 per cent lived in four-roomed houses. These, as well as the remainder of smaller, three- and two-roomed houses, will be dealt with in the next chapter. The greater part of the 60 per cent lived in five-roomed houses. In most towns in the midlands, in the east, and in the south-west and Wales, these made up the bulk of housing, between about half and four-fifths of all dwellings; and in the north they represented a substantial minority. They are often called the 'byelaw type'. The actual calculation of five rooms is somewhat vague. There could be two rooms on the ground floor plus a scullery, or a kitchen-cum-scullery, and there could be two or three bedrooms upstairs. Thus in reality there is a fluctuation between a four-roomed type and a six-roomed type. For the vast majority of these houses there is no hall entrance; but almost all have their separate yard, with their own toilet, ashpit and coalshed (e.g. plate 50).

The next step up is the half-hall-entranced type. It marks the smallest kind of house in the metropolitan south-east, and a slightly better house in the provinces (plates 53, 54). The majority type in the south-east, and to a lesser extent in Bristol, Cardiff and some towns in the southern midlands, was the fully hall-entranced type, with three, sometimes four, bedrooms, with a kitchen and scullery in the back extension, and sometimes a breakfast room in that part as well (plate 48). Most of these houses, from about 1890–1900 onwards, have an upstairs bathroom and toilet.

The type of plan adopted by these houses is largely that which developed in London for the small-medium-sized house after 1850. Only the back extension appears more unified and bulky. Within the standardized confines of the plot and the plan, a number of special solutions develop, partly continuing older methods. Frequent in the south-east is a split-level type, where the back extension has three storeys, and the front part of the house two (plates 48, 55). An unusual type can be found in Muswell Hill, where the three-storey back extension is, so to speak, turned to the side: the service part is now squeezed between the houses,[18] which is reminiscent of some quasi-semidetached and quasi-detached houses (plate 56, cf 148, 149).[19] The most important new tendency is to open the house to the rear garden by placing the largest living-room, usually the dining-room, at the back of the extension and opening it with 'French doors' into the garden. This often led to an even wider and bulkier back extension, which left even less space for the windows at the back of the main part of the house, and we now find the kitchen and sometimes the breakfast room in that position.[20]

Colour plate 8. **Hull**, an
'Avenue' off Mayfield Street,
c. 1870s (see also plates 70 and
67).

The twentieth-century standard type

In fact, the days of the back extension were numbered. There were many signs that it was felt to be cumbersome—the way, for instance, the window at the back of the main part of the house sometimes cut into the back extension.[21] 'Dispense altogether with the ugly back additions,' wrote the *Building News* in 1895.[22] By about 1890, or slightly later, there were already appearing, in outer London suburbs, houses of the standard size generally, but with no back extensions, except perhaps for a short scullery and an outside toilet.[23] The larger part of the back was now free. By 1905–10, most suburban London houses, as well as many in Southend, Portsmouth, Cardiff and other towns, were built in similar ways. This meant some important changes inside: houses for a start, were usually somewhat wider than the standard type so far, the smallest version measuring about 17 feet (5.2 m). The hall was wider but shorter, the stairs mounting in the front part of the house. There was, of course, no long, dark corridor to the back, because the kitchen—which in the small versions included the bath and the scullery—was squeezed next to the dining room; the latter often had its own access to the garden, and there was, of course, always a door to the outside from the kitchen. Likewise, upstairs, the third bedroom is squeezed next to the second bedroom at the back (plates 48, 57).

Predecessors of this plan could be traced in older types of rural cottages and in some housing built by the railway companies; perhaps one can also take some similar houses in Port Sunlight into consideration, which were built by 1890, and also perhaps some semi-detached plans. In any case, it is a type of crucial importance, as it has remained largely unchanged to this day, the standard speculative suburban type of house. The chief reasons for the adoption of this type in London around 1900 were not just a matter of picking up certain influences from other kinds of houses; they were of a more basic kind. Apart from the desire to use the back garden, it was probably the particular socio-economic set-up of housing in the London suburbs generally which produced the new type. Many two-storeyed houses of the standard type were inhabited by two families, and were not properly adapted for it. The smaller new twentieth-century type amounted to little more than half a standard-sized terraced house with a back extension. It was inhabited by one family without a servant; we know of the beginnings of the shortage of servants. It was, unlike the slightly older standard type, purpose-built for one family of limited means. Thus there were probably no objections to combining the kitchen and the scullery and to minimizing the yard, elements which ran counter to the general development of nineteenth-century planning, the tendency towards differentiation and segregation.[24] Another solution to the London problem which had developed slightly earlier was the self-contained 'cottage flat'.

Changes in use and plan

During the nineteenth century the plans of all sizes of dwellings, from the mansion to the cottage, developed in the same direction: seclusion, privacy and convenience. Which, again, are the main changes inside the medium and smaller houses? It was essential to have passages, or corridors, so as not to have to go through another room, as was so often the case in continental dwellings. As we have seen, the great majority of small houses do not possess a hall entrance, though in the north-west there was at least a small porch inside the front door, called the 'vestibule' (plate 91). Many later small houses adopted the middle stairway which provided some separation of the stairs from the front and the back room. These middle stairs, however, usually had the disadvantage that the third bedroom in the back extension could only be reached through the back bedroom in the main part of the house (plate 50). This, to a large extent, cancelled out the primary purpose of having a third bedroom, namely to separate children of the two sexes. In the small London and south-eastern type of house with the side stairs this never happened. Increasingly, a small passage ran along the back bedroom in the middle-stairs type, to solve this problem of separate access. In the newer houses in Burton-on-Trent, for instance, the third bedroom does have this access, as the *Cost of Living Report* assures us.

In slightly better houses the introduction of the half or full hall entrance is the most important change from the earlier pattern. Until about the mid-century, a large cottage would have just a comfortable front room of 4.5 × 4 metres, without any hall, and a small, cramped kitchen at the back, which would also include the scullery and contain the stairway (plate 94). In the later nineteenth century a house might be of the same width, or even narrower, and have a complete corridor. The front room would now measure only about 3.5 × 4 metres (plate 48), though the back room would be bigger than in the old type because the stairs had been taken out of it, and the kitchen had been extended by the scullery. On the whole, the house was now deeper and narrower. Larger windows made up for the loss of light caused by the constriction of the plan. Thus, on the whole, there was more privacy, there were more rooms, but some rooms were smaller. There was another attempt to ensure privacy: the tendency to place the doors of the individual rooms as far apart as possible. On the other hand we have observed developments which ran against privacy: the coupled front doors and the combined back yards; in this case salubrity and economy were more important.[25]

There was more change in the planning of medium and larger houses. One of the most pressing problems was the accommodation of servants. After all, they were people of a different class who had to live under the same roof. They had to be observed; at the same time the masters did not want to be overlooked by them. Bedrooms in the upper storeys seemed to be most useful for their accommodation. But later came the desire to restrict the height of the house: it was more economic to have to clean only two floors when there were not enough servants.[26] Regarding the basement, it was argued that, while cellars for the poor were condemned, the often insalubrious basements of older town houses still seemed acceptable. Many factors spoke for the back extension. In the 1830s the Duke of Devonshire had had his kitchen built behind the house, not underneath it, in order to avoid 'the fry and fat smell usual in a Brighton house'.[27] The back extension seemed the natural place for servants' bedrooms, away from the family bedrooms and closer to the kitchen. It was also the most convenient location for the upstairs bathroom and toilet, for ventilation purposes, as well as for simplified plumbing. It was easy enough to extend the size of the house at the back, while the front could remain the same. Only a two-storey house, that is two main storeys, permitted construction with the minimum thickness of 9 inches (230 mm). To build a basement would have pushed up construction costs without a proportional rise in the area of the accommodation. On the other hand, additional bedrooms could easily be built into the roof. This also became more appropriate for stylistic reasons: steeply pitched roofs had come into fashion, and dormers and gables provided a much desired livening-up of the facade of the slightly larger house. Factors of use, of economy and construction, as well as of architectural style worked hand in hand. Finally, the Domestic Revival brought profound changes in many aspects of domestic design, chiefly a reduction of size and pretensions; for the moment perhaps its influence on speculative housing can already be felt in the development of the 'twentieth-century standard type' in the 1890s (see chapters 13 and 17).

12. The plan: small houses and their regional varieties

The value of sunlight to the human economy cannot be overestimated.

E. Bowmaker, 1895[1]

In our discussion of plans and types we have so far stressed their general similarity; in this chapter we will study chiefly the differences between plans. We could carry on from the last chapter and list houses according to size: in 1901, 21.9 per cent of all families lived in four-roomed houses, 9.8 per cent in three-roomed houses, and 8.2 per cent in houses or dwellings of at most two rooms.[2] But the most interesting fact about the smallest houses is the variety of their plans. It makes a great deal of difference whether a house has a back entrance, or no back entrance as in the case of the back-to-back type; whether the house gives on to a proper street or a court; or how some houses are divided into flats.

The origin of the plan of the regular terraced house lay chiefly with the traditional northern European town house. The origin of the special types of small house lay more with the primitive kinds of rural houses, as well as with the various attempts to crowd the masses as quickly as possible into the towns of the Industrial Revolution. The forces which shaped their plans were not primarily those of convenience, as in the case of the regular house, but those of economy. And yet, in spite of their restricted brief, their builders often produced solutions which were as interesting as those for the larger houses.

The dwellings in this chapter are predominantly those of the working classes in the north. The purpose here is not so much to investigate their vernacular and eighteenth-century origins as J. B. Lowe has done for Wales; the account focuses rather on the later nineteenth century, the way that certain local peculiarities persisted, and the influence of the byelaws. We have already touched briefly on economic, legal and practical aspects of working-class housing. One of the conclusions drawn from the brief investigation of the modes of living among the various classes was that it is hard to draw a firm dividing line between the working classes and the lower-middle classes. Likewise, it is difficult to draw very precise distinctions between middle-class and working-class types of plans. Occasionally, larger versions of our small types—like back-to-backs, or the Tyneside flat— were inhabited by members of the lower-middle classes; while the better-off members of the working classes increasingly lived in smaller versions of the regular type. Furthermore this chapter only marginally deals with 'reform' housing— whether philanthropic or municipal—nor does it consider slum conditions like the overcrowding of old houses, or the substantial margin between the latter and the older, poorer nineteenth-century houses. Neither can an assessment be made as to whether or not a particular type can be considered a satisfactory dwelling in any sense, then or now. Therefore this chapter is only in a limited sense an account of the English working-class house.

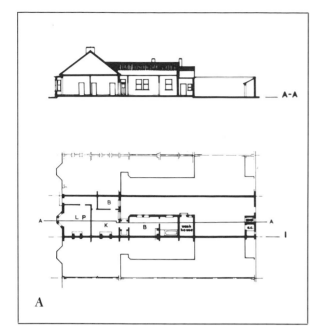

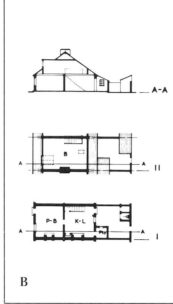

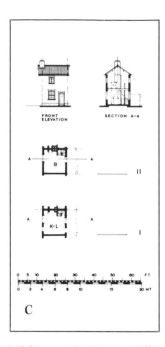

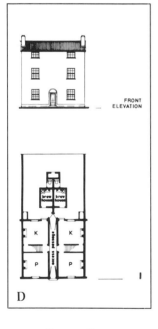

61. **Small types of house**

A: **Sunderland**, late nineteenth-century one-storey 'cottage'. Note the bedroom and the bathroom in the back extension, and the wash-house, which is accessible only from the yard (see p. 138).

B: **Hetton-le-hole**, Caroline Street, miner's house, *c.* 1856, now at Beamish Museum, Stanley, County Durham. One storey with attic. The pantry is really the scullery.

C: The one-room-deep house, built with or without a back yard (Norwich, *c.* 1820, see p. 106).

D: The combined-front-entrance type. A larger house, possibly for subletting and/or workshops. The stairs are arranged as in the standard later type, small version (plate 50), but the entrance is not at the front, but in the centre of the 'tunnel'. The separation of the scullery ('brewhouse') from the rest of the house was typical for the west midlands (Birmingham *c.* 1820–40; see p. 109).

E: **Shotton**, County Durham, miners' colony of the first half of the nineteenth century. Note the generally open surroundings and lack of differentiation between front and back.

62. **Easington.** County Durham, an old photograph of miners' houses, Woolmer, Wheatley Hill, first half of the nineteenth century; they are relatively large, two rooms deep with a small back extension.

One-storey houses; miners' houses in the north-east; Sunderland

We can discount here the most basic type, the one-roomed house, which was probably not built very frequently in England during the nineteenth century. Two-roomed houses were very common, but hardly any seem to survive. Many of the early colliery houses in the north-east seem to have been of one storey only. The earliest houses from the eighteenth century onwards were usually only one room deep, much like small agricultural cottages, and called 'singles' in Northumberland. The attic was accessible for storage, or could serve as a bedroom. Most nineteenth-century miners' houses seem to have been two rooms deep, increasingly with an added kitchen–scullery (cf. plates 20, 61–5). The lean-to roof of the latter was called a cat-slide. Increasingly, larger versions of this type were built, with a larger bedroom in the attic accessible from the back room by a ladder or by steep stairs. Scattered examples survive of this type in all parts of the country. The well-preserved specimens of Francis Street, Hetton-le-Hole, built about 1860, have lately been re-erected at Beamish Museum (plate 61). Later miners' houses were usually two storeys high and belonged to the regular type.

The history of the early mining colonies and their housing still needs to be investigated. Perhaps their most distinct characteristic was their general layout. Their density was usually high, considering that the pressures on land must have been lower than in the towns. As they were mostly built by one employer, their layout was usually fairly regular, yet there were also examples where the houses were strewn around densely but untidily, for instance in Haswell or Black Hill. It is evident from maps, and familiar from descriptions, that there were normally no made-up streets, no paths or fences; with no drainage the ground was usually a quagmire. In Northumberland, on the other hand, most miners' settlements consisted of interminable rows along, one presumes, pre-existing roads, for instance Foreman's Row, Seaton Delaval. From this summary description it follows that these colonies in the first half of the century could hardly be classed as 'reform' housing or 'model villages', of the kind we frequently find among contemporary agricultural settlements.

A major curiosity is Sunderland (plates 61–4), where the one-storey type carried on into the early twentieth century. The long rows of 'cottages', as they are called locally — as distinct from two-storey 'houses' — are an unmistakable feature of that town. The plan of the later examples is usually fairly wide, about 20 feet (6.1 m). There is always a sizeable front room, a hall entrance, and at the back a fairly small kitchen with a small bedroom on its side. Already before the middle of the century most 'cottages' seem to have had their own back yard with their own conveniences, and also a back extension. This extension often contained an extra bedroom — a very unusual feature — as well as a 'wash-house' or scullery. The later houses are often double-fronted, or rather one-and-a-half fronted, with a small bedroom on one side of the entrance. There are also versions with attics, with dormer windows at the front or back or both.

This type has puzzled historians. With the exception of some streets in Darlington[3] and Jarrow, other urban concentrations of one-storeyed houses are unknown in England. There is clearly a basic similarity to the miners' houses just mentioned. But this cannot explain the long continuation of the type in Sunderland; indeed the later miners' houses in the county usually seemed to be the two-storey regular type. More important was the fact that most earlier miners' houses did not have their own yards and toilets. A prominent example of an early miners' colony with its open surroundings and centrally-grouped conveniences, Stobbarts Buildings, Hay's Parade, had been built right in Monkwearmouth itself, and stood in stark contrast to the nearby Sunderland houses. The 1867 Sunderland byelaws are particularly careful in specifying separate conveniences for each house, and also emphasize the specific difference between front and back street,[4] something strikingly lacking in most early miners' colonies.

Many characteristics of the Sunderland 'cottage' can also be found in nearby Tyneside: separate rear facilities, in contrast not only to the miners' colonies, but also to the multi-occupied older houses in both Sunderland and Newcastle. There are always corridors; all rooms have a separate access — a decisive difference between the north-east and the rest of the north of England. Rooms are also unusually high, 9 or 10 feet (2.74–3.05 m) rather than 8 feet (2.43 m), as was normal in England. Finally, both towns show an unusual width in their houses, which leaves space for two rooms side by side at the back and sometimes at the front as well. Many features in both towns are reminiscent of Scotland, such as the height of the rooms — though in Scotland rooms are fewer in number and larger in size. The one-storey house of course occurs frequently in Scotland, and Sunderland further resembles smaller Scottish towns or suburbs in that there are many varieties of dormer window and gable (plate 182). Lastly, Tyneside resembles the larger Scottish towns in insisting on the flat (although they differ completely in their arrangement). But of course this brings us to the striking difference between Sunderland and Tyneside: houses in the Tyneside towns are particularly wide because each floor contains a separate flat, the equivalent of a small house. This serves to emphasize even more the profligacy with space in Sunderland. On the same size plot there are only half the number of dwellings. Perhaps a calculation of the relative costs of land, brick and timber in both areas could provide some explanation for the choice of dwelling type. One important factor is the high degree of subletting in Sunderland.

Certainly the 1867 byelaws greatly encouraged the type, after it had been established firmly by custom. Perhaps the local byelaw-makers were particularly glad not to have to try and outlaw a bad old type of dwelling, as so many other towns had to. Streets in Sunderland with one-storey houses only had to be 30 feet wide (9.15 m) as against 40 feet (12.19 m) for streets with two-storeyed houses. Wall thicknesses could be less, and yards could be proportionally smaller. Precise dimensions were given for attics in order to define clearly the borderlines between

63. **Sunderland.** Mainsforth Terrace West, *c.* 1870s. Note the variation of rooflights (cf. plate 182).

64. **Sunderland.** Canon Cockin Street, *c.* 1890–1900. The backs of similar one-storey houses with their menacingly high walls, often crowned by glass splinters.

65. **Bedlington.** Northumberland, Doctor Terrace (Doctor Row and North Row *c.* 1860s). Compare plate 20. A late example of a row of houses with completely open surroundings. Toilets and coal sheds are across the back street, which is also the main access to the houses, and the front street seems to be very rarely used.

one- and two-storey houses. Thus the Sunderland byelaws contain many details not to be found in the national Acts. Probably the best explanation for the Sunderland 'cottage' is offered by the *Cost of Living Report*: it is the 'favourite of the skilled mechanic'. There are, in fact fully double-fronted 'cottages' with eight or more rooms.[5] Local pride was certainly well-founded.

Two storeys and one room deep

On the whole, the one-room-deep, or 'single pile', plan seems to be at least as frequent as the two-room-deep one. A common variety of this was the double-fronted plan, which predominated especially in the industrial colonies in north Wales. In towns the two-storeyed single-pile house, 10 feet square or more (about 3 m²), with or without a back yard, was probably the most frequent type until the middle of the century (plate 61C). In the long, narrow courts of the older towns like Norwich or Wakefield, they were the only type that could be fitted in easily. London had its share of this kind of planning, like Quicksand Street, near Whitechapel Road,[6] with yards shared by three or four houses. It seems that the north-east continued longer with this sort of house than any other region: Boldon Colliery, Gateshead, Jarrow, or the Hartlepools, where it was called the 'kitchen house'. In a one-room-deep house in Union Street, Wallsend, dating perhaps from around 1870, the straight stairs go up almost immediately behind the front door; the rest of the house is much the same as any other 'through house'. In Liverpool many substantial one-room-deep houses, built between about 1845 and 1860, might, with their back extensions, which probably also provided for another bedroom, be called three-and-a-half-roomed houses. They mark the transition to the two-room-deep, four-roomed regular house of Lancashire which will be discussed below.

    However, most of the small one-room-deep houses had no back extension or back exit; there was simply no space for it, because they were squeezed close to the wall or the buildings of the next yard. Yet there were also a number of small to medium-sized houses which had a back yard and a back door, but no window at the back, at least on the upper floor; for instance in Murray Street, Consett of around 1860–70. In the houses on the north side of Bellevue Grove in Leeds, which were double-fronted and of above-working-class standard, there was a back door, but only the occasional small window at the back (plate 81). This 'blind back' type leads us straight into the major variation of the terraced house: the 'back-to-back'.

Early back-to-backs

There were several straightforward reasons for this type, such as lower land and building costs, and the need to keep warm[7]—the later statutory ventilation ducts were often stuffed up. Another advantage was the uncomplicated utilization of the ends of blocks on corner sites (plate 80). Most industrial towns in the north and the midlands took to the type. By about the mid-century Nottingham had 7000–8000 back-to-backs out of a total stock of 11,000 houses; Sheffield had more than 16,000 back-to-backs; Liverpool 20,000–30,000; Manchester perhaps somewhat fewer; Birmingham continued to build them and had about 40,000 back-to-backs in the 1870s. In the southern midlands and in the south the type was very infrequent, though Bristol and London showed isolated examples;[8] in eastern towns like Great Yarmouth and Norwich, back-to-backs were a little more common. In the north, and to a lesser extent in Wales, they could even be found in small colonies in the countryside.

It is probable that the type had its origins more or less accidentally in the narrow courts of the eighteenth century. But its basic manifestation was that of a straight row, with streets on both sides. There were many early examples of this layout from about the late eighteenth century onwards, in Manchester, Nottingham[9] and elsewhere, and it was to become the dominant layout in north-west Yorkshire.

The plan of the back-to-back was usually very simple: 10–15 feet square ($3.01–4.47$ m²), with the door leading straight into the main living-room, with dark and narrow stairs at the back of it. It most frequently had two storeys, but an attic was very common. In large towns three storeys was the rule. In Liverpool houses always had basements, which usually served as separate dwellings, whereas in other towns these rooms were more like cellars, as in Oldham or Leeds, and used as such, for storage, but also as sculleries and wash-houses. The greatest degree of variation can be found in the position of the toilets. Judging from the maps, for many earlier rows there were virtually no toilets. There might be a cluster of them in the vicinity, or at the end of the row. In other cases they were placed into a gap in the row, or simply inside the row, accessible from outside, often with bedrooms placed directly above (plate 76).

One further element of the back-to-back was the flexible way it could be combined with other types of houses. There are all kinds of arrangements, one such being the following: one 'through house' (a term frequently used in districts where back-to-backs are common), without back extension, alternating with one unit of (two) back-to-backs, which take up the same room as the one 'through house'. There were other combinations of a much more complicated kind on the steep hills of Halifax and Hebden Bridge. Perhaps the most intricate agglomeration ever built, if one can trust the maps, was the combination of twelve houses of varying sizes and shapes into one square block of 60 by 70 feet (18.3×21.2 m) in Albert Street, Todmorden.

In Rochdale (plate 76), a similar combination of types became the hallmark of the town's housing pattern between about 1850 and 1872: a single square of a house—one might say a 'one-up, one-down', or half a back-to-back—was squeezed in the space left between the back extensions of two normal through houses. To help with the class distinction, the former was called a cottage, the latter a house. The houses give on to a normal street; the cottages give on to a 'court', alternating with the back entrances to the houses. The type of house and the manner of arranging the street and access are intimately linked.

Early courts: Birmingham and Liverpool

It has already been stressed that one of the major differences between on the one hand the polite terrace and the more ordered, later working-class developments, and on the other the earlier, cheaper housing, was the lack of proper streets for the latter. There was no proper distinction between front and back. After all, the essential characteristic of the back-to-back was that it had no back. The term 'court' is used here in a very general sense, as tight but undefined space around houses. The long plots of land in older towns, behind the main houses along the old streets, were known as burgage plots. Scores of houses without proper street access were strung along these yards, some stretching to more than 140 yards, for instance in Wakefield. In the poorest parts of London, east of the City and south of the river, there were many short alleys, accessible from the streets (plate 66). Moving further

66. **London.** Bethel Place Area, off Vine Street, near Tooley Street, mainly before 1800.

east, into Stepney and Mile End, this arrangement continued, perhaps until the middle of the century, but gradually the street blocks became larger, the alleys fewer, and the overall density was greatly reduced. It seems that London's contribution to the development of a specific, local type of small house is not very important compared with that of the industrial towns—too many of London's poor and working classes could be crowded into run-down larger houses.

Street blocks in the north were usually smaller and more crowded. In Manchester and Bolton their regularization seems to have started comparatively early, perhaps even before 1800. The sides of the blocks are lined with back-to-backs and through houses; inside there was usually not enough space for more houses (in contrast to Sheffield, about which more below). This meant a certain amount of free space, used for the groups of toilets and for drying. In Manchester these drying spaces carried on occasionally into later periods, even when the houses became larger and more regular. Often the courts were completely enclosed by houses and were accessible through narrow passages called tunnels. This meant a long way to the toilets for those who lived in back-to-back houses along the street, as they had no direct access to the court, but had to go along the street, then through a tunnel, and then past some houses at the back. The plan of some of the houses was confused by the turning of the corner in the enclosed blocks, which led to the most complicated shapes and wriggling party walls.

In some towns, the non-street arrangement carried on longer than in others and was still going strong in the 1840s. It became systematized and regularized. Back-to-backs in courts behind the front streets were the common house form in the older parts of Birmingham (plates 67, 69). During the first half of the nineteenth century the possibilities of this arrangement were further explored, and as a whole this town shows an almost bewildering variety of layouts, and a description of even a small number of types would take up many pages. What does one call a group of four houses, back-to-back, with their 'back extensions' reaching out at both sides: star-shaped? The common terms themselves, judging from the maps, were often used in a confusing fashion. Generally the term 'court' was used for each division within a street block and the courts were numbered, 'Court No. 1', 'Court No. 2', up to twenty or more. But the word could also be used for a normal rear passage along a normal terrace.[10] Even where a decidedly modern-looking plan of a normal, five- or six-roomed house was adopted, this did not always mean the construction of a normal street as well; the terrace could just be put somewhere on open ground.[11] Elsewhere the back extensions were separated from the houses, and the wash-houses and sculleries were, like the conveniences and sheds, sprinkled all over the grounds or gardens between the houses (plates 61, 67). There was a multitude of tunnels from the front streets to the courts (plate 69) and between the courts; their purpose was, also presumably, at least in the later developments, to facilitate ventilation. Overall densities diminished as time went on and the garden areas between the houses became larger and larger. All these elements seemed to continue happily into the 1870s, until the 'byelaw' street was introduced, whereby Birmingham exceeded most towns by demanding a width of 50 feet (15.24 m).

The surrounding midlands towns, Wolverhampton, Walsall, Kidderminster and Coventry, show the same elements as Birmingham, though there were generally fewer back-to-backs.

Conditions in Liverpool were different from the start. Most of the workforce, predominantly dockers, were poorer; housing was restricted at first to a fairly narrow, low-lying stretch of land north of the city centre, close to the docks (plates 67, 68). The density was extremely high, reaching 700 persons per acre (1730 per hectare) in some areas. By 1840, 86,000 people lived in the 'courts'; at that time this was by far the largest area of purpose-built working-class housing anywhere in England, not excepting London. As the reformers saw it, the Liverpool system included all three evils of low-class housing: courts, back-to-backs and cellar dwellings. The typical layout seems to have begun in the late eighteenth century, still in a somewhat irregular fashion (for example, north of Burlington Road), and carried on until regulations gradually phased it out in 1842, 1846 and 1864. In contrast to Birmingham the same pattern prevailed throughout: five to ten three-storey back-to-backs, facing each other over courts which were sometimes only 9 feet wide (2.74 m). These houses had basements, which usually formed separate dwellings with their own access. There was normally a group of toilets at the end of the yard. In most cases there was a narrow opening on one side of the court into the street, between the slightly better houses which lined that street. Sometimes only a tunnel led from the street into the court, 3 feet wide (0.91 m) and 5–6 feet high (1.52–1.83 m). The determination of the builders to carry out this system was shown most strikingly in the narrow strip of development along the Victorial Canal, between Victoria Dock and Stuart Street, only 40 feet (12.2 m) in depth, which had a front row of houses along the street and behind it just 2 × 2 back-to-backs across courts. Occasionally the Liverpool pattern could be found outside the city, even in modern Birkenhead; in Manchester there was an example between Queen Street and King Street, and one cannot help feeling that this was a conscious import from Liverpool, unlikely though this might sound to Mancunians.

67. **Patterns of court layout,** from the *Ordnance Survey Plans* of 1880s. 'Court' chiefly refers to the fact that most of the houses shown are not accessible from normal open carriage streets. The maps contain examples of both the earlier, more irregular layouts and the later highly organized pattern.

Right: **Sheffield.** Most houses are of the regular 'through' type and have normal street access, but their backs are unusually open and are always shared between a group of houses. The blocks of ashpits and toilets are clearly recognizable. Middle to later nineteenth century. See plates 74, 75.

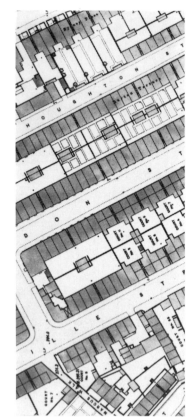

Far right: **Liverpool.** The very organized pattern of back-to-backs facing over courts, of the early nineteenth century. See plate 68.

Right: **Birmingham.** Early to mid-nineteenth century; back-to-backs and other small houses are placed in a variety of patterns behind the normal streets, and are accessible through tunnels underneath the houses along the streets. See also plate 69.

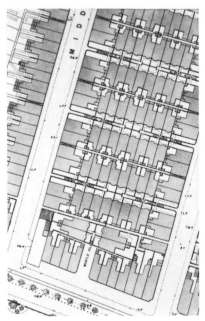

Far right: **Hull.** The typical, highly systematic layout of 'terraces', of 'avenues' of the later nineteenth century; houses are placed along short pathways between streets. See plates 70, 71, colour pl. 8.

68 (facing page). **Liverpool.** Typical court, first half of the nineteenth century. Four houses, back-to-back, with basement dwellings, facing each other across a court, with a view towards a normal street. At the bottom is the back wall of a group of toilets. (Court No. 16, Burlington Street, photo before demolition in the 1930s.)

Later courts: Hull, Nottingham, Sheffield and others

Though the term 'court' was mostly avoided, a small number of important towns carried on with modified arrangements of this kind until after 1900. What it basically amounted to was non-street access.

The city where the defiance of the normal street was most persistent was Hull (plates 67, 70, 71, colour plate 8). On the map it appears that the early, traditional courts (also called yards, squares, alleys, places, entries) were more dense and labyrinthine here than anywhere else. From the eighteenth century a more regularized back-to-back court system emerged, similar to but not as organized or as dense as Liverpool. Then the 1854 byelaws brought decisive changes: every house had to have a space at the back; thus the back-to-back type was phased out and the regular four- or five-roomed house was adopted throughout. All courts had to be 20 feet wide (6.09 m) and had to be completely open to the regular street; thus the earlier tunnel entrance was abolished. The 'terraces', or 'avenues', as the courts were now called, were always placed at right angles to the proper streets; they usually reached through the whole block to the next street, but were cut into two by a fence or wall in the middle. C. A. Forster claims that in the case of Hull the traditional local type won out against the nationally prescribed legislation, which attempted to introduce the regular type to the fullest possible extent. But one can also argue that the 1854 byelaws helped to preserve the local system by making it more salubrious. The later byelaws followed the same line. The byelaws of 1875 brought separate rear access to each house, thus a 'terrace' now had two points of contact with the street: the front entrance and the path along the backs, usually entered by a tunnel from the street. Unlike Nottingham, and more like the old system of Liverpool, the Hull 'terraces' did not usually form a corner with the regular street, but came behind a gap between the better houses along that street—hence the re-appearance of the tunnel for the back access of the 'terraces'. In 1894 a 24-foot minimum width was established for the courts (7.32 m) as well as compulsory front gardens. Although streets became increasingly popular in Hull, as elsewhere, the bulk of small houses carried on with the courts, the last one being built in 1926.

The neighbouring towns Goole and Grimsby did not take part in the Hull pattern but adopted the regular type of terrace and the normal layout, probably because there was no local tradition of a special layout. But Great Yarmouth, an old port like Hull, also had a pattern of extremely narrow alleyways, and continued with a similar disregard for the modern street access, with many rows which can only be reached by garden paths (plate 72).

Nottingham had its share of back-to-backs and courts. Both were outlawed in 1845 and thenceforth only regular through houses were built. Most of these had long front gardens with only a path in between, and at the rear there were short yards, shared or separate, connected by a narrow path again. These 'terraces', or 'avenues', as they were also called, opened with their full width into normal streets, at one end or both (plate 73). Occasionally even terraces of larger houses, such as Clipstone Avenue, off Peel Street, of about 1870–80, were built in a similar way.

The characteristics of the later developments in Sheffield are different from those of the other towns; here it is not a case of non-street access, but of the peculiarities of the back yard. Earlier on, Sheffield was another major example of the court tradition (plates 67, 74, 75). Less varied than Birmingham, less distinctive and systematic than Liverpool, the Sheffield arrangement consisted usually of back-to-backs along streets, with irregularly spaced and divided areas at the back, filled with more houses or just with the toilets and sheds for the whole block. Back-to-backs were not allowed

69. **Birmingham,** typical court; that is, a view of the back row of a group of back-to-backs, facing the court, with a tunnel leading through, presumably to the street. (Court No. 8, Clarkson Street; early to mid-nineteenth century; photo 1930s)

70. **Hull.** Crystal Avenue, off Middleton Street (compare plate 67), *c.* 1870s. The view is along the street with houses of a normal type. Gaps between these houses lead to the so-called terraces or avenues, i.e. courts of limited length, where the houses have no direct street access but give out to gardens and to narrow yards at the back, which one can see on the left, where the houses along the street have been pulled down. The tunnel through the houses on the right shows the normal access to the back of the houses in the avenue (cf. colour plate 8).

71. **Hull.** Devon Grove, off Sculcoates Lane, *c.* 1890s. Later on there was more space and gardens became larger, but the old layout prevailed.

72. **Great Yarmouth**. Middle Market Area, *c.* 1870s. The developments in Yarmouth are much less standardized than in Hull or Liverpool. The access at the front here is particularly narrow, and for the houses on the right there is an equally narrow back alley.

73. **Nottingham**, Ceyde Terrace, off Russell Street, 1870s. This is the end of a 'terrace', but unlike Hull there is normally no row of houses along that street. The gardens and the front of the houses are on the left. The windows in the end wall are typical of Nottingham houses.

74. (below left). **Sheffield**, *c.* 1880s–90s. A typical large communal backyard, for four houses (see page 112).

75. (below right). A view from the street, through the tunnel in the centre of the houses, showing the group of toilets (cf. map, plate 67).

after 1864 and regular four-roomed houses took their place. As elsewhere there was now a clear distinction between the front, the street, and the yard at the back. But what did continue in Sheffield was the lack of division at the back. The old method, familiar also from Birmingham, of numbering the courts within a block 'Court No. 1' etc. continued in Sheffield in some cases where they did not apply to 'courts' in the old sense, but simply back yards. By that time the great majority of new small houses elsewhere had separate back yards for each house, however small, but in Sheffield there are always groups of four, six or more houses sharing a completely open area at the back, with the toilets grouped together in the old court fashion. In most places these had to be a minimum of 3 feet 6 inches (1.07 m) away from the houses and the yards had to be at least 150 square feet (13.94 m²) per house, the normal size. But in Sheffield the toilets are normally much further away, and even further than the 15 feet demanded from the 1880s; and the yards contain a much larger area than the minimum requirements. Even in what must be called lower-middle-class housing there is mostly a shared yard with the same toilet arrangements,[12] and even the municipal flats in Infirmary Road of *c.* 1900 apparently had the WCs grouped away from the block. The reason for keeping the toilets so far away from the house probably lay to some extent with the traditionally backward sewage arrangements in Sheffield. But the openness also seems to stem from a desire for air, for the possibility of a garden. 'Not to be hemmed in, like being put in a suitcase', as an inhabitant put it to the author. 'The toilet arrangement is all right if you get on with the neighbours.' There may be a memory of bad, old, crowded arrangements. Perhaps there was also desire to ensure the inspectability of the working classes, as with the open stairs of philanthropic working-class blocks.

Elements of the Sheffield pattern stretch west and south: to Ashton, Macclesfield, Stockport and Derby; and north and east to Rotherham and Worksop, and even some late nineteenth-century workers' colonies in the countryside have completely open back yards, like Poolsbrook in Derbyshire.

Elsewhere the open back for several houses is much rarer in the second half of the nineteenth century. Yet we frequently find a related element: the rear access of several houses served by one tunnel, for ten houses or more. This means that a path runs along the back of the houses, cutting off, to some extent, their yards from their gardens. The type is particularly frequent in Norwich (plate 37; colour plate 6) and Maidstone. It means that a semi-public space is created at the back of the houses, carefully specified in the deeds, which is often used as the everyday entrance to the houses, particularly as most of them have no hall entrance.

There is one more element which is obviously derived from the tradition of open courts: one could call it the combined-front-entrance type. There are no front doors at the actual front of the house, but there is a tunnel leading from the front to the back yard, and the 'front' doors of two adjacent houses face each other in the centre of this tunnel (plate 61D). Judging from the maps they must have been particularly frequent in the west midlands; later examples can be found in Sheffield, Derby, Lincoln and Grantham.[13]

Later back-to-backs in Yorkshire

Ridiculed and scientifically condemned, chiefly because of their lack of through ventilation, back-to-backs continued in a small part of the country, while elsewhere they had been forbidden and one major town, Manchester, even managed to pull most of its own down by the end of the nineteenth century. In Halifax, Leeds,

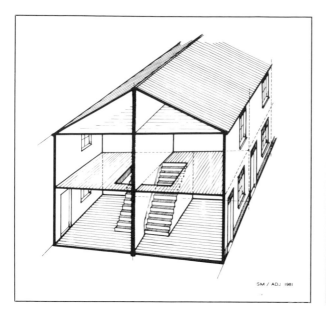

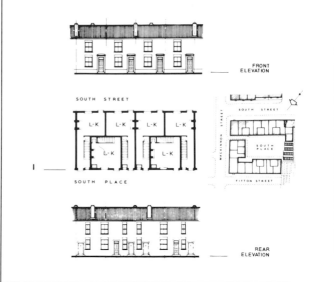

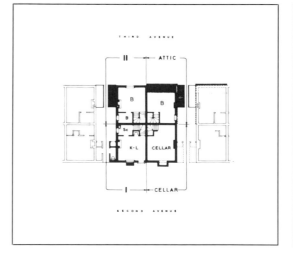

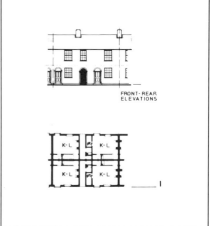

76. **Various back to backs**
Above left: A simplified drawing of the basic kind of back-to-back with just two rooms in each house.
Above right: **Rochdale**, houses and 'cottages', 1872. Here a single unit of a 'back-to-back' is slotted between the back extensions of normal through houses. This is combined with the distinction of street and court: the front of the houses give out to a normal street ('front elevation'), the 'cottages' give out only to a court ('rear elevation').
Centre right: **Keighley**, late nineteenth century, typical groups of four houses, with yards in between. Each house has four storeys in all.
Centre far right: **Manchester**, back-to-backs, before 1840. Note especially the way the toilets are placed in a passage between the houses with bedrooms above.

77. **Keighley**. Second Avenue, c. 1880s–90s. The houses shown in plate 76 are on the left; the corner houses have a different plan.

Bradford and most of the surrounding towns, about 65 per cent of all houses built in the 1880s were still back-to-backs. Bradford had tried to end the custom around 1860, but had to re-allow it in 1864–5, and finally prohibited it only in 1900. In Leeds the (National) Town Planning Act of 1909 put a stop to back-to-backs, but those developments which had obtained permission before that date continued to build the type into the 1930s. It seems, though, that even here the proportion of small through houses increased rapidly after 1900.

We have already discussed the most common types of arrangement of back-to-backs: a row of them along a street, with some sort of court behind, or the row completely surrounded by streets. By and large, this latter type predominated over the later developments. The three blocks of Akroyd's model colony at Copley, Halifax, of the 1840s were of this type, and one of them had the 'novel' arrangement[14] of a scullery under the stairs, and two bedrooms on the upper floor, side by side, accessible separately. As we saw earlier, the position of the toilets was one of the main difficulties in the back-to-back arrangements. In Leeds this was regularized in 1866–9 by a stipulation that a row had to be interrupted after every eight pairs of houses to create an open yard with groups of toilets and bins (plates 78–9). (Today the toilets in this type are mostly placed in the cellar.) Streets had to be 36 feet wide (10.97 m), as elsewhere. Most houses were now somewhat larger than the old, basic type, i.e. they had a wider frontage, which contained the window of the main room, the door and the small window for the scullery (plate 19); one might call this arrangement 'one-and-a-half-fronted'. On the upper floor there were usually two bedrooms, and there was generally an attic and a basement, or cellar (plates 79, 87).

Somewhat different patterns developed in Bradford, probably early in the nineteenth century. Characteristic is the interminable row of back-to-backs, with ample space on both sides, especially in suburban Heaton and Manningham (cf. plate 86).[15] The other type consisted of two rows of back-to-backs facing each other across a kind of back yard, somewhat like the Sheffield type (plates 82–5). Later Bradford solutions carry on the two modes, with some modifications. For the solution with yards the byelaws stipulated tunnels between every two houses to shorten the way to the conveniences in the yard, and to provide some light and ventilation for the scullery windows, which gave out into the centre of the tunnel. In the long rows each house had its own conveniences, half buried in the garden.

Leeds adopted a similar type by law in 1902 for all houses, but wished to differ by placing the toilet in the basement, though it is only accessible from the outside. There are also a great number of minor variations in the plan (plate 87). Streets in Leeds now had to be 42 feet wide (12.80 m) and houses had to have front gardens. What might be considered Leeds's last fling after 1900 was a type which included the most modern features: split-level floors, no basements and an upstairs bathroom. Ingeniously, the split-level 'extension', comparable to those in some London houses of those years, is squeezed in on the side of the house, and contains the scullery, the bathroom, and a small bedroom above; a double flight staircase at the back mediates between the rooms of that 'extension' and the higher rooms in the main part of the house.[16]

Halifax houses have plans like those of Bradford (plate 86) and like the groups of eight in Leeds. Huddersfield adopted an arrangement like Bradford, with tunnels with scullery windows opening into them. In Keighley the byelaws of 1872 were more radical: groups of four houses had to be separated completely from each other by a passage 10 feet wide (3.05 m)—one might also call it a yard—which contained the toilets and sheds for the houses of the block (plates 76, 77)—a type which

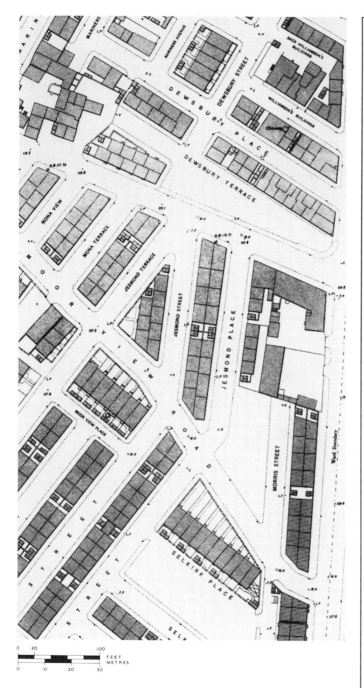

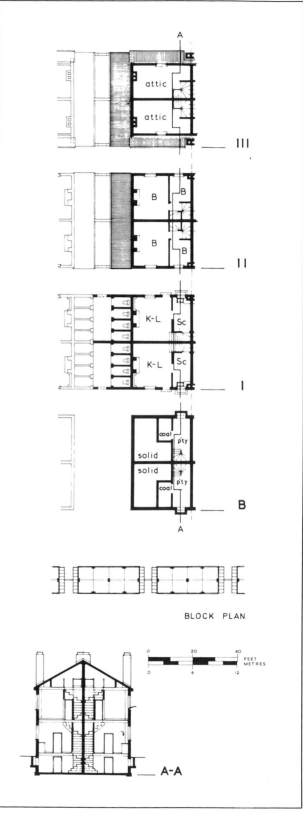

78. Back-to-backs in Leeds

Map: at the top the older, more varied and untidy arrangements; the overriding character of the rest is of openness and wide streets, even in the case of the few 'through houses'.

Plans: the typical Leeds arrangement between *c.* 1870 and 1900: every eight houses the row is interrupted by a gap, which contains toilets and 'yards' for the whole group.

79. **Leeds**. Autumn Place, *c.* 1870s. Four smaller back-to-backs are fitted into the end block on the right; the 'one-and-a-half fronted' type of back-to-back, shown in the plan, is seen further left. Beyond comes the gap between the blocks, with the entry to the shared 'yard'. Most things done in the proper yards of ordinary terraced houses are here done in the street; even the washing is often strung across.

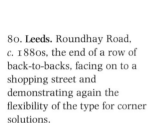

80. **Leeds.** Roundhay Road, *c.* 1880s, the end of a row of back-to-backs, facing on to a shopping street and demonstrating again the flexibility of the type for corner solutions.

81. **Leeds.** Bellevue Grove, *c.* 1880s. Half a row of double-fronted back-to-backs, or 'blind backs' (see p. 106).

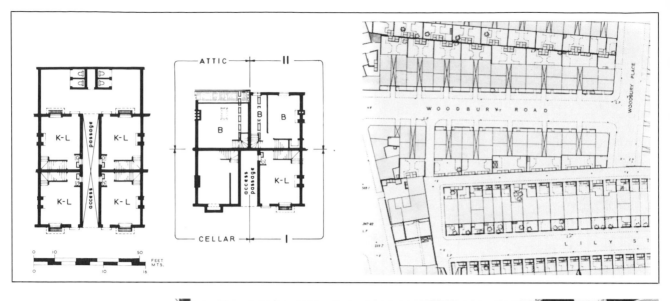

83, 84, 85 (right and below).
Bradford. Back-to-back houses
in the same area. The street
facade showing the houses in
the front row; the passage or
tunnel; the yard, with the
'front' of the houses in the back
row.

82 (left). **Back-to-backs in Bradford**
Map: Manningham area, late nineteenth century, showing the two main variations of plan in Bradford: in the lower part the long uninterrupted row with conveniences in each front 'yard' (cf. plate 86 below), and above, those with tunnels, to give access to the toilets grouped in the back yard.

ATTIC PLAN.

ELEVATION.

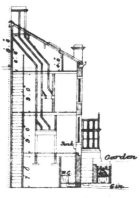

HALF SECTION.
The other side Similar.

Plan: the tunnel version. The plan on the left shows the ground floor of each of the four houses of one unit; the plan on the right shows the same group but each house at a different level; each house has a total of four storeys. The passage through the unit has several other functions (apart from that of giving access to the toilets): to let light into the scullery windows in the centre of the passage, and to provide room for a third, small bedroom in the floor above.

86 (right). **Halifax,** *c.* 1870–80. Back-to-backs of the continuous row type, with conveniences in the front yard of each house. The toilets are placed inside the house, but are accessible only from the outside. The ground floor plan is given twice, showing different levels.

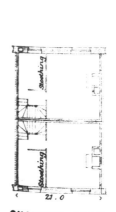

CHAMBER PLAN

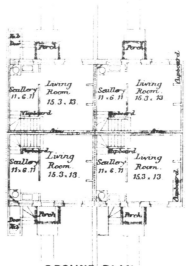

GROUND PLAN.

CELLAR PLAN.

87. **Leeds.** Banstead Grove, *c.* 1905; the typical later Leeds arrangement, with access to the toilet from outside, similar to that shown for Halifax (plate 86).

perhaps no longer qualifies as 'back-to-back' and which—though this might be purely accidental—resembles the four-houses-under-one-square-roof type of the famous Mulhouse workers' colony in Alsace of the 1850s.

Why did this type continue in Yorkshire for so long? Beresford argues that the back-to-backs in Leeds were particularly suited to long, narrow plots.[17] However, most back-to-backs in Leeds are arranged in parallel rows at right angles to the major streets, on what must have been fairly large plots to begin with; the long, single row is more characteristic of Bradford. The fact is that this type is a good space-filler in all situations. All types of row houses are flexible, and as the occupants' demand for space grew generally, they all adapted to it. Later back-to-backs can be larger than early small through houses.

The adversaries of the type claimed that because of the stricter regulations of street width the advantage of back-to-backs was minimal, as there had to be wide streets on all sides of the row. As regards building costs, Barry and Smith calculated the difference to be only a few per cent; but they found that builders' profits were slightly higher in the case of the Halifax back-to-backs—without however elaborating this point further. Rents in through houses of comparable size seemed to amount to between 5 and 20 per cent more. In the Cross Flats area of Leeds the larger back-to-backs cost (in 1914) £13 15s to rent, the smaller through houses nearby £14 15s, and the very small through houses in Harlech Grove not far away must have been cheaper to rent than many larger back-to-backs.

All commentators give the strong impression that these houses were actually liked by their inhabitants. We have already quoted Hole on this. He also cites examples of £20 houses, a decidedly middle-class rental in the provinces in the 1860s. In Bradford there were the curious square blocks of four sizeable houses, back-to-back under one roof, placed into spacious grounds, called St. Hilda's Villas. Were they meant to be a high-class demonstration of the qualities of the plan? In Leeds the back-to-backs juxtaposed to the through houses in Cross Flats actually have larger rooms, though they lack the corridors of the other type.

The most important difference between back-to-backs and through houses was the lack on the part of the former of a back yard, of enclosure, of privacy. But when one looks at the backs of the smaller through houses, one also notices an astonishing lack of privacy: low walls dividing the yards from each other and from the rear lane, which is nearly as wide as the front street. We have also noticed this openness elsewhere in Yorkshire, in Sheffield, and we can note attempts in Wakefield to get small through houses established, with similarly open backs. As we have seen, Bradford continued the older type of back-to-back with some kind of semi-private 'rear' yard for much longer; there are early examples of this arrangement in Leeds as well.[18] But from *c.* 1840 onwards only one basic type was built in Leeds, which is completely surrounded by the same kind of open street. It is here, I think, that the key to the Leeds question can be found. Rimmer cites praise which was lavished by a commentator of the 1840s on developments in Cavalier Hill and Ellerby Lane. These are of the arrangement just described, though not yet as straight and tidy as the later ones. An Act of 1842–3 stipulated that streets should be 30 feet wide (9.14 m)—though this was often neglected, according to Hole. Mair, a strong critic of back-to-backs, remarked in 1910 that the successive legal widening of streets had in fact helped to maintain the type. One is reminded of contemporary arguments in Germany, put forward by Rudolf Eberstadt, that the high blocks of flats were only made possible, and actually to some extent caused by, the regulations stipulating excessive street width.

But the wide open street *was* the thing that was wanted. As a rather late local defender of the Leeds system, F. M. Lupton, put it in 1906: 'there is no backyard in which to deposit filth, a great advantage in the poorest quarters of the town'. It is a late example of an attitude which was most prevalent from the 1830s to the 1870s, when all towns were trying to legislate against hidden untidiness. Birmingham's streets had to be 50 feet wide (15.24 m); Halifax had four classes of streets of different widths. The towns which allowed back yards gave endless stipulations about their construction to ensure cleanliness. The open streets of west Yorkshire, as well as the open yards of Sheffield, stem from the same basic desire.

As we have seen, in some towns byelaws caused a change of type; in others the older type was allowed to continue but was made more salubrious. Hull and Leeds belong to the latter group. The crucial element was the timing. If, as it seems, Leeds managed to reduce density and untidiness generally in new houses from the 1840s onwards, local pressure groups could prevent the introduction of the new regular type. Another question is how conscious commentators actually were, at that time, about the disadvantages of the back-to-back type. An early report on social problems and housing in Leeds in the *Journal of the Royal Statistical Society*[19] does not mention back-to-backs as such. It does not seem to have been until a little later—largely through the detailed central government *Reports* of the 1840s—that the public became more aware of the type, and it could become an element of local concern, but also of local pride, or at least obstinacy. Finally it is ironic that, after so much argument, in 1980 the Government lifted the restrictions on the building of this type!

The 'two-up-two-down' in Lancashire and elsewhere

What can be seen in our survey of regional types to be the most 'modern' form of dwelling was also the oldest one, or at least it was the commonest one: the smallest version of the regular type of terraced house. It was sometimes made out to be characteristic of Lancashire. It did, indeed, supersede the courts and back-to-backs in Lancashire, although it also did this in Sheffield, Hull, Nottingham, Teesside, Cheshire and Staffordshire—though in most of these regions the solutions at the back of the houses were different from those in Lancashire; elements of the court arrangements continued, whereas in Lancashire they were completely abolished (plates 88–99).

The main characteristics of the 'Lancashire' type have already been described in the last chapter; here we have to follow their special development in the region. We must begin here with some important philanthropic, paternalistic work. H. and E. Ashworth, the Bolton cotton manufacturers, began to build four-roomed through houses for their workers in the 1820s at Pinnacle Field and Egerton. Standards seemed very high, 'like houses of middling shopkeepers in towns':[20] there was a fair-sized living-room and the main bedroom in the front, and a small bedroom and small kitchen in the back. There was usually a separate, enclosed yard for each house (plate 94). We have mentioned above mid-century houses in Liverpool which were really only one-room-deep houses with a back extension. The important development at this point was the gradual enlargement of the rooms at the back, when the kitchen became large enough to serve as a kitchen–living-room, so that the front room could be used as a parlour (plates 92, 94). Finally, a small scullery was added to this two-room-deep house, though this did not become common in small houses in Lancashire until the end of the century. One old-fashioned element continued, it seems, longer in Lancashire than in other regions: the stairs in the back

88 (left). **Preston.** Aerial view of the eastern parts of the town in the 1930s; the road in the centre, going towards the centre of the town, is New Hall Lane. Note especially the way the larger roads are lined with somewhat better houses.

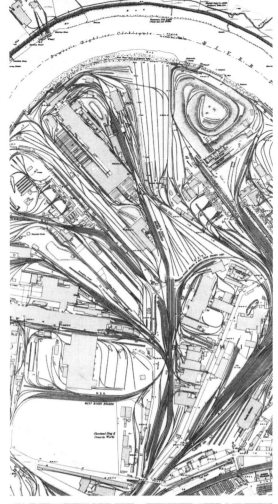

89 (right). **Middlesbrough,** map of 1915. At the top the oldest part, built between 1820 and 1850, a planned town with the market in the centre. South of that the typical later street layout, just spreading outwards, without any apparent overall plan. Yet it was in the oldest part that irregular courts and back-to-backs could still be found, which were completely phased out in the newer parts after 1850 (see also p. 36).

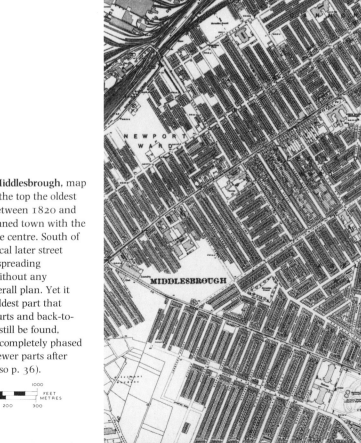

90. **Salford,** area near Church Street, *c.* 1880. Note the variety of back extensions, the varying width of the rear lane and the generally carefully scaled variety of sizes of houses—though each street is homogenous (see p. 26).

91. **Bolton,** a typical 'vestibule'—modern in its details—for the front entrance of the non-hall-entranced type of house in the north-west; a simple way of overcoming some of the problems of entering the front room straight from the street.

room; many other regions adopted the middle stairs type. Across in Yorkshire, the famous post-1850 model workers' colonies provided a wide range of sizes. In Akroydon, 'Block II' and 'Block III' were only one room deep, with smaller and larger back extensions respectively. 'Block IV' had many two-room-deep houses, where the front and the back rooms were approximately of the same size. In West Hill, Halifax, 'Class III' houses had a hall entrance, a rather small parlour, a big kitchen–living-room and a small scullery back extension.[21] We can also observe the gradual enlargement of the back room in ordinary speculative houses in Barrett Street, Bury, of around 1860–70.

Manchester (plates 76, 94), it appears, had more types of small houses to offer than any other large town, not excluding London. We have already mentioned the back-to-backs and the courts. But small versions of our present type also appeared before 1800[22] and many more by 1820:[23] very small but enclosed back yards with very narrow passages between, accessible usually through tunnels. The workings of the early building regulations need much further research, but by stipulating in 1830 that courts and streets had to be 30 feet wide (9.14 m), courts were practically ruled out. In 1844 the Manchester Borough Police Act stated that there should be no new houses without a toilet in the yard or in the house, and that these should have a door and a proper covering. This seems to have made the building of back-to-backs more difficult—though they were only explicitly phased out in 1868. But in any case, the new type already seemed to dominate all new developments. Characteristic of Manchester and Salford remain the orderly but narrow spaces at the back—sometimes the houses are called, misleadingly, back-to-backs. From 1868 streets had to be the usual 36 feet wide (plate 179), but only 70 square feet (6.50 m²) were specified for the back, against the usual 150 square feet. Even larger houses have comparatively narrow yards (plate 98). The 150 square feet specification was only introduced in 1890, and in 1908 this was increased to 250 square feet (22.23 m²), in conjunction with streets 42 feet wide (12.8 m). At this late date, Manchester was overdoing it.

Within this very repetitive general pattern there were only a few variations at the back; the joint ashpit placed between the toilets of two houses was the most frequent feature. Even by 1890 the great majority of houses were still four-roomed, without a scullery back extension (plate 90).

In Liverpool the old system described above was phased out in the 1840s and 1850s. The struggle between legislation, nationally directed, and old local customs was probably stronger here than anywhere else; but the victory of the national type was also more complete. The later nineteenth-century Liverpool houses differ radically from the early nineteenth-century ones. In general they were perhaps somewhat smaller than those in Manchester, with more $3\frac{1}{2}$ roomed houses; the backs appear slightly less narrow, but rear lanes are usually only 4 feet wide (1.22 m) (e.g. plate 92, colour plates 4, 9).

Of the other Lancashire towns, Preston must rate as one of the first to introduce our type on a large scale (plate 88). Generally there were fewer back-to-backs or courts in Preston than in most other towns. The small houses which sprang up close to the early large textile mills just outside the town, from about 1800 onwards, were usually neat rows, at first with open backs.[24] But by 1830–40 two major patterns had already fully emerged: those with a narrow back alley and small separate yards,

92. **Liverpool,** the smallest type of house built in Liverpool around 1900 (see also colour plate 4).

93. **Liverpool,** the yard of a very similar house, late nineteenth century. On the left the toilet and the ash bin (cf. plate 22).

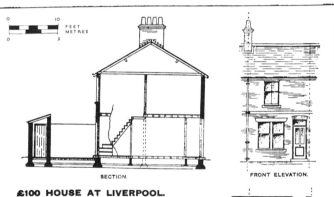

SECTION.   FRONT ELEVATION.

£100 HOUSE AT LIVERPOOL.

IT is stated ("Building World," No. 81, p. 36) that this house, which is erected in Bective Street, Earle Road, Liverpool, actually cost less than £100 to build; that is to say, the cost works out at less than the sum named; for three blocks, each comprising twenty-two such houses, were built. This method of arriving at cost cannot be considered misleading, seeing that such dwellings are seldom or never required to be built singly. The front of the house is built of Premier vitrified buff bricks, relieved with a two-course string of seconds red Ruabon bricks; the arch over the front door being formed of similar bricks to those used for the string-course. Further ornamentation consists of a cornice formed of red headers oversailing, with buff stretchers between. Such decorative brickwork is distinctly more pleasing, and in more legitimate taste, than much of the stucco and stonework ornamentation that forms an obtrusive feature of many modern small dwellings. The windows of these Liverpool houses, however, have sandstone heads and sills. The roofs are covered with 24-in. by 12-in. seconds Llangollen slates, each fixed with two 1⅞-in. galvanised nails; blue ridge tiles being bedded in hair mortar and pointed with cement; while the slates are torched underneath with hair mortar. The outer door frames are of 4½-in. by 3-in. spruce, with moulded stops planted on, the front door being of 2-in. pine, with ¾-in panels, bolection-moulded; a vestibule door, 1⅜-in. thick, having marginal lights in the upper portion. The joists to the living-room are 5 in. by 3 in., those to the bedrooms being 7 in. by 3 in.; while the rafters are 3 in. by 2½ in., supported on a 9-in. by 6-in. purlin formed of two deals bolted together. As regards the planning, it may be sanitary, but is decidedly inconvenient, to place the w.c. at the back of the yard. The rates per hour for labour were: Bricklayer, 9½d.; plasterer, joiner, and mason, 9d.; plumber and boy, 1s.; slater, 10d.; labourer, 6d. The common local bricks were 25s. 6d. per 1,000 delivered; seconds Ruabon, 60s. per 1,000; buff facing bricks, 82s. 6d. per 1,000.

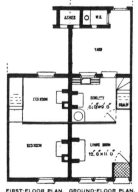

FIRST-FLOOR PLAN. GROUND-FLOOR PLAN.

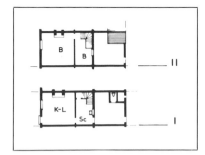

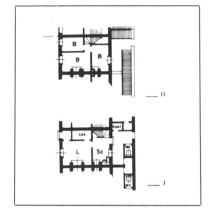

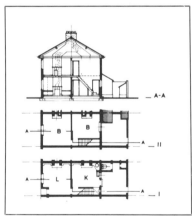

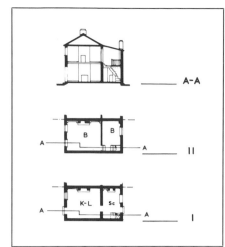

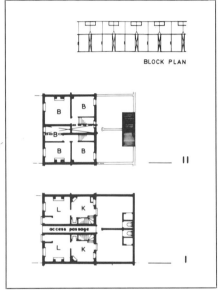

94. Other versions of the two-up-two-down

Egerton (left, above), near Bolton, workers' houses for H. & E. Ashworth, *c.* 1830. The rooms at the back are considerably smaller than those at the front. Specially important for this date is the enclosed back yard with toilet and ashbin for each house (see p. 138 and plates 92, 93).

Saltaire (left, middle) *c.* 1850. Slightly larger than those of the smallest size, this house in Sir Titus Salt's celebrated model town differs very little in general accommodation from the ordinary speculative workers' houses of the period. The walls are thicker than usual because they are built of rough stone.

Manchester (left, below), the later nineteenth-century smallest standard type of the region. Front and back room are now roughly of the same size, although the stairs are still in the back room; there is no scullery back extension (cf. plate 50; see also plate 179, colour plate 27).

Norwich (centre, above), first half of the nineteenth century. A very common plan, urban and rural. The house is really one room deep (though the front rooms are of a very comfortable size, see p. 100), but a small extension at the back, which takes up the whole width of the house, makes it, in effect, two rooms deep. The kitchen-cum-scullery is very cramped indeed, and the back bedroom has no wall separating it from the staircase, and thus is nothing more than a loft.

Preston (centre, below), late nineteenth century. Another version of the small four-roomed house, showing the access for the back of the houses, an economic solution providing every house with its own back door. It also enabled every other house to have a third bedroom at the front. Two houses share a narrow passage to the back (see plates 95–7).

95 & 96 (left), 97 (right).
Preston. Access arrangements
to the backs of small houses; cf.
plans opposite.
Left, above: view through the
tunnel from the street, with the
diagonally placed doors to the
individual yards at the end.
Left, below: view of the yard;
the doors are on the left.
Right: the inside of a street
block as a whole.

98. **Manchester**, late
nineteenth century. The
narrowness of the typical
Manchester back lanes—even
in the case of somewhat larger
houses, on Moss Side, gave rise
to the misleading
characterization 'back-to-back'.

99. **Barrow-in-Furness**
c. 1870s–80s; here the back
streets are uniformly wide.

Colour plate 9. **Liverpool**, Weller Street, *c.* 1860–70.

as in Green Bank Terrace and Moss Rose Road, and those without a back alley, but with a tunnel between every other house, providing a separate street access to every yard, as in East St. Peter's Street or Adelphi Street. This arrangement also gave an additional third bedroom over the tunnel for every other house (plates 94–7). Barrow-in-Furness, the most modern of the big Lancashire towns, which only really began to grow on a large scale in the 1870s, shows more two-storey back extensions than usual in the north (e.g. plate 99); its standards are more those of the south.

Middlesbrough was a new town under strict company rule from its beginnings in the 1820s (plate 89). But only from the 1850s, in the newer parts, were back-to-backs and courts completely banned. The width of the streets had to be that of the height of the houses, with a minimum of 20 feet (6.09 m), and 36 feet (10.97 m) from 1876. Rear lanes were usually rather narrow in Middlesbrough, but somewhat wider in Stockton and Darlington. Thus, in plan and street arrangement, the small houses of the second half of the nineteenth century on Teesside were much the same as in Lancashire. To the south, Macclesfield and Stoke-on-Trent[25] also show a predominance of the three- to four-roomed through house, but the backs are more open in the Sheffield manner.

Flats in terraces: Tyneside and London

The last major provincial variety of dwelling type is the Tyneside flat. Well over half of all the dwellings built on Tyneside in 1900 were still of that type. A small number can or could also be found in Ashington, Sunderland, Hartlepool, Carlisle, Barrow, and perhaps in Manchester.[26] As in the case of the other types, we can only speculate about their origins; it seems though that the flat developed much later than most other plans. One might begin with the proximity of Scotland. There is also an old type of almshouse with separate dwellings on the upper floor, accessible from a gallery.[27] Because many houses were crowded on the steep hills of Newcastle and Gateshead—for closeness to the docks—á tendency for multi-storey structures emerged, where the upper units were accessible from the back. Altogether, multi-occupation and overcrowding seems to have been more frequent in the north-east than, say, in Yorkshire. On the other hand, there were very few back-to-backs and courts to be found on Tyneside. The fashion of subdividing the houses horizontally continued in the medium-sized houses of the 1830s and 1840s in Blandford Street, Wharncliffe Street and George Street. Maps show houses with two doors and even divided back yards. We have seen in Liverpool how basements could serve as separate dwellings. The main question for Newcastle seems to be: when did the separate basement flat become a separate ground-floor flat? Perhaps the Act of 1847, according to which all cellars had to have areas—clearly an attempt to discourage basements—had something to do with this. A plan for some houses in Maple Street of 1854 shows almost all the elements of the Newcastle flat. On the ground floor there are three rooms and two front doors; from one of these the stairs lead straight up to the first-floor flat which has four rooms. At the back there is a door with a stairway leading down to the yard which is separated from that of the ground-floor flat. Each flat has its own convenience in the yard. Only the sculleries at the back of each flat are still rather small. From about the same date are the flats in Percy Street and Middle Street in Tynemouth, and here a basement and an attic enlarge each flat considerably, to nine rooms in the upper one. Even at the end of the century we still find some very large flats.[28] Thus there were middle-class flats, as there were middle-class back-to-backs. At the other end of the scale, there were very much

Colour plate 10. **Burnley**, a typical Lancashire later nineteenth-century back street.

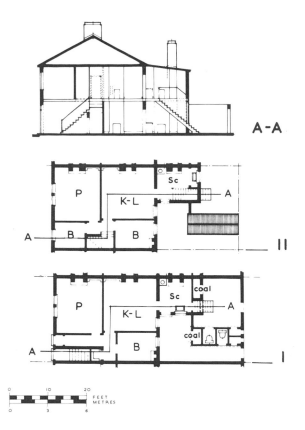

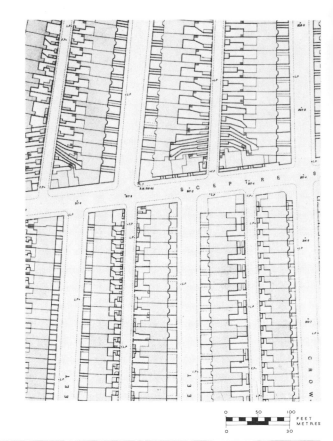

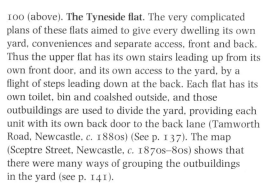

A-A

100 (above). **The Tyneside flat.** The very complicated plans of these flats aimed to give every dwelling its own yard, conveniences and separate access, front and back. Thus the upper flat has its own stairs leading up from its own front door, and its own access to the yard, by a flight of steps leading down at the back. Each flat has its own toilet, bin and coalshed outside, and those outbuildings are used to divide the yard, providing each unit with its own back door to the back lane (Tamworth Road, Newcastle, *c.* 1880s) (See p. 137). The map (Sceptre Street, Newcastle, *c.* 1870s–80s) shows that there were many ways of grouping the outbuildings in the yard (see p. 141).

101. The back yard of a lower flat (Tamworth Road, Newcastle; a house with a slightly different plan).

102. The back yard of an upper flat.

103. The street facade of similar houses in Gateshead.

104. **South Shields**. South Frederick Street, late nineteenth century. Note the high walls separating the lane from the yards and the yards from each other, and the multiplicity of doors to the lane. The back extensions of the houses have here been combined, thus each back extension contains parts of four dwellings.

105. From this follows that here not two but four doors have to be combined (see p. 87).

The London cottage flat

106. London, Longcroft Road, SE9, flats in houses, 1880s. The front does not show any difference from a terrace of houses. (see p.11).

107. The back of the same houses: there is a small flat on each floor. Each has an outside toilet, placed at the end of the extension and reached by an outdoor passage. This conformed to the general rule that lower-class houses should only have an outside toilet (see p. 60). Note also the portable bath tub (cf. plate 26).

108. Advertisements for London cottage flats. They are also frequently called maisonettes; 1907. Cf. also colour plate 11, p. 166.

WHERE TO LIVE IN A HEALTHY DISTRICT
WELL AND CHEAPLY.
Night and Day Train Service, and Cheap Fares.

FRONT VIEW OF FLATS.

WARNER ESTATES
SELF-CONTAINED HALF-HOUSE FLATS,
Separate Entrances, and Gardens Front and Rear,
WALTHAMSTOW AND LEYTON.
Nearest Stations by Great Eastern Railway: St. James' Street and Hoe Street.   By Midland Railway: Blackhorse Road and Walthamstow.   Motor 'Buses from City and Electric Cars pass Letting Offices.

5/6 to 7/- Per Week. Including Rates & Taxes.

APPLY ON THE ESTATES:
13, Pretoria Avenue, High Street.   405, Forest Road (opposite Police Station).
92, Brettenham Road (next Lloyd Park).   392, Markhouse Road (Lea Bridge Road End).

PAMPHLET WITH FULL PARTICULARS ON APPLICATION.

109. Combined front entrances for two flats in each house, characteristic of the later London cottage flat (Hayday Road, E16, early 1900s).

smaller flats, like many of those in Jarrow, which only had two rooms on each floor and shared back yards (plates 100–3).

After 1870 great numbers of flats began to be built. The 1870 Newcastle byelaws acknowledge the type: '. . . the term dwelling house shall include a flat'. Already in 1866 streets had to be 40 feet wide (12.19 m), back streets 20 feet (6.09 m) and rooms 9 feet high (2.74 m). From 1892 houses had to be 18 feet wide (5.49 m) and each habitable room 70 square feet in area (6.50 m²). There were always, as in Sunderland, corridors to all rooms. The scullery at the back became larger, and by 1900 many flats managed to squeeze a bathroom into the extension.[29] Usually back extensions are single; coupled ones necessitated placing the front doors side by side. Here we have, of course, not two, but four doors close to each other (plates 104–5). There were endless variations of the placing of the toilets in the yards. Occasionally there are three flats in one house, as in Gordon Street, Gateshead, of 1899, with three separate back yards. Like some southern towns, such as London and Plymouth, Newcastle built larger houses than usual. A house 20 feet (6.09 m) and two rooms wide, costing about £250 to build, could not have been afforded by the lower classes. It had to be divided, but northern planning ingenuity created a special type, unlike the way it was done in the south, where builders simply carried on with the old types, which were multi-occupied from the start, and were rarely adapted properly.

It took London something like forty to fifty years longer to develop a similar type, the 'cottage flat'. Thoughts about how to adopt the medium standard London house for individual flats probably began in conjunction with the building of high-rise model blocks for the lower classes, which were usually very advanced in sanitary matters. On the other hand these big blocks were not much liked, because of their density, their lack of privacy and their often grim looks. Privately (i.e. speculatively) built block dwellings therefore often adhered to something that at least looked like a normal terraced house (plate 106).[30] Banister Fletcher made elaborate proposals, in his book *Model Houses for the Working Classes* of 1871, to turn regular two-storey

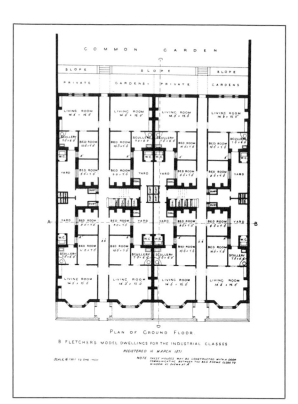

PLAN OF GROUND FLOOR.

B FLETCHERS MODEL DWELLINGS FOR THE INDUSTRIAL CLASSES

REGISTERED 16 MARCH 1871

SCALE 16 FEET TO ONE INCH   NOTE THESE HOUSES MAY BE CONSTRUCTED WITH A DOOR COMMUNICATING BETWEEN THE BED ROOMS CLOSE TO WINDOW AS SHEWN AT B

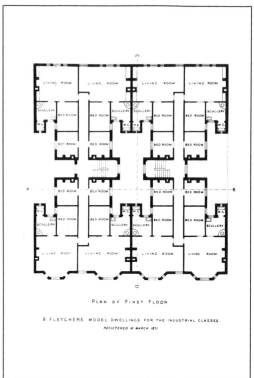

PLAN OF FIRST FLOOR

B FLETCHERS MODEL DWELLINGS FOR THE INDUSTRIAL CLASSES

REGISTERED 16 MARCH 1871

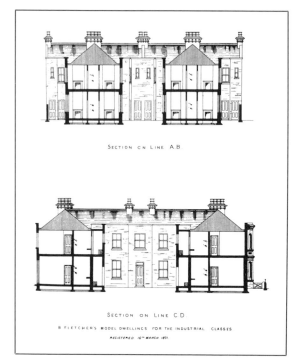

SECTION ON LINE A.B

SECTION ON LINE C.D

B FLETCHERS MODEL DWELLINGS FOR THE INDUSTRIAL CLASSES

REGISTERED 16TH MARCH 1871.

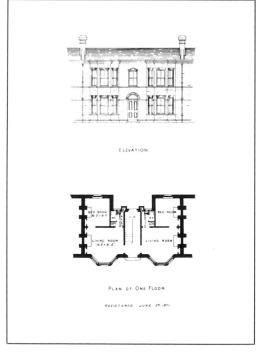

ELEVATION

PLAN OF ONE FLOOR

REGISTERED JUNE 5TH 1871

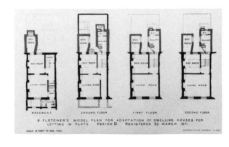

B FLETCHER'S MODEL PLAN FOR ADAPTATION OF DWELLING HOUSES FOR LETTING IN FLATS DESIGN D. REGISTERED 22 MARCH 1871.

BASEMENT   GROUND FLOOR   FIRST FLOOR   SECOND FLOOR

SCALE 16 FEET TO ONE INCH

110. Banister Fletcher, in his book *Model Houses for the Industrial Classes* of 1871, is opposed to high blocks of flats and tries to adapt the two-storey terraced house formula into flats. With these 2 × 4 × 2 three-roomed flats the staircases are placed between the back extensions. Communal corridors upstairs reach through part of the depth of the block, downstairs through the whole of the block. There is a general feeling of openness akin to the contemporary multi-storey blocks of flats. The view of the street facade below emphasizes the similarity to ordinary two-storeyed terraces (see p. 240). The small plan at the bottom (scale about half of those above) shows the adaptation of older Georgian terraced houses through additions at the back.

houses into self-contained flats (plate 110). Perhaps one of the earliest examples of two-storey, purpose-built cottage flats are the very small Victoria and Albert Cottages in Woodseer and Deal Streets, London E1, of 1850–60, with a separate front entrance for the upper flat.[31] By 1881 there were flats with kitchens and sinks on both floors, but shared conveniences in the yard.[32] The arrangement of the stairs at the back in some other flats is reminiscent of the Newcastle types. The mature London type seems to appear around 1890, with coupled back extensions, two bedrooms each, own kitchens, toilets, and, later, own bathrooms. There were always back stairs leading down to the gardens, which were often separated by a small fence (plate 108, colour plate 11). Four entrances were initially placed next to each other;[33] in later flats they are always discreetly placed under one arch, making the whole look even more like an ordinary two-storeyed house. Occasionally there was even an attempt to give the upper flat its own drying ground on the roof of the extension of the lower flat.[34] Many towns adopted the 'cottage flat' after 1900, chiefly for municipal developments.[35] Similar arrangements of separate front stairs for flats are known in Holland.

Changes in use and plan: the open and enclosed back

We have already stressed the important changes of use which went with the increase in the depth of the house; from the old custom of performing all functions in one kitchen–living-room, to that of having two-and-a-half to three rooms, scullery, kitchen–living-room and parlour. All small types of houses, not only the regular 'through' types, but also the back-to-backs and the flats, were gradually enlarged.

The greater differentiation of functions inside the house went with a similar development as regards the different areas outside the house. The front–back divide increased greatly, the front street and the back lane becoming two entirely different spheres. In the previous chapter on the plan of the medium and large houses, we took the enclosed back yard for each house for granted; but for the small house it represented an important new achievement. We have traced the different ways of relating the house to its immediate surroundings: from the older types of back-to-backs and courts, where each house had only one entrance which gave on to something which was the front and the back at the same time, to the 'through' house. At first this had a communal back yard but later mostly an individual enclosed yard. This yard was the essential new element in all Lancashire and north-east houses; however narrow, they are enclosed and private. The stipulation of the 1858 Act, that every house ought to have 150 square feet (13.94 m²) at the back, free from any erection except the toilet block, was probably the most decisive regulation of all (plate 60). Almost all towns followed it. It did not say that the yards should be enclosed by walls, but the local versions of the law in Sunderland and Newcastle specified it, and those walls had to be 8 feet high (2.44 m). It was also here, as we saw, that separate corridor access to all rooms was most strenuously insisted upon. In Tyneside the tendency to separate the yards was probably stronger than anywhere else. The custom of separating the yards belonging to each flat was sometimes taken to astonishing lengths: where the row of the houses turns an angle, the walls of the yards have to be turned as well; here the individual yard degenerates into a long, crooked passage (plate 100).

The yard became an extension to the house, its main purpose being to keep the house clean. Remove dirt 'instantly out of the house' wrote Mrs. Buckton.[36] There was no way of throwing it out of the front door anymore. In Leicester almost all houses had a lobby at the beginning of the back extension, with a door to the yard to provide the most direct access to it from the kitchen and the rest of the house (plate 46). Of course, the yard itself had to be kept clean. The byelaws contain minute details about its construction; storage and collection of refuse became more and more organized. Earlier on, toilets had invariably been shared; now each house had its own, inside the yard; and even with later back-to-back types, toilets were now adjacent to the house. In Sunderland the wash-house in the back extension had to have an entrance from the yard only, chiefly because of the customary back bedroom which came between the wash-house and the rest of the house (plate 61). The coal shed was now almost always outside.

Finally, there had to be a back lane, if the houses had no basement and no corridor. Coal had to be brought to the house, refuse had to be taken away, and so did the contents of the toilets—there were few WCs when the regular house type and the back streets were introduced in the north. In Burnley the back lanes were always 12 feet wide (3.66 m); in Bolton and Barrow mostly 20 feet (6.90 m). Many of these lanes even had small footpaths. There were none of the semi-public back spaces any more, whose exact legal status and right of way had to be cumbersomely stated. The back lane had become almost an additional street, though in status it remained inferior to the front street (plate 99, colour plate 10).

The changes behind the house were perhaps even more decisive than those inside. It was these elements which contributed most to the desired degree of 'self-containedness'. It is, of course, far more difficult to deal with those socio-psychological aspects and their development than with the more practical ones of use. There seems to be a divergence among social historians: some, like Hoggart, find a considerable amount of social contact amongst the residents of a neighbourhood, others, like Seabrook, stress more the restrictions on contact. Most historians of working-class housing categorically deplore the lack of privacy in this early period, seemingly unaware that the notion of privacy was relatively new even in better-class housing.

Occasionally we can find less biased nineteenth-century accounts of life among the lowest classes, such as that of Thomas Wright in *The Great Unwashed* of 1868; twenty houses shared Lock Court in London, and the inhabitants were mainly hawkers, unemployed, or prostitutes. Houses were small and extremely crowded. Hardly any privacy was possible; nor did it seem to be particularly desired. Everybody knew what everybody else was doing. When the author complained about the mob of children which immediately surrounded him upon moving in, he was told they had a right to know what was happening in 'their' court. (This was, of course, in the days before compulsory schooling.) There was a great degree of mutual reliance. Because of the poverty, everyday objects like kitchen utensils were constantly exchanged. In extreme situations like birth or death, the help of the neighbours was essential; there was simply nobody else. Brawling was frequent, and carried out quite openly. With the actual indoor space being so small and overcrowded, as many activities as possible were performed outside, such as meals on the doorstep if the weather permitted.

There must have been an unimaginable sense of territoriality, of enclosure and of a corresponding lack of familiarity with the world outside their immediate surroundings, all the more so when much work was performed in the houses or the courts as well. This was less likely to be the situation in London, but in most provincial towns the sense of belonging to a court or a small street differed little from that in traditional farming communities.

How did the changes in plan affect social life? It was at the back that the old customs prevailed. Whether there were open, communal yards, or individual yards, the back door to the houses usually stayed open, used as a common entrance, partly because houses had no hall entrance at the front. Neighbours came in without prior notice; 'it's only me'. Help in extreme situations remained common into the twentieth century, at least among the poorer families. To the children the differences between the polite street and the common back did not mean very much; they played in both. The big divide was between working-class children who played outside and middle-class children who did not. Neighbourly chats took place both at the front and the back.

On the other hand, more and more middle-class habits began to be adopted. Self-containedness meant a greater stress on the nuclear family, and less dependence on neighbours. More reliance was placed on kin and on public institutions, and to an increasing degree relations were relied upon even if they lived further away. One would pretend not to know about subjects pertaining to one's neighbours' social status and morals, like money and sex. The 'keeping yourself to yourself' attitude gained momentum. In towns where the older types of open yard continued, like Birmingham or Sheffield, we can observe minor attempts to create more privacy, for instance in the way in which the entrances to some toilet blocks were screened by walls. We are told that in Newcastle in the late nineteenth century, families with children took downstairs flats, because of the noise they made.[37] The desire for public and private salubrity contributed to the division into open and private spheres: the act of cleaning was mostly a private affair, and the state of cleanliness served to demonstrate 'respectability' to the outside. Work was now usually separated completely from the dwelling, and was placed further and further away from it. The streets themselves had become more open means of communication for a larger number of people.

At this point it must be stressed that back-to-backs did remain old-fashioned, because of the lack of differentiation between street and back; for instance the washing had to be strung across the street. It is quite possible that some of the debate which has arisen over the degree of sociability in old working-class quarters can be resolved by first observing which type of house we are concerned with in each case. Seabrook, with his sceptical view, is dealing with people in the more modern type of through houses, whereas Hoggart is reminiscing about life in the back-to-backs. The question about cause and effect in these matters—whether, in fact, certain types of plans are kept because certain social patterns are preferred—cannot be answered here; but it brings us to the next section.

The small house: differences and similarities

What makes the story of the small house so complicated is the way in which there is both a distinct pattern of development, and a persistence of regional varieties which often runs against this national development. A clear dividing line can be drawn around 1850: the first half of the nineteenth century saw perhaps the greatest variety of dwellings ever, in the sense that each variety and combination could be found in all major towns throughout the country. After that, we noted a rapid adoption of the regular type in most areas. But at the same time a limited number of important towns consolidated and carried on with one of the earlier types in a regular and systematic manner.

Throughout this chapter, the stress has been on the differences between the various plans. Before we look at some of the basic reasons for these differences, we must attempt a final clarification of what was different and what was similar. If, for instance, we take a purely quantitative stance, the amount of accommodation was much the same in most types. In 1900, a new Manchester two-up-two-down (plate 94), a terraced flat in Newcastle (plate 100), a medium-sized 'cottage' in Sunderland (plate 61), and a medium-sized back-to-back house in Leeds (plate 78) each provided about 500 square feet of living space (46.45 m²), not counting the smaller service rooms and corridors. Standards of living had risen everywhere for most sections of the working class. The chief difference lay in the economy of the use of the plot of land. Manchester and Tyneside came somewhere in the middle, with the floor space being roughly the same as the plot size; Sunderland stood out with the plot size more than double the floor size, and Leeds came at the other end with its plot size being little more than half the floor space. But as we saw earlier, land cost amounted to only about 10 to 20 per cent of the total building costs and the differences in cost through differences in land use were probably less decisive than other variables, like general supply and demand of houses.

All these types usually have four main rooms, used roughly for the same purposes, although their relative sizes vary. What does make a great deal of difference inside the house is whether there are any corridors and the way the stairs are placed. Here, Lancashire and Yorkshire types have much in common, in that both maintain the old-fashioned way of placing the stairway in the back living-room or the scullery; thus there is less privacy inside the house. Tyneside and Sunderland, on the other hand, both insist on separate corridor access to all rooms.

Contrasts between plans are strongest in relation to the use of the outside of the houses. The chief characteristic of the back-to-back is that one has to go outside, through the public street, in order to get to the lavatory. The strongest contrast between any regional types in the later nineteenth century is that between the open, shared yards and the enclosed ones. In that respect south Yorkshire and the west and north midlands belong together, with their open yards, and one can also compare the open streets of west Yorkshire with the open yards of Sheffield (plates 67, 74, 75), although the plans of the houses differ. At the other end of the scale are Lancashire and the north-east (plate 65, 99), and the rest of the country, which adopted enclosed yards.

More considerations of use and comparisons of plans would, no doubt, lead to further differentiation. But a number of differences are recognizable at first sight. Ultimately, explanations for these are difficult. Before the middle of the nineteenth century cheapness must have been the overriding concern in all kinds of houses not belonging to the regular type. After the 1850s, however, it seems very much more difficult to give practical reasons for these differences. The explanation for the 'terraces'—the non-street-access arrangements—of Hull and Nottingham is perhaps the simplest one: the plan and the arrangements at the back conformed to the regular type, and the lack of a proper street in the front was a small saving builders seized upon; at least the access to the court was open and simple. As regards Tyneside flats and Sunderland one-storey houses, one might perhaps be content with pointing to the proximity of Scotland. The major remaining questions seem to be: why did West Yorkshire alone adhere to back-to-backs and why are the backs of Lancashire houses and those of the north-east so different from the back of west and north-west midlands and especially Sheffield houses?

Natural conditions should perhaps be examined first. Yorkshire towns are more hilly than most Lancashire towns, and the more mountainous towns of Lancashire itself, like Rochdale, Blackburn and Oldham, tend to show a greater variety of plans and also more old-fashioned, dense ones. Topographical reasons may play a role, for instance in old port towns; Great Yarmouth, Hull, and the earlier developments of Liverpool share many characteristics.

One might also draw parallels with the pattern of housing and conditions of work. The workshop type of set-up carried on for longer in the west midlands as well as in Sheffield. This meant smaller units and stronger ties of kin and small groups, with the place of work and the house remaining in closer proximity and, one would imagine, more socializing around the houses. Lancashire, on the other hand, was the first county to develop factory work in its cotton industry on a large scale, from around 1800 onwards. Because more members of the family could find relatively stable work, there was more wealth and independence for each family. There was less reliance on kin and localized groups, and more concentration on the nuclear family. It was easier, for instance, for young families to set themselves up independently. The woollen industry of Yorkshire took longer to create a factory system and housing remained more old-fashioned. Significantly, Rochdale (plate 76) was an exception in Lancashire, in that until 1880 its industry was largely wool, as in Yorkshire, and it was also one of the Lancashire towns with relatively old-fashioned and dense types of housing. After about 1870 Rochdale changed over to the regular type of house, and this change of housing might perhaps be explained through the change of industry from wool to cotton. But this kind of explanation is of limited use, because by then Yorkshire had largely gone over to factory work but its basic house type remained the same. Sheffield was developing a large steel industry, but the pattern of housing remained largely the old one, and was quite different from that for steelworkers in Middlesbrough.

We must return to those people more immediately concerned with the houses. The instruments for the changeover after the mid-century were the new housing byelaws. What seems to have varied was the power of the health authorities and of those who drafted the byelaws in each town. Manchester and Liverpool (plates 67, 92), where the type of house changed early and radically, were amongst the earliest and best known local sanitary authorities. In other towns more conservative lobbies, mainly supported by speculative builders, were more powerful, as seems to have been the case in Hull. Yet later in the century byelaws could also be very drastic in the more 'old-fashioned' areas. Sheffield, it was noted, far exceeded other towns in its specified distance of the toilet from the house. We have seen that there was no agreement on the best variety of toilet; analogously, no precise agreements seemed possible as to what constituted a 'salubrious' dwelling. Clearly, privacy in the position of the toilet was desirable; but general cleanliness could perhaps better be achieved where there was a wide open yard. One is reminded of a similar dilemma in the arrangement of the back extension of the better houses: single ones provided more privacy, coupled ones more air.

One cannot help feeling that in many cases builders and speculators were highly conscious of the varieties of plans and sometimes delighted in stressing them. This seems to be the only explanation for some of the excesses of walling in Newcastle (plate 100). And how else could one account for a curious occurrence on the border of Lancashire and Cheshire—one of the most decisive borderlines as regards houses, or rather, types of yards. Some of the small houses in Manchester Road, Hyde, have enclosed yards, the Lancashire way; but their toilets are arranged outside these yards, separately and collectively in a little block, the Sheffield and north-west midlands way.

How conscious were the inhabitants themselves of these differences? Standards of living rose steadily at least from about 1860 onwards. Can one say that for the first time there was an element of choice for working-class people in housing? The better-paid workers could now afford a slightly better type of house; the poor and unskilled remained in the older parts of the towns. Strong status sub-division within the working classes were making themselves felt. The general range of houses which can be found in all towns after 1850 is quite clearly stratified. By the later nineteenth century, there sometimes seemed to be a choice of regional types as well, as in Leeds, between back-to-backs and small through houses of about the same rental. Can the conscious popularity of the later back-to-back, as well as that of the 'cottage' in Sunderland, be explained as a popular aversion to the types dictated by national reforms: a continuation of older types of working-class protest and consciousness, which was otherwise said to have largely died down by then? Thus these 'cottages', and the back-to-backs, carried outward signs of class-consciousness, which had little to do with their practical function. Similarly, the 'Lancashire' type of house seemed a sign of the superior position of the cotton worker. Finally, there was the development of a 'facade' for these houses, to which we shall come back.

It is unlikely that the great differences at the backs of the house can be explained in a similar way. Perhaps the crucial factor for the inhabitants here was the different kinds of housing they had left behind. It was the bad memory of the old narrow courts which led to the open backs (cf. plate 67); it was the openness and generally uncared-for atmosphere of the early miners' settlements in the north-east (plate 20) which led to the tightly enclosed yards in the later houses of that region.

13. The changing plan of the common house

The different forms of dwellings are a complex phenomenon for which no single explanation will suffice.

A. Rapoport[1]

The plan, space and use of a house are malleable subjects; they keep changing according to our viewpoint. After the detailed descriptions of the preceding chapters we must take a more distant look, to summarize what appears valid for most sizes of houses and types of plans. After all, national differences in housing were far greater than those within England.

All categories of houses increased dramatically in size. By the mid-nineteenth century there were terraced houses with more than twenty rooms; at the lowest end of the scale, houses with only one room were probably not built any more. By 1900 very few houses would be built with less than four rooms.

Differentiation in spatial layout and use was seen as the governing principle. It first of all concerned the outside of the house: the polite street versus the back, the latter signifying service. During the second half of the nineteenth century this principle was applied to the meanest new working-class house, though the actual organization of, and access to, the back differed from region to region (plates 37, 67, 90, 94).

Inside, the increased amount of accommodation meant more rooms. It usually did not mean larger rooms; in this respect England differed substantially from Scotland and much of the Continent. Room designation and room use in the eighteenth century still seemed to be somewhat vague, with several 'parlours' and 'drawing rooms' in the largest houses; in the nineteenth century everything seems clear: there was the dining-room, the drawing-room, the study or library, the boudoir. In medium-sized houses the same attempts were made to clarify the difference between kitchen, breakfast, dining-room and drawing-rooms. By the end of the century most working-class people in the south and midlands had a room set apart for 'best', the 'parlour', and many small houses in the north did so, too, though here this could mean real inconvenience in the rest of the rooms. The smaller the size of the whole house, the greater appears to have been the effort, the insistence on, the differentiation of room use.

Social status divisions not only increased between classes and houses, but even within the house. The work of each servant became more clearly defined; the hierarchy amongst the servants became greater; the wages of head servants rose considerably; at the same time there was probably an increase of the employment of the lowest paid, temporary kind of servant. Servants and masters tried to keep apart more rigidly, and there was a general improvement in the living standards and conditions of both.

As in the case of the country house, we do not know enough about the arrangement and use of service rooms of the eighteenth-century town house. The division of the basement appears to have been relatively simple. Again, the nineteenth century brought clearer designations. In large houses, the kitchen and 'offices' could be split into ten or more different kinds of rooms. Even the smallest house by 1900 would be built with separate toilet, ashbin and coalshed and fitted with a number of built-in cupboards in the main rooms.

One of the chief ways of assuring room differentiation was separate corridor access for each room. It also was the chief instrument for achieving privacy. Even in the later eighteenth century we find grand terraced houses where not even all the best rooms were separately accessible, though perhaps more separate servants' stairs were built in that period than later. As regards privacy for each room, here the majority of small English houses did not manage to imitate the medium and larger ones. They had no hall entrance (plate 50), and no corridor, and most of the small third bedrooms in the back extension were only accessible through the other bedroom at the back. On the other hand, for many houses there was some change as regards the position of the stairs, and in most cases there was a way of using the front entrance for strangers and the back door for common entry.

Where was all this increased accommodation to be put? How did the changes of plan reflect changing attitudes to living generally?

An increase in the plot size of the house, in a given area of urban or suburban development, was generally not possible, except for some back-to-backs and the Newcastle flats. In London, in fact, there was, if anything, a decrease in the width of the plot. Here, most terraced houses increased in depth, usually simply by cutting out the garden behind. It was, of course, easiest to extend upwards: Georgian houses normally had three storeys plus basement and perhaps an attic, Victorian ones could have six or even seven storeys in all. Even medium and smaller houses in the newer London suburbs were built with basements into the middle of the nineteenth century. And some back-to-backs in the densest urban areas were sometimes given two or even three storeys plus a basement.

It seems difficult to pin a date to the beginning of the back extension. Many earlier houses spilled out at the back, often with the major reception rooms. In the nineteenth century the back meant service. And when rooms in the basement were felt to be generally insalubrious, that arrangement was abandoned, from about the mid-century onwards, and the backs became bulkier and bulkier. In larger houses they became the equivalent of the country house 'service wing'. There were the servants' bedrooms—away from the family's and closer to the kitchen and scullery. There were the toilet and bathroom, with plumbing that was hygienic, simple and open, instead of being, as previously, hidden inside the main part of the house. The plan of the back extension could be varied more easily than that of the basement. In London the whole back extension was usually placed under one roof, packing as much as possible into it—sometimes at the expense of fresh air between the houses—making nonsense of the principle upon which they had been introduced in the first place. In the provinces the extensions are mostly stepped agglomerations, each part with its own roof, demonstrating, consciously or unconsciously, the hierarchy of functions (plate 51). In the smaller houses in the midlands and the north, conveniences are mostly placed separately, often at some distance, at the end of the yard. In Norwich, for instance, both detached and attached sheds and toilets can be found; in the case of the latter, the bedroom window in the extension above the toilet was not allowed to overlook the back, the space above the toilet (plates 51, 52). In fact, the strict laws brought a degree of hygiene to new working-class houses which could often compare favourably with that of older houses of a better class. This is a phenomenon which can be observed elsewhere in that period; for instance many modern hospitals and even workhouses presented all the innovations of sanitary science to the baffled ratepayer. In fact, it was remarked in 1857 that new London houses by replacing basement with back extension were adopting elements of the smallest local type (cf. plates 48, 53).

At the beginning of this book the question was asked: what are the origins of and the reasons for the persistence of the row house in England? For the first question, a simple answer must suffice here: it is the most basic or one of the most basic types of dwelling, and it has existed for a long time in many countries. We do not know much about the use of houses in the earlier period, or about the socio-psychological values of the house. What the investigation of the varieties of the small house in the nineteenth century has shown is that there was no agreement on the most suitable form of dwelling.

Yet the reasons for the persistence of the general type for the lower classes are more complicated: certainly the experimentation with varieties of the plan played a part, providing higher densities; then there was the distaste for, and distrust of, high block dwellings, and the refusal of the better classes to live in close proximity to the lower classes, as in the early developments of the continental flat system. In the end, both the middle and the lower classes kept their separate house on its separate piece of land. The very poor, however, usually had to multi-occupy the older houses which the other classes left behind, and these could be every bit as overcrowded as the worst continental flats.

Then there is the ideal of the small to medium-sized house, the individual family house. It is compact, tightly fitted around the medium-sized family, owner-occupied, its plan above all manageable and concentrated around the core of the hall and staircase. There are pleasant, well-kept gardens, especially at the back, immediately accessible from the house. The exterior — at first it did not matter so much whether the house was terraced, semi-detached or narrowly detached, tries to mark out the individual house and there is further scope for individuality in the decoration.

Here we come to one of the most important points to be stressed in a history of the terraced house or indeed of the ordinary English dwelling in general: that this notion of the 'ideal' family dwelling is of comparatively recent date. Most of its elements originated with the Domestic Revival during the later nineteenth century and seem to have first found their way into ordinary speculative housing in the south-east by about 1900. It became the basic ideal of the housing reformers after the turn of the century, of the Garden City planners in the whole of Europe, and of all speculative house builders in the interwar period and beyond.

The ideal which preceded it was, in fact, its opposite in many ways. Eighteenth- to mid-nineteenth-century terraced houses — as well as many early versions of the 'semi-detached' and 'detached' houses — were high, and rambling, the backs often chaotic. There was mostly no garden, front or back. The master of the house and his family lived, for much of the time, stuck up, literally and socially, above the ground, separated from the street by a gap, the 'area'; to get to the back was quite complicated, and there was usually nothing worth getting to. For later small houses, too, the back was not meant to be pleasant, but only practical and salubrious. In this lack of emphasis on contact with the ground, the better houses can, at least superficially, be compared with the common continental system of flats with a *bel étage*. The ideals of this type of plan were comfort and convenience in the more material sense of salubrity and the management of servants. Many of these elements continued to be vital in the design of the house, yet because they were taken for granted, they were no longer ideals.

The design ideology of the Domestic Revival as a whole will be discussed briefly in the last chapter; as regards plan and convenience a few elements must be mentioned here. There is a greater concentration on the main living-room, and there was a desire to use it more for the family and less as a showpiece for outsiders. Empty rooms were 'cheerless', ceilings should be lowered.[2] 'There is less morning etiquette than formerly', claims the *Housewife* in 1890, and for larger functions, public halls were more often hired.[3] Stevenson argued in the 1880s against the excessive differentiation of purposes and the multiplicity of rooms advocated by Kerr earlier; houses with fewer rooms seemed more practical. There was even, after 1900, a growing tendency to understate the size of one's house and the number of servants, at least amongst the best circles.[4] In any case, servants had become dearer and harder to get. As regards the actual features of the house, one of the greatest changes can be found with windows. From the later Georgian period onwards windows could not be large enough, but the Domestic Revival preferred them, on the whole, small and placed them very selectively. The Victorians were delighted with the new cheaper and larger panes of glass; but by 1900 small panes were re-introduced for many parts of the windows. Some fairly ordinary, provincial, medium-sized houses in rows and semi-detached arrangements of around 1907, in Eaton and Waverley Roads in Norwich, already have many elements of the new tendencies: low ceilings, broad windows, a kind of wide hall. Although the basic plan remains conventional, there is a much greater feeling of openness, which, of course, was soon to lead to the 'open plan' type of dwelling.

What is probably the most unexpected change is that these new trends no longer directly, or in any simple fashion, paralleled a general economic expansion. This leads us on to the more purely architectural elements of the houses. Here the two phases were not only different, but strongly opposed to each other. The earlier ideal went with the appearance of large size and of the unity of a group of houses; the later one with smaller size and individuality. It is to these elements, as *raisons d'être* for our type and reasons for change, that we must now turn.

As regards the plan and the mode of living, there was, indeed, not one type of terraced house, but several. Ideas about how to live changed frequently and radically, then as now.

14. The facade

Owing to the limited frontage even in the superior class of houses . . . it is exceedingly difficult to plan them with regard to effect as well as convenience.

The Surveyor, Engineer and Architect, 1841[1]

On the whole, the architectural design of the facade and the planning of the house are two very different concerns. Only occasionally did problems of the relationship between the two arise. What mattered above all was the overall composition of the front, based on notions of order and composition in the Classical tradition. Then there were the elements of decoration in detail, the cornices, the surrounds of doors and windows. There was the choice of materials and colours, which will be tackled in the next chapter. Moreover, styles did not stand still in the nineteenth century, and their increasingly rapid changes will be summarized in the subsequent chapter.

There is no parallel anywhere to the architectural splendour of some of the terraces built in Britain before the middle of the nineteenth century, in many parts of London as well as in certain resorts. The public buildings in those towns and in some districts of London are often of minor significance compared with the surrounding houses. In earlier chapters we have attempted to explain how these houses came about: the desire for palatial unity in towns, inherited from the Italian Renaissance; the social exclusivity of the major London estates. Upper-class clients did not mind living fairly close to each other, at least in certain desirable localities. English custom demanded an individual house for every family. Because more and more accommodation was required for each family and its servants, houses grew upwards. Once the economic and social preconditions for such a high and long range of houses had been established, the additional expenses for an ornamental front were comparatively small. Promptly, developers and builders availed themselves of the grandiose forms of Classical and Neo-Classical architecture to beautify such a row of houses. After the middle of the nineteenth century these basic factors changed and the grand terrace as a feat of architecture declined; nothing remotely like the grandeur of the Regency was ever achieved again. Clients, especially the best classes, came to prefer houses which were smaller and lower, which *looked* less grand; they no longer cared to live so close together, and fashions in architectural detail had also changed. We shall investigate the reasons for this complete change of climate in greater detail in the last chapter, in the context of a general discussion of the social meaning of architectural forms in domestic architecture.

There is another important factor in the development of the late Georgian and Regency terrace: landscape. This is, of course, no surprise; the revolutionary new design methods of the landscape garden and the associated concepts of the Picturesque and the Sublime were having a profound influence on every aspect of architecture. What was unique in this development of British architecture was the attempt to introduce 'natural' landscape even into the denser parts of towns. In the Renaissance and earlier Georgian tradition, the palatial front of a group of town houses belonged to the context of tightly enclosed streets and strictly rectangular squares, the 'gridiron' system, as it was later called. In cases where some greenery was introduced, this was restricted to neatly planted trees and shrubs. But from the late eighteenth century onwards the design of the 'park' in the major London squares was handled informally. At the same time, or soon afterwards, first in Bath, then in Regent's Park in London and in the other resorts, the tight urban layout was given up altogether. It was replaced by a loose grouping of individual terraces. The terrace, at least in its grandest version, was now taken out of context and became a separate building in its own right. It was at this point that it developed to its utmost splendour.

From the beginning, the terrace and its architecture was a metropolitan affair. In the earlier eighteenth century it was only Bath, outside London, which also contributed some important models, though Bristol was soon to follow suit. By the late eighteenth and early nineteenth centuries some provincial towns managed to create some streets with ordered facades of houses, like Liverpool (plate 153), Hull, Exeter, and York, and to a lesser extent Newcastle, Leeds, Oxford and Shrewsbury. Other towns, like Norwich, then still the fourth or fifth town in England, contributed hardly anything. Even into the second half of the nineteenth century nothing could equal developments in London and the watering places. And even later, fashions for all elements of facade composition evolved largely in London.

The grand Regency terrace: park and seaside; square and crescent

It was the highest aim of the landscape gardener first of all to discover, then to cultivate and make the most of what was called the *genius loci*, the individual character of a particular place. The great Regency estates were no exception to this: each one tried to take advantage of its situation and differed in its methods from the next. The basic Classical motifs were fixed, but their arrangement varied from place to place. There was both the view of the terrace for the onlooker, and the view from the terrace for the inhabitant. We have already cited the catch phrase 'aspect and prospect' in the context of the healthy dwelling. The nineteenth-century resorts were just as much an expression of the health craze as anything discussed in the chapters on comfort and convenience, in fact they were the first major expression of this fashion, and, as such, they were at first reserved for the better classes.

It was in a resort that aspect and prospect first took on a new, more precise, architectural meaning: the terrace which has nothing opposite it. From John Wood the younger's famous Royal Crescent in Bath, begun in 1767 (plate 125), one not only has a full view of the lawn in front and the valley beyond; the terrace itself can be seen in its full curve and grandeur from many angles and many distances. At the same time Robert Adam seized the opportunity for a grandiose prospect and aspect with his Adelphi Terrace high over the River Thames (plate 9). Later, John Nash gave a grand display on the sloping ground adjacent to the Mall, with the Giant Orders of Carlton House Terrace, begun in 1827. This Order is now detached, forming an enormous, dramatic screen (reminiscent of Carlton House itself) in front of a row of houses of varying sizes. The entrances are from the back, and the front gives out to a large elevated terrace, which also screens the occupants from the view of the street (plate 111).

111. **London.** Carlton House Terrace, The Mall, begun in 1827 by John Nash for the Crown. There are two giant compositions like this, each containing a number of terraced houses of differing sizes. The photograph of 1898 shows the repainting which usually had to be done every three to five years.

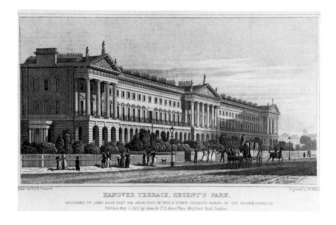

HANOVER TERRACE, REGENT'S PARK.
INSCRIBED TO JOHN NASH ESQ? THE ARCHITECT OF THIS & OTHER SPLENDID WORKS IN ITS NEIGHBOURHOOD
Published May? 1, 1827 by Jones & C? 3, Acton Place, Kingsland Road, London.

SUSSEX PLACE, REGENT'S PARK.

Published Aug? 1, 1828 by Jones & C? 3 Acton Place, Kingsland Road, London.

CORNWALL TERRACE, REGENT'S PARK,
TO THE RESIDENTS OF WHICH THIS PLATE IS RESPECTFULLY DEDICATED.

Published Aug? 18, 1827 by Jones & C? 3, Acton Place, Kingsland Road, London.

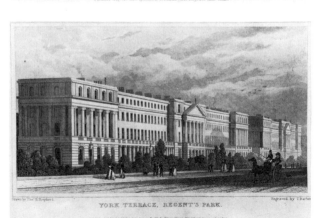

YORK TERRACE, REGENT'S PARK.

Published July 21, 1827, by Jones & C? 3, Acton Place, Kingsland Road, London.

112. **London**. Regent's Park, laid out by John Nash for the Crown,
from *c.* 1811; map of 1870 and views, taken from Elmes, of the
main terraces, mostly built in the 1820s, as they surround the park
from south-west to east (compare plate 136).

ULSTER TERRACE, REGENT'S PARK.
TO THE RESIDENTS OF WHICH THIS PLATE IS RESPECTFULLY INSCRIBED.

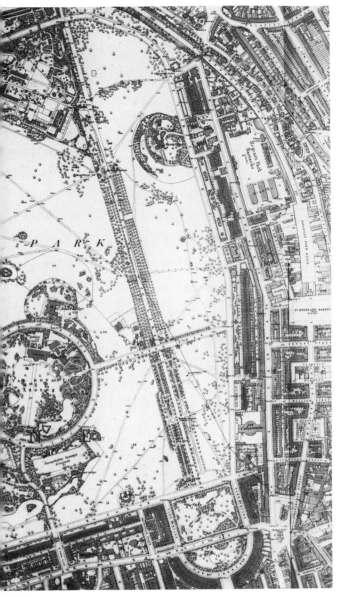

CUMBERLAND TERRACE, REGENT'S PARK.

CHESTER TERRACE, REGENT'S PARK.

CAMBRIDGE TERRACE AND THE COLLISEUM, REGENT'S PARK.

EAST SIDE OF PARK CRESCENT.

EAST SIDE OF PARK SQUARE, AND DIORAMA.

113. **London**. Regent's Park, Chester Terrace, 1825. One of the entrances to the private access road, modelled on a Roman triumphal arch.

115 (facing page, above). **Brighton.** The major squares: on the left, Adelaide Crescent with Palmyra Square and Brunswick Square, flanked by Brunswick Terrace(s) (colour plate 2); on the right, Lewes Crescent and Sussex Square, flanked by Chichester and Arundel Terraces.

116 (facing page, below). **Brighton.** The corner of Chichester Terrace and Lewes Crescent, begun *c.* 1823 by Wilds and Busby for T. R. Kemp.

114. **St. Leonards-on-Sea.** Sussex, begun 1827 by James Burton, architect and builder. This lithograph of 1834 shows in the centre the St. Leonards Hotel, with Baths in the front and the Public Rooms behind, surrounded by other public buildings and terraces.

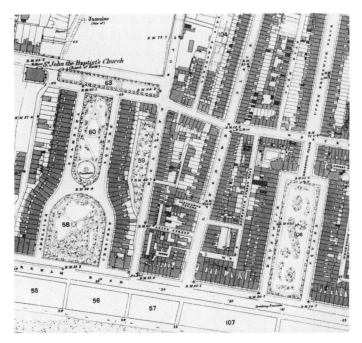
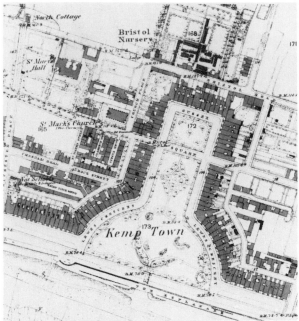

117. **Brighton.** Brunswick Square, begun *c.* 1825 by Wilds and Busby for T. R. Kemp. The curious insertions between the giant bows are by no means arbitrary, but are necessitated by the slope, in order to break the horizontal line of cornices.

119 (facing page) **Brighton.** Brunswick Square, porch. It has to be curved because the bow takes up the whole front of the house.

118. **Brighton.** Adelaide Crescent, begun *c.* 1830 by Decimus Burton for Sir I. Goldsmid. The facades are smooth, to bring out the curve (cf. plates 112 and 116); though again the cornices had to be broken because of the slope.

120, **Brighton.** Houses east of Brunswick Terrace, *c.* 1830, showing the combination of area (see p. 88), bow window and verandah.

121. **Leamington Spa.** The map of a small section of the town shows the characteristic layout with semi-private front lawns and terraces set back from the streets. (1820s onwards, see colour plate 12; plate 217.)

Carlton House Terrace marks the lower end of the Crown's and Nash's grandiose speculative development, Regent Street. The upper end is marked by Regent's Park. The terraces along the street, almost all with shops (and now destroyed), and those on the side of the Park formed one of the grandest examples both of scenic layout and of facade composition ever attempted. An earlier plan for Regent's Park by Thomas Leverton of 1811 still showed the older type of gridiron layout, but Nash in his final design reduced it to a string of terraces around the western, southern and eastern edges of the park (plates 112, 136). Building progressed rapidly from the early to the middle 1820s: Sussex Place with its curved wings and small domed corner accents, nicknamed 'pepperpots'; Cornwall, Hanover and York Terraces with their massive central and side porticoes. Cambridge Terrace had flattish 'Soanian' decor and was replaced by Cambridge Gate in 1875. Chester Terrace is longer than any other; it has a curious, heavy superstructure on its low, almost stumpy order and is flanked by giant triumphal arches at the end (plate 113). The culmination is Cumberland Terrace of 1826 which is raised slightly higher above the Park and not only has an extremely lavish central portico but also three smaller ones on each side, all daringly jutting out and providing Piranesian picturesque views when seen, as is usual, from the side. The completely smooth walls of Park Crescent, built from 1812 to 1822, demonstrate, by contrast, how conscious Nash was of his visual methods. Facing the Park, the houses seen through and above the trees, was what mattered to Nash. Nothing even remotely approaching Regent's Park was ever built in London again. We might however cite Hyde Park Gardens[2] and Lancaster Gate of the 1860s, both overlooking Hyde Park, or the Ladbroke Estate of the 1840s and 1850s which has a more elaborate layout of circles and crescents, with more parkland than usual in London (plate 135).

It was the fashionable seaside which drew the largest projects. One of the first and most daring was St. Leonards on Sea (plate 114), a fairly remote spot near Hastings — which, with its rough cliffs, could hardly have been prepossessing before building started in 1828. Like so many other projects it was never completed. The facades were treated in the by then well-established grandiose manner, with vigorous central and corner accents. We have already mentioned the novel idea of placing the entrance at the back, so as not to obstruct the view — here and in some of the terraces of Regent's Park. The designers of St. Leonards, James and Decimus Burton, had in fact previously worked with Nash in Regent's Park.

Brighton was much more of a success.[3] Notwithstanding its generally slow performance in purely economic terms, several hundred very large houses were built, stretching east and west from the old town for about a mile each way. At first there were a number of smaller developments from the first two decades of the nineteenth century: Royal Crescent, Bedford Square, Regency Square and Marine Square,[4] all sloping upwards, tightly enclosed but open to the sea. From the 1820s onwards many schemes were far more ambitious. First of all there were the long terraces along the seafront, with their vast roads and promenades in front, like Brunswick Terrace East and West. The most exciting layouts were those where an attempt was made as it were to suck the sea air inland (plates 115–20). Brunswick Square stretches up the hill and continues in a street, Brunswick Place, with a stupendous view down to the sea, past its innumerable bow windows. The glory of the Square lies also in these bows (plates 117, 119). They are strong, and a giant Ionic Order with a massive cornice is carried around each one, alternately with columns and pilasters. It makes one forget that Neo-Classical design was ever meant to be flat. Kemp Town, begun in the same years as Brunswick Town, around the mid-1820s, by the same architects, Wilds and Busby, consists of the massive Chichester

122. **Dover.** Wellington Crescent, by P. Hardwick, 1834. It is divided by streets into a long centre range and two shorter ones.

123. **Newcastle upon Tyne.** Leazes Terrace by T. Oliver for R. Grainger 1829–30. The entrances on this, the south-west side, have been altered to suit the building's new role as student residences.

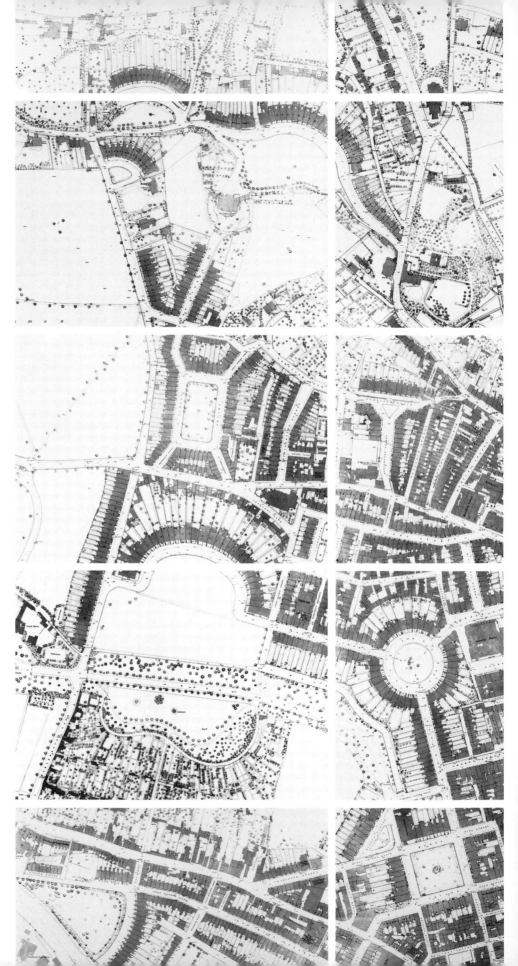

124. **Bath.** A late nineteenth-century map of some of the main districts of the eighteenth century. At the bottom the older layouts: Queen's Square, The Circus (1729–36, 1754–8 by John Wood); then the Royal Crescent, centre left, with St. James Square above and the looser groupings of the later terraces further up.

FEET
METRES

125. **Bath**, the Royal Crescent, by John Wood the Younger, 1767–1775, at the time of building.

126. **Bath,** a view of Cavendish Crescent (by J. Pinch 1817–23) with Somerset Place (*c.* 1790 by J. Eveleigh) barely visible behind, and in the distance, further above, the double curve of Lansdown Crescent (J. Palmer 1789–93).

129. **Bristol.** Worcester Terrace, Clifton (by C. Underwood, 1850s). We are looking at part of the centre projection.

127 (left, above). **Bristol,** a distant view of the crescents of Clifton: topped by Royal York Crescent, forty-five houses long; below, Cornwallis Crescent (both by W. Paty, begun *c.* 1790) and to the left the Paragon (largely by J. Drew, 1809–13) and further below on the left Windsor Terrace (probably by J. Eveleigh, 1790s). Clifton Suspension Bridge looms from behind.

128. (left, below). **Bristol,** map showing the same area.

and Arundel Terraces fronting the sea, and the very large Lewes Crescent, which continues as Sussex Square.[5] The rounded corners of the Crescent give the layout a flowing effect (plate 116). The third large development, (Queen) Adelaide Crescent, built from about 1830 onwards by Decimus Burton,[6] tries to combine elements from Lewes Crescent and Brunswick Square: deeper than the former, and wider than the latter. There are no giant columns or pilasters but smooth walls and a very pronounced cornice, to help the sweep of the curve. This curve of the cornice had of course to be broken because of the slope. There was no perfect solution for the facade of a terrace sloping up a hill (plate 117). At the top, Adelaide Crescent opens into Palmyra Square of *c.* 1860, mid-Victorian in detail, which, in turn, opens into another narrow square, which, again, links up with another street going further uphill. At about a quarter of a mile's distance the sea is more imagined than seen through the trees, but the idea of opening the town towards the sea remains clear (plate 115; colour plate 2).

Other seaside towns were trying hard to keep pace. St. Leonards contributed the magnificent Warrior Square (1843–64) (cf. plate 143), larger than any of the Brighton ones. Folkestone tried a different method of solving the problem of providing a prospect over the sea: long terraces are placed at right angles to the seafront, with bay-windows on both sides.[7] Others, like the Hoe Esplanade in Plymouth, like Eastbourne, Llandudno and Weymouth simply lined the front with a sequence of large terraces; much of the detail on these facades, to which we shall return later, is already mid-Victorian in manner.

Leamington Spa, another major Regency creation, is tightly organized in the London way, with roads and squares, though the houses are generally not as large as in London. Characteristic of Leamington are also the narrow stretches of park or garden between the road and the facade, creating a separate, semi-private driveway. On Warwick Street and Waterloo Place the road is opened like this on both sides (plate 121, colour plate 12).

Next in line are those individual terraces with a particularly commanding position. Perhaps the most memorable is Wellington Crescent, Dover (plate 122), responding to the gentle curve of the harbour, and it is echoed by the longer crescent called Victoria Park, up on the slope of the hill. The list could continue with Pennsylvania Buildings in Exeter, Alverstoke Crescent near Gosport, Hampshire,[8] Hesketh Crescent in Torquay[9] and The Crescent in Scarborough.[10] Finally, there is Newcastle-upon-Tyne, with the only really impressive development outside the metropolis and the watering places. Leazes Terrace,[11] one of Richard Grainger's grand speculations, forms a complete block, surrounded on three sides by parkland. In its magnificent smooth stonework with crisp, angular detailing it betrays the influence of Edinburgh (plate 123).

Later developments in Bath, Clifton and Cheltenham form in some ways a group of their own. Bath continued to attract a considerable number of visitors and new residents until the 1820s. There were particularly vigorous developments before 1800 and after 1815. Two basic methods of arrangement seem to have prevailed, according to the contour of the land: the straight and geometrical layout on flat ground, like Great Pulteney Street, by Thomas Baldwin in 1788, and widely spaced, irregularly curving individual terraces or crescents on hilly terrain, such as Lansdown Crescent of 1789 to 1793 by John Palmer, although how far the latter stems from a comprehensive plan needs further investigation. As regards grand columns and pediments these developments are far more modest than what was to come in London, or indeed than the earlier houses in Bath itself (plates 124–6).

Clifton was particularly successful because it thrived on Bristol's demand for

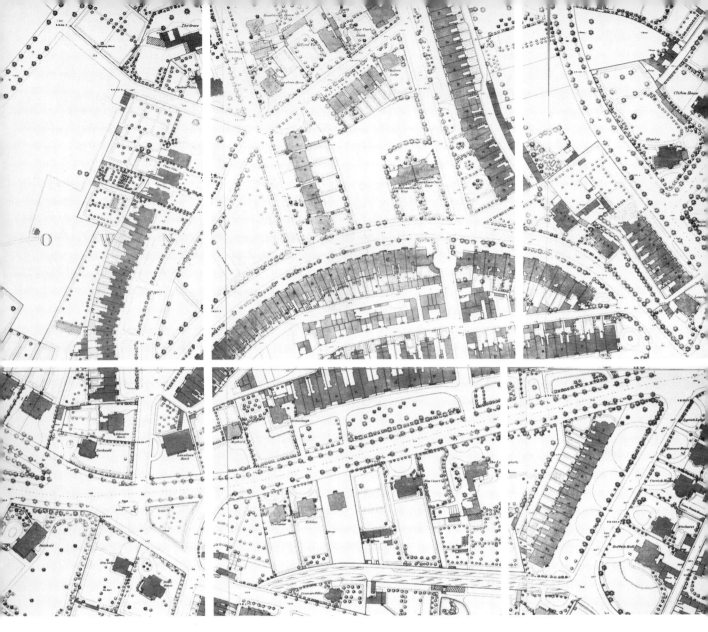

130. **Cheltenham.** Lansdown Estate, 1820s–1840s. The major terraces are: on the left Lansdown Promenade, at the top Lansdown Terrace, and the convex Lansdown Crescent and the slightly concave Lansdown Place in the centre. Lypiatt Terrace is bottom right.

131. **Cheltenham.** Lansdown Place, around 1830. Two houses are combined into one unit, with their coupled entrances recessed—they can thus be called 'quasi-semi-detached' (for the ironwork see plate 205).

132. **Cheltenham.** Lansdown Terrace, around 1830; a variation of the previous arrangement.

133. **Cheltenham.** Lypiatt Terrace, probably by R. W. Jearrad, *c.* 1845. An exceptional terrace in that it can be seen from many sides, thus the back is fitted with extensive barge-boarded gables. The flanking towers make the whole look like an elongated Italian villa.

134. **Cheltenham.** Wellington Square, *c.* 1840s. Gothic details on a Classical frame.

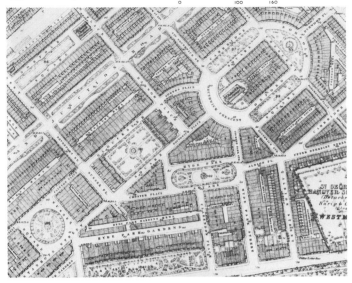

Bayswater, 1830s–40s (see plate 136).

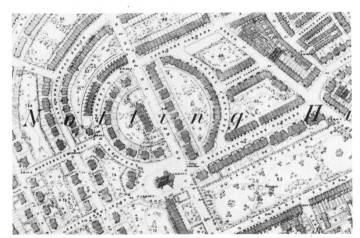

The Ladbroke Estate, North Kensington 1840s and 50s (see p. 156).

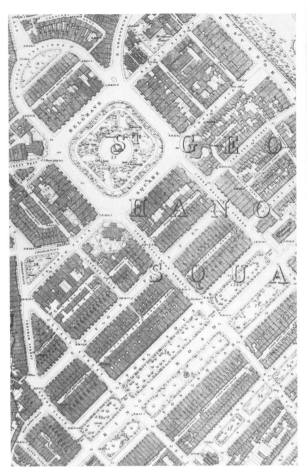

Belgravia, 1820s–40s (see plates 36, 137–8).

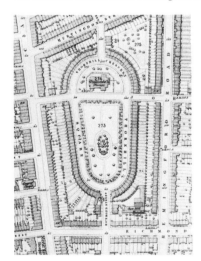

Islington, 1840s–50s.

WC1, c. 1830–40.

NW1, 1820s–30s (demolished).

Paddington, c. 1850 (demolished).

EC2, around 1820.

Walworth, SE1, late eighteenth century (demolished).

North Kensington, W11, 1842–8.

136 (facing page). **London.** Bayswater, looking towards Regents Park in the 1930s (cf. plate 135).

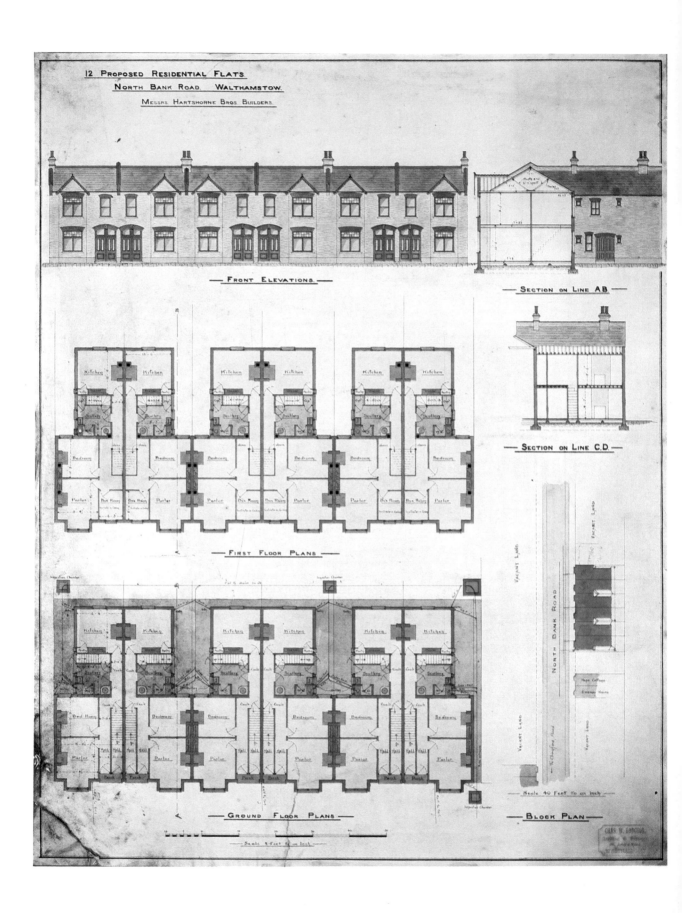

12 PROPOSED RESIDENTIAL FLATS.

NORTH BANK ROAD.   WALTHAMSTOW.

MESSRS HARTSHORNE BROS BUILDERS.

— FRONT ELEVATIONS. —

— SECTION ON LINE A.B —

— SECTION ON LINE C.D. —

— FIRST FLOOR PLANS —

— GROUND FLOOR PLANS —

— BLOCK PLAN —

Scale 40 Feet to an Inch

Scale 8 Feet to an Inch

NORTH BANK ROAD

suburban houses and also kept the image of a spa. Many Clifton terraces make use of the steep slope for grand display (plates 127–8), especially Royal York Crescent, the longest terrace of its kind, begun *c.* 1790 by William Paty. But in strong contrast to London, Clifton shows few attempts to coordinate terraces into squares, let alone sequences of squares. Each terrace stands more or less on its own with a lot of greenery around: The Royal Colonnade,[12] Lansdowne Place, Vyvyan Terrace[13] and Worcester Terrace (plate 129).[14] Their facade treatment is rich, but consists usually of flattish pilasters which give the whole a more subdued character. The last two grand Clifton terraces, Royal Promenade and Victoria Square West, with their mid-Victorian facades, will be mentioned again below.

Even more informal in its effect as a whole is Cheltenham (plates 130–4). The story begins with Royal Crescent of about 1806–10, which although fairly large is notably flat, almost bare in its treatment, and with its very slender windows sets the tone for the smaller terraces. Then there is the very grand terrace on the Promenade, now the Municipal Offices,[15] a full-blown, porticoed Regent's-Park-type composition (plate 32). But the most exhilarating area is the Lansdown Estate, begun in about 1824 by J. W. Papworth for Pearson Thompson and continued by R. W. Jearrad. There are no particular landscape features, no vistas, no areas of water, just lavish parkland. There is very little ordered relationship between each major terrace, which is probably intentional. Lansdown Crescent is extremely long and convex—the only major example of this arrangement. Then there is Lansdown Place, which with its recessed coupled entrances can be called 'quasi-semi-detached', and Lansdown Terrace. Neither are straight, nor curved in any regular way. Nor do they show regularized corner or central accents. With their multiple projections, their broken outline they straggle along gently, appearing and reappearing between the trees. Finally there is Lypiatt Terrace of 1845, probably by the Jearrad brothers: although it is straighter and more tightly organized than the others, it departs from Neo-Classicism altogether by using projecting eaves over gables back and front, as well as turrets at the end; in fact it tries more to look like a series of Italian villas than like a terrace. After all this it is all the more surprising to find the three large houses on the south side of Suffolk Square coordinated in such a way as to form an extremely regular, conventional terrace. In their individuality the large terraces of Cheltenham belong to the highest achievements of their kind, and yet they spell the beginnings of the end of the terrace as a type, as a rigid and organized whole. The individual part of the terrace, the house, becomes in them more important than the whole.

Even in tighter urban situations the best houses give on to greenery. There are, in fact, very few normal streets which are lined by very large houses on both sides; Eaton Place (plate 137)[16] and Stanley Gardens in the Ladbroke Estate (plate 135)[17] are perhaps the most impressive examples. Wherever possible London speculators continued the late Georgian fashion of squares and crescents. Probably second to none (except, of course, Edinburgh) was the elaborate ensemble of squares and crescents in Tyburnia, Bayswater, between Sussex Square and Hyde Park, begun in the 1820s, mainly on the Bishop of London's estate (plates 135, 136);[18] little survives of this district. Belgrave Square (plate 138), begun around 1825 by George Basevi for Lord Grosvenor, is probably the most spacious of all squares; Eaton Square[19] is extremely long but not very wide, in order to let as many houses as possible look out on to greenery. There are the similar later squares in Pimlico: Eccleston and Warwick squares, mostly by Cubitt. Beyond Tyburnia there is Westbourne Terrace of the 1840s and 1850s, which, with its double lines of trees, could be called a boulevard.

In the more distant provinces a square often had a much greater relative

137. **London.** Eaton Place, Belgravia, by T. Cubitt, *c.* 1830–40. Decoration without the use of Giant Orders.

138. **London.** Belgrave Square, north side, around 1830 (largely by George Basevi).

139. **London.** Northdown Street, N1, *c.* 1840. There is no symmetry in the relationship between porches, ground floor window and portico (see p. 181).

Colour plate 12. **Leamington Spa**, Lansdowne Crescent, *c.* 1830–40. Note the way the crescent is treated like a terrace with a centre projection (compare Nash's Regents Park Crescent, plate 112).

Colour plate 13. **Cheltenham**, Back Albert Place, *c.* 1840s.

importance than in London. Hamilton Square in Birkenhead is civic as well as residential.[20] Eldon Square in Newcastle[21] makes use of the grand coordination with Giant Orders, but the houses are relatively small. Earlier on, South Parade and Johns Square in Wakefield adhered more strictly to London Georgian models.[22] On a much smaller scale, Southfield and Hanover Square in Bradford and Trafalgar Square in Scarborough of the 1850s and 1860s are charming in their informality.

We must go back to London for some of the more unusual layouts (plate 135). There is the complete circle, Percy Circus[23] and the complete oval, Finsbury Circus.[24] There was even an actual circle, or an approximation to it, the Polygon near Euston.[25] Thornhill Crescent and Square in Barnsbury consist of two crescents with a trapezoid 'square' in between. Crescents by themselves come in all sizes and shapes (cf. plate 31): the short but elegant Pelham Crescent in Hastings, the flattish Royal Crescent in Ramsgate; the near-horseshoe of the Royal Crescent in Harrogate, of the 1870s, with its ends treated like semi-detached villas; and the minute Victoria Crescent in Dover. A special problem was encountered by the designer of the Royal Crescent, Holland Park (plate 135):[26] its apex was broken by a road. An attractive feature was made of this by letting the corners bulge out into complicated turrets, which are answered by similar turrets at both ends of the Crescent. In general, designers shied away from corner solutions and often did not quite know what to do with the side elevations of terraces—Cubitt's work in Pimlico is one of the few exceptions.

The terrace, in essence, has a single front. Almost all the terraces and squares and crescents described here adhered to the later Georgian method of giving special accents to the ends and the centre of the block. Even some of the rare examples of terraces with Gothic details have these clear accents (plate 134).[27] By the end of the century, however, porticoes and columns had gone out of fashion, and the projections of the corners of even very large terraces, like those of Eccleston Square and Warwick Square in Pimlico, were very slight. Later in the nineteenth century, many terraces, often of medium-sized houses only, had accents at the ends, usually with gables, for instance in Birkenhead and Cardiff (cf. plates 134, 171).

One special problem arose with the centre accentuation of the earlier terraces. When, as we explained earlier, the centre was taken up by a wider house, the pediment could be placed above the central door of that house. But in those cases—the vast majority—where the house in the centre was of the same width as the rest of the houses and of the normal one-door-on-the-side-plus-two-windows disposition, a conflict arose between the symmetrical pediment and the asymmetrical house (plate 1). In Park Square East and West in Regent's Park, Nash was wrestling with the problem; one or two decades later we find different solutions in Northdown Street (plates 139, cf. 6) and Cambridge Terrace in Grantbridge Road in Islington.[28]

Facade treatment, Regency to mid-Victorian

Terraces from the years 1815–40 largely adhered to the late Georgian formulae: plain surfaces for most of the houses; the time-honoured proportions for windows and doors, a porch, or an ornamental door; the whole facade crowned by a vigorous cornice or a high parapet. But with the new demand for height new problems were encountered. In an incisive article in the *Surveyor, Engineer and Architect* of 1841[29] we find a contemporary view of the situation. With a height of four or five storeys there was a danger that a house would appear to be a narrow strip. Thus the coordinating forms of the terrace facade such as pilasters and porticoes were even

140. **London.** Lancaster Gate, towards the east, 1863–6, by J. Kelk (builder) for J. Johnson (architect). Compare plate 43.

141 (below left). **Bristol.** Victoria Square West, Clifton, by Foster and Wood, 1855.

142 (below right). **Lowestoft.** Wellington Esplanade, 1850s. Most of the decoration is in red and white brick and moulded brickwork.

more needed than before. On the other hand, porticoes need breadth as well as height; it is difficult to accommodate traditional Classical proportions to structures with more than two or three storeys. Generally the 'lanky' strips of giant columns and pilasters were beginning to be despised. The new solution was to decorate just individual parts of the facade; mainly those parts, the article says, which are there for practical purposes anyway, namely the windows. This springs partly from a rationalist frame of mind, and also from a general desire to liven up blank surfaces. The broad, plain surfaces of Georgian architecture were now thought to be monotonous. We can thus see a tremendous variety of window surrounds, round, segmental, or stilted segmental arches, and pediments of all sizes, also called *aediculae*, that is, a small temple front surrounding a window (plate 43). There was also now more emphasis on horizontals, not only on the main cornice or the baseline of the *piano nobile*, but on the subsidiary horizontals between the other storeys, or between the windows. There were now also many more balconies and balustrades, for ornamental, as much as for practical purposes. Lastly, there was far more rustication, not only for the ground floor, in the traditional Georgian way, but for the corners of the upper part of the buildings as well. In short, there was a multitude of small accents, instead of a few large ones.

Nash had already introduced various kinds of window surrounds on his otherwise plainer elevations of the smaller terraces of Park Square East and Ulster Terrace in Regent's Park. Basevi's Belgrave Square shows a lessening of the impact of the Giant Order and an increase of small-scale ornament, especially on the cornice. The article just mentioned praises the 'astylar' elevation of Lowndes Square by Lewis Cubitt of 1841–3 (cf. plates 138, 140), the term referring to the lack of a Giant Order. Most of Thomas Cubitt's later terraces rely on the same method, as does, in the provinces, John Dobson's Royal Crescent in Whitby of 1850. In Clifton, Vyvyan Terrace and Worcester Terrace (plate 129), already mentioned, apply Giant Orders, but in a flattish way and closely interlinked with the horizontal divisions. The very exceptional Milner Square in Islington,[30] designed by Roumieu and Gough around 1840, makes the rather abstracted Giant Order identical with the strips of wall between the windows, and there is no other overall coordination.

After 1850 decoration becomes more overtly Renaissance and more festive in character. There is a tendency to move away from repeating the same standard opening at regular intervals all along the facade. Princes Gate, of about 1850,[31] goes further in grouping three windows into one unit, with special emphasis on the centre one. The great stuccoed terraces of the 1850s and 1860s in Queen's Gate (plate 43), Cromwell Road, in Paddington and North Kensington elaborate this style further (plate 140). Elliot Terrace in Plymouth, and some of the terraces on Warrior Square, St. Leonards kept pace with London (cf. plate 143). In Clifton, the Royal Promenade[32] and at right angles to it Victoria Square (West) (plate 141)[33] show the vigour that is possible with the endless repetition of relatively small elements of rich decor.

On a scale somewhat below this highest class of terraces are the heavily rusticated terraces of Lowestoft of around 1850 (plate 142), of Princes Road, Leicester of around 1860, and of some of the terraces in Princes Road, Liverpool. Blenheim Mount, Manningham Lane in Bradford[34] shows more delicate elements in stone. The difference is largely due to the different materials being used in each case—to which we shall come back in the next chapter.

Bows and bays

A new motif for all sizes and types of houses was the bay window. The term 'bay' is the same as the general one for any interval between two supports in a building, whether they are columns, beams or strips of wall. A projecting window between two supports was a common motif in much traditional architecture. But several factors restricted its use in the seventeenth and eighteenth centuries: the general Classical and Neo-Palladian desire for flatness and the look of solidity, sensitivity about the building line, the window tax, to be lifted in the 1850s, and the prohibition of the use of wood on the facade, especially in London. By the late eighteenth century many 'Gothick' architects had begun to revive the bay window for country houses and villas. In Classical buildings we occasionally find a bow, that is, a rounded bay, even in terraces. Small bow windows were becoming popular for shop fronts. Oriel windows, as we call those bays or bows which are not built from the ground upwards, are rare on terraces, except for some houses in Brighton (plate 158).

The main reason for reviving the bay on terraces was the craze for fresh air, especially at the seaside. Henry Holland's first Brighton Pavilion of the 1780s had bays and first floor verandahs, and this was precisely the model for the first major terrace in Brighton's Royal Crescent of 1799. But this Crescent, with its old-fashioned and somewhat flimsy woodwork, was not taken very seriously by those who undertook the grand developments described above, and only Brunswick Square (plate 117) and Brunswick Place took up the idea, with bows—and very solid ones at that. It is the medium and smaller houses of Brighton that are hardly ever without a bay, which ensures a glimpse of the sea when the street is placed at right angles to the coastline (plates 117, 158). Only by about 1840 does the bay become *de rigueur* in all the larger terraces in Brighton as well. It often takes up the whole breadth of the facade, which leads to curious solutions for the porch (plate 118). Elsewhere bays are often narrower, for instance in the case of the slender bows of Liverpool Terrace in Worthing or York Place in Scarborough (cf. plates 151–2). Llandudno had a soft spot for bows for a long time. London was hesitant at first, although there always were many bows at the back of terraces. The bows of Gloucester Terrace of the 1840s,[35] with their curious way of linking up with the cornice, are a magnificent exception. Only about the mid-1860s did square or polygonal bays of one, two, or three storeys become the rule in suburban houses (plate 160). Above all, bays meant an extra space in front of the house.

Verandahs are related (plates 32, 43, 45, 152, colour plate 12). In many Georgian and Regency terraces they amounted just to large 'French windows', where one could step out as far as the 'window guard'. On the south coast we find many elaborate verandahs and balconies with iron roofs, often curved around a bow. From the middle and later Victorian period onwards the desire to participate with what was going on in the street was greatly diminished and balconies went out of fashion; they were revived at the end of the century in resorts.

The story of porches belongs in this context of the gradual livening-up of the flat Georgian facade. Increasingly, Regency houses erected wooden, brick and stucco—or occasionally stone—porticoes (plate 137). The portico normally consisted of two columns or piers which carried a roof, with or without a gable, which covered the bridge above the area. In later Victorian houses, where the basement, and thus the area, were given up, the tendency was to place the porch inside, within the confines of the building (plates 118, 168, 170, colour plate 16). Again, around 1900 there was a revival of porches, or simply of hoods over the door, but now they were usually built in a picturesque cottagey style (plate 214).

144 (above left). **Scarborough.** Avenue Victoria, *c.* 1870s. Carefully controlled polychrome stone decoration in the High Victorian Gothic manner.

145 (above right). **London.** Sloane Gardens, SW1, *c.* 1890. Gothic verticality combined with 'Queen Anne Revival' Classical details, all in a variety of red and moulded bricks (cf. colour plate 7).

146 (right). **Southend-on-Sea**, Palmeira Avenue, *c.* 1902. These houses are, in fact, 'quasi-detached' (cf. plate 149).

Later Victorian large facades

We shall deal with the different styles of the later Victorian period in the last chapters and also with materials, which more and more determined the shape and details of all the facades. Here we only need to pinpoint some general compositional elements. The changes of styles were rapid. The characteristic treatment of the large facades of Brighton (plate 207), Eastbourne (plate 45) and Plymouth from about 1850 was extremely solid, usually with polygonal bays in brick and plaster; by contrast the stone bays of Blackpool were very much more slender. In London, Grosvenor Gardens[36] continued in some ways the Kensington manner from the late 1860s onwards, but also introduced some new elements. The houses were even more slender, the aim being to emphasize height, whereas earlier on the aim was to disguise it. There was now a very pronounced roof, and the chimneys were shown prominently. Similar terraces, but with more of a High Victorian Gothic type of polychromy, can be found in Scarborough (plate 144).[37] A little later came the Tudor Revival, which meant a prominent gable for each house and large mullioned and transomed windows; characteristic examples can, again, be found in Scarborough[38] and in Harrogate. All this was already outmoded by the late 1870s, when the 'Queen Anne Revival' or 'Pont Street Dutch' conquered West London (plate 145), combining as it did Gothic verticality and irregularity with small Classical motifs. The last style of nineteenth-century domestic architecture—the timberframing, or half-timbering, and tile-hung imitation of the old manor house type—can occasionally be found in terraces (cf. colour plate 15).[39] In Southend, Palmeira Avenue of 1902 (plate 146), with its exuberant wooden balconies and its great variety of forms, generally marks the end of strict coordination of the facade. The uniform terrace had long ceased to be a fashionable type of dwelling.

Medium-sized to late standard

It is, of course, difficult to define the medium-sized house exactly but it normally contains seven to eleven rooms. There are also several special varieties of plan and facade which usually fall between those two brackets which cannot be dealt with here, like the double-fronted (plate 47), the quasi-detached, or the quasi-semi-detached (plates 147–9, cf. 56).[40] The latter two are characterized by the fact that the service rooms are placed at the side of the house, and as they are smaller and treated less ostentatiously, the main part of the house is more prominent, thus producing some impression of detachment. We shall have to come back to the influence of the semi-detached, the tendency to give an impression of separateness, as a crucial element in the later terraced house.

What clearly distinguish the grand from the medium-sized house, at least early in our period, are the compositional problems experienced in the design of the facade. The link between the plan and the facade was more immediate in the medium house; only rarely could builders afford the special features, the columns and porticoes of the grand facade. By and large, the 'problems' were those indicated by the motto of this chapter, relating to the limited frontage of the terraced house. We have so far assumed that the openings of a facade are perfectly regular, in the sense that they are placed exactly on top of each other, or aligned. In the provinces we find this alignment in virtually all medium-sized houses. In the north, terraced houses (plate 154) are often particularly widely spaced, for instance in Northumberland Square in North Shields,[41] which is perhaps influenced by Scottish practice. Even smaller

Semis and quasi-semis

147. **Cheltenham.** Queen's Road, a pair of semi-detached houses, *c.* 1840. Note the entrance on the side (cf. plan 47). But the facades are still treated very much in the manner of a traditional terrace facade.

148. **London.** Wharton Street, *c.* 1840; 'quasi-semi-detached' houses; the entrances are combined and recessed, the main parts of the houses are combined under one stately gable (cf. colour plate 1).

149. **London.** Altenburg Gardens, SW11, 1890s. 'Quasi-detached' houses of medium to large size. The link between the houses contains the 'service wing' (cf. plate 51) above an unusual, wide passage to the back.

150. **Worthing.** Warwick Place, *c.* 1820–30s; small attached porches are the only decor.

152 (facing page). **Ramsgate.** Augusta Road, *c.* 1840s. Bows and bays are now indispensable in seaside towns and are often combined with verandahs.

151. **Ramsgate.** Guildford Lawn, *c.* 1840. The term 'lawn' for a terrace seems peculiar to Ramsgate.

153. **Liverpool.** Rodney Street, *c.* 1800. Outside London, Bath and Bristol, only Liverpool has kept extensive late Georgian streets of a stately width, with medium-sized and large terraces.

154. **Newcastle-upon-Tyne.** St. Thomas Crescent, *c.* 1840s. There are only two main storeys but each house is rather wide, characteristic of the north and Scotland.

155. **Cheltenham.** Royal Parade, Bayshill Road, *c.* 1840. The indecision about the size of the windows on the upper floor is probably due to memories of the first-floor drawing-room (see p. 183).

houses in the provinces usually have their windows aligned, although in narrow houses this means that the windows are pushed right to the side of the facade, which produces a rather awkward corner position of the window from within, while making the best sense constructionally.

But in the generally narrower houses in London the pattern was different, and was shown to be so by the handbooks by Nicholson/Elsam and Simon (plates 2, 40, 41, 139). The First Class of houses had all windows aligned, but the three classes below did not. There were two windows on the first and upper floors, placed symmetrically into the facade, or one window in the case of the smaller houses. The ground floor, however, usually had only one window, which was placed not in the centre of the whole facade but in the centre of that part of the facade which was left beside the door. This window was thus completely out of line with the windows above. The door, too, was not aligned with the openings above. It was obvious that if you put the door underneath one of the symmetrically placed windows above, you would have a disproportionally wide hall entrance and at the same time cut off valuable space from the front room. There are some variations of this London pattern with three windows on the upper floor and two windows on the ground floor and vice versa.[42] Nash obviously experimented with these problems, as in St. Andrew's Place and Park Square East in Regent's Park. The former shows the ground floor windows completely out of line; in the latter each house has three windows on each floor and all openings are aligned. But as the houses are not very large, there is very little wall space left between the openings. It was a method which became popular in the 1830s and 1840s in Islington, London, and occasionally in the provinces. However, it was soon felt to lack solidity.[43] The tendency towards greater enrichment in detail which we saw in the development of the grand terrace applied just as much to medium-sized facades. The ground floor was increasingly covered in stucco, with horizontal lines to indicate rustication, and thus the base line of the first floor was also emphasized more strongly. As regards the alignment problem, this meant that the ground floor was more distinct from the upper floors and the impact of asymmetry was reduced (plate 173).

The only other town where similar distinctions between the sizes of houses applied consistently was Bristol (plates 156–9, 177). Most facades, though, were narrower than the London ones, and many houses, even three-storeyed ones, had only one window on each floor. As a result, the asymmetrical position of the door was even more pronounced. Moreover, Bristol customarily divided each house from the next by a pilaster strip, a tradition derived from the seventeenth century, and there was much less of a horizontal dividing line above the ground floor than in London. Thus we find the door squeezed to the side and the windows almost floating in the surface of the wall (plate 157). The surface was normally unified by its material, ashlar facing, whereas London houses tended to divide their facades by juxtaposing different surface treatments.

The real solution to these problems came through a fundamental change in the method of dividing the facade of each house, the most important such change in the whole history of the type. The facade, the front of the house, was in fact divided into two units: a wider one with the window, and a narrower one with the door. It is quite likely that there was a strong influence from the semi-detached house (plate 47), where the entrance on the side is often recessed. The builder of the group of nos. 99, 100 and 103 Cotham Brow in Bristol in the 1860s obviously had a struggle with his alignment: there was no problem with the end houses, as the door is put on the side, and thus taken out of the facade, but in the centre house everything is out of line (plate 159). In London the beginning of the new facade can be found in those

156. **Bristol.** Granby Hill, 1790s. Medium-sized houses; note the narrowness of the front and the varieties in the placement of doors and windows.

157 (right). **Bristol.** Byron Place, by Pope, Bindon & Clark, 1852. Many medium-sized houses have only one window on each floor but are higher than the usual Georgian house of this type. The door appears to be squeezed in on the side.

158 (far right). **Brighton.** Charles Street, early nineteenth century. Slender stuccoed or tile-covered bay windows — no problems of alignment on the facades.

159. **Bristol.** Cotham Brow, later 1860s: The problems of alignment on the facades (cf. plates 2, 47).

terraces of the 1860s where the main part of each house, which contains the window, projects very slightly (plate 49).

This new kind of accentuation was soon to go with two new features in most houses: the bay window and the gable. Characteristic of the medium-sized houses from the late 1860s onwards in Clifton and Redland—many of them, in fact, semi-detached houses—are the extremely large and solid polygonal bays, mostly with hipped gables. Earlier most bay windows on medium-sized houses consisted of rather flimsy wooden attachments. Now they formed part of the whole fabric. Gables were used occasionally in Gothicizing terraces[44] but they normally appear artificially placed above a cornice. Later gables are always shown to be a continuation of the wall below. Many gables were now bargeboarded (plate 194, colour plate 20), that is, ornamental wooden planks accompany the line of the roof, which normally projects over the edge of the wall. Bristol differed from London in that the gables could easily be attached to the old type of transverse roof, which had never really been given up there, whereas in London, gables usually had to have a special short roof built behind them, which was joined in a complicated way on to the main roof, which ran parallel with the terrace.

The new treatment of the roofline must generally be seen in this context. We have already outlined the possibilities of roof construction in the chapter on the fabric. In London, Bristol, and also in Cheltenham, the idea of a Classical cornice was rigidly adhered to until the 1870s (plate 29). This meant that a parapet, or 'blocking course' completely hid the roof from the viewer in the street. It was then given up in favour of the older method of letting the roof project over the wall ('eaves drop') which was due to the fashion of reviving cottagey elements in domestic architecture, as well as to the general desire to liven-up the traditionally flat facade of the terraced house. In houses which were set back, the roof could project even further.[45] A frequent later solution in the provinces—where the old traditional eaves drop had never really been given up—was to project the top courses of the brickwork, or masonry and to rest the overhanging roof on those (plate 181).

What these new features amounted to was nothing less than the abandonment of the time-honoured concept of the terrace as a unit, in which each house formed only a subsidiary part, in favour of stressing precisely the separateness of the individual house. One often hears the expression 'a terrace of villas' for these houses. What had announced itself cautiously in the 1830s in the large terraces of Cheltenham, by the 1870s could be found in most medium-sized houses. Naturally, for reasons of economy and standardization generally, each house within a row was exactly the same.

One more problem of the medium-sized facade needed solving: the position, or rather, the accentuation by means of larger windows, of the drawing room; in short, the *piano nobile* (e.g. plates 1, 41). In houses with more than three storeys its position on the first floor was firm and hardly changed. The same can be said of houses with three storeys and a basement. But with houses with three storeys without a basement the position becomes more difficult. There were few houses of this type in London, earlier on; but in the provinces, terraces like Byron Place, Bristol (plate 157), do not indicate by the size of their windows what the first floor was used for. The next stage down is two storeys and a basement, more especially those with an elevated basement. Here we sometimes find ornate windows and a kind of balcony usually reserved for the *piano nobile* of larger houses, as at Royal Parade in Cheltenham of *c.* 1840 (plate 155). Clearly the main living-rooms, whether they include a drawing-room or not, are on this floor, and on the floor above, the top floor, are the bedrooms. Yet, curiously, the windows on the top floor of some of the houses

160. **London.** Riversdale Road, N5, *c.* 1880. A convenient demonstration of the change in London facade design: the tendency is towards the alignment of openings, as well as showing the eaves and the roof, instead of hiding them behind a parapet (cf. plates 29, 49). There is also a new manner (cf. plates 197, 198) of embedding structural and decorative parts, like lintels over windows, flush into the walls, instead of letting them project.

161. **London.** Brecknock Road, N19. Left 1910–11; centre and right 1860s–70s. Basically all houses are much the same size, but they show how dramatically styles changed. The most striking element is height, which the later houses did not seem to care for any more.

162 (right). **London.** Coleman Road, SE5, 1880s. An early version of the ubiquitous late nineteenth-century London standard house. (For later versions see plates 30, 55.)

163 (far right). **Bristol.** Coronation Road, *c.* 1890. Typical later Bristol contrast of stone trim and rubble facing (see p. 201).

Colour plate 14. **Liverpool**, Princes Avenue, late 1880s. Double-fronted with lavish moulded brick.

Colour plate 15. **Bristol**, Downleaze, narrowly semidetached houses, by H. Dace Bryan, 1893, with 'Old English' and Domestic Revival features.

164. **Plymouth.** Bedford Park, *c.* 1890. An unusual solution for the facade of the late standard type of house: square bay windows with oriel windows on the first floor.

165. **Cardiff.** Tydfil Place, 1904 (compare the porch in colour plate 17). The very large gables mark the slightly above-standard-size of these four-bedroomed houses.

166 (facing page). **Portsmouth.** Laburnum Grove, *c.* 1905–10. It was nicknamed 'brass-buttoned alley' referring to the naval officers who were said to have lived there. The covering of the facade with white, glazed bricks is an exception. There is a fair display of decoration of the Queen Anne Revival (cf. plate 145), or the half-timbering of the 'Old English' Revival (cf. colour plate 15) but it is strictly regularized.

Porches around 1900

Colour plate 16. **London**, Nansen Road, SW11. The grey bricks here are called gault bricks *c.* 1890.

Colour plate 17. **Cardiff**, Tydfil Place, 1904 (cf. plate 165).

Colour plate 18. **Portsmouth**, Chichester Road, *c.* 1900. The stone decor is usually painted.

Colour plate 19. **Cardiff**, Albany Road, *c.* 1905.

167 (above). **Manchester.** Platt Lane, *c.* 1910.

168 (above right). **London.** Woodberry Crescent, N10, *c.* 1907–11. 'Period' details are now replaced by purely cottagey features, like roughcast or pebble-dash, and simpler half-timbering. The facades are now made to look small rather than grand, horizontal rather than vertical.

169 (right). **Cardiff.** Albany Road, *c.* 1900–5. There are many ways of filling the space between the footpath and the front door, and in this area of Cardiff they are particularly elaborate.

170. **Worthing.** Stanley Road, *c.* 1880s. In a most unusual way, at least for its date, the bay window is set within and behind a ground floor arcade, which also contains the porches.

171. **Reading.** Liverpool Road,
c. 1900. There is an
exceptional degree of co-
ordination is this terrace of
small to medium-sized houses,
with gables at regular intervals.
(For the spectacular Reading
brick colours cf. colour plates
29, 30.)

in the same terrace are higher than the others. Are they meant to be just a formal reminiscence of the first-floor drawing-room of a larger house? By the later nineteenth century the problem was not really solved, but forgotten. The typical new three-storeyed London house (plate 160) shows a ground floor and a first floor of the same height, perhaps also a reflection of the fact that most of these houses were inhabited by several families. The late Victorian standard type of house had normally only two floors and they were both of the same height; additional rooms could be put into the now much more prominent roof. When we discussed the general development of the plans of these houses, we noted the fundamental change at the back of the house: much accommodation could now be put into the back extension. The front of the house, even the larger house, tends to be relatively low; an imposing size was no longer fashionable.

We likewise noticed a new attitude to the garden: it was the desire for direct access to the garden which helped to phase out the custom of placing the main living-rooms on the first floor. This was true for all types and sizes of houses, the country house, the villa, the larger to medium-sized terrace. Naturally, in smaller houses and terraces, there never had been a *piano nobile*, and the ground floor was always the main floor. It was the second major change in the general disposition of the house: by the 1870s the Classical tradition was abandoned, and the modern, or at least the common idea of a house was established or, one might say, re-established: two storeys and a roof, the upper storey of about the same height as the lower one. The history of the common house sounds simple, but this does not mean that there were no changes (cf. plate 161).

Two storeys with a square or polygonal bay, with a proper gable or a hipped gable (plates 48, 55, 162–7): these are everywhere the basic characteristics of the late nineteenth-century standard type of medium-sized house. The first mature examples date back to the late 1870s or early 1880s, at least in London: Brook Road, Hackney, N16, areas of Peckham (plate 162) or Brixton. By 1890 the type had spread to Brighton, Portsmouth, Plymouth and Cardiff. There was still scope for variations and for towns to develop certain minor characteristics of their own. Plymouth and Southend generally adhered to the square bay and a generally solid look, in contrast to, say, Bristol (plate 163) and Portsmouth (plate 166)[46] with their more delicate stone detail. Occasionally more specialized solutions of the facade occur: two adjacent bays placed under one gable,[47] a strong reminder of the semi-detached house; more rarely, the continuation of the projecting roof over the rest of the facade between the bays (colour plate 1, cf. plate 148).[48] In Newcastle the elegant bows of Devonshire Place are reminiscent of Scottish practice.

After 1905 the elements of the fully-fledged Domestic Revival took over very rapidly: lavish Queen-Anne-Revival pargetting work was already frequent in Muswell Hill (plate 56); half-timbering was increasing; finally a sub-Voysey kind of pebble-dash covered many facades (plates 161, 168).[49] There was an apparently irresistible temptation to make each house look different, even if it only meant a slight variation in the placing of the half-timbering. A row of four houses in Crawford Gardens, Cliftonville, Margate of 1905 can hardly be called a terrace any more, as each house has a completely different facade.

The small house and its facade

172. **Reading.** Pell Street,
c. 1890. A method occasionally
used on short, angled streets is
to stagger the houses, instead
of running the facades parallel
to the street.

To begin with, there is a basic question: do small houses have facades at all; do they come into the same category of architecture discussed up to now? There is no ready

173 (above). **London.** Westport Street, E1, *c.* 1840. The common small London house (cf. plate 41) is brought up-to-date with the stucco covering.

174 (above right). **Stafford.** Goal Road, terrace *c.* 1820–1860. Small, but by no means pinched, with features and proportions aspiring to the polite Classical.

175 (right). **Cambridge.** Jesus Terrace and New Square, *c.* 1830. The houses are smaller than the terrace in Stafford, but the effort to emulate the grand Classical is greater.

176 (facing page). **Leamington.** Rugby Road, *c.* 1830.

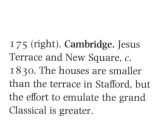

177. Bristol. Windsor Terrace, Totterdown, *c.* 1870. Bristol was almost as consistent as London in not adopting alignment in all houses below the best class until the later nineteenth century. Note also the division between each house, characteristic of Bristol, from the seventeenth century onwards.

178. Aberaman near **Aberdare**, South Wales, North View Terrace, late nineteenth century; part of an industrialized countryside.

179. **Manchester.** Wren Street and Nut Street, 1880s. Houses of the minimum width with standardized lintels and windows produce elegant proportions almost automatically (cf. colour plate 27).

180. **Barrow Hill.** Derbyshire, the endless street of an isolated industrial settlement (*c.* 1900–5).

181 (right). **Birmingham.** Walford Road, *c.* 1900.

182 (far right). **Sunderland.** Wharncliffe Street, *c.* 1850s: the great exception among English towns in that most small houses here have only one storey (cf. plate 63); most slightly larger houses show gables.

answer. The subject is made more difficult by the fact that almost all the early houses have been destroyed. We cannot here reach back into the vernacular origins of forms and methods, and we will be looking in more detail at the later period, and at the way the small houses adopted elements from the better houses (plates 173–83).

During the first half of the nineteenth century, houses could still look like primitive hovels, of low contour, with a broad, thatched roof, with smallish, often randomly placed windows, and with a characteristically diminutive upper floor. There was little difference between the rural and the urban cottage. In the new, denser agglomerations of urban dwellings, however, a more orderly look seems to have been common; many houses were three storeys in height, though again the upper floor would be lower than in comparable better houses. They had a rather low-pitched roof; most of them had sash windows, some of which were of standard Georgian proportions (plate 61). The sashes were usually hung in the old-fashioned way, with the frame near the outer surface of the wall (plate 69), not inside as in the better houses. There was rarely any attached decoration on these houses, except perhaps some imitation rustication over the windows, or a somewhat rickety wooden hood over the door (cf. plate 201). It would be hard to decide whether these fronts could be called 'facades' in the Classical sense.

Occasionally some distinctive vernacular practices continued into the second half of the century. A row of houses on a steep slope would not be stepped, in order for all roof lines to be horizontal, but the eaves and ridges would be inclined, simply running parallel with the slope in continuous lines. This can be seen to survive particularly strongly in Rochdale and Oldham, where the incline is often so steep that it can cause a cut, or a chamfering off, on the ceiling of the upstairs room (cf. plate 62). Doors of cottages were traditionally broad and of low proportions, something which can still be seen in many later houses in Bury and Carlisle (cf. colour plate 5). Lintels across windows were traditionally constructed with rather coarse methods, with primitive brick arches, or flattish pieces of stone. The latter method continued for a long time in Bradford; it was simply a matter of using a convenient local stone (plate 83).

At the other end of the spectrum of competence there were small houses for agricultural workers, and very occasionally industrial workers, which were carefully designed by architects, in the context of a paternalistic philanthropic estate. Their style could be more advanced than that of many contemporary better houses. These designs were, of course, very rare exceptions. It is, on the other hand, often impossible to make a rigid distinction between those highly 'designed' houses and the mass of 'illiterate' small houses. There were many grades between these extremes. In towns with a high degree of overall planning and where a lot of care was taken generally, like the resorts, the builders of all houses must have been fairly closely controlled; we only need to look at the sparkingly neat, white terraces of very small houses in Leamington or Cheltenham (e.g. Sandford Street) (cf. plate 176). In Cambridge some colleges, as developers, stipulated regularity particularly for small houses in the 1820s to 1840s, which produced, around New Square, some of the attractive and regular streets of comparatively very small houses (plate 175). In London the situation varied. Generally the small houses situated among the better streets, such as Kelly Street in Camden (cf. plate 173),[50] are elegantly stuccoed and even carry some kind of flat pediment on the top of their cornices, the sort of reminiscence of the larger terrace which can also be found in some early model towns. In the generally poorer parts of London, however, much less care was taken architecturally and often the most incongruous designs carried on into the 1860s at least (plate 216).

183. **Norwich.** Wellington Road, 1880s.

There was one element of the front, though, which all small houses in London (plates 173, 216), and also those in Bristol (plate 177), shared with the better facades until about 1880: the Classical parapet, or blocking course, which hid the roof proper, whereas in the provinces the traditional exposure of the roof and the eaves prevailed. On the other hand, the small houses in London and Bristol, equally consistently, carried on with the non-aligned facade, again in contrast to the rest of the country. Even in the outlying districts of London, which did not form part of the London area earlier on, we find examples of the provincial type of small house, with the windows aligned and the normal type of 'eaves drop' roof. We shall have to come back to the problem of the hierarchy of status in the facades of London houses in the last chapter.

The second half of the nineteenth century brought, as we have seen, the widespread adoption of the regular plan. It brought a process of regularization for the front of the houses as well, not only for the regular type but for those small houses which adhered to older plan types, such as the back-to-back. From about 1860 or 1870 onwards one can speak more positively of the 'facade' of the smallest house.

There were several non-aesthetic, non-artistic factors which spawned this development. Most important, there was the byelaw stipulation about room heights; from the late 1850s, or at least from the 1870s onwards, no rooms in the main part of the house were allowed to be less than 8 feet (2.44 m) in height. Houses also appeared higher because the floor-boards were no longer allowed to lie flat on the ground, but had to have a 6 inch (0.15 m) ventilation space underneath. The third element was the standardization in the production of the windows and many of the decorative parts of the facade. And lastly, a narrow house was more economic in terms of land use and street costs (e.g. plate 179).

As a result of these elements, as well as a desire to imitate the facades of the better houses, we now have the universal standard facade of the late nineteenth-century small house. Also roofs are now usually steeper than they were during the mid-nineteenth century, regardless of the material they are covered with (e.g. plate 183); thus they are more dominant and give a more restful character to the terrace as a whole. Proportions are always slender; doors are small, and thus they are often very narrow (plate 175, colour plate 9). Windows follow the standard Georgian proportions. All doors and windows carry proper lintels, that is, their heads are not flat, but of a certain height, so as to be reminiscent of the Classical architrave. Finally one must not forget the made-up street, the orderly footpath, straightened, paved and drained, in front of each terrace.

The most important additional 'extra' to which so many small houses aspired was the bay window. There are many gradations; from just an enlarged lintel for the ground-floor window, to a tripartite window (colour plate 22); then there were the small wooden bays (cf. plates 14, 183), so common in Birmingham (plate 181), and the larger, more structural stone or artificial stone bays in London (plate 53)—all strictly of one storey only for the small house. The detailed decorations of the facade, even more than in the case of the larger houses, are determined by the nature of the materials used. It is to these aspects of craftsmanship that we now turn.

15. Decoration: materials and techniques

. . . architecture is itself a real thing.

John Ruskin[1]

The way a building is built is a subject often neglected by those interested in architecture. It is sometimes the architect's idea that matters most, the way he visualizes the building, long before it is turned into bricks and mortar. But for the more ordinary kinds of structures which are the concern of this book, the architect's concept was of lesser importance, if one could speak of such a thing at all. The overall design was usually predetermined by tradition and convention; the element of choice often lay in materials and techniques and the detailed decoration. This choice was usually made by those who were involved in the actual building, the tradesmen and craftsmen.

Because of the overall importance of this aspect of architecture, this chapter is the most general one of the book. What will be said of the development of construction and decoration will not only be valid for terraces, but also for minor villas and semi-detached houses as well and even minor commercial buildings. It is characteristic of the whole of the architecture of the nineteenth and twentieth centuries that preferences for materials changed very rapidly. One only needs to be reminded of the very decisive changes between about 1960 and 1980 with the move from concrete to brick. We must also be aware that there are always a number of factions. There are, firstly, those who judge buildings from an Arts and Crafts point of view, that is, with the eyes of William Morris and Ernest Gimson; they will always search for subdued colours, for simple, rough stonework and for the roughest kinds of old brickwork. To them, the smooth red or yellow pressed brick of the late nineteenth century will be anathema. The Gothic Revivalists and all those influenced by Pugin and his disciples will always insist on 'bare' masonry, and will view any covering with plaster and the like as immoral. Thus there was plenty of contemporary controversy in the nineteenth century. The fate of stucco is only one example: it was 'in' around 1830; it was almost totally rejected in 1870–80; but was revived in a limited way about 1890–1900. It clearly follows that we would do well to put our own preferences aside when studying the development of each material in turn. Broader changes in the preferences for materials and techniques and the architectural styles and ideologies which governed them will be discussed in the following chapters.

We have already dealt with the general changes in the organization of building: from local crafts to national industries; the growing mechanization of production, and the resulting standardization as regards quality and price. We have also pointed to the revolution in transport and retailing. Although we have to explain the different techniques individually, according to each material, what emerges most clearly overall is the growing variety of materials and techniques in any given place (colour plate 20). As early as the 1850s stone and brick were fiercely competitive, according to George Gilbert Scott.[2] By the end of the century bay windows could be supplied competitively in brick, stone or wood, and one can see them side by side in places like Grantham, Doncaster or Leicester. Earlier, there were some areas where stone and brick were used alternately, or in close proximity, as in Leeds or Sheffield, but normally this was not exploited visually. There was little concern for the integrity and identity of a material. Certain materials were used to imitate others of a higher status: stucco had to look like stone; woodwork was echoing ironwork in verandahs (plate 215); conversely, there were cases of iron imitating wood: the very thin Regency wooden sash bars were sometimes executed in metal and then painted to look like wood (cf. plate 201). In the later nineteenth century materials were always juxtaposed: limestone with brick, or rubble-stone facing with Ruabon pressed bricks; the list of variations could extend to a considerable length. In Plymouth there are late nineteenth-century standard-sized houses[3] with two colours of brick, the rough bluish local limestone and smooth, brown, Bath-type limestone, as well as timber and rough-casting, plus a number of minor features in other materials. And the facades of even the smallest houses, whether they are in Norwich, Manchester, Portsmouth or Carlisle, have solid stone lintels placed in brick. What must also be stressed is that in most cases there were not only new imports from other regions, but also a more vigorous exploitation of what was available locally.

How much this development was a reflection of the general patterns of trade remains to be investigated. Earlier on, the tradition of the autonomy of each trade and each material was still strong. Although individual trades might try and encroach on each others' territory, to snatch business away from each other by imitation, or by the supply of cheap substitutes, one would not expect an actual mixture of materials. Later on, when more crafts could be united in one undertaking, there was no hesitation in combining several materials in one building. There was no need for one craft to pretend to be any other. No other period of English building witnessed a greater variety of materials than the years 1870 to 1910.

Stone

Naturally, stonework as such does not change. However, we have noted that brickwork replaced stone for most structural work because it was more practical and because it had become relatively cheaper. But stone dramatically increased its share in facade-work. At no other time was so much stone used in Britain as between 1860 and 1930. This was due chiefly to improved quarrying, cutting and transport. The status of stone did not change like that of other materials, but certain kinds of stonework were preferred at certain times, mainly because of changing colour preferences. During the eighteenth and early nineteenth centuries, Portland stone was greatly preferred because of its whiteness, though it could hardly ever be afforded in terraces; during the middle and late nineteenth century yellow Bath and brown York stone were in fashion, strong colour and colour variety then being considered desirable generally in architecture; after 1900 the best public and commercial buildings returned to Portland stone. For the vast range of kinds and the methods of working stone we must refer to Clifton-Taylor; here we can only concentrate on a few major areas.

There were few towns where good craftsmanship in stone was widely available. Here Bristol was outstanding. We have already noted its own peculiar traditions in

184. **Bristol.** Lower Redland Road, *c.* 1870s. A tradition of smooth ashlaring and fine carving with Neo-Classical and Mid-Victorian floral motifs, as well as some influence of South Kensington flat pattern decor.

185. **Bristol.** All Saints Road, Clifton, 1872. Free stone and rubble, with unusually elaborate Gothic decoration on this narrowly detached house.

the designing of facades, second only to the metropolis in importance; but in some branches of craftsmanship it far surpassed London. Of course, Bath (lime) stone was relatively easy to work. First of all there was the continuing tradition of exceedingly smooth ashlaring (cf. plates 2, 125, 129, 141, 155, 157, 184, colour plate 21)[4]: large blocks of the same size and colour, with paper-thin joints. There are mid-century terraces with completely smooth fronts, with only the door and window surrounds slightly projecting as flat bands.[5] Then there are the most delicately carved cornices, balcony railings and similar decorations.[6] There is an abundance of figurative carving, much of it of Gothic inspiration, and also of a more abstract 'South Kensington' character (plates 184–5).[7]

The other major kind of surface treatment is 'rubble' work, or rough stonework (plate 186). Its use in the nineteenth century has several roots. Firstly, it was simply a cheaper method than ashlaring and as such it was used in all kinds of work. Secondly, it did have a place on the facade of even the best buildings, as rustication, though the individual blocks were usually expensively large and often carefully smoothed at the edges. Then there was the Picturesque movement which preferred rubble simply because it was rough, more varied and natural. For most minor nineteenth-century rubble buildings in traditional stone areas, it would, of course, be impossible to determine which one of the reasons was decisive. But by about 1850 we can observe in some of the largest houses in Clifton a pronounced turning away from ashlar and stucco. Probably the first to reintroduce rubble work in a (small) country house was Nash, in Luscombe.[8] Later, Pugin claimed in his *True Principles* of 1841 that construction with small irregular stones was more solid, and Stevenson felt that rubble was more 'homely' than ashlar.[9] Bristol rubble was invariably the home-grown 'Pennant' sandstone, bluish, or purplish-grey, which formed a strong contrast with the limestone ashlar facing of the corners, window surrounds and doors (colour plate 15). This framework was increasingly used, in a rather Gothic fashion (plate 163), to give special emphasis to the main outlines of the facade, especially the bay windows.

Weston-super-Mare followed Bristol in its general handling of stone decoration. Booming late Victorian and Edwardian Cardiff can also be seen as a sequel to Bristol. Earlier houses there were usually nondescript brick or rubble, plastered over and

186. The growing acceptance and popularity of rubble walls, for large and small houses alike, in the later nineteenth century. There were many grades of roughness. However, much of the new 'rubble' was a thin facing on much rougher walls or on brick.

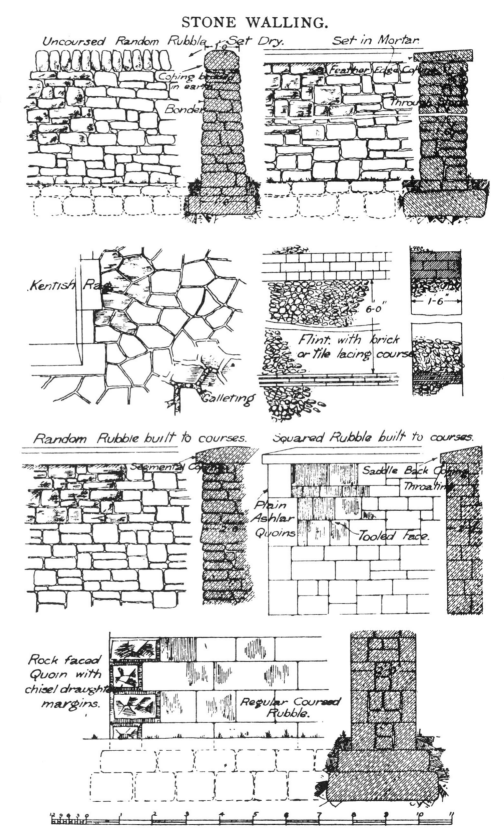

187 (facing page, above). **Cardiff.** Cathedral Road, *c.* 1890; part of the side elevation of one of the large terraces.

188 (facing page, centre). **Consett.** *c.* 1900. Heavy local stone, note especially the 'quoins', the corner blocks.

189 (facing page, below). **Huddersfield**, late nineteenth-century variation of rough stonework.

rendered. But with the example of Clifton, and with John Prichard's and William Burges's strong Neo-Gothic influence in Cardiff itself, the local blue-grey 'Pennant Grit' was used as carefully applied rubble (on brick) and combined with Bath stone facing for corners and frames. Cardiff was even more exuberant than Bristol in combining rubble with pressed brick facing, polished granite shafts and other materials (plate 165, colour plates 17, 22). The normal rubble of Bristol and Cardiff appears smooth in comparison with this wild variation of sizes and colours perhaps initiated by E. W. Godwin;[10] there are several examples of this work later on in Cardiff (plate 187).

The other great stone area in England is 'York', which in its most general sense refers to a sandstone belt reaching from the mountainous parts of Yorkshire and further north and into Nottinghamshire and Derbyshire, as well as east Lancashire. It is harder and more difficult to work than Bath, thus there is less of a tradition of carving, and profiles and mouldings are usually sharp but simple (plate 123, colour plate 23). On the other hand, there seems to be a greater variety of, and degrees in, dressing the surface. The place for the greatest variety in domestic work is Harrogate. What strikes one first of all is the heaviness of many facades, for instance the enormously solid piers and frames of the bays of nos. 7–19 Park View, of the 1870s–1880s. There is a great deal of rustication of all kinds, such as vermiculation ('worm tracks') and very heavy quoining. There is an abundance of heavy, Classically-inspired profiles, but also the smoother, uniform rubble stone with 'flush' quoining for the doors and windows in a more Gothic fashion (colour plate 23).[11] It is, of course, even more difficult here to decide where traditional rubble ends and revived rubble begins, but a comparison between early and later larger houses does reveal a considerable increase in rubble, as well as a greater differentiation between the work on the front, on the side, and on the back (plate 189).[12]

Later nineteenth-century smaller houses in that part of England also continue and elaborate the rubble tradition. At the same time there was an increase in dressed stone. A crucial borderline between the primitive and the more developed house is the dressed jamb for doors and windows. Then there is the thin slab, the 'head' or lintel over doors and windows, which changes from a flattish to an upright piece of stone, faintly reminiscent of an architrave (plates 83–4). Newcastle used solid piers and lintels in two-part windows for all houses (plate 103). Furthermore, by the late nineteenth century the different grades of rubble were used for contrasting back and front even in the smallest houses, as in Burnley (colour plate 10), Accrington, Huddersfield and Consett (plate 188, cf. colour plate 22). A few strongholds of stone remained, areas where few buildings were built of brick. The _Tudor Walters Report_ refers to some areas with local customs of too much 'dressing', which make small houses unnecessarily costly.[13] It does not say where, but the remark could well be linked with one in the _Cost of Living Report_[14] on the relatively expensive walling in Huddersfield, to the effect that 'local brick, a cheaper material, is said to be of not sufficient quality for the construction of the outer walls' (plates 77, 83, 189).

We have already mentioned the greater availability, from the mid-century onwards, of stone for the heavy-duty parts of a building, such as steps or sills. Extraction of stone became more and more mechanized, and by 1900 the largest quarries used steam engines and travelling cranes; pneumatic drills began a little later. Small railways had already been used in the Bath stone quarries in the eighteenth century. By 1824 James Tulloch of Esher Street, Millbank, London[15] had steam-powered saws for rubbing, dressing and polishing stone. By 1857 most marble was sawn by machine.[16] Later machines, like the 'Stonemason', could deal with 'all kinds of stone'.[17] From 1880 there was a tremendous increase in the use of granite, though this seldom affected the smaller house (colour plate 17). Traditionally, in non-stone areas like London, stone was not used for anything but the facades of the best public buildings. Essentially only Bath, Portland and York stone were available in London. After about 1850 there was a tremendous increase both in quantity and in variety, at first in commercial buildings and by about 1880 in all domestic work as well. The same is true for other non-stone areas. In Leicester some small late nineteenth-century houses have lintels of Bath stone, window sills of Derbyshire Grit and steps in York stone.[18] Late nineteenth-century door surrounds in Preston and seemingly also in Blackburn had to be of stone (plate 212). The price of stone as such remained much the same throughout the century—apart from a steep rise and fall in the 1870s—but what mattered was that the price difference according to the distance from the quarry was greatly reduced. Even in a brick stronghold, like Norwich, a stone lintel was reputed to have cost two-thirds as much as a brick arch. These lintels were normally about one brick thick and three or four bricks high, and could thus easily be put into position by a bricklayer.

There was another major factor in the cheapening of decorative stone: 'quarry working'. How much stone exactly was treated in that way is very hard to assess, as it did not change the style of ornament, but it must have been considerable at the lower end of the market. We know that London masons protested against it in the late nineteenth century.[19] Yet one has to remember that, in any case, the tradition of working stone in the yard, rather than *in situ*, was always strong in England, as compared, for instance, with France.[20] Already in the Catalogue of 1849 Randall & Saunders of Bath offer 'machine made mouldings at moderate prices' and in 1856 we read of their 'patent facing sawn and dressed ready for fixing'.[21] The Bath Stone Firms of 1887, a very large company, 'make it a speciality of working stone on the spot'.[22] Indeed, Bath stone was softer to work when fresh and wet from the quarry, and wages were lower here than in the towns. There was also less weight in transport and the waste could be sold for other purposes. The worked stone could be sent direct to the building site and bypass the local mason's yard. Only occasionally do we find local stone-carving blossoming as it did, literally, with the floral and animal decor in Church Road, Moseley, Birmingham.

Bath stone was probably imported to greatest effect at Portsmouth. It must have come ready cut by rail, as there are houses with exactly the same kind of decor in Winchester and Southampton.[23] It was only used for domestic and minor commercial work. Houses are of the late standard types, with bays of one or two storeys. Not only the piers of these bays were of stone, but also all lintels and even the balustrades of the upper windows. There is also an elaborate cornice-panel feature over the door. The design, which varies very little, combines the slender Gothic forms of mid-century villas with the 'bracketed' forms of T. E. Owen's smaller houses in Southsea of the 1850s. (Bracketing is the exaggeration of projecting supports, such as consols, beam-ends, and others, ultimately derived from the wooden cottage-ornée (cf. colour plate 20).) The first mature examples of the new stonework occur around 1880.[24] It was, of course, the late Victorian build-up of the Navy which helped to produce street after street of two-storeyed relative magnificence—hardly less impressive as a whole than the earlier seaside resorts (plate 166, colour plate 18). Will it ever be possible to find out who designed the detailed decor and where exactly it was made?

Brick

With brick everything kept changing: technology, legislation, availability, colour,

Fig. 3.

Fig. 1.

Fig. 5.

Fig. 6.

Fig. 2.

Fig. 4.

Scale of

Feet.

A Pair of seven roomed Villas Italian. Pl. 5 Details.

status. Its shape, colour and surface texture could so easily be varied. More than with any other material there was always a variety of grades and qualities available, due chiefly to the unpredictability of the burning process. Brick enjoyed its highest reputation in the seventeenth and eighteenth centuries. Even in stone towns like Bristol we find red brick facing on some of the best late eighteenth-century terraces.[25] In some southern towns, older, timberframed buildings were faced with a thin cladding which looked like brick, the so-called Mathematical tiles, until the early nineteenth century.[26] Soon afterwards brick reached a low point in its reputation, in the 1820s to 1840s, when better houses were invariably faced on their fronts with stone substitutes. The High Victorian Gothic mode drew attention to the possibilities of multi-coloured brick from the mid-century onwards, though this concept only gradually found its way to the facades of ordinary houses (colour plates 20, 24). In the 1870s the Queen Anne Revivalists rediscovered the charms of strong red brick. The main aspect of our investigation is the way brick varies from region to region. Our attempt at an account will be regional as well as chronological.

Change was slow in the time-honoured craft of bricklaying itself. Attempts since the seventeenth century to standardize the size of brick by law had led to a common size of $9 \times 2\frac{1}{2} \times 4$ inches ($230 \times 60 \times 100$ mm), but many variations still occurred and in the north bricks were usually thicker. Of the two major kinds of bonding, English bond was considered sounder, but Flemish bond was preferred for aesthetic reasons from the Georgian period onwards. English bond consisted of a layer of stretchers alternating with a row of headers. Flemish bond is more complicated: headers and stretchers alternate in each layer, and the layers are placed upon each other in such a way that a header comes symmetrically above a stretcher, and vice versa. The north, again, preferred to differ: at least in most smaller houses we observe four or five courses of stretchers followed by one course of headers (plate 68).

The most elaborate piece of work was usually the arch. The more primitive heads of windows are normally at least partly supported by the wooden frame underneath (plate 60, colour plate 5); by 'arch' we usually mean any covering of an opening which is self-supporting. The most frequent solution is the 'flat arch', which was also called, in brickwork, the 'skewback arch' (plates 40–1). Then there were several kinds of segmental arches, including the 'camber arch' with a very slight curve. The doors in all but the smallest houses were covered by a semi-circular arch. In all buildings of any pretension from the seventeenth and eighteenth centuries onwards these arches had to be gauged (also spelled guaged, or gaged). It meant that the bricks were shaped radially, in order to spread the load of the masonry sideways. These gauged bricks were specially made of finer clay, and burnt short of vitrification so as to be softer. Normally the arch would be drawn out in full scale on the floor and the bricks would be cut and rubbed to fit together very neatly—thus the term 'rubbed arch' was also used. Only a very thin joint would show, which was filled not with mortar, but with lime or putty (plate 190, colour plate 24). Ultimately this technique of neat facing was derived from ashlar work. It was the degree of contrast between the thin joints of the gauged work and the wider joints of the surrounding ordinary brickwork which marked the quality of the former. The tradition was strongest in the south-east; we shall come back later to developments in Norfolk. It declined in London from the Regency period onwards; there are many later elaborate but roughly constructed arches (plates 139, 216, colour plate 25). After 1850 most other parts of the country lost interest, too, and other materials and techniques became more popular for the same kinds of jobs, such as stucco and, later, ready-cut stone, as well as the many new moulded bricks. In London, fine red gauged work and other eighteenth-century brick techniques were largely limited in

the Queen Anne Revival to the better houses in the West End (plate 145).

London was the hub of common English brickwork, but it remained strangely conservative during most of the nineteenth century as regards the making and especially the burning of brick. The clay was turned to paste with a lot of water in a 'pug mill'—by manpower, horse or machine—and was then moulded by hand on a table (colour plate 24), brick by brick, which then had to be dried for a long time. It was then burnt in heaps called 'clamps' with coal and ashes placed in between. Ashes were also mixed with the paste itself, to help further with the burning process—one of the reasons for the often mottled colour of the London bricks. Usually bricks were produced near the site of a new construction and when it was finished the gang of brickmakers moved on to the next. Gradually this came to be considered a nuisance, and more and more London bricks were produced outside, for instance in Shoeburyness in Essex and Sittingbourne, Kent. They travelled on barges up the river and the canals, and on the way back these barges carried ashes and refuse for the burning process. Again, it was the stench of the works and also the competition of the cheap Flettons that extinguished these brickfields after 1900, and thereby abolished the typical London brick altogether.

Because of the primitive burning process and also because of changing colour preferences generally, London bricks were produced in a wide range of varieties, with a very complicated development and with a confusing terminology into which a lot more research has to be done. The cheapest and roughest bricks, for hidden walls only, were red and were usually called 'place' bricks. The bricks for normal facing were the 'stocks', so called after the table they were moulded on. It has remained the name for the typical London brick generally, although it was occasionally used for different kinds of bricks in the provinces, for instance in Manchester. In the eighteenth century there were also the 'red stocks', referring largely to the rubbed, smooth facing bricks and those for arches—the dearest bricks of all. Then there were the 'grey stocks', usually ranging from brown to yellow and occasionally to grey. After 1800 red stocks were virtually phased out—perhaps the red arches in Bedford Place are among the last examples—and only grey stocks remained. This colour corresponded to Palladian preferences for lightness, purity and Portland stone colour, shared 'by all persons of refined judgement',[27] and all those persons were strongly opposed to red bricks. Initially, the grey and yellow colours resulted from the admixture of a chalky clay, 'malm' or 'marl' and a special sand from the Thames at Woolwich, which prevented the iron in the clay from turning red. But this special clay and sand became rare and was more and more restricted to dearer bricks. Thus a new category of grey or light yellowish bricks emerged, the 'malms', and replaced the old category of red stocks as the best bricks (colour plate 25). With the cheap red 'place' bricks still at the bottom of the hierarchy, 'stocks' now formed the middle price range. They were usually made yellow or greyish by adding chalk to the ordinary clay. These London stocks were advanced in that their colour was manipulated, whereas most of the rest of the country stuck to the more natural red. In addition to the choice of colour there was a vast range of gradations from 'best picked' downwards, which was used for the differentiation of the different classes of houses.[28] Later, there came an additional kind of purer grey without the yellow tinge, the 'gault', which can be found, for instance, in Queen's Gate Place in the 1860s, and later on in many smaller houses, especially in south London (colour plate 16). It came from the 1850s onwards, by rail for instance from R. Beard's works in Arlesey, Bedfordshire, and also from a yard in Aylesford, Kent, which was started by Cubitt.[29] To the even dearer 'Suffolk White' we shall come below. The reason for the conservatism of London brickwork is perhaps due to the

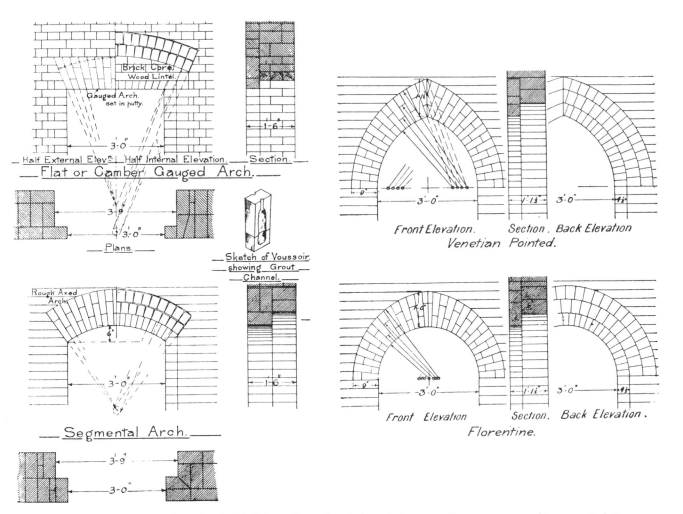

Brick Core
Wood Lintel.

Gauged Arch.
set in putty.

3'-0"

Half External Elev⁵·| Half Internal Elevation.

Section.

1'-6

__Flat or Camber Gauged Arch.__

3'-9

3'-0"

__Plans.__

__ Sketch of Voussoir.
showing Grout
Channel. __

Rough Axed
Arch.

6"

3'-0"

1'-6"

__ Segmental Arch. __

3'-9"

3'-0"

Front Elevation.   Section. Back Elevation

3'-0"   1'-1½"   3'-0"   1½"

Venetian Pointed.

Front Elevation   Section. Back Elevation.

9"   3'-0"   1'-11"   3'-0"   1½

Florentine.

190. **Gauged arches**; the Gothic types are less frequently used in terraced housing.

fact that brick did not have the status of stucco earlier, or stone and terracotta later. When red brick was again universally appreciated later in the century, it was also used for the facades of the better houses in London (cf. colour plates 1, 7). Many of the best reds came from Fareham or Bracknell.[30] Taste in colour had changed again and become somewhat simplified, with red reappearing at the top of the range.

There are two major differences between London and the rest of the country: bricks elsewhere were not clamp-burnt but kiln-burnt, at first in more primitive 'clamp kilns' and then in updraught 'Scotch' kilns, surrounded by walls. This method generally made for much more even shaping and colouring. There were, however, a few major exceptions to this: common bricks in Kent, Sussex and Portsmouth continued to be clamp-burnt as in London, though their colour was usually reddish-black.

The second difference concerns colour: red remained the dominant colour in most of the provinces for cheap *and* best bricks. Again, there is at least one major exception to this: the 'white' bricks of East Anglia, usually a dirty grey, but whitish-yellow when cleaned.[31] Most houses in Cambridge (plate 175), Ipswich and Lowestoft from about 1820 onwards are white-grey brick throughout. In Cambridge there is much pressed white brick after 1870, later called Cambridge Gault or Burwell White.

In Norfolk white brick was used only for facades. It was combined here with the continuing tradition of gauged work. Possibly John Soane's country house Shottesham Park of the 1780s in white brick, with its very extensive use of gauged arches, was a model for the local architects and builders. On the whole, there was

191. **Norwich.** Gladstone Street, 1865. Good 'gauged' (or, more precisely, moulded and rubbed) work, as well as the technique of the 'reveal', that is the half-brick projection of part of the wall, can be found in large and small Norwich houses alike.

singularly little use of stucco in Norfolk; stone was very expensive and wooden decor was, by 1840, restricted to the smaller houses. Thus the bricklayers had the field to themselves. In Norwich, the large houses in Newmarket Road abound in complicated brick arches, and from the 1850s even medium to small, non-hall-entranced houses invariably sport these arches, hardly inferior in their work-manship to their larger neighbours (plates 183, 191). In addition to gauged work there is the 'reveal', a half-brick layer which projects from the wall and surrounds doors and windows, and sometimes serves as a kind of pilaster without capital. There is little difference between the colour, surface, and quality of the arched bricks and the rest of the facade bricks; the joints of the latter are also comparatively narrow. In fact, in many cases the facing bricks are slightly larger than the walling bricks behind, which often meant a lack of bonding between the two. Builders were obviously striving hard to find a method of brick facing akin to the carefully lined face of an ashlar wall. There were probably two other factors behind the spread of this method into the cheaper houses after 1850: the abolition of the brick tax, which was particularly heavy on all larger bricks, and, possibly, a considerable degree of pre-moulding of the arch bricks.

Indeed, gauged work was already being superseded by 'moulded' work, that is, relatively complicated ornaments cast in ordinary brick earth. In the terraces of neighbouring Lowestoft from about 1850 onwards the flat character gave way to more vigorous profiles around windows, along cornices and on corners, the so-called quoins. The whole Classical vocabulary of small details was recreated by these moulds. Outside East Anglia there were occasional bursts of white brick, as for instance in some estates of the 1860s to 1880s in Hove, which can be understood as a protest against stucco Brighton.

In Norwich red brick had been relegated to the backs of the houses; in Lowestoft, however, we see the beginnings of the exploitation of colour contrast on the facade (plate 142). We shall have to return to the use of different colour bricks as signs of social status in the last chapter: here we are interested in colour as such. The initial idea of contrasting bricks of different colours came chiefly from the High Victorian Gothic churches of the 1850s and 1860s. In the last three decades of the nineteenth century it was taken up by smaller houses and the greatest variety can be found in a belt around London, from Bedfordshire to Hampshire.

Bedford has red and yellow bricks, and by the late nineteenth century there is also the mottled red-white Fletton type for the back of the house. Luton produced another colour in addition to these: the dark-grey or light-grey purple. This colour stemmed from a reaction of small amounts of flint with iron oxide, plus possibly manganese. Most walls, from those of minor public buildings down to small houses, are faced with purple, and even the backs are faced with a slightly inferior kind of the same brick. The arches are usually red, though there is little gauged work (colour plates 31–2). The colour effects are further helped by a special kind of pointing.

Reading's pride is the silver grey brick (colour plates 29–30), which was already familiar earlier as the 'Sussex Grey'. It affects only that side of the brick which is shown on the face of the wall, usually a header (plate 171). The colouring was achieved earlier on with the ashes of the wood used in the burning process and later, when coal firing was introduced generally, by adding rock salt during burning.[32] S. & E. Collier proudly called theirs 'Waterloo Silver Grey'. Another town with a great variety of brick colours was Maidstone, with London-type clamps, gaults, and red and white decorations. The desire for colour contrasts, particularly in Luton and Reading, carried on into this century, regardless of the new fashions for uniform red brick mentioned earlier on.

192 (above left). **Birkenhead.**
Wycliffe Street, *c.* 1890. A
mode of decoration of
doorways frequent in that area,
especially in Manchester.
'Pressed', smooth facing bricks
and some 'moulded',
ornamental bricks.

193 (above right). **Liverpool.**
Briar Street, *c.* 1880s. Red and
buff bricks plus moulded brick
decor.

194. An advertisement of
1894.

STANLEY BROS., NUNEATON

Illustrated Catalogue
(containing more than
1 000 designs) on
application.

SAMPLES
SUPPLIED FREE.

MANUFACTURERS OF
BLUE BRICKS, COPING, KERBING, &c.
Superior Blue, Red, Buff, Black, and Chocolate Quarries.
(Specially suitable for Churches, Entrance Halls, Conservatories, &c.)
RED, BROWN, AND BLUE, ROOFING, AND RIDGE TILES;
GLAZED PIPES, SEWER-GAS TRAPS, &c.
ORNAMENTAL RED CRESTINGS & FINIALS; RED AND BUFF ORNAMENTAL TERRA-COTTA.
Red and Buff Chimney Pots; Fire Bricks, Quarries, and Lumps; Glazed Bricks
and Sinks; Buff Bricks, Vases, and Statuary.
VENTILATING BRICKS AND MALT-KILN TILES.

In the West Country bricks played a less prominent role, though the red and yellow ones from Bridgwater and Cattybrook were popular later in the century, especially in brick towns like Newport, Monmouthshire. Bricks in most of the rest of the country remained uniformly red. As Nicholson remarked, it was 'difficult to get grey in the country'.[33] A widespread method, especially in the south midlands, for instance in Oxford, was to place whitish headers into Flemish Bond or into black burnt ones, so as to give a checkerboard effect (plate 201). Very fine gauged work suddenly flourished in Birmingham around 1840–80.[34] The lowland parts of Yorkshire share some characteristics with East Anglia, but the variety of techniques and colours seems less pronounced. Middlesbrough had its own type of vigorous brick arches and jambs (plate 33).

At this point we come to a chronological and geological halt. Beyond the regions discussed so far lie those parts of the country where brick was not traditionally made— which also brings us to new methods of brickmaking. First of all, the harder and older 'plastic' clays had to be used, especially those of the coal measures—thus we often find coal-mining and brick-making in one place, which also often meant that there was rail for transport. These clays had to be ground more fully by new methods, with rollers rather than in a pugmill. The paste was denser and dryer, which saved time and fuel in drying and burning. Much of the early progress seems to have been made in the Potteries alongside innovations in making pottery itself. Mechanical brick-making was begun probably in the 1820s but only really caught on in the 1850s with the 'wire cuts', where a long bar of paste came out of the pug mill, to be divided into ten or more bricks by a wire frame. These bricks were mostly used for walling only. Another method was to squeeze the paste into a number of moulds on a rotary table.[35] All these devices for 'machine bricks' were at first usually driven by manpower or horsepower. Equally important were the new efficient methods of drying and burning; the continuous Hoffmann kiln was introduced in Britain by H. Chamberlain at Wakefield in 1859.

Another problem was that of producing bricks with a smooth surface and sharp edges ('arris'). Earlier bricks were sometimes 'dressed' on one side, like stone. Later on, a much smoother finish could be achieved by pressing; in 1831 R. S. Bakewell of Manchester invented this process by applying two tons of pressure on one half-dried brick. Later pressing was mostly done more cheaply by machines. Very little is known about the early firms using this method. Hole mentions 'pressed brick' facades in 1866 for the new Langham Street Model Cottages in Leeds. There was the Nottingham E. Gripper Patent Brick from 1867, also used for St. Pancras Station and Hotel, which was probably pressed. There were 'Leicestershire Reds' by Heather & Co. from Counthesthorpe. In Birmingham[36] pressed bricks were used for all facades from about 1880 onwards (plate 181). Lastly, the best known, heavy-pressed bricks were the 'Staffordshire Blues', which replaced the traditional 'Dutch Clinkers' for heavy-duty work, but were also used for colour variation. By 1900 probably the most important firms for pressed facings were in Ruabon, near Wrexham, notably Edwards and H. Dennis; their bricks were of a bright, almost scarlet red, and there were also buff yellow ones. Ruabon bricks travelled as far as Reading, Cardiff (colour plate 33) and Newcastle upon Tyne. In Lancashire there was the more expensive Accrington brick; and apparently it was here that in the 1860s for the first time the almost dry clay was crushed and pressed with great strength to make the 'stiff plastic', 'semi plastic', 'semi dry' brick, which was used with incredible success from the 1880s onwards in the Fletton region—from Peterborough to Bedford—where a specially oily clay also greatly cheapened burning.

Most of the ordinary bricks of the midlands and northern regions, as well as the

Brick and stone combined

196 (above left). **Nottingham**, Noel Street, *c.* 1885. Tough and sharp decoration in stone and brick.

197 (centre). **Leicester**. St. Peter's Road, 1880. a rather extreme example of laying bands of stone 'flush' with the wall surface so that water could flow off easily.

198 (right). **Leicester**. Guildford Street, *c.* 1890. The same can be said of the innumerable stone lintels set in brick in so many small houses in most parts of the country (see p. 204). The ornament also follows Pugin and the South Kensington fashion in being highly stylized—as well as cheap to cut.

195 (facing page). **Birmingham**, Trafalgar Road, Moseley, *c.* 1870s. There can be few Victorian streets in Britain with a greater variety of styles and materials of decoration.

Flettons, with their usually mottled colour, were not considered to be of much use for the facade. Thus the pressed, uniformly red facings (plates 91, 192, colour plate 9) assume a much more important role here than in the southern and eastern clay areas where homogeneity was not a problem (cf. colour plate 28). From the 1870s or 1880s onwards the better houses, and from the 1890s all smaller houses in Liverpool and Manchester, carry a facing brick. The facade of a 1900 two-up-two-down in Liverpool is faced with 'Premier vitrified buff bricks, relieved with a course of seconds red Ruabon bricks' (plate 92). A convenient end to our story is provided in 1900 by some firms advertizing alongside their machine-made bricks 'hand made' ones,[37] and the traditional brick sometimes acquires the adjective 'sandfaced'.[38] By that time the fronts of some of the better houses in Cambridge were faced with traditional bricks, and the pressed bricks were relegated to the back.

Stucco

Of all nineteenth-century materials stucco was the one most violently subjected to the changes of fashion; with its peak in the 1830s, a nadir in the 1870s and 1880s and a mild revival around 1900.[39] The use of the term for external work is somewhat unusual in a European context, as is 'plaster', but it serves to show the origin of the craft in the inside of buildings: decorative work in the case of stucco, and smoothed surfaces in the case of plaster. The term 'cement' was also used, deriving from the actual material used in many cases. 'Composition' or 'compo' denotes the process of making the ornament, though that term was later also used for roughcasting.

The covering of walls, especially rough ones, with rendering and roughcast for protection, frequent at the back of buildings, does not interest us here. Yet the impetus for extensive stucco covering at the front does, to some extent, result from the practicality of covering up cheaper bricks, and from the scarcity of stone. The cost factor was vital: stucco was considered cheaper than stone by two-thirds or three-quarters, and could even be cheaper than wood. There were, of course, many grades of qualities within stucco itself. An additional element spurring its early adoption in London was that the Building Acts forbade the use of wood on the facade. The impact of the new manner of decorating facades in the 1820s must have been tremendous; as Nicholson put it in 1837: '. . . the facility of their adaptation . . . their cheapness, has tended greatly to foster the art of design, and produce a diversity of architectural display which heretofore was never dreamt of, as an inspection of Regent Street and the terraces in Regent's Park will fully substantiate' (e.g. plates 39, 41, 111, 137, 150, 173, colour plates 2, 12).[40]

The ingredients of stucco are not that different from brick, but unlike brick the ornament is not burnt after it is shaped. The most basic kind 'in country places'[41] consisted of burnt stone lime plus sand, and Walsh says that even small cornices can be run with this mixture. But for more ambitious work new methods had to be used. It was all part of the scientific climate of the day. The story begins with lawsuits in the 1770s between Robert Adam and two of his competitors, a Swiss clergyman called Liardet, and John Johnson, over new patents for stucco (cf. plate 9). The first really successful external method was patented somewhat later, in 1796, by James Parker of Northfleet,[42] working in conjunction with Charles Wyatt. 'Parker's', 'Roman', 'London', and possibly also 'Stourbridge' usually denote the same cement. In contrast to most lime mixtures, cement has more hydraulic qualities; we have already discussed its importance for a new kind of mortar. It is basically, like most kinds of plaster, made of ground clay balls, or septaria, which are burnt and mixed with three parts of clean sharp sand. Hair can be added for greater coherence. 'Roman' cement was held to be very hard and quick setting, but had a brownish colour which was considered disagreeable and always had to be painted over. The main production centres were Harwich and the Isle of Sheppey in Kent. In the early 1800s William Atkinson of Whitby introduced his cement, which was more expensive but more hydraulic and of a lighter colour ('dark Bath'). Nash used Parker's stucco at first but from about 1820 onwards mainly Hamelin & Dehl's mastic, a more oily mixture.[43] All these cements were soon to be superseded by Portland Cement, patented in 1824 by Joseph Aspdin from Yorkshire. The clay and chalk was burnt at a very high temperature, and it was stronger and yet more hydraulic. It was fairly dear, but more sand could be mixed with it. The name was chosen because it resembled the fashionable grey Portland stone and it was at first also used as a finish on Parker's cement.[44]

199. **London.** Cumberland Street, Pimlico, *c.* 1860. The anatomy of stucco decor: underneath the smooth covering we find bricks, tiles and iron straps to hold the ornament in place.

200. **Swansea.** Vivian Street, *c.* 1900. A comparatively late flowering of flattish stucco decor in South Wales (except Cardiff), derived from Classical rustication. The pebbledash is perhaps a later addition.

Stucco was used, according to Nicholson in 1837, '. . . to finish a plain face, to be jointed to imitate stone, and also for the formation of ornament of every description'.[45] To cover the walls, they were at first soaked, before the $\frac{3}{4}$ inch (19 mm) coat was quickly thrown on. Most minor ornaments were pressed in or 'run' at the same time. For features projecting further out, bricks had to be inserted into the wall, and often thin roof tiles were used behind the finer decorations, and for porches and balconies hidden, or sometimes open, iron ties or brackets (plate 199). Larger and more elaborate ornaments were, just as those for inside, pre-moulded or cast. From the frontispiece of Pugin's book *Contrasts* of 1836 we know that there was a boundless variety of forms. George Jackson and Sons claimed in a catalogue of the same year to be '. . . Composition ornament and improved papier mâché manufacturers, modellers, carvers and workers in ornamental Roman cements and plaster of Paris'. However, many of these decorations were of burnt clay and therefore belong to the next section on ornamental brick.

The strongholds of stucco were the south coast and London. Only around the mid-century is there a spread to most parts of the country — even Bristol,[46] usually in the best houses — as a sign of some metropolitan ambition. With Cubitt's work we can observe the development from the earlier, cautious application of stucco pilasters in Bloomsbury[47] to the full covering of almost all houses in Belgravia and Pimlico. Cheltenham, which is part stucco, part stone, seems to reserve the more vigorous work for stone and the plaster ornaments are often extremely delicate, as in the key pattern around the doors of Montpelier Spa Buildings, a terrace of about 1820. But vigour and bulk was certainly the watchword in mid-Victorian Plymouth (plates 47, 213),[48] in Eastbourne and in Hastings. Warrior Gardens in St. Leonards, with its multitude of stucco-covered porches, gables and bays is probably the most spectacular of all Victorian terraces (plate 143).

There are many smaller features in stucco. The most important is rustication, which is usually flat, with simple incisions. Often there are only horizontal ones, in which case the rustication is also called channelling (plates 39, 41, 173). Later, when the rejection of stucco had already set in, there were often flat bands of stucco alternating with brickwork[49] — a method also universally applied to Dutch houses in that period, and derived from the Dutch Renaissance. Another popular kind of rustication, mainly on corners ('quoining'), was vermiculation, literally 'worm tracks', an old motif, which was particularly frequent in Brighton and also in Medway. In Swansea we find a surprisingly late flowering of this manner in the small houses around 1900 (plate 200). Then there are the small stucco features applied to brick facades. There is a profusion of plaster heads over windows and doors in Birmingham.[50] The scroll-bracket under a pediment or door hood is one of the most common forms of decoration on houses from the seventeenth to the nineteenth centuries. For smaller houses this was one step up from the usually more primitively shaped wooden door decoration. The most basic, common stucco feature is probably the imitation of a flat arch, consisting of a few stones splayed outwards at the top, with a slightly projecting keystone, ultimately also derived from rustication (plate 201). Below that even more primitive features occasionally survive, like the thin band of stucco marking a 'pediment' on a broad stone lintel in Weir Street, Todmorden, of perhaps the middle of the century.

More sophisticated figurative decor occurs occasionally in stucco; whether it is of cement or of burnt clay is hard to tell. Regency Brighton has the greatest variety of this work; the herms, that is busts, carrying a porch, in 3–5 Lansdown Place; the lions in Hanover Crescent,[51] or the curious 'ammonite' capitals, a pun on the Ionic capital on the part of Amon H. Wilds, the Brighton architect.[52] Later on, we find less

201. **Macclesfield.** High Street, *c.* 1850. The ubiquitous rusticated window head, usually stucco imitating stone; here in Macclesfield they are usually of stone, but then often covered in stucco and painted, perhaps to sharpen the contours. The arch over the door is usually stucco, a frequent motif in North Staffordshire.

of this kind of work: the little dog heads repeated *ad nauseam* in Park Street, Dover, or the more impressive Neptune heads in Derby Road, Southampton (plate 203).

After 1850–60 new kinds of forms were attempted.[53] Coarse lines and blunt angles were now disliked, and flatness and sharply stamped out ornaments were preferred. James Knowles's terraces on Clapham Common, of 1860,[54] or the houses in St. Helen's Road, Hastings and Connaught Avenue, Plymouth are good examples of this manner. A special liking developed in the 1870s for exposed grey Portland cement surfaces.[55] The Queen Anne and late nineteenth-century stucco revivals spring from a rather different frame of mind in that they turn back to older, more elaborate vernacular methods, such as 'pargetting', for instance in Muswell Hill in 1900 (plate 56), and roughcasting. The latter has already been mentioned as a practical method of covering the sides and the backs of houses; it is a mixture of cement and coarse sand, or, in the case of pebble-dash, small stones. From the 1890s it appears in conjunction with mock half-timber work on the gables of standard-type houses in Brighton, Southend and elsewhere (plate 166). Finally, pebble-dash replaced other surface treatments in many houses from about 1908–10 onwards (plates 161, 168),[56] and eventually became *the* interwar style for most kinds of house.

Ornamental brick and terracotta

There is a vast range of ornaments in 'baked earth'. Most simply one could vary the position of ordinary bricks (plates 142, 192). The range of ornaments began with those of common brick earth, reaching into fine clays, with high degrees of firing, just as in pottery itself. There were also the 'fireclay' refractory bricks for fireplaces, chimneytops and ridge tiles (plate 194). As we saw in the previous section, many of the more vigorously projecting decorations underneath stucco and paint were cast and burnt in some kind of brick earth. After 1850 all kinds of brick and brick decorations could be shown again, uncovered by paint, after the dislike of red had ceased and stucco had begun its decline. At the same time new technologies began to produce harder and more neatly shaped bricks which replaced the expensive Georgian precision of rubbed brickwork.[57] There was a new liking for those kinds of ornament which helped to create relief on the facade. Prosser of Birmingham in the 1840s, and some Suffolk White yards in the 1850s, as well as Beart at Arlesey and Cubitt at Aylesford, were among the early producers of 'moulded bricks'. In Leicester, ornamental brickwork on a large scale seems to begin with the better houses in the Walk area around 1860; and in the 1870s and 1880s it became common for almost all smaller houses in Birmingham (plate 181), Nottingham and elsewhere. By about 1900 James Brown of Whitechapel produced three hundred varieties of profile alone, for cornices, string courses etc. (What remains to be done, of course, is to link the ubiquitous examples with the different firms.) In Liverpool (plate 193, colour plate 14) ornamental brick was frequent and lavish; much of it came from the Ruabon manufacturers, where even the Liverpool firm of Monk & Newell had works. Ornamental brick was also an important element in the Queen Anne Revival, though the revival of the more special kinds of seventeenth- and eighteenth-century soft red, rubbed or carved brick, was of very limited usefulness for ordinary houses.

One of the most interesting of all nineteenth-century building and decorative materials was terracotta. The use of the word was by no means consistent; sometimes it was used for all ornaments in 'baked earth'. An early variety was 'Coade Stone'.[58] Mrs. Eleanor Coade founded the firm in 1769 in Lambeth and

202 (far left). **Newark-on-Trent,** mid-nineteenth century. Stucco imitates brick: the very rough brick 'arch' covering a window is receded about one centimetre, and then filled with a layer of cement or lime, which is coloured a pinkish red and incised with lines (now barely visible) to suggest a gauged brick arch.

203 (left). **Southampton.** Derby Road, 1870s. This large decorative head in stucco or earthenware occurs several times.

supplied a great variety of decorative elements, from the small features on the doors of Bedford Square (plate 1) to large free-standing sculptures; though an imitation stone, Coade stone was far from being just a down-market concern. (The firm faded out in 1840 and was taken over by Blanchards.) Other major terracotta firms were Edwards' of Ruabon, Blashfield's of Stamford, Lincolnshire, who had taken over from Parker-Wyatt's cement firm, and Doulton's, who probably sold the most comprehensive range of all clay products, everything from 'art pottery' to sewage-pipes.[59]

It was only in the 1860s that terracotta, in the narrow sense of the term, really came into its own. The paste was burnt at very high temperatures, after it had been very carefully selected and mixed; terracotta was thus a relatively artificial and non-localized material. It was claimed to be stronger than stone or brick, and it could be used for structural work as well. It was lighter than the other materials, as the blocks could be hollowed out. It was, in short, a complete system of building and decoration. Its surface was now always exposed—'honestly confessing to be artificial', as Stevenson put it[60]—and the colour could be manipulated from light yellow to bluish red. However, there were disadvantages; the unpredictable shrinking in the burning process caused an irregularity of shape which necessitated wide joints in construction, and the complicated production process in general meant that breakages could not be replaced easily and speedily enough. Thus it was rarely used in ordinary houses (colour plate 26). The facades of Manilla Road in Bristol of 1888 are a prominent example. There are others in Ruabon, and in Glasscote Terrace in Tamworth, close to the workshops of another of the major manufacturers, Gibbs and Canning.[61] Cheaper kinds of terracotta were, however, used widely over doors and windows and for bays, especially in the south-east for the late standard type of house. They are now usually thickly painted over, which makes their coarse ornaments even more blurred; one is often uncertain whether there is terracotta, stucco, or stonework underneath the paint (plate 109).

Other varieties of artificial stone, like Victoria Stone, were used mainly as substitutes for hard York stones, for floors and steps. 'Coke breeze' has already been mentioned. Encaustic ornamental floor tiles were sometimes used for outside decoration.[62] Highly ornamental patterns in glazed tiles can be found in Edwardian porches in London and especially in Cardiff (colour plates 17, 19). Lastly, there are odd examples of bricks covered with a white glaze over the whole facade, as in the Edwardian Laburnum Grove in Portsmouth (plate 166).

Painting and pointing

The custom of painting the outside of the house, especially the front, was more widespread than we are inclined to think today. There was also the more utilitarian 'rendering', meaning roughcasting, limewhiting or limewash. All the stucco work and much of the decorative brickwork and even much decorative stonework was covered with paint. In the case of the grand Regency terraces, covenants stipulated the colour, and also that fronts had to be repainted usually every three years (plate 111). Plain white was increasingly disliked; 'unpleasant to persons of taste', writes Webster, and he claims that painters had now acquired skill and a 'good eye for colours'.[63] One must remember that colours were usually not yet ready bought, but had to be mixed individually by the painter. Ochre and 'stone colour' were usually applied; in London it was often termed 'Bath'. In addition, ashlar joints were incised, or simply drawn on and tinted, in order to produce 'an exact imitation of any

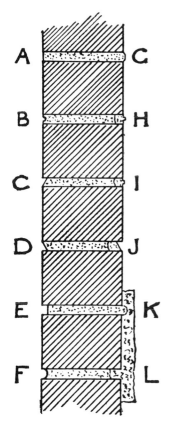

204. Various kinds of pointing; early twentieth century:
A. Flat or flush joint
B. Flat joint jointed
C, D. Struck joint
E. Recessed joint
F. Keyed joint
G. Mason's V-joint
H. Tuck pointing
I. Bastard tuck pointing
J. Pointed weather struck joint
K. L. Keying for plastering

particular stone which may be required'.[64] Only now was the stuccoed Regency facade complete. Earlier, facades were often frescoed,[65] but by the 1830s linseed oil and white lead seem to have become the common ingredients. Woodwork, which had earlier been painted white, was now often 'grained' to imitate English oak — in the same way that slates on fireplace surrounds were painted like marble.

We know almost nothing about the developments of external colouring in the Victorian period. Perhaps the south-west of England, with its multitude of stuccoed and coloured houses can give us an idea. Stronger colours still seemed popular around 1900, on woodwork and ironwork, when Raymond Unwin criticized them: '. . . bright green next to chocolate red' (cf. colour plate 8).[66] Even brickwork was often painted. It must be remembered that evenly shaped and uniformly coloured bricks were expensive, and 'to obtain uniform appearance'[67] at least a light coat of paint, usually reddish, was applied. It is still a habit, especially in the north, to paint inferior, or slightly inferior bricks, in a colour approximating Ruabon Reds, or in a more purplish colour (colour plate 27).

Earlier on, this was often done in conjunction with pointing. Finer mortars were often used to fill the joints between the bricks on the facade, and Elsam mentions Roman cement for pointing. Pointing, as distinct from jointing, refers to the treatment or covering of the joint on the face of the wall. In good work the joints would usually be raked out about half an inch deep and filled again with special 'stopping'. More expensive, but still frequently found today, was 'tuck pointing'. According to Elsam it was already 'much in fashion' in the 1820s.[68] A line, $\frac{1}{4}$ inch thick (6.4 mm) and $\frac{1}{16}$ of an inch (1.6 mm) deep, of putty was placed neatly on the pointing. It could be red, white, or black. In Luton, where the tradition is still strong, a white line is usually put on the pointing of purple brick; between the red bricks the whole pointing is usually coloured red, which often goes over the actual red brick as well, to intensify its colour and the colour contrasts on the facade as a whole: unnecessary detail, we might think, but we do know how different kinds of pointing can change the appearance of the same brick (plate 204, colour plate 31).

Roof tiles and slates

Our last brick earth product is roof tiles. These were largely made by bricklayers, to be laid by bricklayers, but the brick earth was usually more carefully selected and mixed, and also kiln burnt. Tiles were at a disadvantage *vis-à-vis* slates in many ways: plain tiles needed a much steeper pitch, which was unpopular for economic and aesthetic reasons. Much more economical were pan tiles, originating in the Netherlands; they were larger and needed only a fairly low roof. In the 1820s they were little more than half as dear as the cheapest slates and were probably still used very frequently in a lower class of work. Also their colour could be improved with 'blue anti-corrosion paint'.[69] Towards the later nineteenth century their price in London seems to have increased somewhat and they were very rarely used.[70] Only in a few corners of the provinces did they continue to be used on any scale, as in Norwich, with blue ones for the front of the house and red ones for the back (colour plate 28), the former mostly glazed.

Tiles continued to develop, and from the mid-nineteenth century Shropshire and Staffordshire 'dry' and 'pressed' tiles became widely available, especially 'Broseley' tiles — a brand as well as a generic name. They were lighter, thinner and less absorbent. In addition there were the abundant earthenware roof ornamentations, like crestings and finials on gable ends, produced by all the big terracotta firms. The initial impetus for these came from High Victorian Gothic Revival work, but the real boost was provided by the new liking for a prominent roof and all its details generally. By about 1880 these new ornaments were available for medium-sized houses, especially those with bays. As the slate industry had nothing to offer in this line, ornamental tiles were used on slate roofs just as much as on tiled roofs, adding to the general variety of materials (plate 194).

The story of the success of slates from north Wales from the late eighteenth century onwards has been told by Clifton-Taylor. They were propagated by Robert Adam in London, and transported by sea; they were light, smooth, fashionably grey in colour and non-absorbent, and the roof pitch could be very low. They were marketed in three standard qualities and in about a dozen standard sizes: 'Duchesses', 24 × 12 inches (610 × 305 mm); 'Countesses', 20 × 10 inches (508 × 254 mm); and 'Ladies', 16 × 8 inches (406 × 203 mm) were the most popular ones. By 1900 even tile strongholds like Hull had been largely or entirely conquered by slates. In general, however, it must be repeated here that all roofs became very much steeper again after 1850, which was not related to the availability of materials, but to style and fashion.

Finally, slates and roof tiles concern us marginally as a method of covering walls externally. Slate hanging was mainly a practical method of keeping the wet out, and is to be found at the back of buildings, for instance in Portsmouth. The custom seems to have died out by the end of the century. (There does not seem to have been in England an equivalent to the ornamental slate coverings on walls of the kind traditional in some parts of western Germany. In fact, German Arts-and-Crafts-minded architects like Carl Schäfer complained about the import of British slates which they held were destroying old German craftsmanship.) Indeed, English Arts-and-Crafts architects also disliked big Welsh slates and went for the green Westmoreland slates, which were smaller and less regular, but, of course, much more expensive. Plain tiles, on the other hand, were used again by the Domestic Revivalists like Philip Webb from the 1860s onwards and by 1900 they appear on the fronts of the later standard type, especially on gables (colour plate 15).[71]

Iron

We have already found that there was relatively little structural ironwork—internally and externally—in English houses. By the late eighteenth century the fashion for larger drawing-room windows was spreading, and it is again Adam who is said to have started the use of a new material in this context: cast iron—which so far had been mainly used for railings around the area. We can still see his window guards in 7 Adam Street, Adelphi, of the 1770s. The anthemia or 'heart and honeysuckle' motif was cast by the Carron Company in Falkirk, in which Adam's brother John had shares. Subsequently Carron cornered a very large share of the market throughout Britain.

The greatest place for Regency ironwork is Cheltenham. It appears to have been made largely by local craftsmen, like R. E. & C. Marshall & Co.[72] Their work is not cast, but wrought, and its delicacy and elegance was hardly ever surpassed. It can be seen in the large verandahs of Lansdown Place (plate 205), the hanging 'trellis work' of Priory Parade on London Road, or even the porches of the very small houses in Sandford Road.

But cast iron was bound to become popular not only because of its cheapness but also because taste in the 1840s was turning to more solid forms. There was a very

205. **Cheltenham.** Lansdown Place, *c.* 1830: first floor balconies (compare plate 131). Wrought iron (in the upper parts) and also cast iron with the popular heart and honeysuckle motif, produced usually by the Carron Company.

206 (below left). **Hastings.** Pelham Crescent, by J. Kay, 1824–8. Cast and possibly also wrought iron in the balcony railings. the curved roofs are typical for verandahs of medium to large-sized houses on the south coast.

207 (below right). **Brighton.** St. Michael's Place, 1870s; the more solid-looking cast-iron work, typical of the later nineteenth century.

YOUNG & MARTEN, Ltd., Merchants and Manufacturers,

Ornamental Verandahs.

No. C4728.—VERANDAH.

No. C4823.

Set of Ironwork for Verandah, 12 ft. wide × 3 ft. to 4 ft. projection, as shown, fitted ready for re-erection, prepared to receive wood beam and wood astragals for glass.

No. C4728.

VERANDAH SET.

Comprises:—

3 Verandah Columns, 8 ft. 6 in. high; with Entablatures.

3 pairs Brackets for same.

1 pair Brackets for wall.

Frieze, 4½ in. × 3 in. Moulded Gutter, and Cresting for front and returns.

2 Terminals.

£11 5s. per set.

No. C5728.—VERANDAH.

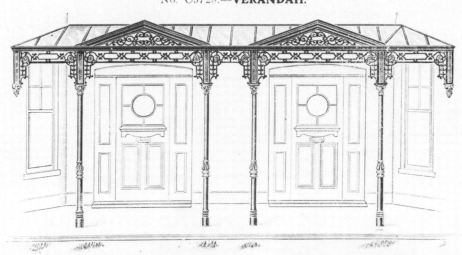

No. C5728. Set of Ironwork for Verandah, 23 ft. wide overall by 2 ft. projection, as shown, or similar arrangement, fitted ready for re-erection, with Ironwork for Roof, ready for Glazing, comprising:—

3 Verandah Columns, 8 ft. 9 in. high; with Entablatures, Brackets, Frieze, Gutter, and Pediments.

£21 per Set.

STRATFORD, Walthamstow, Leytonstone, Millwall, & Brentford.   [167 widespread use of the same patterns, not only through the firms and their catalogues, but also through pattern books, like those by L. N. Cottingham and Henry Shaw. Apart from Carron, another large supplier was the Coalbrookdale Company. From the 1820s to the 1840s ironwork flourished in Brighton, Leamington, Scarborough and elsewhere, and in London to a lesser extent (plates 41, 43, 117, 152, 206, colour plates 2, 12). The variety of styles became greater, in spite of the standardization of production: smallish Neo-Rococo floral motifs, late Neo-Classical squarish work and even Gothic forms. But after the mid-century ironwork was not liked any more: those 'hideous iron railings', as the *Builder* remarked in 1864.[73] In large London terraces the balconies and sometimes even the 'area' railings are of solid brick and plaster. Iron continued to be used in the fencing around smaller front gardens (most of it removed during the second world war)[74] and in porches for front doors, especially in the south (plate 208). Sometimes bay windows had corner supports of iron.[75] There was now also an influence of High Victorian Gothic ironwork (plate 86), in that the blurred forms of much earlier cast work were avoided in favour of crisper contours and more naturalistic floral motifs, as in the products of Walter Macfarlane of Glasgow, one of the biggest suppliers from the 1850s onwards. Iron was also replacing lead for gutters and drainpipes, which were now also made into more of a decorative feature. Lead lived on, or was revived, chiefly in ornamental glazing in front doors (colour plate 19).[76]

Wood

Whereas there was little change in carpentry and joinery inside the house, the decline of wood outside had already begun in the seventeenth century, and it was phased out by successive Acts in London in the eighteenth century and in Newcastle in the nineteenth century. In many provincial towns ornate wooden door surrounds can be found until the early nineteenth century (plates 6, 153). Minor structural uses continued in the provinces, and wooden lintels can sometimes be found until the end of the century; in Ipswich they remain general for small houses until after 1850. And, of course, wood remained behind paint and stucco in the innumerable smaller Brighton bay windows. Often wood was substituted for iron in Regency verandahs (plate 215). Lower prices generally after the 1870s and the already mentioned great advances in machine sawing did not seem to outweigh the unpopularity of wooden decor on the outside. One of the few elements which must be mentioned here are the bay windows which could be bought from big firms 'ready for fixing',[77] and they are fairly common in small to medium-sized houses in Birmingham, Leicester and elsewhere. There is the occasional elaboration of wooden panelling surrounding front doors, in the style of the heavily panelled door itself (plate 210).[78] It was in the smallest houses that wooden decor continued, as with the simple sloping roof over the door placed in somewhat rickety fashion over two simple brackets. By about 1850 this was phased out and later doors for small houses are usually slender, with full pilasters, simplified capitals and a fairly heavy cornice (plate 174). Apart from the brick arch and some cheap stucco motifs this was the most frequent decoration for the small and medium-sized facade.

Only two areas remained surprisingly faithful to wood. Firstly, east Yorkshire, with York, Grimsby and especially Hull. Because of the shipbuilding tradition, carving was particularly strong here. There is an abundance of Neo-Classical woodwork.[79] By 1850–60 Classical severity had turned into mid-Victorian exuberance, as around Spring Bank (plate 209) and a little later Eldon Grove.

Colour plate 25 (above left). **London**, Matham Grove, SE22, 1880s. Late nineteenth-century London brickwork, in 'stock' bricks with yellow 'malm' arches, somewhat Gothic.

Colour plate 26 (above centre). **Great Yarmouth**, Palgrave Road, c. 1905. Edwardian Baroque in terracotta (probably supplied by Hathern Station Brick and Terracotta Company, Leicestershire).

Colour plate 27 (above right). **Manchester**, Lynn Street, 1880s. The pressed brick facing is locally called 'stock'. Red paint is commonly applied. The leading on the windows is more recent.

Colour plate 28. **Norwich**, Earlham Road, c. 1894. At the front/side are local 'Suffolk White' bricks and slates, and at the back are red bricks and local pan tiles. The contemporary houses opposite have red brick throughout (See p. 239).

Colour plate 29 (above left). **Reading**, Alexandra Road, semi-detached houses, *c.* 1870s. Apart from the red, yellow and black bricks (the latter probably Staffordshire 'Blues') there is the celebrated Reading 'Silver Grey'. (See also plates 171, 172.)

Colour plate 30 (above centre). **Reading**, River Road, late 1890s. A very individual motif on the side gable of a small house.

Colour plate 31 (above right). **Luton**, North Road, late 1880s. The great majority of houses in Luton are of purple brick with red trim, as in plate 32, but a few reverse this pattern.

Colour plate 32. **Luton**, Albert Road, 1890s.

209 (far left). **Hull.** Spring Back, *c.* 1870; carved woodwork and cast iron cresting.

210 (left). **Oldham.** Pitt Street, *c.* 1870–80. A door with unusual ornamentation of the door frame.

211 (below). **Sunderland.** Azalea Terrace, 1870s; castellated woodwork, an unusual form in that material and an unusual feature on a terraced house.

Porches and bays were equally affected (colour plate 8). To some extent, carving was replaced by a kind of *papier mâché* using wood powder, first used for interior work in the late eighteenth century. Perhaps designs were also burnt into wood.[80] The other region was Sunderland, where probably much the same conditions existed as in Hull. Again, one can observe the same transition from Neo-Classical bulk to mid-Victorian floral exuberance (plates 163, 211). More ornate wooden doors can be found in Darlington, South Shields (plate 105) and the Hartlepools.

The actual motifs of the decorations in Hull and Sunderland might be called old-fashioned. On the other hand, we are also entering a new phase stylistically: we have already discussed the new turn towards wooden eaves lines and gables, especially in the metropolis. By the 1870s and 1880s the heavy bargeboarded gable had percolated from the 'cottage ornée' via the villa (colour plate 20) and the semi-detached house down to many terraces in Harrogate, Sheffield,[81] Bristol and elsewhere (cf. plate 164). Verandahs seemed to be liked again in seaside towns, as in Egbert Road, Westgate-on-Sea in the 1880s. Greatly encouraged by the Domestic Revival, in conjunction with half-timbering, wood dominates larger houses around 1900 in Ramsgate, Brighton, Bournemouth and Southend (plate 146). Now, finally, lightness was a positive element again, and we are sometimes reminded of the Far East—or at least of the Far East flavour of Scheveningen.

16. The changing styles of the facade

By the employment of style in an edifice the Architect . . . gains a positive beauty at once, because thousands of spectators in Europe and America, for example, have some crude ideas of what is Grecian and what is Gothic . . . Style, therefore, ought never to be neglected by Architects who wish to gain general applause.

J. C. Loudon[1]

We have so far looked at the facades of terraced houses from two separate points of view; the broad division, or the composition, of an elevation, and the techniques of detailed decoration. But, of course, these two aspects need to be seen together. What determines the particular combination of composition and ornament in one facade, the underlying element in both the whole and its detail and even to some extent the choice of materials, can be termed 'style'. Each terraced facade can thus be categorized according to a style or a mixture of styles. There are two kinds of style: those which denote the particular period of the nineteenth century, like Regency or Mid-Victorian, and those signifying a style of the past which was imitated in the nineteenth century, like Neo-Classical or Queen Anne Revival. Any investigation of nineteenth-century architecture needs to consider both.

However, in the definition of 'style' generally there is considerable breadth and controversy. What Loudon wanted to pinpoint was the general availability of a small set of features which added a pleasant variety and could be easily applied to any building; it also meant that the underlying structure did not need much adjustment. It was a view particularly prevalent in the early and middle nineteenth century and emphasizes the symbolic, historical, message of each individual motif; you attach, for example, a pointed arch somewhere, and the building conjures up the later Middle Ages—a practice which was particularly widespread with medium-sized villas and cottages.

Classical, Neo-Classical, Regency, Neo-Renaissance

For our terraces we need a wider and more thorough definition of 'style', which concerns both the underlying division and the added ornamentation. This is specially relevant for Classical facades. What Georgian and most Regency facades were really based on was the principle of the column. The ordinary Georgian facade, where no actual columns appear, is a perfect example of what we mean by the 'underlying division'. The low rusticated ground floor represents, in character and proportion, the pedestal of the column and the base of the temple; the column, the Order, is represented by the main floor and the small floor above. Then follows an actual part of the Classical decoration, the cornice; and above it the blocking course, or a further small storey, corresponds at least vaguely to the frieze or the gable. In addition there were, of course, smaller features like the ornamental doorway, which could be put on or left off, according to finance or inclination in each case (e.g. plates 1, 2).

The term 'Classical architecture' refers to a long tradition of designing and building, influenced by Italy and France. Sorting out the precise contributions of each period is an extremely complicated undertaking for the historian. So much of nineteenth-century architecture is simply part of an unreflecting Classical tradition, which in England goes back to the sixteenth and seventeenth centuries. When, for instance, a trade and teaching manual like Charles F. Mitchell's *Building Construction and Drawing*, in the edition of 1902, says: 'Most groups of mouldings used by the joiner consist of combinations of some of the Greek or of the eight Roman examples . . .',[2] this is still part of that tradition (plate 210), which carried on in joinery into the 1930s or even 1940s. Similar traditions carried through the nineteenth century in the proportioning of windows, and in the use of rustication. The most basic element was of course, the overall orderly and symmetrical layout, which everybody strived so hard to achieve; a surveyor in the Norfolk Estate in London stipulated it as late as 1881.[3]

In the eighteenth century the English Palladian movement—the middle and later Georgians, if we talk about urban houses—also insisted on overall coordination, but more specifically prescribed decoration for the centre and end blocks of a terrace or a country house, whereas in between too much detailed decoration was felt to be distracting. Thus one of their main contributions was to draw the eye to the merits of broad sweeps of wall surface, with windows cut in simply and sharply. These walls could, as we have seen, be faced with smooth ashlar (e.g. plate 2), with smooth, regularly laid 'white', or 'grey' brick (e.g. plate 191), or with even smoother stucco (e.g. plate 176), usually painted cream to represent the best kinds of stone.

But already by the end of the eighteenth century fashions were changing rapidly. Robert Adam denounced the eternal repetition of the same traditional Classical elements (plate 9). Neo-Classicism meant, first of all, a more intensive study of the actual monuments of antiquity, and this meant greater variety, of Orders and of decoration. Architects and critics liked to cite more precise precedents for their buildings; for instance, Elmes speaks of 'Paestum Doric'[4] for Nash's Ulster Terrace (plate 112). Neo-Classicism meant, secondly, in most cases a tendency towards greater massiveness, towards greater plastic accentuation of the facade; it was 'movement' which seemed so desirable in the great facades of Nash and of Kemp, in Brunswick Square in Brighton and in Cheltenham. This new desire for 'power' and strong accentuation cannot, however, simply be classified as Neo-Classicism: it stems also from the new English eighteenth-century aesthetic of the Picturesque and Sublime (plates 111, 117, 120, 132). And there we run into a further complication of the definition of style: these new basic aesthetic concepts—the first signifying, broadly, variety, the second, powerful size—were not only applied to Classical buildings, but to other styles as well, including Gothic.

From the 1830s we begin to move gently from Regency to Early Victorian. Elmes already frequently mentions 'Italian'; it became an important label, but was even less specific than 'Classical'. What it basically meant was the abandonment of the Giant Classical orders in favour of a multitude of smaller Classical decorative appendages (e.g. plate 137). 'Astylar' was another word which covered the same process. The great model of all 'astylar' buildings of the early and mid-Victorian periods was Charles Barry's Reform Club of 1837, which meant that the main precedent was no longer Classical Antiquity, but the Italian Renaissance of the sixteenth century. The main stress of the elevations is no longer the vertical Order of columns and pilasters, but the horizontal cornice, or a multitude of cornices (plates 43, 140). It was felt that the growing number of storeys in a Victorian terrace could be more easily decorated by horizontal divisions than by vertical ones. Exactly the same problems were experienced by the designers of the new large commercial structures and hotels. In addition, decor was lavished around windows and doors; the tops of the facades were crowned by balustrades. On the whole, straight contours and flat surfaces were to be avoided; Georgian and much of Regency architecture was thought to be monotonous. Again, stucco decoration, the new kinds of more durable cements, as well as the countless kinds of ornaments in baked earth, came in extremely useful. However, on the whole they were still covered by paint, which still unified the facades, at least in their colour. It was only after 1850 that brick and brick ornaments were again exposed in their natural colours.

By that date we are moving, equally gradually, into the mid-Victorian period. The variety of motifs used grew steadily. Increasingly, forms from the Mannerist period—of Italian or Northern origin, or both—were taken up. A riot of all-Classical motifs, many of them impossible to label properly, is presented in the 1860s and 1870s in terraces like Warrior Gardens in Hastings (plate 143). When it comes to further varieties of style, a more fruitful field would be the villa, or the country house. But occasionally terraces adopt special styles on their facades. The Royal Promenade in Bristol verges on the Quattrocento, or even the Romanesque or 'Rundbogenstil'; and there are examples of Elizabethan or Jacobean detailing in Prince Albert Road on the north side of Regent's Park, in the 1840s and 1850s. Another generally Northern motif was the curved or 'Dutch' gable (plate 145).[5] In the 1860s we encounter the 'Second Empire' mode, chiefly consisting of a revival, by the second Napoleon in France, of the French Baroque motif of the mansarded roof (plate 144).[6] Occasionally, the Neo-Rococo, so popular in interior decoration, found its way on to the facade (plate 43). Finally there is the rustic variety of the 'Italian', meaning an imitation of the rougher and more massive treatment of Italian country villas, 'simple, bold and massive' as James Hole termed it in 1866.[7] An example of terraces under the influence of this trend was Knowles's work at Clapham Common in 1860. Iron was not liked for a while because it looked thin.

Gothic

The most important challenge to the superiority of Classical styles came with the Gothic revival. It was' .. calculated for producing emotion ...', Loudon[8] maintained, like so many other early writers on Gothic. But no other type of building adopted Gothic in such a modest fashion as the terrace. Charming, rather than dramatic, one might call the 'Gothick' decor over the doors in Byrom Street, Manchester, on what are otherwise quite normal Georgian Classical terraced houses of the early nineteenth century. Nevertheless, a small, but distinguished number of larger Gothic terraces of individual, one-off designs, were built between the 1820s and 1860s. There was St. Mary's Place of 1827 by John Dobson, next to his ingenious Gothic St. Thomas's church in Newcastle, or Queen's Terrace, Exeter, somewhat later: both rely largely on Tudor square hoodmoulds over the windows as well as gables, which were the most frequent motifs of the early Gothic Revival. The same applies to the terraces on Clarence and Wellington Squares in Cheltenham of the 1840s (plate 134). There are lesser Gothic terraces in Herne Bay and Tunbridge Wells. It must be stressed that all these terraces show a Gothic dress on a basic Georgian–Classical structure. Much more original is Chartham Terrace of 1850, next to Pugin's own church at Ramsgate, with its steep, cottagy roof; did the great master have a hand in its design? Perhaps his son Edward was involved with the spectacular Gothic terrace in Albert Road, also in Ramsgate, of the 1860s. Above all Gothic meant variety and movement; the straight contour and flat facade were condemned. Bay windows and gables were basically there for their picturesque qualities.

From about the 1860s smaller Gothic elements or Gothic-derived elements were on the increase, especially the ubiquitous flat segmental arch, often placed on top of a stretch of vertical frame, and thus called a stilted segmental arch (plate 144, cf. 106). There was also the pointed segmental arch, especially frequent in Birkenhead. The actual pointed arch is not so often met with, though there are many late nineteenth-century examples in Cardiff. Furthermore there is much leaf carving, which does not resemble any standard Classical forms. Occasionally some areas, like south London around the Crystal Palace, or Upper Tollington Park in north London of around 1880, show more Gothic elements than usual (cf. colour plate 23).

But there is more to Gothic than arches and gables. From about the 1860s there is a new preference for slenderness generally, especially in bay windows. There is no doubt about their stability, because all forms fit into a clear vertical framework (e.g. plates 145, 160). On the other hand, the solid look of a continuous wall surface is also stressed. In the 1860s and 1870s larger terraces and villas generally avoided too many openings in the facade at the expense of solid walls. In stone areas there was a turn towards a coarser kind of rubble work, which included substantial houses where previously one would not have avoided the extra expense of ashlaring (e.g. colour plate 15). This preference for the 'natural'—another example is the stress on undisguised brick—was also part of the Italian 'rustic' style. Most decorative features are now set neatly flush with the surface of the wall, neither projecting nor receding (e.g. plates 160, 197). This has, again, practical and economic advantages, but also conforms to High Victorian preferences for flat pattern design, as first expounded in the writings of Ruskin and the buildings of Butterfield. Likewise the tendency to contrast the colours and textures of different materials, which in ordinary houses came to the fore in the 1880s, sprang directly from the theories of Pugin and Ruskin, and from the work of the High Victorian Gothic church architects, with whom it was already out of fashion by that time (colour plate 20). As regards small-scale decoration like that on friezes and many capitals, on the face of arches and elsewhere, the tendency was also towards abstraction, with stylized floral patterns, leaves and so on (plate 185). They were based on Neo-Classical Greek flat pattern design *à la* John Soane or Thomas Hope, and later on Pugin's and Henry Shaw's Gothic, as well as on the flat-pattern theories of the South Kensington decorative designers, like Owen Jones, R. Redgrave, Christopher Dresser, and many others (plates 184, 198, colour plate 20).

Late Victorian mixed styles

Clearly, by this time it is hard to distinguish properly between the different Revivals; also the distinction drawn earlier between fundamental and superficial definitions of 'style' hardly applies any more. For better houses, villas, and country houses, but also in most commercial structures, there was no agreement as to the most suitable single style and thus many styles were amalgamated or just set side by side as in East Park Parade, Northampton. It must be remembered, though, that for most provincial terraces, as well as for most provincial minor villas and country houses, the early and mid-Victorian versions of the Classical carried on into the 1880s and 1890s.

The influence of Gothic was still on the increase, though mixed with Italian, Elizabethan and other Northern Renaissance elements, and the 'cottagy' style, which expressed itself largely in the increase of wood on the facade, on gables, or for roofs over doors. The neo-Adam style and the Japanese style of the 1870s and 1880s mainly concerned the interior, though some Far Eastern influence can perhaps be detected in external woodwork, especially balconies, around 1900. Art Nouveau elements can be found in the ornamental leadwork of doors of 1900 and later, though this is of minor importance when compared with the blossoming of this style in the villas of many Continental countries. Edwardian Baroque occasionally left traces, such as the flat oval window or bulgy pilasters (cf. colour plate 26).[9]

There were two principal new styles for domestic architecture. The Queen Anne Revival began in the 1860s and blossomed in the 1870s and 1880s. On a simple level, it concerned itself with the combination of Gothic verticality with Classical detail. It also revived the custom of the all-red-brick facade. Wooden parts, in contrast, were painted a strong white. But 'Queen Anne' also works on a more sophisticated level: not the most competent, elegant and 'correct' examples of the past are revived, but the quaint, or the curiously proportioned features. In that sense the Revival remained the realm of the better London architects and some of the best provincial practitioners, and also of some of the largest west London speculative houses (plate 145, cf. colour plate 7) but rarely of smaller houses (cf. plate 56).[10]

The companion movement, so to speak, of the Queen Anne style, was the Old English Revival. It concerned itself with crude-looking half-timbering, tile-hung and rough stone walls. Like 'Queen Anne', it took its models not from the major structures of the past, but from medium-rank and minor country houses. A kind of manor-house look was adopted, in conjunction with the most rambling kinds of plans and vast, complicated roofs. Both revivals are also called vernacular revivals, and they are linked with the new attitudes to domestic planning and design of the Domestic Revival.

Again, not much of the Old English could be transferred to the ordinary terrace facade, though there are some examples of very large terraces in Bristol (colour plate 15), Scarborough, and Brighton[11] attempting to vary the facade relief in the most forceful way with a tremendous display of porches, bays and balconies. Smaller versions of this manner can be found in Muswell Hill (plate 168). However, there are a few elements in which the late Victorian Picturesque—to use yet another label— influenced the ordinary medium-sized terrace in order to give the houses individuality. The vast majority of gables on these houses are no longer built just in brick or stone, but are either timber-framed or tile-hung, or completely covered with roughcast. Timber-framing begins to appear in speculative houses in the 1880s[12] and is frequent by the 1890s; tile-hanging probably began in the 1890s and can universally be found after 1900 (plate 165). Roughcast occurs mostly in the infill between the wood. It is hard to distinguish whether the details of this work stem from the 1870s 'Old English', or from the earlier cottage revivals. But the way they were adopted by builders for medium-sized speculative houses was undoubtedly prompted by the fashionable suburban country houses by Norman Shaw and others. Of course, there was still a long way to go to the 'semis' of the interwar period; proportions were still generally slender, there were still large sash-window and much applied ornament; the overall effect of the house could hardly be called 'cottagy'. But after about 1905 half-timbering increased, and a sub-Voysey kind of pebble-dash (plate 168), covering large parts of the facade, became more frequent. For at least sixty years the Georgian style had been fiercely condemned as monotonous, but by 1910 we are, finally, back to the style we began with. The Neo-Georgian meant a new emphasis on repetition, simplicity and horizontality.[13] Significantly, the now more individualized speculative house was not yet to be touched by this new style.

No doubt a closer search will reveal examples of all the revivals of the nineteenth century in our terraces. Yet the general run of speculative developers did not want to commit themselves to a detailed symbolism, apart from those in the Classical style. There are few proper Gothic terraces with pointed arches, because builders did not want their houses to look like churches. There was rarely time for a 'battle of styles', or for the persistent questioning of style which Robert Kerr undertook in his book on the individualized detached house. Nevertheless, the underlying ideas of the Picturesque and of some aspects of the Gothic Revival were as important and influential on the terraced houses as they were in every other type of architecture in England. We shall come back to them in the next chapter.

17. Social and architectural hierarchy

No rule can be laid down by which the different classes of dwellings can be accurately separated and defined; yet there is, and ought to be, a general feeling of propriety as to the character which each should possess.

T. Webster & Mrs. W. Parkes[1]

Architectural taste, like manners, travels downwards.

H. J. Dyos[2]

Art in our houses is so helpless and hopeless . . . Our wealth, instead of helping us, may be the cause of failure . . . We think our position in society requires a certain amount of display . . . The variety of our knowledge confuses us.

J. J. Stevenson, 1880[3]

Class differentiation, ornament and style

Throughout this book we have dealt, explicitly or implicitly, with the hierarchical division of society. It was normally a simple economic equation which expressed itself by the end of the nineteenth century in finely differentiated sizes of houses, with equally carefully calculated rentals. We must now turn to some more socio-historical elements of class-structure. On the whole, the gap between rich and poor was widening in the nineteenth century. But there were also now more steps on the social ladder, and the steps came at smaller intervals. More and more sub-groups desired to set themselves above the next group down, as in the case of the 'middle'-middle classes and the lower clerks; or the higher-paid artisans and the poorer unskilled working classes. On the whole, divisions by pay replaced the earlier pattern of divisions by trade.[4]

What interests us here is how architectural elements, that is, elements of facade composition and decoration, or the type of dwelling (as opposed to the size), express this social hierarchy and the changes within the hierarchy. A distinction has to be drawn from the outset: between the purely economic correspondence of such-and-such an income with such-and-such a type of house on the one hand, and, on the other hand, a more arbitrary correspondence of status and style. The former remains the same; the latter can change.

The prevailing opinion was that, in every respect, each class should keep to itself as much as possible; and the system of many continental cities, where several classes lived literally on top of each other, was despised and held to cause 'distress and shame'.[5] Earlier, the large London Estates usually had pockets of low-class inhabitants, traders or craftsmen. In the nineteenth century the estate planners tried to carefully contain these classes, by allocating special streets for them, as in the unexecuted plan by Charles Barry for a large estate in Hove in the 1820s,[6] or by moving them out altogether. We have mentioned the meticulous wording of the restrictive covenants to exclude almost all kinds of trade. Later on, the solution was thought to be suburban travel: improved houses for the lower classes and the same, plus seclusion, for the better classes. We can often see attempts to separate the classes as much as possible by the way streets are actually cut off by a wall, or laid out so as not to connect where one would expect them to.[7] The notion of a street as the shortest connection between A and B, to be used by everybody, could still not be taken for granted. Very occasionally there is even a dividing wall running along the back lane between houses of a different class.[8] It was exceedingly rare later on in the century to alternate substantially the sizes of houses within one street or one area; although one might have thought this to be advantageous from the point of view of a quick sale. In the end, it was the class-homogeneity of a street which was its most saleable element. A change of class meant moving house, moving into another district. Mobility was extremely high. Conversely, it could be the district that was moving downwards in class; again one had to move, 'as soon as the brass handle was tarnished'.[9] Neighbours had to be of the same class, or better.

However, all this is of interest chiefly to the historian of towns, while the architectural historian is more concerned with the way the houses are contrasted when they are in close juxtaposition—though as we shall see, the growing separation in space was itself to have an effect on the style of the houses.

The stress on propriety, on decorum, was universal. As Mark Girouard writes,[10] the rules of good society became stricter so that they did not get blurred with the increased mobility between classes; and we have seen that some of the agreements for middling houses in the middle of the century contain more stipulations than those for the best houses, to make doubly sure that 'standards' were kept, the standards at each level of the hierarchy. Similarly, the attempts to differentiate room use appeared more insistent with smaller houses. Standards were concerned with housing, with entertainment, with dress, and even the spread of cooking appliances, which was, according to Ravetz, 'more than anything else a sign of social emulation'.[11] Differences tended to be exaggerated. The author's own street in Norwich was held to be 'decidedly superior' to the one around the corner, although rentals were only 10s more, £9 rather than £8 10s. The only significant difference is in the plan, in that there are more tunnels to the back and thus a greater degree of privacy in the £9 street (cf. plate 37). Thus there were two important aspects of the process of class differentiation: standards did travel downwards, because of rapidly increasing wealth; but once achieved, they were 'kept up' strenuously, even jealously.

As was remarked in the first chapter, there was no status differentiation in the type as such, its basic plan remaining the same for all classes; but there were a host of other possibilities. We can begin with the layout, with the very names of the streets: 'road' being superior to 'street'; and 'place', 'crescent' and some others being reserved for the best developments, at least earlier on. The size of the house and the size of the plot were, of course, obvious indicators of wealth, whereas height underwent a change to which we shall come back. The most important traditional quantitative element is the amount of decoration. Because this seemed so obvious, the traditional Renaissance demand for keeping the hierarchy of decorum is seldom restated. Apart from Webster, whom we quoted at the beginning of this chapter, we can cite Hole where he comments on a new Model Lodging House for the Poor in Leeds: 'no attempt was made at architectural effect, such as would frighten at the very entrance those whom the home was intended to benefit'.[12] Throughout his book Webster tried his utmost to pinpoint what is 'high' and what is 'low'.

212. **Preston**, doorways: various stages of elaboration of Neo-Classical motifs, according to the size of the house.
Left to right:
Ribblesdale Place, *c.* 1840s.
Chaddock Street, *c.* 1850s.
Kingswood Street, late nineteenth century.
Avenham Road, *c.* 1860–80.

Traditionally the widest scale of differentiation can perhaps be found in joinery with its endless variation of ornament, especially mouldings. In the later nineteenth-century stone door surrounds of Preston, one sees a very full hierarchy, from the most elaborate Classical versions in Ribblesdale Place to their abstracted imitations in the smallest houses (plate 212). Most specifications would use terms like 'best', 'good' and 'common' work, which often corresponds to actual price scales. Then there are the different forms of construction. According to Webster, low segmental brick arches are 'ordinary', and flat camber arches are 'best'. Short, square, yellow chimney tops are preferred to long, round, red ones. In London and Bristol there was—as we have seen—the hierarchy of alignment of the facade openings (plates 40–1). In London this hierarchy was strictly adhered to until the later part of the nineteenth century, whereas the situation in the eighteenth century appears to have been much less clear.

There was also the most minute differentiation of brickwork. According to Simon, Class I houses had to have all exterior walls of 'best picked grey stock brick' and 'all arches with malm bricks and gaged', Class II: 'best grey stock bricks', 'the arches to be gaged'; Class III: the same as regards bricks, but differences in pointing; Class IV: 'best hard stock bricks'—and nothing more. By the 1870s this sounded rather old-fashioned and in the 1880s the Noel Park Estate in north London adopted a differentiation by colour of brick: fronts wholly red; fronts partially grey stocks; fronts wholly grey stocks with red trimmings only. Although these scales seemed generally adhered to in London, it is difficult to find coherent patterns everywhere. Charting consistent class differentiation, for instance with the help of Booth's famous maps of London streets according to classes, is very difficult. Clearly, it was the kind of carefully planned large estate, like Noel Park and like previous workers' colonies, such as Saltaire, where consistency is most likely to be found. There are some larger towns with a strong degree of estate control throughout, like Cardiff. In the late nineteenth-century area around Cathedral Road, the largest houses show careful rubble facing on front and sides. The medium-sized houses in the side streets show the same sort of work on their fronts, but their sides are only faced with good bricks. Then the smallest houses, in the side streets off other side streets, show similar good bricks on their fronts only. Another method was the variation of the depth of the front garden. One can observe their gradual scaling down as one goes southwards from the best areas in Princes Road, Liverpool, towards the poorer area of Park Road. Finally, there was what the inhabitants themselves could do to make their houses look more ornamental and 'respectable': cleaning the steps, whitening the sills, polishing the brass hook, or painting it if it was made of cast iron. Ornaments placed on the window sill inside can function as ornaments for the street.

The most straightforward 'class' contrast was that which occurred within every house itself: the contrast between its front and its back. We have already discussed many aspects of the front–back divide: the polite street front versus the common yard; the parlour and drawing-room versus the service and servants' quarters. 'Queen Anne front and Mary Ann back' had been a saying for some time; and we concluded in the chapter on changes in plan and use of the house that this contrast had, if anything, increased during the Victorian period (plates 6, 7, 44–5, 117). There is certainly nothing more confusing than the occasional break with this principle, as for instance in Bolton, where many stone lintels at the rear are painted like those on the front. We have also mentioned the difficulties builders usually had with finding a solution for the sides of the building, though many later houses carefully differentiate between *three* grades of material for front, side and back.[13]

There were many ways of providing a contrast. Between about the 1830s and the 1880s, many smaller houses in Norwich adopted modern sashes for the front, but kept old-fashioned casements for the back. Also in Norwich, slates never managed to phase out pantiles entirely, so most of the backs kept them, but covenants for most houses above the smallest size usually specified slates for the front (colour plate 28). Those houses with pantiles at the front and the back differentiate them by colour, dark ones for the front and lighter ones for the back. In rubble stonework there was an endless scale of degrees of working. We have cited examples in Harrogate, and even the smallest, late nineteenth-century houses in Burnley, Huddersfield and Accrington explore these methods (plates 188–9, colour plate 10).

The most effective contrasts occur in brickwork. Differentiation is almost a foregone conclusion, because bricks were always produced in a range of qualities. The nineteenth century added variety of colour. In East Anglia, white brick was fashionable between 1830 and 1890. It was somewhat more expensive than red and was thus used for fronts only. Sometimes, when a chimney was seen from the front and from one other side as well, both these sides would be of white brick, the others, like the back of the whole house, being of red brick. Shortly after came — in Norwich, as elsewhere — a return to red brick for the front, and there is no more colour contrast (colour plate 28). Lowestoft and Cambridge differed from Norwich, in that there did not seem to be a price difference between red and white, and thus most houses show white brick on all sides. Later on, in Lowestoft, as elsewhere, the new fashion for red led to some facing with good red bricks, while the back of the house remained white. Thus we have the reverse of the pattern in Norwich earlier on. The situation in London was somewhat different, and the question how much of the methods of differentiation between the houses of various classes were used for the contrast between back and front needs further investigation. Later on, all better houses have red brick facades, and smaller houses red trimmings around windows and corners. Luton seems to correspond to the London patterns in that the facing brick for all sides of the house is different from the walling brick: inferior purple for the back and sides, and selected purple for the front. In later houses in the north there is invariably a neat red or yellow facing, contrasting strongly with the more drab general walling brick at the back (colour plate 27). In the case of the small Liverpool houses with Ruabon 'premier vitrified buff bricks' for the front, the extra cost of these special bricks was around £1.50, within a total building cost of £100 (plate 92). Decoration was no longer expensive.

It can probably be said that, at least in the case of the smaller house, the contrast between front and back was the most important rationale in the design of the outside of the house. The growing desire to accentuate class differences and the growing variety and availability of materials reinforced each other. But there was also a fundamental change in the relationship between status and colour: with the earlier method there was a desire to hide what was considered an inferior colour, whereas the later method exploited colour variety for its own sake, not only in the contrast between facade and back, but also on the facade itself (e.g. colour plate 29). The result was that the facade–back contrast was often blurred, and by the end of the nineteenth century was largely given up. Another reason was, of course, the change of use at the back.

The relationship between social class and architectural treatment was in fact becoming extremely complicated and even contradictory. Traditionally there was a natural hierarchy of size, of the amount of decor, of the degrees of competence on the part of the designer and builder. As this hierarchy was weakened, deliberately devised methods of differentiation were used. The increase in the front–back contrast is probably a result of this development. The same can probably be said of the continuation of the curious London pattern of lack of alignment for the lower classes of houses—a measure that seemed especially necessary in the metropolis, where the danger of blurring the borderlines between classes seemed more acute than in the provinces.

On the other hand, there was also an actual trend towards the evening out of differences. We have discussed the convergence of plan types, as regards size and sanitary facilities at the lower end of the social scale. We have traced the development of the facade of the smallest house, which had been non-existent earlier. By 1900 all small houses, even the smallest types such as back-to-backs, show relatively well-proportioned facades, faced with a better material. There is universal disapproval of the drab look of earlier working-class districts. The *Cost of Living Report* at one point actually says that 'the small, old houses . . . are . . . generally too poor in character to be considered as typical working class dwellings'.[14] Ornamentation of working-class block dwellings was considered by some to be 'a wise expenditure all round'.[15] and in 1886 C. B. Allen felt he had to add a chapter on matters artistic to a new edition of his cheap practical book *Cottage Building.*

We can trace this rise of the small dwelling further back. In his book *Model Houses for the Industrial Classes* of 1871 Banister Fletcher was not just concerned with salubrity and cheapness but also with privacy and comfort, which, he argues, the working class deserved as much as anybody else. We have already quoted the builder Dudley on his flats in terraced houses. Both argue against high blocks and courts. While for the later London standard house there were still some elements of class differentiation on the facade, such as the one-storey bay window and lack of alignment for the smallest type, the 'cottage flats' looked almost exactly like the better two-storey-bay-window medium standard houses (colour plates 1, 11). And we have seen how by the late nineteenth century the old distinctions between Class I and Classes II–III were blurred, as the latter also 'acquired' alignment for its facade. The distinction of the *piano nobile* had also been given up. Fletcher stresses himself that his proposed cottage flats looked identical with the 'residence of some respectable member of the lower middle classes . . . which effect is further supported by a low dwarf wall in front with stone coping surmounted by simple iron bar and standards' (plate 110).[16] We have noticed in Leeds the way each area adopts the whole range of English street names—road, place, crescent, etc.—for the same sort of houses makes nonsense of the hierarchy of those terms. And while as regards their size and outline the cottage flats *pretend* to be the same as the standard medium-sized house, the amount and the style of the external decoration *is* the same.

All this can be contrasted with cases from the decades before where we find just

213. **Plymouth.** Benbow Street, Devonport, *c.* 1870s; medium-sized houses with solitary piers reminiscences of grand terraces.

214. **Portsmouth.** Somerset Road, Southsea. The facades were added some time around 1850s onto cottages built in the 1830s. This probably took place when the larger and smarter stuccoed houses in adjacent Beach Road were built.

the occasional token of decor derived from much larger houses, like the curious single pilasters in Tidy Street, Brighton, or Benbow Street, Plymouth (plate 213). Very occasionally small houses are hidden behind incongruously rich facades, as in Somerset Road, Southsea (plate 214). Akroyd describes a case where his own workers at first tried to argue against the 'paternalism' of gables with which their employer was to ornament their houses in Halifax. By the later nineteenth century the decoration of small houses — as that of larger houses — formed much more a part of the structure as a whole. There was a change towards a more rationalist approach, which cannot any longer be understood by studying the amount of decoration in the different strata of houses, nor by investigating the varying degrees of competence in the application of ornament; but another element must be brought in at this point: changes in style.

As we know, styles changed with increasing rapidity. Sometimes this could even affect the economic performance of a development, as in the 1880s in Queens Gate, when more modern Queen-Anne-type houses sold more quickly than old-fashioned stucco ones, some of which later received a Queen Anne facing.[17] Slightly larger houses in later normal London suburban areas, such as in Seven Kings, Ilford, adopted the 'new', informal, cottage tile-hanging for parts of their facade, while the smaller houses nearby clung to brick-colour decoration. On the other hand, run-of-the-mill houses rarely adopt the more extreme varieties of the new revivals, but plan and elevation changed in more general terms and this was related to the more fundamental ideals of the revivals.

We must recapitulate the development of the hierarchy of decorum so far. Most notable was the increase of decoration at its lower end. Indeed, a working-class house in 1900 usually showed more decoration than that of a middle-class house in 1800, or at least as much. The history of the terraced house in the nineteenth century could almost be summed up by saying simply that the house remained the same but the class of its inhabitants changed. This seemed the logical outcome of the fact that in most ways its occupier was as well or better off. It was also the result of some modes of decoration having become cheaper. But by eliminating the simple and primitive house at the bottom of the hierarchy, the logic of the whole system had been upset. What was to be done? A totally new set of criteria emerged: radical simplicity and the greatest apparent solidity.

The simplicity of English Palladian and Neo-Classical architecture was already based on the rejection of exuberant decoration; the way decoration was handled by the Baroque was felt to be lacking order and seriousness. The medium-sized, plain-fronted Georgian town-house also came low in the hierarchy of decoration. On the other hand, it is misleading to insist too much on the simplicity of the Georgian houses — as has so often been done in this century — as they are mostly bound into a larger, stately whole, and because the regularity of the facade required a great degree of expensive organization and craftsmanship. The sudden rise of decoration for this kind of house after 1815 can again be explained by the general increase in wealth and the availability of cheaper materials, as well as the purely aesthetic demand for greater variety of surface forms. Perhaps increased competition also called for more 'advertising' externally. However, criticism set in almost immediately. Nash had already censured recent developments on the Portland Estate for bad workmanship hidden behind lavish facades,[18] a criticism soon to be levelled against his own work. The article in the *Surveyor, Engineer and Architect* of 1841 used the most vitriolic language against Nash and others. 'Trumpery' became a fashionable word. Gradually terms of esteem such as taste, beauty, respectability and even gentlemanliness became associated with chastity, simplicity and 'truth'. It was felt that grand decorations, pilasters, pediments and the like ought not to be found on private houses, but only on public buildings. Too much ornament was liable to be considered showy and vulgar. Like many others, Stevenson regretted that the hierarchy of decorum had been upset, '. . . the foolish desire to be grander than we really are'.[19] The most drastic result of all this was the almost complete phasing out of external stucco in London by the 1870s and 1880s and in Brighton by *c.* 1890. Areas like Cliftonville, Hove, with its yellow brick throughout, or the huge terrace in Bath stone, Cambridge Gate of 1875, rudely interrupting Nash's stucco in Regent's Park, must be seen as protests against plaster. Walsh proposed his largest model house with an all-brick front in the 'solid Italian style'.

It seems clear that, at first, 'genuineness' was reserved for the best class of buildings. Webster is still ambiguous; on the one hand he recommends many kinds of substitutes, like 'graining' (i.e. painting wood to look like oak), yet all 'good work ought to be genuine'.[20] Talking about deception, the *Builder* of 1869 says that stucco decoration in smaller houses is 'not altogether to be despised', but with 'all buildings of a high class . . . the rules ought to be like the Dekalogue: thou shall not . . .'.[21] Yet, like everything else, this new concept had already begun to travel down the social ladder. Jennie Calder quotes from the *Ladies Cabinet* of 1844 a remark that 'humble dwellings' should observe 'simplicity and good taste, superior to silly ambition'.

It was the Gothic Revivalists from Pugin onwards, as well as the South Kensington theorists and designers with their strict views on flat pattern decoration, who most strenuously insisted on rationalism, or 'truth' in decoration. Moreover, to Pugin and Butterfield truth was closely related to propriety and both insisted on the most minute differentiation of status in their churches, schools and houses. But there is a decisive difference between their hierarchy and the traditional one, which was still voiced so clearly by Webster in those same years: the lowest and simplest buildings in the hierarchy, like cottages and stables, exist in their own right. They are not just 'common' and undeserving of notice; they can be considered beautiful and visually attractive, because they are handled truthfully, like all the other grades, and because of the new and increased liking for colours, surfaces and materials for their own sake, something in which all buildings take part. Most Victorian paternalistic cottage-estates stress the simple but solid. Of course, as we have demonstrated, later Victorian small urban houses are no longer simple but rather ornate. But what matters most in this context is that the decoration does not amount to a paternalistic crumb, like one pilaster, or a couple of scrolls. Nor does it imitate higher-class decorations in cheap and crumbling materials; instead the decoration forms part of the essential structure, as in the new houses of the class above, conforming to the modern notions of 'truth to construction'. Ernst Gombrich explains in *The Sense of Order*, as Thorstein Veblen did earlier on, how time and again the lower classes, or the nouveaux riches, had imitated high-class ornament and exaggerated its forms, only to be subsequently condemned as lacking taste and solidity. The new situation in the later nineteenth century was that the lower classes with their rich decoration could no longer be accused of lack of solidity. There was no need to hide anything any more (cf. plate 214). The meaning of 'respectability' had now been extended, as the *Oxford Dictionary* put it: '*Respectable* of persons: of good or fair social standing and having the moral qualities appropriate to this. Hence, in later use, honest and decent in character or conduct, without reference to social position, or in spite of being in humble circumstances.' Rationalism was among these new classless virtues, as was cleanliness; no-one could afford to neglect these.

This is not to claim that the old dialectic was completely phased out; it might still apply to other fields of design, such as furniture, where a simple but solid piece could

215. **Ramsgate.** Spencer Square, *c.* 1820–30. It must be remembered that the great majority of developments before about the middle of the nineteenth century did not achieve a great deal of regularity, be it through slow progress, lack of initiative and control, or both.

be contrasted with one that was ornate but flimsily made. But in building this contrast was now less likely to be met with. Doubtless bad building still occurred, but generally a high degree of cheapness *and* solidity in construction seems to have been reached. Walls thicker than the standard 'byelaw' wall were not necessarily better walls in all respects. Much of the new solid look of the facade was just a new kind of facing of standard construction.

Mark Girouard has summarized the changing relationship between the upper and the middle classes. In the face of rapidly growing middle-class success through industry and intelligence, the upper classes could no longer afford to present an image of idleness and profligacy.[22] In addition there was the threat from the lowest orders, especially in the 1840s, and thus the upper classes 'came down' to the middle classes in adopting their virtues of 'respectability', while imparting to the middle classes some of the older elements of 'respectability', or nobility, be it through intermarriage or in the form of richly appointed houses. In a similar way the second half of the nineteenth century saw an adoption of the supposed virtues of the lower classes, like thrift and simplicity, by the middle classes, while the lower classes, in turn, adopted some middle-class trappings of wealth.

It must, finally, be stressed here that this new richness of the facade of the small house differs in many respects from the new richness in other types of buildings, mainly frequented by the lower classes, the pubs and music halls. Here, a different set of values was in operation; the stress was not on rationalism and order but on entertainment, on gaiety; there was, for instance, a far greater amount of figurative decoration on these buildings. As regards the streets with smaller houses, the Georgian ideals of strict proportion and order, ultimately derived from the ideal towns of the Renaissance, continued to be influential until after 1900. The street, the public space, newly achieved for the lower classes, seemed to demand this kind of order.

The general ordering of the facades of small houses around 1900 in Preston, Swansea and Reading dates back several centuries. More specifically, the doorways of Preston and the stucco vermiculation in Swansea can be traced back at least to Neo-Classicism or the Neo-Renaissance (see Chapter 16); and the polychromy of the Reading facades to the 1850s. Can these elements be called 'popular art' — inasmuch as by that date the middle classes no longer availed themselves of these styles?

Fashions kept changing relentlessly. Very soon there were splits between the purely moneyed and the more intellectual middle classes, the dandy and the snob. Individuality and unorthodox tastes were sought, for instance, by writers of the Aesthetic movement like Mrs. Haweis and Mrs. Panton, from the 1870s onwards. Soon the term vulgar widened its meaning: earlier it was directed against what seemed so rakish and flimsy in the Regency period, now it was also aimed at the mid-Victorian solid and stolid. 'Respectability' was beginning to be looked down upon. In setting the scene for *Candida* in outer suburban London in 1894, G. B. Shaw describes salubrious, but monotonous and 'unlovely' houses, filled with 'unfashionable middle-class life', led by 'respectably ill dressed people . . .' In the more advanced artistic circles around Whistler and Oscar Wilde, the notion of 'Art for Art's sake' fought against the earlier concerns for truthfulness and the moral message. As a result, exuberant carved brickwork and fanciful wood and stucco decor from earlier periods were revived, which appeared rather doubtful by High Victorian standards of solidity and honesty (cf. plate 156). In many of the early houses of the Domestic Revival elegant proportioning or alignment were disregarded in favour of strong irregularity and low, squat proportions, for instance in the shaping of doors; just at a

216. **London.** Chandos Road, Stratford, E15, early 1860s. Little of the generally very coarse building of the smaller London houses has survived. These houses, by no means of the smallest type in plan, were built in what was then an outlying new suburb. Was the lack of order on the facade perhaps deliberate? It would have been unthinkable anywhere twenty or even ten years later.

Colour plate 33. **Cardiff**, Paget
Street, 1890s. Three colours of
pressed brick (See p. 213).

time when remote provincial builders came round to understanding the basics of the
Classical systems of ordering and proportioning.

We witness in the 'vernacular revival' a new love for features of more modest
buildings, the 'quaint', the primitive, the small rather than the grand, tile-hanging
rather than stone carving. In earlier chapters we mentioned how the new 'home'
ideology of the Domestic Revival, with its new emphasis on close family togetherness
superseded the earlier, largely restrictive values of separation in the sense of privacy
and salubrity. Likewise, in the style and design of the house, the more positive values
and explicit symbolisms of, for instance, the 'cottage' and 'rural' life, or the 'quaint'
old English manor house, replaced the merely restrictive doctrines of rationalism and
chastity of mid-nineteenth century Gothic Revival (colour plate 15). 'Simplicity' no
longer meant chiefly bareness and sharpness, like the 'flush' surface decor of Neo-
Gothic, but became associated with, for instance, old fashioned materials, like plain
tiles, or small old-fashioned casement windows with primitive outside wooden
shutters.

But all this can be seen as a desperate attempt on the part of the 'fashionable world'
to reinstate some kind of hierarchy—a hierarchy which, in a way, was turned
upside down, an anti-hierarchy, where the humble and the quaint were glorified.
Our story of the development of the relationship, or the contrast, between front and
back can be concluded by citing two new varieties: in Bath, the city of ashlar on all
facades, we now find, around 1900, houses where the side and backs are faced with
beautifully clean, large ashlar blocks, while the front carries a mixture of rough and
smooth rubble of small stones. In Cambridge, at about the same time, the better
houses relegate the modern smooth pressed brick to the sides and backs, and use an
older type of rougher brick to mark out the front. However, very soon these
differentiations were abandoned completely. And as regards the actual juxtaposition
of houses of a different class, this became a non-issue. The growing suburban spread
of houses meant that different types and sizes were less and less in sight of each other;
there was no real need for a 'facade' any more.

The Domestic Revival and the end of the terrace

Throughout, the Domestic Revival has appeared to mark the end of all the
developments we have discussed. What do we actually mean by 'Domestic Revival'?
We have sketched the evolution of its architectural styles. In its broadest sense, the
Domestic Revival goes back at least as far as the 'cottage ornée', around 1800, with
its idea of the occasional retreat into remoteness, nature, smallness, individuality.
Evangelical moral fervour and rationalism militated against what was considered
showy and overdone Classical design. Pugin contributed the notion of the cosiness of
medieval life; to him it meant comfort and humanity, which he set against the
mechanical utilitarianism of the modern industrial world. In a similar way Ruskin
searched for poetry and individuality in ages and countries far away; and although
neither Pugin nor Ruskin were particularly interested in the domestic house, their
anti-Victorian attitudes were extremely influential. In some of the works of the Pre-
Raphaelites, especially in Rossetti's and Burne-Jones's medievalizing watercolours
of the 1850s, we find new kinds of mysterious and emotional symbolism of the
domestic interior. They soon found their way into the decoration of the Morris firm.
Another outcome was the boundless figurative decoration of the houses and 'castles'
of William Burges; as was the new primitivism in the interior designs of Charles L.
Eastlake and his followers in the 1870s, which was also based on the rationalist,

moralist demands of Pugin, Street and the other Gothicists. In the country houses of Webb and Shaw new elements of home life were emphasized: the great hall as the family meeting place, with the small, cosy inglenook around the revived big, old (and less efficient) fireplace. By now the Domestic Revival had been fully developed— though it was never codified in one major book. The health movement of the 1870s, in conjunction with the Aesthetic Movement and the Japanese fashion, combatted more fiercely 'unnecessary' ornament in the interior. Colour and colour contrast had, to some extent taken the place of applied decoration. (Another example of the idea of the quaint and simple life in the country, combined with the studied, almost withdrawn, simplicity of the Aesthetic Movement can be found in the illustrations of Kate Greenaway, whose naive and happy children symbolize another new facet of the same ideal world.) Houses now tended to be sedate, smallish-looking, hidden behind greenery. There are no proper 'Terraces' in Bedford Park, the model estate of these circles built in a western suburb of London from the late 1870s by Godwin and Shaw, nor can we find there pinched, basemented villas or 'semis'. As regards the lower classes, the new group of housing reformers from 1900 onwards, like Raymond Unwin, held that simpler country cottage styles were more suitable for their houses, and precisely not the imitation of middle-class elements which Banister Fletcher, for instance, advocated in the 1870s.

By 1900 some of the individualized, ruralized, Arts-and-Crafts-type houses by Baillie Scott and Voysey appear as the antithesis of most of what is discussed in this book. Many of these ideas and ideals seem, indeed, to lie outside of what is conceivable or practical, for the common house. And yet their influence had already begun to filter down the social scale. In the chapter on the changing plan of the row houses we noted the beginnings of the tendency to reduce the size and especially the height of the houses; in the sections on the facade and the styles of decoration and their significance we described the tendency to reduce outward pretension and splendour. Eventually the new modes brought about a fundamental change of the whole type of the house.

Throughout the book, throughout the story of the common dwelling, there is one major, consistent line of development: suburbanization, from the sixteenth century onwards almost to the present day. This was so basic a desire and development that it transcended particular types of dwellings. In the first chapter we maintained that, initially at least, the common row house was not specifically characteristic of any particular type of surrounding, whether urban, rural, or suburban, and that exactly the same type of house could be found in all kinds of environments. But in the following chapter we also claimed the grand Georgian terrace to be a contribution to 'urban' architecture, although in the first chapter it was characterized in practical-functional respects as suburban with its emphasis on distance from work and trade. The analysis of the facade and decoration can now help to clarify this uncertain role, in that it can be shown that it was only in the course of the nineteenth century that a clear 'look' or symbolism of the suburban house emerged. The detached small villa, or the 'cottage ornée' were at first seen as images from remote rural surroundings. But gradually, and by the end of the nineteenth century rather rapidly, they were adopted for suburban surroundings. This occurred because of the reduced appeal of Classical size and unity, and the desire for stronger, more individual and varied symbolism. Classical houses might vary in plan, but the style and meaning of their decoration were basically the same whether they were built in town, country, or suburb. There was also the rapidly growing desire for gardens. Even the inhabitants of the largest cities thought themselves entitled to one, if not at the back, then at least a narrow one at the front. The modern house could be small, or look small, if the gardens could look lavish instead. The desire for 'self-containedness' had developed into a desire for seclusion. The unifying element in any settlement was no longer the tight coordination of houses, but simply greenery. Now the detached or the semi-detached house was becoming *the* type of suburban dwelling; the terrace was more firmly seen as belonging in urban surroundings.

As early as 1840 the terrace had ceased to be fashionable. The often-cited article in *Surveyor, Engineer and Architect* of 1841 found insuperable compositional difficulties in the arrangement and decoration of a terrace facade, and recommended its break-up into smaller units; we have traced the process of individualization in the composition of the facades after 1850. The plaques which so often proclaimed So-and-so Terrace as the name of a range of houses had no real meaning when one could not properly mark out the beginning and the end of the 'terrace' (plate 37). These houses form, strictly speaking, part of a row, not of a terrace. In many later rows, the plaque for a terrace was replaced by individual names for each house (colour plate 18). In common parlance today, 'terrace' refers to a row of common houses, those which are neither detached or semidetached. Surprise is often expressed when a connection between this sort of row of houses and the grand terraces of the Regency period is made. As early as 1883, in his book on estate development, Maitland divides the types and classes simply and sharply: terraces for the lower orders, villas for the better classes. In 1857 Nathaniel Hawthorne remarked about some terraces in Leamington: '. . . magnificent, but some unreal finery . . .'; and A. J. Beresford-Hope put it more bluntly: 'We want houses instead of terraces.'[23]

The architects of the Domestic Revival would, of course, exercise their ingenuity when it came to fitting a terraced house into a narrow site, as Shaw did, for instance, with no. 196 Queens Gate, South Kensington in 1874.[24] But the ideal was now a detached, or at least a semidetached house, spreading outwards rather than growing upwards. If it could be afforded, this kind of house was now built even in denser surroundings; one only has to observe how in Grand Avenue, Hove, a lowish Edwardian house in the heaviest red brick antagonizes its multi-storeyed, slender Victorian terraced neighbours (cf. plate 161). It should be possible to trace upper- and middle-class families in their moves from older, grander houses to newer smaller houses, as, in a way, it happened with the 'family wing' in some country houses.

There were instances, in the early changeover from terraced to detached house, when there could be a definite economic advantage for the builder in the choice. A villa standing by itself could be more saleable than a house in an otherwise unfinished terrace. Indeed, Clarendon Place, Leamington can probably be quoted as a demonstration: at both ends we find what we could call the 'stubs', or the stuccoed beginnings of a short crescent, but the rest is filled in by solid later-style villas (plate 217). McGovern writes that the rental (and that means size and status) is often more difficult to tell for a villa than for a terraced house,[25] and in 1834 a Leamington covenant specified terraced houses of not below £1000, but detached ones not below £800.[26]

Whatever were the precise motivations for building villas and 'semis' in any given case, their numbers grew very rapidly. The London Eyre Estate in 1794, north-west of Regent's Park, was according to Summerson the first large area to adopt the 'semi' on a large scale. Many major suburban areas followed suit, like Clifton, at first very gradually, but then very decidedly, from the 1840s onwards. There were some resorts which began to grow shortly afterwards, where hardly any terraces can be found, like Bournemouth; Southport is consistently built up with 'semis'. In Lowestoft, a magnificent and very regular row of detached villas and 'semis' adorned

217. **Leamington.** Clarendon
Place. This appears as a kind of
terrace, or crescent, begun
about 1820–30, where only
the ends, or corner blocks, were
completed according to the
Regency design. The rest was
filled in, around 1870, by
narrowly detached houses (see
plate 121).

the seafront in the 1840s and 1850s, with the terraces behind. The prestigious new
suburban estates of major provincial towns did not adopt the terrace plan any more.

We have mentioned some of the early influences of the new types on the form and
facade of the terrace, and shown some of the combinations of terraced and detached
type of house. Conversely it must be stressed that early 'semis' and villas often
adhered to many elements of the terrace plan and the character of imposing height
and uprightness; to cite only one early example of 'semis', nos. 6–7 Queens Road in
Cheltenham. There were also cases where terraces replaced planned villas, as with
Lansdown Parade, Cheltenham.[27] There is further interaction, so to speak, between
terraces and flats; to cite a high-class example, Belgrave Mansions within the
Grosvenor Gardens development near Victoria Station of around 1870 look like
terraced houses, but are, in fact, divided into apartments. The 'cottage flat' has been
dealt with at length above. And in Scotland and Ireland we find abundant examples
of combinations of bungalow and terrace (plates 106, 147).

Finally, it would go against one of the basic tenets of this book to claim a gap as
wide as the one suggested just now between the ideal dwelling and the speculative
reality. Very soon speculators began to avail themselves of many features of the
Domestic Revival. Between the wars the quintessence of the speculative 'semi' were
many of those features, which stood for 'anti-spec' before 1900. Very soon our new
types of houses went out of fashion as well, the villa, the 'semi', the 'estate' and the
'suburb', and finally even the bungalow, while the terraced house, as the 'town
house' has now finally come back again.

Builder and architect

Having looked at the status hierarchy in bricks and mortar we must now turn to the status hierarchy amongst those who designed and built the houses. This brings us to what many readers must have felt to be a glaring gap in this book: hardly ever is the name of the designer mentioned. Sometimes, when a name is given, it is not clear whether it is that of the designer or the speculator. The reason is partly that in this general book on a type of building the careers of individuals are less important. It is also because of a lack of detailed research. But it is chiefly due to the fact that even a diligent search would not reveal the name of a designer in most cases.

Increasingly, the best architects turned away from terraced housing and all other kinds of speculative housing. This is particularly true for London from the 1830s and 1840s onwards. Even in those cases where a high-class architect was involved with speculative houses he often concerned himself only with the general layout and the facades; an interest in domestic planning *per se*, in all its aspects, came only with the Domestic Revival. The separation between architect and builder, between craftsman and entrepreneur in England only dates back to the eighteenth century. The brothers Adam still acted in every one of these capacities. The separation was, in fact, increased through what were seen as bad examples of an involvement of the architect with the business side of building, in the case of Nash, Burton father and son, and others. The architect's aim was high social status, 'professional' integrity, and above all a concern for art, history and perhaps science, but not for building and finance. For these aspects the new species of quantity surveyors, clerks of works and foremen were employed. Yet the majority of architects were far from achieving all this right away. After all, anybody could call himself or herself an 'architect' until the 1930s. As in all professions, a many-tiered structure emerged: the top class, designing churches, public buildings and country houses; the middle rank for good commercial and medium domestic work. In addition, there was the older type of set-up, the surveyors and architects in the continuous employment of large corporations and estates, including large speculative housing estates, like the Cundy family for Lord Grosvenor. The lowest class of architect is hard to delineate, but those who drew plans and elevations of houses for builders came under it—though later in the century the main purpose of their contribution would be to get the drainage passed by the authorities. The larger builder could do the plans himself, or he would employ a draughtsman for that purpose. In the medium and smaller provincial towns, with fewer local architects, the range would, of course, be much less strongly observed. Mid-nineteenth-century Bristol must, however, be treated as an exception, as the major local practitioners, like R. S. Pope and the Foster family, designed public buildings of national importance, as well as terraced houses. The latter probably also still acted as masons and builders.[28]

But the builders were equally subjected to the general process of specialization and professionalization. As Summerson writes, the best builders of Georgian London were already men of considerable ability in matters of drawing and business. In the nineteenth century a small number of high-class builders, the 'master builders' or 'contractors', emerged. Cubitt proved that even a daring speculative builder could build up a reputation for solid professionalism. When he was offered a knighthood, he refused, preferring to remain plain 'Mr. Cubitt'. Soon the head of this kind of firm was usually recruited from other similar firms, and no longer from individual building trades. Parallel to this, a range of interior decorating firms emerged; later there were the highly reputable specialist firms of plumbers and electricians. Sometimes in those circles the architect was considered an unnecessary and expensive 'extra'.[29] Even Stevenson's book, which in many ways was jealous of the builders' share in the housing market, had to admit that they were generally efficient, and the *Building News* in 1895[30] estimated that a builder could run up a house 50 per cent more cheaply than an architect.

Throughout the book we have assumed a growth in the competence, and the professionalism of all builders. It is very difficult to substantiate this when looking at the history of the profession. The length of training in the trades varied considerably. It was lengthy for carpenters and joiners and later on for plumbers, but shorter for other trades. In fact, due to increasing speed and competition, London builders could hardly afford to employ apprentices and largely drew their young workers from the provinces. All training was on site and in the workshops. Of course, lack of rigid training could also mean greater freedom in the choice of work and a greater flexibility in the building process. One has to remember that in England even architectural training was only in its infancy. After 1870 some sort of elementary art training under the strict and methodical supervision of South Kensington would be available to most children, but secondary schooling and more specialist training had a slow start, apart from some evening classes. By the 1890s, however, many building manuals, like Rivingtons' and Mitchell, are arranged according to the South Kensington Syllabus and the stages of examinations reflected the hierarchy among builders and architects.

Books, on the whole, played a more important role. Again, the large range of books reflected the range of purchasing power and the various groupings of those interested in the subject. There were the very lavish archaeological publications for the rich client and the architect. There were the new kinds of comprehensive books on architecture and building, which included a lot on domestic economy, like Loudon and Webster, chiefly aimed at the client and the non-specialist speculator. Because of the increase in contracting there were many books containing detailed specifications; also, the growing complications of building regulations needed ample description. For the better craftsmen there were lavish versions of manuals like Nicholson; but there were also an increasing number of cheap books on individual crafts, like Dobson on bricks. A. Hammond in *Bricklaying* (1885) wants to write specifically in a 'simple language'. Banister F. Fletcher's monumental and well-known *History and Architecture* was advertised as useful for the 'student, craftsman and amateur' and cost 21s.[31] By that time most books on house-building concerned themselves primarily with hygiene and plumbing.

The role of publications as 'pattern books' underwent changes. In 1824 Cottingham remarked in his book of cast iron patterns that for the 'mechanic' it would be 'excellent practice to draw the smaller ornaments three or four times the size of the work'. But increasingly the builders would know how to draw simpler facades and patterns themselves. Occasionally there were medium-expensive books illustrating ordinary houses and their details, like *The Builders' Practical Director* of c. 1855 or the books by Blackburne. But with rapidly changing fashions these could not be relied on for very long. The latter books made use of the new process of chromolithography—as did many of the very influential South Kensington handbooks on ornament. The 'pattern book' was, in fact, largely replaced by a new kind of publication, the catalogue of a firm producing or selling building details. Lastly, there were the new kinds of books on domestic design, chiefly on the interior, like Eastlake, which did not primarily address themselves to the trade, but mainly to the client, and especially to women. And finally, all books lost ground to the much more up-to-date specialist magazines—which, again, by the late nineteenth century, presented in their range the well-known hierarchy.

After the buildings themselves, the clearest expression of the growth of professional competence is in drawing. Traditionally, most houses were built without any drawings. But from about 1850, and at the latest from the late 1870s onwards, plans for even the smallest new building and alterations had to be handed in to the authorities. Very often sections were given in as well, and increasingly elevations. More and more these would be attractively drawn — even for the smallest houses — with colour wash and shading (plate 50, colour plate 11). There was a colour coding for plans, which had to be mastered by all, and handbooks even dealt with ornamental lettering for these plans. Various cheap reproduction methods for plans were developed from the 1870s onwards — apart from lithography, which had occasionally been used for large projects earlier.

We still know far too little about the processes of designing and craftsmanship. Early on in our period, it has been said that men like Robert Adam greatly extended the architect's control, as a designer, over the individual craftsman, for instance in stucco and ironwork. Later in the nineteenth century Hermann Muthesius could remark about the ornamental art producers: 'All factories have lately enlarged and completed their stocks in such a way that the architect is put into an embarrassing position.'[32] No doubt, much of the designing was done not on site for a particular building, but by or for the firms, whether by eminent architects like Adam, or later by unknown designers trained in South Kensington principles. On the other hand, individual craftsmanship was also on the increase, at least in some fields, as in the innumerable carved stone capitals for doors and bay windows.

Growing standardization, which we have traced throughout the book, concerned all phases of design and production. There was the convergence of types towards the medium size of the 'late standard' types. The compulsory drawing of detailed plans must have helped considerably with standardization. Constructional details, especially the 'scantlings', the standard measurements for timber parts, were equally influential. In judging standardization from aesthetic and moral angles, we must carefully differentiate between a Classical point of view, in which regularization and uniformity was a virtue, and the later more romantic point of view, when it was a vice — let alone those twentieth-century views which try and differentiate between good and bad standardization. In any case, one has to remember that, while components were more standardized, the growing number of them in total also meant greater possibilities of combination.

Those who have attempted to pinpoint one style for one builder, or speculator, have largely admitted defeat,[33] while this is hardly a difficult task in the case of even a medium-competent Victorian church architect. This is not surprising, for the way the designs came about was often a very complicated and haphazard process. Two examples must suffice here to illustrate this. In 1856 it was specified in the restrictive covenants for small houses in Napier Street, Norwich, that 'all doors in front should be arched and should not be made with frontispieces, porches or similar projections'. The reason for this stipulation was probably the then particularly prevalent desire to keep the building line. There might also have been the intention to give the buildings a more solid look. There might have been competition between bricklayers and carpenters. The man most likely to have inserted this stipulation was S. H. Meachen, a Norwich builder from humble background — and who remained in relatively humble circumstances, judging from the kind of houses he lived in. We have already met some of his 1860s speculations. What matters most here is that there is a strong likelihood that it was this remark, buried in the deeds of a street long pulled down, which helped to change the face of the small streets of Norwich by phasing out the customary wooden bracketed door hoods and replacing them by good gauged arches (cf. plate 191). The story of the design of the facades of 44–52 Queens Gate, the 'Albert Houses', which we have mentioned so often, has been told in the *Survey of London* (plate 43). In 1859 Charles Aldin, a generally powerful builder, encountered the usual difficulties, and had to sell the unfinished houses to a 'client', James

Whatman, a former MP, with as his architect, the tolerably well-known C. J. Richardson. In the background there was also Prince Albert whom everybody wanted to please and who served as kind of advertisement. The main purpose of the facade design was to help with a quick sale. As the *Survey* says, there was even a kind of speculative agreement between the client and the architect—the quicker the sale, the higher the latter's profit. But it is very difficult to determine to whom the design is actually due. The *Builder*[34] reported that it was Whatman who decided on the large quantity of ironwork. As iron was not particularly popular in London at that time, one suspects here a plug for the industry. Later, when sales did not proceed as expected, the architect and the patron accused each other of profligacy in court; while earlier the client had been so pleased with the design that he wanted to patent it. There was little notion of the unity of the design, or of the 'integrity' of the designer. As many contemporary critics would put it, the houses were not the product of 'art', but of 'trade'.

More and more the Victorian upper classes had to accept the successful businessman as an equal. But they did so reluctantly. And in the case of the speculative builder we can see a backlash against him, a kind of revenge. From about 1850–60 onwards, architectural critics completely rejected his houses, socially and artistically. Earlier complaints about the absence of strength and salubrity in some speculative developments were carried on and were combined with the condemnation of the plan, the style and the whole type. Olsen, in his book on Victorian London, gives a great number of quotations, especially from the architectural periodicals (in spite of their calling themselves *Builder* and *Building News*). Stevenson complains about how modern building believes in large glass panes, which to him destroy the continuity of the wall. His preference is the Gothic and Georgian small-pane division of windows, and, he claims, 'it rests for the architects to find an expression for it', and they are 'not likely to become popular'.[35] He was, of course, wrong; by 1890–1900 almost all houses revert to small panes, at least for part of the window—but the snobbery in the remark is characteristic. By 1900 even Booth gave the definition of the architect as: 'in the first place an artist, responsible for beauty, for unity of conception and completeness of design'.[36] The architect directs taste, the builder follows it. Today, we use the curious term 'architect-designed' as a distinction in house building. Already late in the nineteenth century high-class specifications could say 'no stock mouldings'.[37] No other country seems to have this kind of hierarchy.

As we have remarked before, the Domestic Revival addressed itself not primarily to the trade, or to the speculator, but to the designers and the inhabitants. It was crucial to the High Art and the Aesthetic Movements from the 1870s that clients should concern themselves with art and with the choosing of a modern designer, on a more individual basis. This meant a complete change in the social position of the artist. It was only in the 1870s and 1880s that artists—writers, actors, architects or interior designers, like E. W. Godwin—were really accepted in the 'best' circles. Previously there had, of course, been exceptions, but the status of the architect, the decorator and the builder was normally that of the professional and the better tradesman, at best comparable to the doctor and lawyer. 'Professional' meant just that: one conferred with them only when their services were needed, and if they were competent and efficient, so much the better. Robert Kerr's detailed instructions for planning are those of a professional in house planning, providing a maximum of physical comforts. Hence Stevenson's scepticism and his search for the more emotional and less tangible values of 'home'. The trade supplied the latest scientific improvements; the Domestic Revival took them for granted. The building industry provided an ever-increasing variety of competent external and internal decorations; hence Stevenson's condemnation of knowledge as the precondition of art, and the Arts and Crafts Movement's tendency to reduce variety and their search for simple, old work. The trade, the speculators, wanted to demonstrate sound finance and economic success, the client, the inhabitant, wanted to be assured of that competence; and thus no house within one development could appear inferior to the rest. This was ultimately the reason for the sameness of the houses in one terrace; the Domestic Revival, in contrast, cared for individuality.

Arguments and judgements about architecture and building, about art, trade and crafts and about 'popular' architecture cannot be pursued here any further. If one takes the simpler, traditional values of Classical architecture, like 'good' proportion, 'elegance', finish and rich ornamentation, there is no argument: many builders of ordinary terraces did achieve these qualities. It was something that could be acquired through copying and study. If, however, we adopt the more complicated aesthetic value systems developed from the eighteenth century onwards, those of the Picturesque and the Sublime, as well as the more complicated romantic notions of creativity, then the problem of evaluating the work of nineteenth-century builders of terraces is a very difficult one. The way in which in some towns, like Cardiff or Portsmouth, the designs of a particular architect were taken up in some detail in the masses of smaller houses is perfectly legitimate, judged by the first set of standards, but doubtful if judged by the second. If we apply those standards, again, in the case of the terraces in Norwich and London just described, we have grave doubts as to the artistic integrity of the design process, not being clear about the identity of the designer. But judged by more traditional standards, the traders and craftsmen delivered a job which can at least be called competent.

Uvedale Price, Pugin, Butterfield and Norman Shaw taught us to see beauty in the picturesque forms of small old houses; it was Ruskin, Morris and Unwin who finally taught us to appreciate all vernacular design and workmanship—that which lies

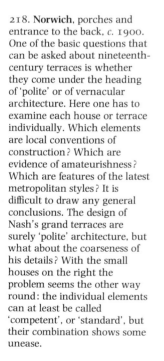

218. **Norwich**, porches and entrance to the back, *c.* 1900. One of the basic questions that can be asked about nineteenth-century terraces is whether they come under the heading of 'polite' or of vernacular architecture. Here one has to examine each house or terrace individually. Which elements are local conventions of construction? Which are evidence of amateurishness? Which are features of the latest metropolitan styles? It is difficult to draw any general conclusions. The design of Nash's grand terraces are surely 'polite' architecture, but what about the coarseness of his details? With the small houses on the right the problem seems the other way round: the individual elements can at least be called 'competent', or 'standard', but their combination shows some unease.

before the threshold of polite architecture, to use an expression from the historians of vernacular architecture. But at the same time Morris and Unwin condemned millions of houses with their countless items of craftsmanship belonging to the polite vernacular—if such a formulation is permissible—because they did not reach the thresholds of the new kinds of romantic and individualized art. One cannot help feeling that the pulling down of so many nineteenth-century houses in recent years has not only been due to actual, or presumed, obsolescence in practical terms, but also to artistic disregard. There does not seem a solution to the dilemma of creativity versus love of the old in architecture. We now regret letting those houses come down which Morris regretted going up. The middle classes today have begun to consider even smaller nineteenth-century houses as antiques, as 'period homes'. Lower-middle-class house-owners, on the other hand, still think, on the whole, that they ought to change and modernize the facades of their older houses. The look of the old would not suit their newly acquired status.

Class differences in art, in craftsmanship and in the environment remain a problem today. In the early periods, splendid palaces and miserable huts often existed in close proximity, to be seen and accepted by all. During the nineteenth century, the rapid progress in building legislation and in the building industry benefitted the upper as well as the lower classes. This seemed to lead to a more minutely detailed accentuation of class differences, for instance with the choice between mahogany and plain deal for lavatory seats. Today, we find it impossible to take these distinctions seriously. The point, however, about today's situation is that there is less of a need to demonstrate class differences, because in the outer suburban areas different classes rarely live within sight of each other. And yet, within the last decade or so, one very strong class contrast, even antagonism, has emerged, the high-rise flat versus the individual house. More than ever before, these different types also symbolize different kinds of ownership, the council-owned block versus the owner-occupied single dwelling.

We do find voices earlier which did not join in with the standard demand for class separation. James Hobrecht, the notable planner of Berlin's rapid expansion after the middle of the nineteenth century, was well aware of the English manner of spreading out suburban houses, and propagated what he saw as one the virtues of the continental system of high blocks with flats of different sizes: the different classes would be constantly aware of each others' existence.[38] Housing reformers, however, soon turned against this pattern of dwelling, largely because high densities did not accord with more stringent sanitary standards. Yet just after 1900 the Manchester critic and town planner Thomas Horsfall also praised the German system for precisely the same reasons as Hobrecht.[39] Today we reject the paternalism of this attempt to integrate the classes. On the whole, the housing reformers of the Garden City faction did not follow it, opting as they did for extremely low densities and for large-scale planning, and thus predetermination in any settlement.

This book does not try to advocate a wholesale return to one of the housing patterns of the past. On the contrary, it tries to show that the past also had its problems. Class differentiation and distancing of housing began in the seventeenth century, and continued and increased in the nineteenth century, more radically from the late nineteenth century onwards. It went hand in hand with suburbanization, a process which few would argue to be entirely avoidable. However, periodically the past itself 'changes'; it appears in a new light. In contrast with the high level of class separation in recent housing, the class differentiation of most nineteenth-century housng now appears less clear than it did at the time the houses were built. In fact, in the case of the older, larger terraces the pattern in

219. **London.** Clapton Passage, Hackney E5 in 1885. Michael Hunter has suggested that the man in the frock coat is the builder of the houses, Christopher Ruthven, and the others are his assistants.

England has moved closer to that in the continental towns, in that the houses are almost always split up into a number of flats. The smaller streets and terraces are inhabited today by a much greater mixture of classes than ever before. Could perhaps the preservation and adaptation of nineteenth-century terraces help us to overcome some of the extremes of class difference today?

Illustration sources

For complete references see Bibliography.

O.S. = Ordnance Survey Maps, 25 inches to the mile.

O.S.T. = Ordnance Survey Town Plans, 10 feet to the mile, surveyed in the late 1880s.

1 O.S. XXXIV, 1870; plans: S. E. Rasmussen. 3 O.S. XXXV, XXVI, XXXIV, XXXV, 1870–1. 4 Engraving by Sutton Nicholls, British Library. 8 Covent Garden: Colen Campbell, *Vitruvius Britannicus*, London 1717, Vol. II; A. Palladio, *Quattro Libri dell' Architettura*, Vol. II. 9 R. Adam, *Works in Architecture*, 1778. 10 Norfolk Museum Service, Cromer Museum. 16 Laxton, 1886. 17 Middleton I, 116. 18 Mrs. Rundell, *Modern Domestic Cookery*, 1855 (Science Museum). 19 Leeds City Libraries. 20 Photo Wm. Ward, Bedlington. 21 W. H. Maxwell. 23 According to Hellyer, Lamb, Palmer, Robertson, Wright. 24 Simon. 25 *Illustrated Carpenter and Builder*, 25 Oct. 1907. 26 Beamish Museum. 27 The Munby Collection; the Master and Fellows of Trinity College, Cambridge. 29 Mitchell, 1902, p 212. 32 H. Davies, *Cheltenham, Past and Present, c.* 1843. 34 Rochdale Reference Library (J. Milne, *Rochdale as it Was*, Nelson, Lancs. 1973). 37 O.S.T. LXIII, 10.20. 42 Antony Dale. 43 *Survey of London, South Kensington*. 47 Bristol plans from Bristol City Archives. 48 London: 'Splitlevel', H. Muthesius, Vol. II; Southend: Hasluck. 50 Norfolk and Norwich Record Office, ph. M. Brandon-Jones. 53 Hasluck. 54 *Builder* 30 June 1883. 58 O.S. Essex, *New Series*, 1919 LXXVIII. 60 Knight. 61 Hetton: Cooper; Shotton, O.S. Durham 1897, XXVIII, 6. 62 *Farewell Squalor*, Easington Rural District Council, 1947. 66 London County Council, *London Housing*, 1937. 67 O.S.T. Sheffield CCXCIV 8.2.; Liverpool CVI 10.7.; Birmingham (Prescott Street) XIII 4.19.; Hull CCXL 2.3. 68 Liverpool City Engineers' Department. 69 Birmingham Central Libraries. 76 O.S.T. Rochdale LXXXXIX 1.7.; Manchester, *Buildings Regulations Report* 1842 (see Official Publications). 78 O.S.T. CCXVIII 10.1.; plans: Lupton. 82 O.S.T. CCXVI 3.10.; for the plans compare also *Building News* Vol. 62, 1892, p 289. 86 Barry and Smith. 88 Aerofilms Limited. 89 O.S. Yorkshire VI, 14, 1915. 92 Hasluck. 94 Ashworth Houses, see Boysen (*Sanitary Conditions, Report* 1842); Manchester, Marr. 100 O.S.T. ed. of 1896, 63. 111 National Monuments Record, London. 112 O.S. XXIV, XXV 1870. 114 Lithography, J. Foulden 1834. 115 O.S. Sussex LXVI 9., LXVI 14., 1875. 121 O.S.T. XXXIII 11.7.; XXXIII 11.8.; XXXIII 11.12.; XXXIII 11.13. 124 O.S.T. XIV 1.13.; XIV 1.14.; XIV 1.18.; XIV 1.19.; XIV 1.23.; XIV 1.24.; XIV 5.43.; XIV 5.4.; XIV 5.8.; XIV 5.9. 125 Drawing by Thomas Malton, *c.* 1770–80 courtesy Victoria Art Gallery, Bath Museum Services. 127; LXXI 15.25.; LXXI 16.21.; LXXV 3.5.; LXXV 4.1.; 130 O.S.T. XXVI 7.18.; XXVI 7.23.; XXVI 7.19.; XXVI 7.24. 135 O.S. Belgravia XLIII, 1869; Paddington XXXIII, 1867–8; Notting Hill, Ladbroke Estate XXXII 1863–5; Islington XVII, 1871; Percy Circus XXVI, 1871; Polygon XXV, 1870; Blomfield Crescent XXXIII, 1867–8; Finsbury Circus XXXVI, 1873; Paragon XLV, 1872; Royal Crescent XLI, 1865–6. 136 Aerofilms Limited. 156 Watercolour by Lt. Col. W. Booth, 1822, Bristol Museums, 186 Mitchell 1902, 190 Mitchell 1902. 193 Laxton 1894. 204 Middleton I, 128, 208 Young & Marten, London, firm's catalogue not dated, (no. 29) Vol II, p 767. 218 Centerprise Trust Ltd. Colour plate 11, London, Vestry Museum, Borough of Waltham Forest, Clarke-Orme Collection.

Notes

1. The common English row house

1 Eberstadt, *Bodenparzellierung*, p 57
2 Few languages can have developed such a large number of terms for the house. The term 'row' is sometimes used misleadingly for a terrace, though 'row house' as such is more an American usage. The names on the plaques on terraces often bring more confusion by calling the row so-and-so 'villas'. Even 'house' can have different meanings: in Scotland it denotes usually a flat, in Leeds it can mean the main living-room in a small dwelling—also called 'house-place'. Then one finds 'cottage', referring to smaller houses generally, usually older ones, but in Rochdale and in Sunderland they denote a specific local, small, urban type, as distinct from 'houses', which are larger. James Hole attempted to apply a rigid classification on these lines: 'cottage' for the smaller, three-roomed dwelling without a parlour, and 'house' for all sizes above. But this was not much adhered to, and even six-roomed terraced houses were often referred to as 'cottages'. Another word is 'tenement', sometimes applied to small rented properties, including terraced houses, chiefly those where the rates, referred to as 'compound rate', were paid collectively by the owner, and not individually by the occupier. A special local use is found in the south-west, where the back extensions of terraced houses are sometimes called 'tenements'. Increasingly though, 'tenemented' referred more specifically to the subletting of larger houses. Finally, there is the word 'dwelling', which the statisticians of the nineteenth century preferred for any kind of abode.
3 But see Sutcliffe, Worsdall, Eberstadt. Wagner-Rieger & Reissberger
4 *Builder*, 1883, Vol. I, p 880
5 Aug. D. Webb, *The new Dictionary of Statistics of the World to the Year 1911*, London 1911, p 301
6 Bright, p 252
7 White, pp 48, 60
8 See Wagner-Rieger & Reissberger
9 *Report of the Royal Commission on the Housing of the Working Classes*, 1884–5, Minute 13141

2. The Georgian terrace and its Classical origins

1 Rasmussen, p 202
2 Elmes, p 19

3. Demand and supply

1 Eberstadt, *Bodenparzellierung*, p 56
2 Dobraszczyc
3 White, p 29
4 Daunton, pp 112–13
5 Dearle, p 37
6 Dyos, *Victorian Suburb*, p 219
7 For example, Lewis and Daunton
8 See Dale, *Fashionable Brighton*
9 See Summerson, *Life and Work of John Nash*
10 See Hobhouse
11 See Chalklin
12 Norfolk and Norwich Archives, Norwich
13 Vestry Museum Archives, Walthamstow, London

4. The economics of building

1 Hole, p 57
2 White, pp 33–4
3 *Architectural Magazine*, 1834, p 14
4 Hobhouse, p 287 etc.
5 *Builder*, 1854, p 2
6 Cox, p 37
7 Kelly, 1874 and 1902
8 Laxton, 1886, p 41; see G. T. Jones
9 Kelly, 1898, p 98
10 Kelly, 1886
11 H. Muthesius, Vol. III, p 130
12 *Builder*, 1857, p 220
13 Maitland, p 65

5. Control

1 Hole, p 26
2 Olsen, *Town Planning*, p 101
3 Laxton, 1886, p 88
4 Dyos, *Victorian Suburb*, p 212
5 *Eastern Evening News*, 17 January 1980
6 Marr, pp 72–3
7 Summerson, *Georgian London*, p 126
8 *Punch*, 11 Oct. 1890
9 Quoted in Ashworth, p 91
10 See *Manchester Building Byelaws*...

6. The house and the home

1 Beeton, 1859–61, p 1
2 These could be seen in Hillfields and Kingfields, built in the 1850s; see J. Prest, *The Industrial Revolution in Coventry*, 1960
3 Stevenson, Vol. II, p 154

4 Stevenson, Vol. II, p 152 (italics SM)
5 *Clari, The Maid of Milan*, 1823; the composer of the music was H. R. Bishop
6 Quoted in Rubinstein, p 117
7 Hamilton, p 75
8 See Burnett; G. Best *Mid-Victorian Britain 1851–75*, London 1971; and others
9 *Report on the Royal Commission on the Housing of the Working Classes*, 1884–5, Minute 5282
10 Stacpoole, pp 45–6
11 See Hasluck, p 9
12 For plans see *Builder* 1883, 30 June; Tarn, *5 Per Cent Philanthropy*; plate 57.
13 Marr, p 38
14 Hole, p 11
15 *Cost of Living Report*, p 191

7. Comfort

1 Webster & Parkes, p 45
2 Laxton, 1886, p 307
3 Simon, p 168
4 Walsh, p 115
5 H. Muthesius, Vol. II, p 233
6 Fletcher, *Architectural Hygiene* pp 168, 145
7 Webster & Parkes, p 89
8 Stevenson, Vol. II, p 213
9 *Building News*, 1888, Vol. I, p 65
10 Walsh, p 111
11 Middleton, Vol. III p 137
12 See Ravetz
13 Simon

8. Sanitation

1 *Builder*, 1904, *Vol. II*, p. 514
2 Hellyer, p 1
3 See Morton
4 Humber, p 229
5 *Plumber and Journal of Heating*, January 1908
6 Hole, p 152
7 Quoted in Dixon *et al.*, *Changing Kibblesworth*
8 See *Tudor Walters Report*, Paragraph 169
9 Webster and Parkes, p 1, 216
10 *Builder*, 1879, p 1217
N.B. I also owe information to Andrew Saint

9. Improving the fabric

1 Barry and Smith, p 22
2 H. Muthesius, *Vol. II*, p 178
3 *Tudor Walters Report*, Paragraphs 173, 174
4 Webster and Parkes, p 33
5 Vequeray Street, Coventry, *c.* 1900
6 Walsh, p 27
7 E.g. Medway Street, SW1, early nineteenth century
8 Hasluck, *Cheap Dwellings*, p 24
9 Webster and Parkes, p 41
10 Sexton Street, Gillingham, *c.* 1850–60
N.B. I also owe information to Andrew Saint

10. Outside the house

1 E.g. some Railway Cottages at Tilbury, Essex
2 Lowe, pp 50–1
3 Maslen, p 216
4 Marr, pp 72–3
5 Rubinstein, p 135
6 Maitland, p 35
7 *Builder*, 1857, p 221
8 Dueckershoff, p 59
9 Laxton, 1886, p 19 (Advertisements)
10 White, p 47
11 Stevenson, Vol. II, p 153
12 *c.* 1836, by J. Foster jnr (?)
13 Sillwood Road, Brighton, *c.* 1840; West Hill, Halifax, e.g. Cromwell Terrace, *c.* 1860s
14 Maitland, p 33
15 Fletcher, *Model houses*; see p 249
16 White, p 52; see also *Builder*, 1857, p 221
17 See Toplis
18 *Building News*, 1858, p 606
19 See also plate 146

11. The plan: the regular type

1 Hooper
2 1863–6 by J. Kelk, for J. Johnson, architect
3 'Albert Houses', Queens Gate; Bedford Square, Brighton
4 For Norman Shaw see p 249 for 27 Grosvenor Square by Wimperis, see *Survey of London, The Grosvenor Estate*, Parts I and II
5 Radstock Road, Reading
6 Aylsham Road, Norwich, 1872
7 Also Sandringham Road, Norwich, *c.* 1880
8 Gibraltar Place, Chatham, 1791, or High Street, Dover
9 Also Wellington Crescent, Ramsgate, 1819
10 Calverley Crescent, Tunbridge Wells, 1830 (originally meant to be a row of shops)
11 Wenmot Cottage, Shrubland Road, London E8, 1855
12 Balfe Street, formerly Albion Street, London N1, *c.* 1840
13 Royal Crescent, Cheltenham, *c.* 1806–10; Lewes Crescent, Brighton
14 The Crescent, Norwich, 1820s; East Terrace, Gravesend, *c.* 1830; Royal Crescent, Harrogate, 1870s
15 'Semis' in South Park Road, Harrogate
16 But see also Toward Road, Sunderland
17 E.g. Stepney Green, E1; see also *Builder*, 1857, p 220
18 London N10, e.g. Church Crescent, *c.* 1900
19 See also plate 146
20 E.g. Nassau Road, Barnes, SW13, *c.* 1908
21 Laburnum Grove, Portsmouth, after 1900; Leicester, Raymond Road, *c.* 1900
22 *Building News*, 1895, Vol. i, p 577; cf. RIBA Jnl. 28 Apr. 1934.
23 E.g. Dangan Road, Wanstead, E11
24 There were also larger versions with upstairs bathroom and a room for a servant, virtually a double-fronted type; e.g. Seven Kings Road, Ilford, Essex, *c.* 1905–10
25 See pp 86–7
26 *Building News*, 1881, Vol. I, p 639
27 Quoted in Dale, *Fashionable Brighton*, p 98

12. The plan: small houses and their regional variations

1 Bowmaker, p 115
2 *Cost of Living Report*
3 E.g. Eastbourne Road, Darlington
4 See p 11
5 Ripon Street, Sunderland
6 See also *Architectural Magazine*, 1834, p 38
7 Hole, p 11
8 Apollo Buildings, Gloucester Street, London SW1
9 Sneinton Market area, Nottingham; St. Stephen's Street, Manchester
10 Godwin Street, Aston
11 Kensington Place, Birmingham
12 129–43 Whitham Road and Upper Hanover Street, Sheffield, *c.* 1860s–70s
13 Upper Hanover Street, Sheffield; Peach Street, Derby; Ripon Street, Lincoln
14 Hole, p 71
15 Greenhill Road and White Abbey Road, Bradford, before 1850
16 East Park Mount, Leeds, cf. plate 56
17 In Chapman, *Working Class Housing*
18 East of Mars Lane, Burmantofts, Leeds, before 1821
19 *Journal of the [Royal] Statistical Society*, Vol. II, 1839
20 Quoted in Boysen, p 119
21 Plans in Hole and Tarn
22 Portland Street, Silver Street, Ashton Street and Bank Top, Manchester
23 E.g. Hodson and Ravald Street, Salford
24 Singleton Row, Preston
25 See J. G. Jenkins
26 E.g. between Raby Street and Great Western Street, Stretford
27 E.g. near Newcastle: Frenchmens' Row, Hetton-on-the-Wall, built in 1796 as miners' houses, then served as houses for prisoners of war; now replaced by new houses
28 St. Aidan's Street, South Shields
29 E.g. Coniston Avenue, Jesmond, Newcastle upon Tyne
30 See above p 11
31 Formerly Pelham and Albert Streets
32 Crownfield Road Estate, Stratford; *Builder*, 1881, Vol. I, p 165
33 E.g. Francis Road, Leyton E10, begun 1894
34 E.g. Goldsborough Road, SW8, *c.* 1885
35 See W. Thompson
36 Buckton, p 3
37 Dueckershoff, p 47

13. The changing plan of the common house

1 Rapoport, p 46
2 Stevenson, Vol. II, pp 55, 145–6
3 *The Housewife*, 1890, p 363; see also McGovern, p 8
4 Franklin, p 90

14. The facade

1 *The Surveyor, Engineer and Architect*, 1841, p 198
2 Formerly Hyde Park Terrace, begun 1837, see Toplis
3 See Dale, *Fashionable Brighton*
4 Royal Crescent, 1797–1807; Bedford Square, 1807–18; Regency Square, 1818–28; Marine Square, 1824

5 'Brunswick Town' and 'Kemp Town' for T. R. Kemp, developer; see p 22
6 For Sir I. L. Goldsmit
7 1850s–60s, designed by Sidney Smirke
8 Near Gosport, Hampshire, *c.* 1826
9 W. & J. T. Harvey, 1846
10 R. H. & S. Sharp, 1832–57
11 By T. Oliver, 1829–34
12 On Victoria Square, *c.* 1835
13 By R. S. Pope, *c.* 1840
14 By C. Underwood, *c.* 1851–3
15 Begun *c.* 1825
16 Formerly New Street, *c.* 1825–40
17 W11, 1840s–50s
18 Cambridge Square, Hyde Park Crescent, Norfolk Crescent, begun *c.* 1825
19 Formerly Eaton Place
20 By J. G. Graham of Edinburgh
21 By J. Dobson for R. Grainger, 1825, now largely destroyed
22 South Parade and Johns Square, from 1790s onwards
23 Near King's Cross, WC1, *c.* 1828–53.
24 EC2, 1819, now rebuilt
25 NW1, *c.* 1820–30, destroyed.
26 Formerly Norland Crescent, W11, 1842–8
27 See below, p 232
28 By T. Cubitt, *c.* 1840
29 *Surveyor, Engineer and Architect*, 1841, pp 169–70
30 N1; see Pevsner, *Buildings of England*, London, Vol. II, 1952, ill. 51
31 London SW7, by Johnston
32 By Thomas Foster and Son, *c.* 1845
33 By Foster and Wood, *c.* 1855
34 By S. Jackson, *c.* 1865
35 London WC2
36 Designed by the Cundy family for Lord Grosvenor
37 Esplanade and Avenue Victoria, *c.* 1870s
38 No. 60 etc., Esplanade, Scarborough, *c.* 1880s
39 E.g. Scarborough, Belvedere Road, *c.* 1900; Brighton, Hove, Fourth Avenue and further west
40 E.g. Park Crescent, Brighton, 1829; Gloucester Crescent, near Regent's Park, London NW1, *c.* 1840
41 Also Victoria Place, Carlisle
42 See Cruickshank and Wyld
43 See *Surveyor, Engineer and Architect*, 1841, p 198
44 Wellington Park, Bristol, by S. B. Gabriel 1857
45 Compare 11 and 13 Victoria Park Road, Hackney, E9
46 See p 204
47 Frome Road, Wood Green, London N22
48 Grosvenor Street, Cardiff
49 Woodberry Crescent, London N10, *c.* 1907
50 London NW1, *c.* 1840

15. Decoration: materials and techniques

1 Ruskin, *The Seven Lamps of Architecture*, 1849, 'The Lamp of Beauty', Paragraph XXXV
2 G. G. Scott, p 97
3 Victoria Terrace, Plymouth
4 See also earlier, Buckingham Place, *c.* 1830
5 Lansdown Road, Redland, Bristol 6, *c.* 1860
6 E.g. Hanbury Road, Bristol, *c.* 1870

7 Nos. 9 and 11 All Saints' Road, *c.* 1870s, and houses opposite
8 Devon, *c.* 1800
9 Stevenson, Vol. II, p 170
10 Nos. 10–11 Rockleaze, Bristol, 1865
11 West End Avenue, Harrogate
12 E.g. house at corner of Victoria and Lancaster Road
13 *Tudor Walters Report*, Paragraph 224
14 *Cost of Living Report*, p 224
15 Bale, *Stone Working Machinery*, p 27
16 Walsh, p 24
17 By Coulters of Batley, advertisement in Kelly, 1886
18 Hasluck, *Cheap Dwellings*, p 28
19 Booth, p 132
20 White, p 37
21 Quoted in Hudson, *Fashionable Stone*, p 85
22 *The Quarry*, June 1896, pp 101–4
23 50–70 Fairfield Road, Winchester; St. Edmund's Road, Southampton
24 Margate Road, Portsmouth
25 Berkeley Crescent, Bristol, 1787
26 E.g. Royal Crescent, Brighton
27 Elsam, p 106
28 See p 238
29 Hobhouse, p 310
30 E.g. 'TLB Rubbers', by Lawrence & Co., Bracknell
31 E.g. Rosher & Co., Ipswich; G. T. Lucas, Somerleyton, initially for S. M. Peto; Gunton of Costessey (or 'Cossey') near Norwich
32 Information from Jane Wight
33 Nicholson, 1823, p 346
34 E.g. Trafalgar Road, Moseley, and Park Hill, both in Birmingham
35 R. Bradley and W. Craven, 1853 etc.; see Woodforde, *Bricks*, p 122
36 Adderley Park Co. and others
37 Wallgrange, Longsdon; see Kelly, 1898
38 *Building News*, 1905, Vol. II, p 207
39 See Booth, p 77; I owe a lot of information to unpublished papers by Frank Kelsall of the Greater London Historic Buildings Department. See also Clifton-Taylor, *Pattern of English Building*
40 Nicholson, 1837, p 184
41 Elsam, p 137
42 See Colvin
43 The same as 'Hamelin'?; Webster and Parkes, p 26
44 *Builder*, 1845, p 160
45 Nicholson, 1837, p 184
46 Oakfield and Pembroke Roads, Bristol, *c.* 1850
47 E.g. Tavistock Square, London WC1, 1820s
48 E.g. Ford Park, Plymouth
49 E.g. Bolton Gardens, London NW10, *c.* 1870–80
50 E.g. Lozell's Street, Birmingham
51 1820s–30s
52 Montpelier Crescent, Brighton, 1840s; also Rotherfield Street, London N1
53 *Builder*, 1869, p 497; 1854, p 388; 1871, p 485
54 SW4; see P. Metcalf, *James Knowles, Victorian Editor and Architect*, Oxford 1980
55 E.g. St. Helen's Crescent, Hastings
56 E.g. Vera Road, London SW6, *c.* 1908–10
57 *Builder*, 1861, p 252

58 See Ruch and A. Kelly
59 See Atterbury and Irvine
60 Stevenson, Vol. II, p 179
61 Information from Michael Stratton
62 E.g. Beresford Road, Stoke on Trent, 1870s; Tollington Park, London N4, *c.* 1870; Shirley Road, Southampton
63 Webster and Parkes, pp 37, 53
64 Nicholson, 1837, p 185
65 Elsam, p 137
66 R. Unwin, *The Art of Building a Home*, London, 1901, p 107
67 Laxton, 1886, p 16
68 Elsam, p 118
69 Elsam, pp 119, 144
70 Some can still be seen at the backs of houses near Victoria Park
71 E.g. in Shirley Road, Cardiff
72 See Chatwin
73 *Builder*, 1864, p 742
74 Some good examples are left in Lincoln, e.g. Arboretum Avenue
75 E.g. Swete Street, London E13
76 See also above p 50
77 John Brown of Grimsby; Kelly, 1886
78 Examples also in St. Helen's, Lancs.
79 See Hall and Hall
80 Webster and Parkes mention a method by Braithwaite, p 59
81 E.g. Moor Oaks Road, Sheffield

16. The changing styles of the facade
1 Loudon, p 1122
2 Mitchell, p 259
3 Olsen, *Town Planning*, p 17
4 Elmes, p 80
5 E.g. Lansdowne Road, North Kensington, 1852–64
6 Grosvenor Gardens, London SW1, *c.* 1870
7 Hole, p 66
8 Loudon, p 1123
9 E.g. Kimberley Road, Cardiff, *c.* 1910
10 E.g. Stapleton Hall Road, London N4, 1881
11 See p 261 note 39
12 E.g. the quasi-semis in Park Crescent, Northampton, 1884
13 E.g. S. P. Adshead's Kennington Estate, Cardigan Street, SE11, 1913, for Duchy of Cornwall

17. Social and architectural hierarchy
1 Webster and Parkes, p 5
2 Dyos, *Victorian Suburb*, p 83
3 Stevenson, Vol. I, pp 21, 22
4 Daunton, *Coal Metropolis*, p 133
5 Quoted in Olsen, *Victorian London*, p 116
6 Drawings Collection of Royal Institute of British Architects, London
7 E.g. Thorn Grove and Cedar Grove, Manchester, and College Road and Denbigh Road, Norwich
8 Coltard Road and Handel Street, Liverpool
9 Booth, p 177
10 *Life in the English Country House*, p 268
11 Ravetz, p 459
12 Hole, pp 52–3

13 E.g. Heywood, Lancs, houses on the road to Bury
14 *Cost of Living Report*, p 430
15 *Report of the Royal Commission on the Housing of the Working Classes*, 1884–5, Minute 7068
16 Fletcher, *Model Houses*, p 9
17 *Survey of London, South Kensington*, p 305
18 Elmes, p 18
19 Stevenson, Vol. II, p 180
20 Webster and Parkes, pp 53, 49
21 *Builder*, 1869, p 498
22 Girouard, *Life in the English Country House*, p 270
23 Simpson and Lloyd, p 115; *Builder*, 1861, p 315
24 See Saint
25 McGovern, p 8
26 Simpson and Lloyd, p 139
27 *c.* 1840, compare H. S. Merrett's map of Cheltenham, 1834
28 See Gomme *et al.*
29 *Building News*, 1878, Vol. II, p 283
30 *Building News*, 1895, Vol. I, p 577
31 Advertisement in Fletcher, *Specifications*, London, 1903
32 H. Muthesius, 1898, p 622
33 Gomme *et al.*, p 276; Hobhouse, pp 66, 116, 269
34 *Builder*, 1861, pp 109–11
35 Stevenson, Vol. II, p 196
36 Booth, p 47
37 Macey, 1898, p 9
38 For Hobrecht see W. Hegemann, *Das steinerne Berlin*, Berlin, 1963
39 C. T. Horsfall, *The Improvement of the Dwellings and Surroundings of the People: the Example of Germany*, Manchester, 1904

Bibliography

Some directions for research

The most important source of documentation for a house, a terrace, or an estate are the deeds. In some cases old deeds are now deposited in Local Record Offices or Archives, or local history libraries, where most of the other documents and literature is also kept: photos of demolished houses; town plans and county maps; directories; rate books; copies of the Census Enumerator Books; Building Control Plans (or Town Engineer's Plans), or Drainage Plans in the older parts of London; local newspapers with advertisements; local byelaws; publications about local traders; insurance documents.

For a bibliographical guide to places and subjects turn to the general index; page numbers beyond p 264 refer to titles in the Bibliography.

Journals

Builder
Builder's Journal and Architectural Review
Building News
Building World
Country Life
Housewife
Illustrated Carpenter and Builder
Illustrated Journal of Patented Inventions
Industrial Archaeology
Local Historian
Nineteenth Century
Public Health
Surveyor, Engineer and Architect
Urban History Yearbook
Urbi
Victorian Studies

vide Willing's Press Guide for specialist trade journals

Official publications

Cd., C.	= Command Number
HL	= House of Lords
Rep.	= Report
R.Com.	= Royal Commission
Sel. Cttee Rep.	= Select Committee Report

Manufactures, Commerce and Shipping. Sel. Cttee Rep.; 1833 (690) vi

Health of Towns. Sel. Cttee Rep.; 1840 (384) xi

Regulation of Buildings and the Improvement of Boroughs. Sel. Cttee Rep.; 1842 (372) x

Sanitary Condition of the Labouring Population. Poor Law Commissioners. England and Wales. Local Reps.; 1842 HL xxvii

Sanitary Condition of the Labouring Population. Poor Law Commissioners. Rep. (E. Chadwick); 1842 HL xxvi (Reprint. Edinburgh University Press, 1965)

State of Large Towns and Populous Districts. R.Com. 1st Rep. 1844 [572] xvii; 2nd Rep. 1845 [602] [610] xviii

Local Government Act 1858, 21 and 23 Victoria Chap. 98 Sec. 34

Model Byelaws issued by the Local Government Board for the Use of Sanitary Authorities, IV, New Streets and Buildings, 1877

Artizans' and Labourers' Dwellings and other Acts. Sel. Cttee. Rep. 1881 (358) vii; Further Rep. 1882 (235) vii (Cross Committee)

Housing of the Working Classes. R.Com. 1st–3rd Rep.; 1884–5 C.4402: C.4409: C.4547 xxx; xxxi

Town Holdings. Sel. Cttee Reps.; 1886 Sess. I (213) xii; 1887 (260) xiii; 1888 (313) xxii; 1889 (251) xv

Working Class Rents, Housing, Retail Prices and Standard Rate of Wages in the United Kingdom. Rep. of an Inquiry by the Board of Trade; 1908 Cd.3864 cvii (Cost of Living Report)

Report on Back-to-Back Houses, by Dr. L. W. Darra Mair . . . ; 1910 Cd.5314 xxxviii

Working Class Rents, Housing, Retail Prices and Standard Rate of Wages in the United Kingdom. Rep. of an Inquiry by the Board of Trade; 1913 Cd.6955 lxvi

Questions of Building Construction in connection with the Provision of Dwellings for the Working Classes in England and Wales, and Scotland. Cttee. Rep.; 1918 Cd.9191 vii (Tudor Walters Report)

General bibliography

Actes du Colloque 1979 à l'Abbaye de Royaumont; typologie opérationelle de l'habitat ancien 1850–1948, Paris (Ministère de l'environement et du cadre de vie) 1979

H. Adams, Building Construction (24 Weekly Parts, Cassells'), London 1907 onwards

R. Adam, *Works in Architecture*, London 1778

G. Adamson, *Machines at Home*, Guildford 1969

S. O. Addy, *The Evolution of the English House*, London 1933

E. Akroyd, *On Improved Dwellings for the Working Classes*, London 1862

C. B. Allen, *Cottage Building, or Hints for Improving the Dwellings of the Labouring Classes*, London 1849–50, 1854, 1867, 1873, 1886

R. Altick, *Victorian People and Ideas*, London 1974

M. Anderson, *Family Structure in Nineteenth Century Lancashire*, Cambridge 1971

W. Ashworth, *The Genesis of Modern British Town Planning*, London 1954

P. J. Aspinall, 'The Building applications and the building industry in 19th century towns, the scope for statistical analysis', *Research Memorandum 68*, Centre for Urban and Regional Studies, University of Birmingham 1978

P. J. Aspinall, 'Speculative Builders and the Development of Cleethorpes, 1850–1900', *Lincolnshire History and Archaeology*, Vol. 11, 1976, pp 43–52

P. J. Aspinall and J. W. R. Whitehand, 'Building Plans: a major source for urban studies', *Area*, XII, 1980, pp 199–203

E. Asmus, *Wie Europa baut und wohnt, Typen Eingebauter Wohnhäuser*, Hamburg 1883

P. Atterbury and L. Irvine, *The Doulton Story*, London (Victoria and Albert Museum) 1979

J. and B. Austwick, *The Decorated Tile*, London 1980

R. Bailey, *The Homeless and the Empty Houses*, Harmondsworth 1977

J. M. Baines, *Burton's St. Leonards*, Hastings Museum 1956

M. Powis Bale, 'On Brickmakers and Brickmaking Machines', *Building News*, Vol. 58, 1890, pp 533 etc.

M. Powis Bale, *Stone Working Machinery*, London 1898

R. Banham, *The Architecture of the Well-Tempered Environment*, London 1969

M. W. Barley, *The House and Home, A Review of 900 Years of House Planning and Furnishing in Britain*, London 1963

Barry and P.G. Smith, *Joint Report by Dr. Barry and Mr. P. Gordon Smith, on Back to Back Houses*, Local Government Board (Reports of Medical Inspectors after Local Inquiries) 1888

G. Beard, *Decorative Plasterwork in Great Britain*, London 1975

I. M. Beeton, *The Book of Household Management*, London 1859–61, 1868, 1879–80, 1892, 1906, 1915

C. and R. Bell, *City Fathers, The Early History of Town Planning in Britain*, Harmondsworth 1969

Benwell Community Project, Final Report Series, No. 3: Private Housing and the Working Classes, Birmingham 1978

J. L. Berbiers, 'Back to Back Housing in Halifax', *Official Architecture and Planning*, December 1968

James Bishop, *New and Popular Abstract of the English Laws respecting Landlords, Tenants and Lodgers*, c. 1845–72

E. L. Blackburne, *The Mason's, Bricklayer's, Plasterer's and Decorator's Practical Guide*, London 1859–62

E. L. Blackburne, *Suburban and Rural Architecture*, London 1869

Charles Booth, *Life and Labour of the People in London. 2nd Series: Industries, Vol. I: The Building Trades*, London 1902–4 (reprint)

H. P. Boulnois, *Housing of Labouring Classes and Back to Back Houses*, London 1896

P. Bourdieu, *La distinction critique et social du jugement*, Paris 1979

M. Bowley, *The British Building Industry*, Cambridge 1966

M. Bowley, *Innovations in Building Materials*, London 1960

E. Bowmaker, *The Housing of the Working Classes*, London 1895

J. Bowyer, *Guide to Domestic Building Surveys*, London 1971

R. Boysen, *The Ashworth Cotton Enterprise*, Oxford 1970

T. Bright, *The Development of Building Estates*, London 1910

S. H. Brooks, *Rudimentary Treatise on the Erection of Dwelling Houses*, London 1860

Brown (The Rev.), 'The Domestic Character of Englishmen', *Evangelical Magazine* Vol. 10, 1868, pp 583–7

R. W. Brunskill, *Houses*, London 1982

R. W. Brunskill, *Illustrated Handbook of Vernacular Architecture*, London and Boston 1971

R. W. Brunskill and A. Clifton-Taylor, *English Brickwork*, London 1977

C. M. Buckton, *Our Dwellings, Healthy and Unhealthy*, London 1885

The Builder's Practical Director, for Buildings of all Classes, Leipzig and Dresden (H. H. Payne) and London (J. Hagger) c. 1855

Building News, 'How to Estimate' (series), 1901

'Building Trades Journal Centenary' (i.e. extracts from *Illustrated Carpenter and Builder* from 1877 onwards), *Building Trades Journal*, 15 July 1977, pp 5–108

N. Bullock and J. Read, *The Movements for Housing Reform in Germany and France, 1840–1914*, Cambridge (forthcoming)

J. Burnett, *A Social History of Housing*, Newton Abbott 1978

Business Archives Council, London, Various lists of firms' records

J. Calder, *The Victorian and Edwardian Home from Old Photographs*, London 1979

J. Calder, *The Victorian Home*, London 1977

E. Camesasca, *Storia della Casa*, Milan 1968

D. Cannadine, *Lords and Landlords, The Aristocracy and the Towns 1774–1967*, Leicester 1980

Cassell's Building Construction, see Adams

Cassell's Carpentry and Joinery (ed. Paul N. Hasluck), London c. 1900

Cassell's Household Guide, London 1869–71 (and later editions)

C. W. Chalklin, *The Provincial Towns of Georgian England, A Study of the Building Process 1740–1820*, London 1974

E. B. Chancellor, *The History of the Squares of London, Topographical and Historical*, London 1907

D. Chapman, *The Home and Social Status*, London 1955

S. D. Chapman, *The History of Working Class Housing, A Symposium*, Newton Abbot 1971 (A. S. Wohl, London; J. Butt, Glasgow; W. M. Beresford, Leeds; S. D. Chapman, Nottingham; J. H. Treble, Liverpool; S. D. Chapman and J. N. Bartlett, Birmingham; W. J. Smith, Lancashire; F. J. Ball, Ebbw Vale)

A. Chatwin, *Cheltenham's Ornamental Ironwork*, Cheltenham 1975

F. Choay, *The Modern City, Planning in the 19th Century*, London 1969

J. J. Clarke, *The Housing Problem, its History, Growth, Legislation and Procedure*, London 1920

A. Clifton-Taylor, *The Pattern of English Building*, London 1972

A. Clifton-Taylor, see also R. W. Brunskill

L. J. Collier, 'Development and Location of the Clay Brickmaking Industry in the South East Midlands of England', PhD Thesis, University of London 1966

H. Colvin, *A Biographical Dictionary of British Architects, 1600–1840*, London 1978

E. W. Cooney, 'The Building Industry, in Ed. R. Church, *The Dynamics of Victorian Business*, London 1980.

K. Cooper, 'A Consideration of some aspects of the construction and use of miners' dwellings and related domestic buildings in County Durham 1840–70', 1975, MS in Beamish Museum, Stanley, County Durham

W. H. Corfield, *Dwelling Houses, their Sanitary Construction and Arrangements*, London 1885

W. Cowburn, 'Popular Housing', *Arena, Journal of the Architectural Association*, Vol. 82, Sept.–Oct. 1966, pp 76–81

A. Cox, *Survey of Bedfordshire Brickmaking, a History and Gazetteer* (Bedfordshire County Council and Royal Commission on Historical Monuments) 1979

S. W. Cranfield and H. I. Potter, *Houses for the Working Classes in Urban Districts*, London 1900

W. Creese, *The Search for Environment, the Garden City Before and After*, New Haven and London 1966

G. Crossick, *An Artisan Elite in Victorian Society, Kentish London 1840–80*, London 1978

G. Crossick, ed., *The Lower Middle Class in Britain 1870–1914*, London 1977

D. Cruickshank and P. Wyld, *London: The Art of Georgian Building*, London 1975

H. Cubitt, *Building in London*, London 1911

F. G. D'Aeth, 'Present Tendencies of Class Differentiation', *The Sociological Review*, III, 1910, pp 267–76

A. Dale, *Fashionable Brighton, 1820–60*, London 1947

A. Dale, *The History and Architecture of Brighton*, Brighton 1950

G. Darley, *Villages of Vision*, London 1975 (for the development of model agriculture and industrial colonies)

M. J. Daunton, 'The Building Cycle and the Urban Fringe in Victorian Cities', *Journal of Historical Geography*, Vol. 4, 1978, pp 175–81

M. J. Daunton, *Coal Metropolis, Cardiff 1870–1914*, Leicester 1977

M. J. Daunton, 'Miners' Houses: South Wales and the Great Northern Coalfield 1880–1914', *International Review of Social History*, XXV 1980, pp 143–75

M. J. Daunton, *Residence and Revenue, Working-Class Housing in the City, 1850–1914*, forthcoming

N. Davey, *Building in Britain*, London 1964

N. Davey, *A History of Building Materials*, London 1961

L. Davidoff, *The Best Circles, Society, Etiquette and the Season*, London 1973

G. J. Crosbie Dawson, 'Street Pavements', *Journal of The Liverpool Polytechnic Society*, 28 Feb. 1876

N. B. Dearle, *Problems of Unemployment in the London Building Trades*, London 1908

O. Delisle, 'Studien über Bauweisen an englischen Einfamilienhäusern', *Centralblatt der Bauverwaltung*, 1900, pp 549–52

E. R. Dewsnup, *The Housing Problem in England*, Manchester 1907

R. Dixon, E. McMillan and L. Turnbull, *Changing Kibblesworth*, Gateshead M.B.C., Department of Education, Local Studies Series No. 5, c. 1978

R. Dixon and S. Muthesius, *Victorian Architecture*, London 1978

J. Dobai, *Die Kunstliteratur des Klassizismus und der Romantik in England 1700–1840*, Berne 1974–7

A. Dobraszczyc, 'The Ownership and Management of Working Class Housing in England and Wales, 1780–1914', Cardiff and Swansea Conference of Urban Historians, 1978

E. Dobson, *A Rudimentary Treatise on Brick and Tiles*, 4th ed., London 1864

L. Duckworth, *Consumers' Handbook, Gas, Water, Electric*, London 1899

E. Dueckershoff, *How the English Workman Lives*, London 1899 (*Wie der englische Arbeiter lebt*, Dresden 1898)

R. Dutton, *The Victorian Home*, London 1954

H. J. Dyos, 'The Speculative Builders and Developers of Victorian London', *Victorian Studies*, XI, 1968, pp 640–90

H. J. Dyos, ed., *The Study of Urban History*, London 1968

H. J. Dyos, *Victorian Suburb, A Study of the Growth of Camberwell*, Leicester 1961

H. J. Dyos and M. Wolff, eds., *The Victorian City*, London 1973

R. Eberstadt, *Handbuch des Wohnungswesens und der Wohnungsfrage*, Jena 1909

R. Eberstadt, *Die Kleinwohnungen und das städtebauliche System in Brüssel und Antwerpen*, Jena 1919

R. Eberstadt, *Städtebau und Wohnungswesen in Holland*, Jena 1914

R. Eberstadt, *Die städtische Bordenparzellierung in England*, Berlin 1908 (for the practice of suburban development in London, Ipswich and Felixstowe)

P. Eden, *Small Houses in England 1520–1820*, The Historical Association, H.75, 1969

Arthur M. Edwards, *The Design of Suburbia*, London 1981

A. Trystan Edwards, *Modern Terrace Houses*, London 1946

J. Elmes, *Metropolitan Improvements of London in the Nineteenth Century*, London 1827

R. Elsam, *The Practical Builder's Perpetual Price Book*, London 1825 (this is usually bound with Nicholson's *Practical Builder* (see below) and variously cited as Elsam or Nicholson)

A. Emden, *The Law Relating to Building Leases and Building Contracts*, London 1882 and later editions

F. Engels, *Die Lage der arbeitenden Klasse in England*, Leipzig 1845 (*The Condition of the Working Classes in England*, London 1968)

G. E. Engerts, *Nederlandse en Amsterdamse Bouwactiviteiten 1850–1914*, Deventer 1977

K. A. Esdaile, 'The Small House and its Amenities in the architectural Handbooks 1749–1847', *Transactions of the Bibliographical Society*, XV, 1917–19

S. Everard, *The History of the Gas Light and Coke Company*, London 1949

G. Fehl & C. Vierneisel,' Wohnungsbau in England', *Bauwelt* 1976, No. 3

R. Field, *Byelaws and Regulations with reference to House Drainage*, London 1877

B. Fletcher, *Architectural Hygiene or Sanitary Science as applied to buildings*, London 1899

B. Fletcher, *The London Building Act 1849 and the Amendment Act 1898*, London 1901

B. Fletcher, *Model Houses for the Industrial Classes*, London 1871

C. A. Foster, *Court Housing in Kingston upon Hull, University of Hull Occasional Papers in Geography, No. 19*, Hull 1972

C. A. Forster, 'The historical development and present day signficance of byelaw housing morphology, with particular reference to Hull, York and Middlesbrough', PhD Thesis, University of Hull 1969

J. Franklin, *The Gentleman's Country House and its Plan, 1835–1914*, London 1981

M. Gallet, *Paris Domestic Architecture of the 18th Century*, London 1972

S. M. Gaskell, *vide* Crossick, *The Lower Middle Class in Britain 1870–1914*

E. Gauldie, *Cruel Habitations, a History of Working Class Housing*, London 1974

M. Girouard, *Life in the English Country House*, New Haven and London 1978

M. Girouard, *Sweetness and Light, The Queen Anne Movement 1860–1900*, Oxford 1977

M. Girouard, *The Victorian Country House*, Oxford 1971

M. Girouard, *Victorian Pubs*, London 1975

J. Gloag, *Victorian Comfort, A Social History of Design from 1830–1900*, London 1961

Glossarium Artis, Deutsch-Französisch-englisches Definitionswörterbuch zur Kunst, eds. R. Huber and R. Rieth, Tübingen 1973, in progress

W. Goldstraw, *A Manual of Building Regulations in Force in the City of Liverpool*, Liverpool 1902

E. Gombrich, *The Sense of Order, A Study in the Psychology of Decorative Art*, London 1979

A. Gomme, M. Jenner and B. Little, *Bristol, an Architectural History*, London 1979

A. G. Granville, *The Spas of England, and Principal Sea-Bathing places*, London 1841 (reprinted Bath 1971)

G. and W. Grossmith, *Diary of a Nobody*, London 1894

J. Gwynn, *London and Westminster Improved*, London 1766 (reprint Farnborough 1969)

I. and E. Hall, *Georgian Hull*, York 1978/9

H. L. Hamilton, *Household Management for the Labouring Classes*, London 1882

A. Hammond, *Bricklaying*, London 1885

D. Handlin, *The American Home, Architecture and Society 1815–1915*, Boston 1979

H. J. Hanham, *Bibliography of British History 1851–1914*, Oxford 1976

P. N. Hasluck, *Cassell's House Decoration*, London 1908

P. N. Hasluck, *Cheap Dwellings, . . . plans selected from Building World*, London 1905

W. Hazelwood, *House Journals*, London 1963

G. Heller, *Propre en ordre, Habitation et vie domestique 1850–1930: l'example vaudois*, Lausanne 1979

S. S. Hellyer, *The Plumber and Sanitary Houses*, London 1877 and later editions

G. L. Hersey, *High Victorian Gothic, a Study in Associationism*, Baltimore and London 1972

A. Hickmott, *Houses for the People*, London 1897

H. R. Hitchcock, *Early Victorian Architecture in Britain*, New Haven and London 1954

H. Hobhouse, *Thomas Cubitt, Master Builder*, London 1971

R. Hoggart, *The Uses of Literacy, Aspects of Working Class Life*, London 1957

J. Hole, *The Homes of the Working Classes*, London 1866

F. Hooper, *The Planning of Town Houses*, Architectural Association Lecture, 1887

R. Huber and R. Rieth, eds., *vide Glossarium Artis*

K. Hudson, *The Fashionable Stone*, Bath 1971 (on Bath stone)

F. E. Huggett, *Life Below Stairs, Domestic Servants in England from Victorian times*, London 1977

W. Humber, *A Comprehensive Treatise on the Water Supply of Cities and Towns*, London 1876

M. Hunter, *The Victorian Villas of Hackney*, London (The Hackney Society) 1981

D. Iredale, *Discovering This Old House, A Pocket Guide to the History of Your Home*, Tring 1968

W. Ison, *The Georgian Buildings of Bath*, London 1948

A. Jackson, *Semidetached London, Suburban Development, Life and Transport 1900–39*, London 1973

J. T. Jackson, '19th Century Housing in Wigan and St. Helens', *Transactions of the Historical Societies of Lancashire and Cheshire*, Vol. 129, 1979

J. T. Jackson, *Working Class Housing in 19th Century Great Britain, A Bibliography*, Vance Bibliographies, Post Office Box 229, Monticello, Ill., USA, 1979

K. Jackson, 'Working Class Housing and Building in the 19th Century', PhD Thesis, University of Kent 1979

N. Jackson. 'The Speculative House in 19th Century London', PhD Thesis, Polytechnic of the South Bank, London 1982

J. G. Jenkins, *A History of the County of Stafford* (*Victorian County History*, VIII), Oxford 1963

S. Jenkins, *Landlords to London*, London 1975

G. T. Jones, 'The London Building Industry 1845–1913', in ed. C. Clark, *Increasing Return*, Cambridge 1933

J. R. Jones, *The Welsh Builders on Merseyside*, Liverpool 1946

P. N. Jones, *Colliery Settlements in the South Wales Coalfield 1850–1926, University of Hull Occasional Papers in Geography*, No. 14, Hull 1969

Karlsruhe, Universität, Fakultat fur Architektur, *Die Wohnungs-frage in London, 1840–1970, Materialien zur Entwicklung des sozialen Wohnungsbaus in England*, 1982

J. R. Kellett, *The Impact of Railways on Victorian Cities*, London 1969

D. Kelsall, 'London House Plans', *Post-Medieval Archaeology*, VIII, 1974, pp 80–91

Kelly's/Post Office, *Directory of the Building Trades*, 1870 and subsequent editions

A. Kelly, 'A Camouflage Queen by the River. Mrs. Coade at Greenwich', *Country Life*, CLXV, 25 Jan. 1979, pp 244–5

R. Kerr, *The Gentleman's House*, London 1864 (reprint 1972)

R. Kerr, 'Observations on the plan of Dwelling Houses in Towns', *Journal of the Royal Institute of British Architects*, 3rd Series, I, 1894, pp 201–31

A. King, ed., *Buildings and Society, Essays on the Social Development of the Built Environment*, London 1980

P. W. Kingsford, *Building and Building Workers*, London 1973

(Charles) Knight, *Annotated Model Byelaws*, 7th ed., London 1905

H. A. J. Lamb, 'Sanitation, An Historical Survey', *The Architect's Journal*, 4 March 1937

S. Lasdun, *Victorians at Home*, London 1981

H. Laxton, *The Builder's Price Book*, 1826, and later editions

J. P. Lewis, *Building Cycles and Britain's Growth*, London 1965

D. Linstrum, *West Yorkshire Architects and Architecture*, London 1979

T. H. Lloyd, see Simpson and Lloyd

C. Lockwood, *Bricks and Brownstone, the New York Row House, 1785–1929*, New York 1972

London County Council, *London Housing*, London 1937

J. C. Loudon, *An Encyclopedia of Cottage, Farm and Villa Architecture*, London 1833, and later editions

J. B. Lowe, *Welsh Industrial Workers' Housing 1775–1875*, Cardiff (National Museum of Wales) 1977

R. Lowe, *How our Working People Live*, London c. 1882

J. Lowerson, *Cliftonville, Hove, A Victorian Suburb*, University of Sussex (Centre for Continuing Education) 1977

F. M. Lupton, *Housing Improvement*, Leeds 1906

F. W. Macey, *Specifications in Detail*, 3rd ed. London 1899

F. Maitland, *Building Estates, A Rudimentary Treatise on the development, sale and general management of building land*, London 1883 and later editions

L. W. D. Mair, see official publications

K. Maiwald, 'An Index of Building Costs in the UK 1845–1938', *Economic History Review*, 2nd Series, Vol. VII, 1954

Manchester and Salford Sanitary Association; Manchester Society of Architects, *Papers on the Manchester Building Byelaws*, Manchester 1887

Maps, see Ordnance Survey

P. L. Marks, *The Principles of Planning*, London 1901

T. R. Marr, *Housing Conditions in Manchester and Salford*, Manchester and London 1904

T. J. Maslen, *Suggestions for the Improvement of our Towns and Houses*, London 1843

Mass Observation: 'Report by Mass Observation for the Advertising Service Guild', *An Enquiry into People's Homes*, London 1943

H. P. Massey, 'Colliery Housing in North West Durham, 1850–1930', BA Architectural Thesis, University of Newcastle, 1976

J. D. Mathews, 'The Model Byelaws as a basis of a general building act', *Sess. Papers of the Royal Institute of British Architects*, 1877–8, pp 277–96

W. H. Maxwell, *The Construction of Roads and Streets*, London 1899

J. H. McGovern, *Suggestions for . . . Laying out Building Estates*, Liverpool 1885

P. Metcalf, *The Park Town Estate and the Battersea Triangle: A Peculiar Piece of Victorian London Property Development and Its Background*. London Topographical Society 1978

G. A. T. Middleton, *Modern Buildings, their Planning, Construction and Equipment*, 6 vols, London c. 1905

Charles F. Mitchell, *Building Construction and Drawing*, 6th ed. London 1902

E. C. S. Moore, *Sanitary Engineering*, London 1901

M. Morton, *Historical Sources in Geography*, London 1979

H. C. Morton, 'A Technical study of Housing in Liverpool, 1760–1938', MA Thesis University of Liverpool, Department of Architecture, 1967 (3 vols.)

Michael Müller, *Die Verdrängung des Ornaments; zum Verhältnis von Architektur und Lebenspraxis*, Frankfurt 1977

S. F. Murphy, *Our Homes and How to Make them Healthy*, London 1883

H. Muthesius, *Das englische Haus*, Berlin 1904–5 (*The English House*, London 1979)

H. Muthesius, 'Die neuzeitliche Ziegelbauweise in England', *Centralblatt der Bauverwaltung*, 1898, pp 581–3, 593–5, 605–7, 622–3

S. Muthesius, *Das englische Vorbild, Eine Studie zu den deutschen Reformbewegungen in Architektur, Wohnbau und Kunstgewerbe im späteren 19. Jahrhundert*, Munich 1974

S. Muthesius, *The High Victorian Movement in Architecture 1850–70*, London 1972

S. Muthesius, 'Progress Terrace, A re-appraisal of late Victorian and Edwardian Housing', *Architectural Review*, CLXVI, 1979, pp 93–7

S. Muthesius, see also Dixon

R. S. Neale, *Bath 1680–1850, a Social History*, London 1981

R. S. Neale, *Class in English History*, Oxford 1981

J. S. Nettlefold, *Practical Housing*, Letchworth 1908

Newcastle Weekly Chronicle, Extracts, 'Our Colliery Villages', 1873 (Newcastle Public Library)

A New System of Domestic Economy founded on modern Discoveries and the private communications of persons of experience, London c. 1820, 1823, 1824, 1825

R. B. Nichol, 'Colliery Housing in Ashington and South East Northumberland, 1848–1926', BA Architectural Thesis, University of Newcastle, 1980

P. Nicholson, *Architectural Dictionary*, London 1819 and later editions

P. Nicholson, *The New and Improved Practical Builder and Workman's Companion*, London 1823

L. Niethammer, ed., *Wohnen im Wandel, Beiträge zur Geschichte des Alltages in der bürgerlichen Gesellschaft*, Wuppertal 1979

Notes on Building Construction (Rivington's Series), 3rd ed., London 1896

P. Oliver, I. Davis and I. Bentley, *Dunroamin, the Suburban Semi and its Enemies*, London 1981

D. Olsen, *The Growth of Victorian London*, London 1976

D. Olsen, *Town Planning in London, the 18th and 19th Centuries*, New Haven and London 1964

Ordnance Survey Maps. Maps used for this book begin after c. 1840, with 6-inch maps for some counties, especially in the north. There are also 5-foot plans for most northern towns from that period. The first editions of 25-inch maps date mostly from the 1870s and 1880s. Most of the 10-foot town plans date from the later 1880s, some from the 1870s. London maps come in 6 inches, 25 inches and 5 foot.
6 inches to the mile: 1 km = 9.47 cm or 1 cm = 105.59 m (c. 1:10,000)
25 inches to the mile: 1 km = 39.46 cm or 1 cm = 25.34 m (c. 1:2,500)
5 feet to the mile: 1 km = 94.70 cm or 1 cm = 10.55 m (c. 1:1,000)
10 feet to the mile: 1 km = 189.40 cm or 1 cm = 5.28 m (c. 1:500)
See J. B. Harley and C. W. Philips, *The Historian's Guide to Ordnance Survey Maps*, London 1964

W. Pain, *The British Palladio; or, Builder's General Assistant*, London 1786

R. Palmer, *The Water Closet, A New History*, Newton Abbot 1973

J. E. Panton, *From Kitchen to Garrett, Hints for young householders*, London 1890

J. W. Papworth, 'On Houses as they were, they are and they ought to be', *Journal of the Royal Society of Arts*, 1857, p 317; *The Builder*, 1857, p 220

Vanessa Parker, *The English House in the Nineteenth Century*, Historical Association H.78, 1970

J. Parsons, *Housing by Voluntary Enterprise*, London 1903

M. Pawley, *Home Ownership*, London 1978

Penguin Dictionary of Building (J. S. Scott), Harmondsworth 1964

S. Pepper, *Housing Improvement*, London 1971

J. W. Perkins, A. T. Brooks, A. E. McR. Pearce, *Bath Stone, a Quarry History*, Bath 1979

S. Perks, *Residential Flats of all Classes*, London 1905

P. Peters, *Häuser in Reihen*, Munich 1973

N. Pevsner, *Buildings of England Series*, Harmondsworth, from 1951

W. F. Pickering, 'The West Brighton Estate, Hove, A Study in Victorian Urban Development', *Sussex Industrial History*, V, 1972

D. Pilcher, *The Regency Style*, London 1947

G. V. Poore, *The Dwelling House*, London 1897

C. G. Powell, *An Economic History of the British Building Industry, 1815–1979*, London 1980

R. B. Powell, *Housekeeping in the 18th Century*, London 1956

H. E. Priestley, *The English Home*, London 1970

J. Prizeman, *Your House, the Outside View*, London 1975

M. and C. H. B. Quennell, *A History of Everyday Things in England*, London 1959

A. Rapoport, *House Form and Culture*, Englewood Cliffs, N.J. 1969

S. E. Rasmussen, *London, The Unique City*, London 1934

J. R. Ravensdale, *History on your Doorstep*, BBC, London 1982

A. Ravetz, 'The Victorian Coal Kitchen and its Reformers', *Victorian Studies*, XI, 1968, pp 435–60

D. A. Reeder, 'The politics of urban leaseholds in late Victorian England', *International Review of Social History*, Vol. VI, 1961, pp 413–30

W. G. Rimmer, 'Working Men's Cottages in Leeds 1770–1840', *Thoresby Society*, XLVI, 1960, pp 165–99

Rivington's Series, see *Notes on Building Construction*

R. Roberts, *The Classic Slum, Salford Life in the first quarter of the century*, Harmondsworth 1971

E. G. Robertson and J. Robertson, *Cast Iron Decoration, A World Survey*, London 1977

W. Robertson and C. Porter, *Sanitary Law and Practice*, London 1905

J. M. Robinson, *The Wyatts, An Architectural Dynasty*, Oxford 1979

M. Rose, 'Dwelling and Ornament in the East End', *Architectural Review*, CIII, 1948, pp 241–6

Royal Commission on Historic Monuments, *England. The City of York*, Vol. III, Vol. IV, HMSO, London 1972, 1975

D. Rubinstein, ed., *Victorian Homes*, Newton Abbot 1974 (extracts from nineteenth-century writings)

J. E. Ruch, 'Regency Coade', *Architectural History*, 1968, pp 34–56

A. Saint, *Richard Norman Shaw*, New Haven and London 1976

S. B. Saul, 'House Building in England 1890–1914', *Economic History Review*, Second Series, XV, 1962–3, pp 119–37

A. Saunders, *Regent's Park*, Newton Abbot 1969

A. Sayle, *The Houses of the Workers*, London 1924

Science Museum, London: Domestic Appliances Gallery, *Catalogue*, n.d..

G. G. Scott, *Remarks on Secular and Domestic Architecture*, London 1858

J. S. Scott, see *Penguin Dictionary of Building*

J. Seabrook, *The Unprivileged, A hundred years of family life and tradition in a working class street*, London 1967

A. R. Sennett, *Garden Cities in Theory and Practice*, London 1905

A. Service, *Edwardian Architecture*, London 1967

F. H. W. Sheppard, see *Survey of London*

S. M. Sigsworth, 'The Home Boom of the 1890s', *Yorkshire Bulletin*, XVII (I), 1965

J. D. Simon, *The House-Owner's Estimator, or 'What will it cost to build, alter, or repair?'*, London 1875

M. A. Simpson and T. H. Lloyd, *Middle Class Housing in Britain*, Newton Abbot 1977 (R. Newton, Exeter; M. A. Simpson Glasgow; F. M. L. Thompson, Hampstead; T. H. Lloyd, Leamington; K. C. Edwards, Nottingham; J. N. Tarn, Sheffield)

M. Smets, *L'avènement de la cité jardin en Belgique*, Liège c. 1976

G. L. Soliday, *History of Family and Kinship, an International Bibliography*, New York 1980

Spon's *Household Manual*, London 1891

F. Stacpoole, *Handbook of Housekeeping for small Incomes*, London 1898

D. Stephenson, 'Balcony Railings in Kent', *Archeologia Cantiana*, LXXXVI, 1971, pp 173–91

J. J. Stevenson, *House Architecture*, 2 vols., London 1880

D. Stroud, *The South Kensington Estate of Henry Smith's Charity*, London (The Trustees of Henry Smith's Charity) 1975

J. Stübben, *Der Städtebau*, 3rd ed., Leipzig 1924 (*Handbuch der Architektur*, IV, 9)

J. Summerson, *Architecture in Britain 1530–1830*, Harmondsworth 1953

J. Summerson, *The Classical Language of Architecture*, new ed. London 1980

J. Summerson, *Georgian London*, London 1945

J. Summerson, *The Life and Work of John Nash*, London 1980

J. Summerson, *The London Building World of the Eighteen-Sixties*, London 1973

Survey of London, General Editor F. H. W. Sheppard: XXXVII, *Northern Kensington*, London 1973; XXXVIII, *The Museum Area of South Kensington and Westminster*, London 1975; XXXIX, XL, *The Grosvenor Estate in Mayfair*, London 1980

The Surveyor, Engineer and Architect (article on Lowndes Square), 2nd. Series, 1841, pp 154–5, 169–70, 198–201

A. Sutcliffe, *Multistorey Living, the British Working Class Experience*, London 1974

A. Sutcliffe, 'Working-Class Housing in Nineteenth Century Britain: A Review of Recent Research', *Bulletin, Society for the Study of Labour History*, 1972, No. 24, pp 40–51

G. L. Sutcliffe, *Modern Plumbing and Sanitary Engineering*, London 1907

G. L. Sutcliffe, *Principles and Practice of Modern House Construction*, London 1899

E. L. Tarbuck, *Encyclopedia of Practical Carpentry and Joinery*, Leipzig and London c. 1860

J. N. Tarn, *5 per cent Philanthropy, An Account of Houses in Urban Areas 1840–1914*, Cambridge 1975

J. N. Tarn, 'Some Pioneering Suburban Housing Estates (London)', *Architectural Review*, Vol. 143, 1968, pp 367–70

J. N. Tarn, *Working Class Housing in 19th Century Britain*, London 1971

I. C. Taylor, 'The Court and Cellar Dwelling, 18th Century Origins of the Liverpool Slum', *Transactions of the Historical Societies of Lancashire and Cheshire*, Vol. 122, 1970, pp 67–91

I. and J. Taylor, *Builders' Price Book*, London editions 1776, 1787, 1794, 1810, 1813

N. Taylor, *The Village in the City*, London 1973

T. P. Teale, *Dangers to Health, A Pictorial Guide to Domestic Sanitary Defects*, London 1879

T. P. Teale, *A Discourse on the Principles of Domestic Fireplace Construction*, Lecture delivered to the Royal Institution, London 1886

F. M. L. Thompson, *Hampstead, Building a Borough, 1650–1964*, London 1974

P. Thompson, *The Edwardians*, London 1977

W. Thompson, *The Housing Handbook*, London 1903

J. G. Timmins, *Handloom Weavers' Cottages in Central Lancashire*, Centre for North West Regional Studies, University of Lancaster, Occasional Papers No. 3, 1977

G. Toplis, 'Urban Classicism in Decline' (on Tyburnia, London), *Country Life*, 15, 22 Nov. 1973, pp 1526–8, 1708–10

T. Tredgold, *Elementary Principles of Carpentry*, London 1840 and later editions

L. Turnbull and S. Womack, *Home Sweet Home, A Look at Housing in the North East from 1800 to 1977*, Gateshead Metropolitan Borough Council Department of Education Local Studies Series (ed. L. Turnbull), c. 1978

A. Ure, *A Dictionary of Arts, Manufactures and Mines*, London 1839

T. B. Veblen, *The Theory of the Leisure Class*, New York 1899

Victoria County History, Staffordshire, see Jenkins

M. C. Wadhams, 'Witham Housing 1550–1880', *Post-Medieval Archeology*, VI, 1972

R. Wagner-Rieger and M. Reissberger, *Theophil von Hansen*, Wiesbaden 1980

J. H. Walsh, *A Manual of Domestic Economy, suited to Families spending from £100–£1,000 p.a.*, London 1857, 1889

I. Ware, *A Complete Body of Architecture*, London 1756

M. Ware, *A Handy Book of Sanitary Law*, London (Society of Arts and Manufactures) 1866

E. Warren, *A young Wife's perplexities with Hints on the training and instruction of young servants*, London 1886

B. Weber, 'A New Index of Residential Construction and Long Cycles in House Building in Great Britain 1838–1950', *Scottish Journal of Political Economy*, II, 1955, pp 104–32

T. Webster and Mrs. W. Parkes, *An Encyclopedia of Domestic Economy*, London 1844

B. Weinreb Architectural Books Ltd, *The Small English House, A Catalogue of Books*, London 1977

J. White, *Rothschild Buildings: Life in an East End Tenement Block 1887–1920*, London 1980

W. H. White, 'Middle Class Houses in Paris and Central London', *Sessional Papers of the Royal Institute of British Architects*, 1877–8, pp 21–65

J. W. R. Whitehand, 'Building Activity and intensity of development at the urban fringe: London Suburbs in the 19th Century', *Journal of Historical Geography*, I, 1975, pp. 211–24

J. W. R. Whitehand (ed.), *The Urban Landscape, Historical Development and Management* (Papers by M. R. G. Conzen), London 1981

N. Whittaker, *The House and Cottage Handbook*, Durham (Civic Trust for the North East) 1977

L. Wilkes, *John Dobson*, London 1980

L. Wilkes and G, Dodds, *Tyneside Classical*, London 1964

J. A. Williams, *Building and Builders*, London 1968

F. G. Wilmott. *Bricks and Brickies*, Rainham (Kent) 1972 (on brick making in Kent)

John Wood the Younger, *A Series of Plans for Habitations for the Labourer, adapted as well to towns as to the country*, 1781

J. Woodforde, *Bricks to Build a House*, London 1976

J. Woodforde, *Georgian Houses for All*, London 1978

H. Woolmer, 'Low-rise or High-rise, A 19th Century Argument renewed', *Town and Country Planning*, Vol. 37, 1969, pp 567–71

S. Worden, 'Furniture for the Living Room. An Investigation of the Interaction between Society, Industry and Design in Britain from 1919 to 1939'. PhD Thesis, Brighton Polytechnic 1980

F. Worsdall, *The Tenement, A Way of Life, A social, historical and architectural study of housing in Glasgow*, London 1979

T. L. Worthington, *The Dwellings of the Poor and Weekly Wage Earners in and around Towns*, London 1893

L. Wright, 'Dublin', *Architectural Review*, CLVI, 1974, pp 325–30

L. Wright, *Clean and Decent, the Fascinating History of the Bathroom and the WC*, London 1960

L. Wright, *Home Fires Burning, the History of Domestic Heating and Cooking*, London 1964

L. Wright, *Warm and Snug, A History of the Bed*, London 1962

P. Wyld, see Cruickshank and Wyld

D. Yarwood, *The British Kitchen*, London 1981

ADDENDA:

J. Cornforth, *English Interiors 1790–1848, The Quest for Comfort*, London 1978

S. Farrant, *The Growth of Brighton and Hove 1840–1939*, Brighton 1981

C. C. Knowles and P. H. Pitt, *The History of Building Regulations in London, 1189–1972*, London 1972

N. Morgan, *An Introduction to the Social History of Housing in Victorian Preston* (publ. by Lancashire Education Committee, Preston Curriculum Development Centre, Preston, 1982)

General Index